Contending Voices

Contending Voices

Biographical Explorations of the American Past

VOLUME I:
TO 1877

John Hollitz
Community College of Southern Nevada

A. James Fuller
University of Indianapolis

Houghton Mifflin   Boston New York

Editor-in-Chief: Jean Woy
Sponsoring Editor: Mary Dougherty
Assistant Editor: Michael Kerns
Senior Project Editor: Florence Kilgo
Production Editorial Assistant: Marlowe Shaeffer
Production/Design Coordinator: Lisa Jelly
Senior Manufacturing Coordinator: Priscilla Bailey
Senior Marketing Manager: Sandra McGuire
Marketing Associate: Jim David

Printed in the U.S.A.

Library of Congress Catalog Number: 2001133280

ISBN: 0-395-98068-2

23456789-VHG-06 05 04 03

Contents

Volume 1

CHAPTER 4

The Price of Patriotism:
Jonathan Sewall and John Adams

↝ 57 ↜

CHAPTER 5

The Conflict over the Constitution:
Patrick Henry and James Madison

↝ 75 ↜

CHAPTER 6

Agrarians and Capitalists in the Early Republic:
John Taylor and Alexander Hamilton

↝ 93 ↜

CHAPTER 7

Resistance and Western Expansion:
Tecumseh and William Henry Harrison

࠾. 111 ࠾

CHAPTER 8

Gradualism, Colonization, and Militant Abolitionism:
Benjamin Lundy and David Walker

࠾. 127 ࠾

CHAPTER 9

Liberation and Control in Antebellum Culture:
Fanny Wright and Catharine Beecher

࠾. 145 ࠾

CHAPTER 13

Free Blacks and the Struggle for Equality:
Mary Ann Shadd and Henry Bibb

∽ 224 ᔓ

CHAPTER 14

Mr. Lincoln's War:
Clement Vallandigham and Benjamin Wade

∽ 243 ᔓ

CHAPTER 15

Race and Redemption in the Reconstructed South:
Robert Smalls and Carl Schurz

∽ 263 ᔓ

Preface

Contending Voices: Biographical Explorations of the American Past uses paired biographies to bring alive the debates and disagreements that have shaped American history. It is based on the assumption that students find history more engaging when they realize that it is full of conflict. Through biography, individual men and women emerge from the tangle of events, dates, and facts that often make history so challenging for students.

Following the organization of most survey texts, each chapter examines two individuals who stood on different sides of an important issue. Their stories, combined with a small set of primary sources in each chapter, show students how individuals—from the pre-English settlement of the New World to the presidential election of 2000—influenced their times and were influenced by them. At the same time, the book's biographical approach naturally incorporates political, social, economic, cultural, religious, and diplomatic histories while underscoring the diversity of those who shaped the past. This biographical approach highlights competing perspectives, prompting students to think about issues from multiple viewpoints. The biographical essays that preface the sources were written with these pedagogical goals in mind.

Although students will encounter familiar names in these pages, many of the thirty individuals in each of Contending Voices' two volumes rarely appear in survey texts. All of them, however, addressed significant events and issues of their times. In Volume I, sixteenth-century conquistador Hernán Cortés and Dominican priest Bartolomé de Las Casas contest the fate of Native Americans. In the seventeenth century, the pitched battles between Governor William Berkeley and rebel Nathaniel Bacon reveal forces shaping early Virginia. Other chapters illuminate the Great Awakening, the American Revolution, and the ratification of the Constitution. Later, the life-and-death conflict between William Henry Harrison and Tecumseh reflects the larger struggle between whites and Indians sparked by westward expansion in the early nineteenth century. Likewise, abolitionist militant David Walker and antislavery moderate Benjamin Lundy highlight the disagreements among abolitionists over the best way to end slavery, while Catharine Beecher and Fanny Wright square off over the proper place of women in antebellum society. In the same period, chapters pairing union organizer Sarah Bagley with industrialist Nathan Appleton, Governor Juan Bautista Alvarado of Mexican California with merchant Thomas Larkin, and former slave Henry Bibb with abolitionist Mary Ann Shadd focus on the rise of the factory system, manifest destiny, and the challenges confronting free blacks before the Civil War. At midcentury, George Fitzhugh and Hinton Rowan Helper debate slavery's impact on the South and reveal deep fears at the heart of a growing sectional conflict. Still later, antiwar Democrat Clement Vallandigham and radical Republican Benjamin Wade demonstrate the limits of dissent during the Civil War, while black congressman Robert Smalls and white senator Carl Schurz underscore the limits of Reconstruction.

Volume II offers a similar diversity of individuals and topics. In the late nineteenth century, tycoon Jay Gould and union leader Terence Powderly face off in a bloody conflict between capital and labor. In the early twentieth century, the radically different views of home economics pioneer Ellen Richards and anarchist Emma Goldman illuminate both progressive reform and the changing role of women in American society. Antiwar critic Randolph Bourne and war propagandist George Creel further illuminate aspects of progressive reform, as well as the new power of advertising and the effects of World War I on American society. Chapters covering the 1920s pair black nationalist Marcus Garvey with labor leader A. Philip Randolph and back-to-the-land advocate Ralph Borsodi with advertising man Bruce Barton. They highlight competing visions guiding the postwar struggle for racial equality and the era's new consumer economy. During World War II, Japanese-American internee Harry Ueno and internment director Dillon Myer illustrate the issue of Japanese relocation during World War II. Later battles are brought to life in chapters pairing civil rights activist Fannie Lou Hamer with black leader Roy Wilkins, women's rights champion Betty Friedan with feminist Gloria Steinem, and Interior Secretary James Watt with novelist Edward Abbey. They illustrate the challenges confronting the civil rights, women's, and environmental movements and the conflicts dividing them. Finally, "godfather" of neoconservatism, Irving Kristol, and consumer activist Ralph Nader advance competing visions about the regulation of business—views that helped shape policy in the late twentieth century and continue to guide political discussion today.

While permitting easy access to often unfamiliar topics, *Contending Voices* is also designed to build students' critical thinking skills. Each chapter begins with a brief essay providing an introduction to the lives and ideas of the two individuals who held conflicting views on an important issue. The essay does not offer a complete accounting of the subjects' lives—an impossible task—but focuses instead on aspects that illuminate the chapter's main topic. Each essay begins with a short vignette designed to capture the reader's attention and includes a running glossary, which defines terms that may be unfamiliar to many survey students. A set of four to six primary sources illustrating and amplifying the chapter's central themes follows each essay. These sources demonstrate the variety of evidence historians use to understand the past and reflect another premise behind this book—that the best way for students to learn history is to explore it themselves. Their explorations are assisted by a brief set of Questions to Consider following the primary sources. In addition, references to the primary sources appear in the essays, helping to integrate the primary and secondary material. A brief introduction to each primary source also aids student analysis. Finally, a brief Further Reading section at the end of each chapter contains both biographical and general works that will help interested students explore each topic further.

Many people made valuable contributions to these volumes. DeAnna Beachley, Michael Green, and Charles Okeke, colleagues at the Community College of Southern Nevada (CCSN), offered useful suggestions and encouragement. Susana Contreras de Finch generously gave of her time with computer assistance, for which I am deeply indebted. As usual, CCSN Interlibrary Loan librarian Marion Martin provided invaluable and unfailingly pleasant help. CCSN administrative assistants Venus Ramirez and Michele Sanders cheerfully and efficiently typed portions of the manuscript. Stanley Kutler of the University of Wisconsin more than once generously offered his wise counsel. Larry Harshman of the University of Nebraska lent support and a sympathetic ear from afar. I owe thanks to many people at Houghton Mifflin as well. Michael Kerns guided the development of this book with a keen eye and sound suggestions. He was a pleasure to work with, and his efforts undoubtedly made the final result far better. Colleen Shanley Kyle nurtured this project in its initial stages and helped refine its approach, while Mary Dougherty saw it through to completion. Jean Woy backed it and smoothed bumps along the way. Florence Kilgo efficiently handled the production stage, and Barbara Jatkola skillfully copyedited the manuscript.

Numerous colleagues around the country read and reviewed some or all of the chapters. I was repeatedly impressed by their commitment to this project. Their insights and suggestions improved this book immeasurably, and I am grateful for them. They included Alfred Hunt, Purchase College, State University of New York; Teresa Kaminski, University of Wisconsin—Stevens Point; Arlene Lazarowitz, California State University, Long Beach; Stephen Middleton, North Carolina State University; Fred Nielsen, University of Nebraska at Omaha; Virginia Noelke, Angelo State University; Clifford H. Scott, Indiana University— Purdue University Fort Wayne; and Tommy Stringer, Navarro College.

Once again, my biggest debt is to Patty. She endured far more than a reasonable husband ever could expect. Without her support, this book would not have been completed, and to her, therefore, it is dedicated.

—J.H.

The Cross and the Sword in Spain's New World:
Bartolomé de Las Casas and Hernán Cortés

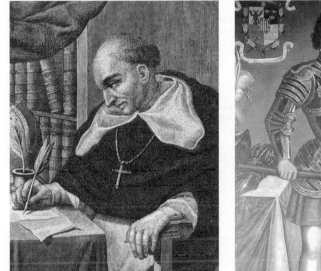

Bartolomé de Las Casas   Hernán Cortés

The pulse of the sixty-six-year-old Bartolomé de Las Casas quickened as he stepped into the court of King Charles I of Spain in 1540. The Catholic friar could not suppress his nervous anticipation. After all, he carried to Charles a story of bloody conquest and naked exploitation that the monarch would surely find shocking. In the half century since Columbus's voyage of discovery in 1492, Spanish conquerors had claimed vast portions of the New World and put millions of its native inhabitants under Spain's yoke. Las Casas knew that none of these men had figured more prominently in Spain's conquest than Hernán Cortés. In 1519, the young conquistador had marched fewer than six hundred Spanish soldiers into the Aztec Empire in central Mexico and taken it over. In little time, the area had represented the heart of Spain's vast empire in the New World. Las Casas was aware that Cortés and other conquerors had brought great wealth and glory to His Majesty's realm. Yet he believed that there was much more to the story of Spain's conquest of the New World.

Las Casas was no stranger to the New World. After arriving in the West Indies in 1502, he lived there on and off for the next four decades. He sought passage to the Indies to make his fortune and along with many other Spaniards secured the right to control the labor of numerous Indians for his own benefit.

As a young colonist, he seemed destined to live as a prosperous West Indian planter. Life in the New World took a strange turn, though. Less than a decade after his arrival there, Las Casas heard the call of the priesthood. Then a few years after his ordination, he heeded another call. Increasingly troubled by the cruelty of many Spaniards toward the Indians, Las Casas denounced the system by which his countrymen held many native people and renounced his own grant of Indian laborers. Then he proceeded to make it his life's work to defend the Indians and challenge the Spaniards' treatment of them.

Now as he stepped into the royal court, he was ready to lay before his king the gruesome details of the Spanish extermination of the Indians and the con- quistadors' brutal rule over the survivors. Among the "tyrants" he singled out was the founder of New Spain, Hernán Cortés. Impressed as Cortés was by the way the Aztecs lived, Mexico's conqueror had no doubt that they should be converted by the sword and then be made to serve his—and his nation's—ends. After conquering the Aztecs, Cortés grew rich and powerful from his exploitation of Native American labor, inspiring other Spaniards to conquer millions more Indians. The conquistadors exacted an awful price from their victims, and now Las Casas pleaded with the Spanish king to take control of the Indians away from these greedy men. As he stood in His Majesty's court, he believed that the fate of the New World's native population was at stake.

"The Indians Have Slain Las Casas!"

Bartolomé de Las Casas's connections to the New World and its native inhabi- tants began almost as soon as Spain's encounter with them. Las Casas was born in 1474 in the southwestern Spanish town of Seville. The son of a merchant who had fallen on hard times, Bartolomé was eighteen years old in 1493 when he witnessed Columbus's triumphant procession through the streets of his home- town after the latter had returned from his first voyage to the New World. Later that same year, Las Casas's father and uncle shipped out with Columbus on his second voyage and were among the first colonists to settle in Hispaniola.* When Bartolomé's father returned to Spain in 1498, he brought along a present for his son: a servant in the form of a Taino Indian from Hispaniola. We do not know the young man's reaction to this gift, but his imagination must have been fired by tales of Columbus's adventures.

In 1502, when he was twenty-eight, Las Casas sailed with his father to the West Indies. With a university education in Latin, he was qualified to hold the position of *doctrinero,* or teacher of Christian doctrine. As such, he would earn an ample salary and was able to acquire property. As soon as Las Casas's ship reached Santo Domingo,* he discovered that there were plenty of opportunities to do just that. He immediately heard the news that gold had been discovered on the island and that a war with the Tainos had produced a large number of slaves to mine it. Years before, the Tainos had impressed Columbus with their meekness and hospitality. It had not taken long, however, for friendly relations

Hispaniola: The island east of Cuba that is now occupied by Haiti and the Dominican Re- public.

Santo Domingo: A seaport and the principal Spanish settlement on Hispaniola.

between the Spaniards and Tainos to descend into a nightmare of slaughter and enslavement.

Here and elsewhere in the West Indies, Columbus had set in motion a series of events that would have devastating consequences for the New World's native peoples. Periodically, his men kidnapped Tainos "to learn the secrets of the land." In 1494, Columbus dispatched his first human cargo from the New World to be sold at the slave market in Seville. Later that year, his men launched a savage attack on the Tainos that resulted in the destruction of villages, the killing of countless people, and the shipment of five hundred more slaves to Spain. By the time Las Casas arrived in Hispaniola, many Tainos were working as forced laborers for the Spaniards in the mines and fields.

These practices may shock modern sensibilities, but they reflected the attitudes of Spanish culture at the time. Unlike most of Europe, southern Spain had not done away with slavery by the late fifteenth century. That area had been a stronghold of the Moors—Muslims from North Africa who had invaded Spain in the eighth century and occupied parts of it until the late fifteenth century. The Spaniards viewed the invaders as infidels—that is, non-Christians—and as such inferior. They applied the same views to the native inhabitants of the Caribbean islands. To the Spaniards, these people—living without cities, clothes, private property, or any concept of economically productive work—appeared utterly irresponsible and uncivilized. Moreover, as Christians, the Spaniards saw these strangers who worshiped numerous gods as heathens.

By the late fifteenth century, the Spaniards, who viewed Africans in the same way, began to import African slaves to the West Indies to replace the native workers who had succumbed to Old World diseases and Spanish cruelty. In the fifty years following Columbus's arrival, the Indian population declined by perhaps 90 percent. In the fifteenth century alone, Spanish and Portuguese slave traders shipped as many as a quarter of a million Africans to the West Indies to fill this void.

As Las Casas settled down in the West Indies, he gave no indication that he disagreed with the Spaniards' attitudes toward the Indians. Shortly after arriving there, he helped to suppress several Indian uprisings and was rewarded with an *encomienda*—a grant of land and the native people living on it. In theory, the *encomenderos*—the recipients of these grants—were responsible for the protection of the people entrusted to them and for their introduction to Christianity. But in reality, the *encomienda* system was nothing more than slavery. Ambitious and energetic, Las Casas had few qualms about this arrangement. In fact, when a group of Dominican* friars arrived on Hispaniola in 1510, Las Casas was unmoved by their arguments against the colonists' mistreatment of the Indians.

Even Las Casas's decision to become a priest the same year did not lead immediately to his rejection of the *encomienda* system. In early 1512, he joined an expedition led by a military adventurer named Diego Velásquez that was already engaged in the conquest of the neighboring island of Cuba. Serving as chaplain, he witnessed the slaughter of hundreds of Indians that, he said, left "a stream of blood running . . . as if a great number of cows had perished." Las Casas

*Dominican: A member of a Catholic religious order founded in the thirteenth century.

attempted to stop the massacre, but without success. Afterward, however, he accepted an *encomienda* on Cuba, where he prospered by farming and raising cattle.

Within a few years, Las Casas began to have doubts about the treatment of the native people. The turning point came as he was preparing a sermon after discussing the plight of the Indians with some Dominicans who shared his concerns. As he thumbed through the Bible, his eyes fell on this passage: "Tainted his gifts who offers in sacrifice ill-gotten goods." Las Casas was unable to get these words out of his mind, and he finally concluded that everything done to the people of the West Indies was "unjust and tyrannical." Committed now to giving up his own Indian slaves, he soon delivered his first sermon denouncing the treatment of the islanders.

In fact, the Indians posed a thorny problem for Spanish Christians. Like the Moors, the New World's natives were outsiders captured in battle. Unlike the Moors, they were not stubborn infidels, but people capable of salvation. At the same time, Indian labor was the key to extracting the New World's wealth. Indeed, making the natives economically productive was essential to "civilizing" them. Two years earlier, King Ferdinand had called a group of jurists and theologians together to consider what to do about the Indians. The group called for the teaching of Christian doctrine to the native people, but it also offered Ferdinand a powerful justification for Indian service. Because of their "natural lack of understanding," the Indians were unable to rule themselves. They could not be considered slaves, but for their own good, they would have to "work for those who govern them."

In 1512, Ferdinand issued the Laws of Burgos, the first royal confirmation of the *encomienda* system. These laws contained provisions to prevent the abuse of Indian laborers, but those provisions were largely ignored. Spain was a poor country, and the impoverished Spanish crown had an obvious interest in the gold mines of the West Indies. Moreover, numerous royal officials had a vested interest in the *encomienda* system. Indeed, Ferdinand was the largest holder of Indians in the New World. Thus the Laws of Burgos salved Spanish consciences, but wealth continued to flow out of the West Indies, and the natives continued to die in the mines and fields.

In contrast to most of his countrymen, Las Casas believed that the Indians, despite their primitive mode of living, were rational beings with "excellent, subtle, and very capable minds." Like other clerics, he never doubted the need to save the Indians by making them economically productive. But he also knew that their way of life poorly fitted them for servitude. Slavery did not "civilize" the Indians; it killed them. They could be converted and civilized only through "love and tenderness." Determined to see the *encomienda* system destroyed, Las Casas returned to Spain in 1515 and gained an audience with Ferdinand. Within weeks, however, Ferdinand was dead. When Las Casas then took his case to officials in charge of Spanish affairs in the New World, he got the cold shoulder.

In response, Las Casas devised a remarkable plan to save the people of the New World by scrapping the *encomienda* system. Under his plan, the Indians would live in their own villages, learn to govern themselves, and claim a share of the profits of their labor. They also would be treated in a humane manner, although they would continue to work for the Spanish settlers and produce revenue for the Crown. For Hispaniola, where the native population had already been largely destroyed, he proposed an alternative plan. Spanish peasants would be sent to the island to work alongside, and eventually intermarry with, the surviving Indians. Las Casas endorsed the importation of African slaves to do heavy labor and to compensate the colonists who had lost their *encomiendas*. He seemed to have few qualms about enslaving Africans, perhaps because he believed that Africans could better endure the rigors of slavery, or perhaps because Africans were more "outlandish" to him than the Native Americans he was so eager to save.

Already rebuffed by colonial officials in Spain, Las Casas presented his plan to Francisco Jiménez, the cardinal of Spain and the regent* of the young King Charles I.* In response to Las Casas's proposals, Jiménez named him "Protector of the Indians" and sent some friars to the West Indies to investigate the situation. When Las Casas arrived back in Santo Domingo, he realized that the cardinal's investigators were no more interested in his complaints than the Spanish colonists were in giving up their control over the Indians. After he returned to Spain to press his case again, royal authorities issued orders granting free passage and land to Spanish peasants who immigrated to the West Indies. For the second time, wily officials had approved one of his reforms, but again there was a catch. Las Casas soon learned that the great landowners in Spain had no desire to lose their tenants, and as a result of their powerful opposition, he was forced to abandon his plan.

Now Las Casas developed an even grander scheme to save the Indians. Battling colonial agents at court for a year, he finally secured a grant of land running about eight hundred miles along the coast of Venezuela. Only a few missionaries had penetrated the area, and thus the native inhabitants had been spared the fate of the Tainos. Under Las Casas's plan, the Indians would be converted and live in towns. He knew that any successful effort to save the Indians had to profit the Spaniards, so he promised to the Crown handsome revenues resulting from the production of gold and various trade items.

Las Casas's model community was doomed to failure, however. When he set sail from Spain in 1520, he was accompanied by seventy condemned men escaping punishment. Shortly after he arrived in Venezuela, he sailed to Santo Domingo in an attempt to stop Spanish slave traders' continued attacks on the Indians there. A few days after he left Venezuela, the Indians killed several Spaniards and burned a monastery. When his ship landed at the wrong end of Hispaniola, he was forced to walk across the island to Santo Domingo. As he walked, people told him the news from Venezuela: "The Indians . . . have slain the cleric Bartolomé de Las Casas and all his household!"

Las Casas was stunned. He had compromised his principles, he believed,

---

Regent: An individual appointed to rule in a monarchy when the sovereign is too young or otherwise unable to govern. The appointment of a cardinal to this position indicates that church and state were inseparable in sixteenth-century Spain.

Charles I: The grandson of Ferdinand and Isabella. Because his mother was insane and his father had died, Charles inherited the Spanish throne while still a boy.

when he threw in with the Spaniards, who were interested only in money. Taking the news from Venezuela as "a divine judgment," and no longer confident that he had been chosen to save the Indians, he decided to turn his back on the world. In 1522, he entered the Dominican monastery in Santo Domingo and the next year took his vows as a Dominican friar. To "all appearances," as Las Casas himself put it, for the next eleven years he "slept." As he dozed off, Hernán Cortés was putting millions of Indians under Spain's yoke.

"A Vast Multitude of Corpses"

Hernán Cortés was a restless man of action. Born in Medellín* in 1485, the son of an army commander, young Hernán was sent off to study Latin and law at the same university attended by Las Casas. Two years later, at the age of sixteen, he returned to Medellín, convinced that his future lay in the military. In 1504, still only nineteen, Cortés sailed for the West Indies, landing in Santo Domingo. Soon after his arrival, like Las Casas, he participated in an expedition under the command of Diego Velásquez to crush an Indian revolt. He distinguished himself in the fighting and, again like Las Casas, was rewarded with an *encomienda*. For six years, he enjoyed life as a planter. Then in 1511, he accompanied Velásquez's expedition to conquer Cuba—the same expedition that left Las Casas shocked by the carnage he witnessed. Rewarded with another *encomienda*, Cortés settled in the seaport of Santiago, in southwestern Cuba.

In the years since Columbus's first voyage to the New World, the Spaniards had seized control of the West Indies, visited Florida, and probed the coasts of Central and South America. Strangely, however, they had never sailed due west from Cuba. Then in 1517, an expedition in search of more Indians to work Cuba's mines and fields had done just that, landing on the Yucatán, a peninsula extending northward into the Caribbean Sea from southern Mexico. When the expedition returned to Cuba the following year with gold and other treasure, Velásquez immediately outfitted another group, which returned with still more gold and the knowledge that the Yucatán was not, as previously thought, an island. Determined to discover what lay to the north of this peninsula, Velásquez turned to Cortés to lead a third expedition. The restless *encomendero* seized the opportunity. To finance the voyage, he borrowed heavily and even pledged his *encomienda* as collateral.

Cortés set sail in early 1519 with an armada of eleven ships carrying 553 soldiers, 4 cannon, and a banner that read, "Friends, let us follow the cross with true faith, with which we will conquer." His orders were to explore further, rescue any Spaniards captured by the Indians during the earlier expeditions, find any gold and silver he could, and colonize the area if conditions were favorable. The fleet made its way to Cozumel, an island off the northeastern tip of the Yucatán. There Cortés encountered people living very differently from the primitive West Indians. For the first time, he saw native cities and evidence of a highly organized society. These Indians were descendants of the Mayas, who had built a complex civilization in southern Mexico and Guatemala between

---

Medellín: A town in southwestern Spain.

the sixth and tenth centuries. Like other Mesoamerican* peoples, the Mayas built stone structures, lived in cities, and used sophisticated agricultural techniques. They also worshiped numerous gods and practiced human sacrifice, both of which were shocking and incomprehensible to the Spaniards. Although he was no priest, Cortés took his Catholic faith seriously. The product of a militantly religious society, he was driven by his duty as a Christian warrior to bring these heathens to God. After entering one blood-splattered temple, for example, he smashed the idols inside, erected a cross, and ordered a priest to say Mass. Before his conquest was over, he would strike down many more Native American idols.

Sailing on, Cortés's party soon landed near the mouth of the Tabasco River on the Gulf of Mexico. When the native Tabascans gave the Spaniards a hostile reception, the Spaniards brought their horses and superior arms to bear, killing more than eight hundred Tabascans. The Indians then presented Cortés with gold and twenty young women. One of the women spoke Mayan and Nahuatl, the Aztec language. Named Malinche, she had been born into a noble Aztec family. After her father died, her mother remarried and bore a son. To make sure this son received his inheritance, her mother and stepfather sold Malinche into slavery. Now handed over by the Tabascans, she soon became Cortés's faithful helper and lover. She also played another important role, translating Nahuatl into Mayan, which a priest rescued from the Yucatán then translated into Spanish. Cortés now had the means to communicate with the emperor of Mexico.

As the expedition continued along the coast, Cortés heard tales of a magnificent kingdom in the interior. Anchoring at the site of modern-day Veracruz, he soon received a chief bearing gifts of gold from the Aztec emperor, Montezuma II. The Aztec leader had already heard about the battle with the Tabascans and no doubt wanted to learn more about these newcomers, their strange animals, and their weapons that made a deafening roar. Cortés told the emissary that he represented a great monarch on the other side of the ocean, information that confirmed an important Aztec myth. The Aztecs believed that a white-skinned, bearded god named Quetzalcoatl had founded the Indian race and then sailed away to the east, promising to return and reestablish his rule. The Aztec emperor may or may not have believed this myth, but he surely did not want to give up his power. The ambassador told Cortés that Montezuma did not want to see him. Cortés was undeterred. If he returned to Cuba without enough gold to pay for the voyage, he would lose his *encomienda*. Facing disgrace and financial ruin, he knew there was no turning back. After executing two conspirators who wished to head home, he had his men unload all the ships' provisions; then he ordered the vessels burned. Without the possibility of retreat, the choice was now simple: the conquest of Montezuma's empire or death.

In this desperate hour, messengers arrived from the chief of the Totonacs, another Mesoamerican people who had recently been defeated by Montezuma's warriors. Cortés was encouraged by evidence of dissension among the Indians.

---

*Mesoamerican: The term applied to the Native Americans, including the Mayas and Aztecs, who lived in present-day Mexico and Central America.

In August 1519, the Spaniards set off with thirteen hundred Totonac warriors for Tenochtitlán,* the capital of the Aztec Empire. It was an arduous and bloody trek. More than two hundred miles lay between the coast and the heart of Montezuma's empire on Mexico's central plateau. Getting there required a climb to more than 7,300 feet above sea level. Along the way, the expedition came under attack by the Tlaxcalans, another people in central Mexico subject to Aztec rule. Overwhelmed by the Spaniards' superior arms, the Tlaxcalans decided to join the invaders.

By the time Cortés marched into the Aztec religious center of Cholula, about sixty miles southeast of Tenochtitlán, his army had swollen to six thousand men. They were met by more than twenty thousand people. Warned by Malinche that the Cholulans were planning an ambush, Cortés struck first. With the aid of their Tlaxcalan allies, the Spaniards fell on the Cholulans and slaughtered them. Two days later, six thousand men, women, and children lay dead. Cortés pressed on to Tenochtitlán, arriving at its outskirts in early November.

Realizing that he could not prevent the Spaniards from entering his domain, Montezuma invited the visitors into the city. The capital of an empire numbering perhaps 16 million people, Tenochtitlán was an awesome sight. With some 300,000 residents, it was larger than any city the Spaniards had ever seen. In many ways, it was also the most sophisticated. Built on an island in Lake Texcoco, it was supplied with water by an aqueduct linked to the mainland. People and goods entered the city across three viaducts, each fortified with drawbridges. Its plaza, the site of a weekly market, could accommodate 60,000 people. In short, Tenochtitlán was the creation of a highly organized civilization. Dominated by pyramids that seemed to touch the sky, it amazed even the hard-bitten Spanish soldiers. Montezuma's gifts of gold, silver, and jewels had the same impact.

The emperor no doubt hoped that the Spaniards would be impressed by his power and generosity and then depart. Cortés had no intention of leaving, however. The Aztecs astounded Cortés with their magnificent achievements and highly organized social structure, which was similar to that of Spain. But in Cortés's eyes, they were still barbarians. In every town on their trek to Tenochtitlán, his men had seen temples where humans were sacrificed to appease the unpredictable gods. In the Aztec capital, Montezuma took Cortés to the top of the highest pyramid, the temple of the war god Huitzilopochtli, where Cortés saw a fearsome idol covered with dried human blood. Witness to such sights, Cortés never doubted that the Aztecs were heathens—or the justice of bringing them to God by the sword. [See Source 1.]

Not intimidated by Montezuma's power, Cortés seized the emperor and held him hostage. He justified the action by claiming that some Spaniards left in defense of Veracruz had been killed by Montezuma's men. Cortés detained the emperor for five months, while the Spaniards studied the Aztecs and surveyed their empire. Then he ordered Montezuma to gather his nobles and announce that he was submitting to the Spanish monarch. As tribute, the Spanish took

---

Tenochtitlán: Pronounced "the-noach-*tee*-tlan," the city was built on the site of present-day Mexico City.

huge quantities of gold objects. It seemed that Cortés had accomplished the un-thinkable: the peaceful conquest of the Aztec Empire.

The Aztecs began to grow, restless, however, and Cortés received word that a Spanish fleet had arrived at Veracruz with orders from Diego Velásquez to re-turn to Cuba immediately. Leaving a small force in the Aztec capital, Cortés re-turned to the coast to persuade this force to join him. While he was away, more than six hundred Aztec nobles and some three thousand spectators assembled in Tenochtitlán's temple area for sacred dances. Fearing an insurrection, Span-ish troops under Pedro Alvarado fell on the crowd. When they were finished, the courtyard was littered with bodies, and the leading Aztec nobles had been wiped out. **[See Source 2.]**

When Cortés returned from the coast, the Aztecs were up in arms. Desper-ate, he forced Montezuma to appear before his people and plead for peace. But the move backfired. Many Aztecs, disillusioned with the emperor's apparent cowardice, turned on Montezuma with stones and arrows, fatally wounding him. With his valuable hostage lost, Cortés retreated. As the Spaniards tried to escape, the Aztecs, led by Montezuma's brother Cuitlahuac, attacked. Bogged down by gold and other loot, the Spaniards lost 450 men, 4,000 Indian confed-erates, and dozens of horses. In the confusion of battle, they also lost much of their treasure.

Cortés barely escaped, but the Aztecs had not seen the last of him. The in-vaders returned to their Tlaxcalan allies, who had amassed a force of 150,000. They marched back to Tenochtitlán, slaughtering all who resisted. As smallpox raged through the empire, killing Cuitlahuac, Cortés and his army laid siege to the capital. When the Aztecs continued to hold out, Cortés decided that the only way to defeat them was to systematically destroy the city. With the assistance of his Indian allies, the Spaniards laid waste to Tenochtitlán. The siege and cam-paign of destruction lasted for seventy-five days. When it was over in August 1521, the Aztecs had lost perhaps 140,000 people. Their once magnificent capi-tal was reduced to rubble, and its streets and canals were littered with "a vast multitude of corpses."

The victorious Spaniards were quickly disappointed, however. Searching for more Aztec wealth, they found little. Even torturing Cuitlahuac's twenty-three-year-old successor, the last Aztec emperor, produced no treasure. Frus-trated in his hopes for immediate riches, Cortés organized expeditions to the outer reaches of the Aztec domain, speeding the Spanish discovery of more Mexican territory and the founding of new cities. In short order, all of the Aztec empire was under Cortés's command. The decimation of the Aztec lords and priests, who were often burned at the stake, hastened the consolidation of Span-ish control. Accustomed to authoritarian rule, the surviving Indians quietly submitted to their new masters.

The outlines of a new society quickly emerged from the ashes of the old. One characteristic—a racially mixed population—began to appear when Mal-inche presented Cortés with a son shortly after the conquest. Because most of the early Spanish immigrants to Mexico were male, sexual liaisons and some-times even marriages between Spaniards and Native American women were common. Therefore, many more mestizos (mixed-blood children) were born. Just as Mexico City was built on the site of the destroyed Aztec capital, the new society was based on the exploitation of Indian labor. Like Mexico City, the *encomiendas*, which Cortés generously distributed to himself and his officers, were a symbol of one culture's conquest of another. **[See Source 3.]** His own grants included twenty-two towns and perhaps as many as ninety thousand Indian vassals. Appointed governor of New Spain in 1522, Cortés lived regally. "I did not come here," he declared, "to till the land like a peasant."

A "Tyrannical Pestilence"

As Cortés built New Spain, Bartolomé de Las Casas studied and contemplated behind monastery walls. After eleven years in retreat, he was ready to resume his role as "Protector of the Indians." Turning to Central America, he founded a Dominican monastery in Nicaragua in 1534. After attacking the Spanish governor's efforts to conquer the Indians there, he left to evangelize the people of Guatemala. As three military expeditions had failed to convert them, Guatemala's governor granted Las Casas permission to use peaceful means instead. When his efforts began to bear fruit, he published *The Only Method of Attracting All People to the True Faith* (1537), an assault on the assumption of Cortés and other conquistadors that the Indians could not be converted unless conquered. **[See Source 4.]**

His confidence restored, Las Casas again took up his fight against the *encomienda* system. After winning an audience with King Charles in 1540, Las Casas read at court his account of Spanish atrocities against the Indians. Determined to shock the king, he related revolting details of the Spaniards' "murder and destruction" of the Indians and the "tyrannical pestilence" introduced among them. Then he called on Charles to take the revolutionary step of abolishing the *encomienda* system, the very basis of Spanish control of the Indians. **[See Source 5.]** In 1542, Charles responded by issuing the New Laws, which prohibited the enslavement of any more Indians, stripped officials of their *encomiendas*, and transferred other *encomiendas* to the Crown upon the death of their owners. The New Laws emancipated the Indians from the plantations and set them on the path to freedom.

Getting the New Laws on the books was one thing, but enforcing them was quite another. When Las Casas returned to the New World, he encountered the wrath of Spanish settlers. When he arrived in southern Mexico, where church officials had offered him a bishopric, local *encomenderos* were up in arms over the New Laws, and colonial officials refused to enforce them. So he set off again for Spain. On his way, he visited Mexico City, where he defended the New Laws and denounced the *encomienda* system before political authorities and fellow bishops. Word of his actions reached Spain, and in 1547 officials there rebuked him. Las Casas refused to back down, and the New Laws stayed on the books.

By that time, the man directly responsible for the virtual enslavement of New Spain's Indians had suffered a reversal of fortune. Cortés's fabulous success in Mexico had sparked tremendous interest in New Spain. On the heels of his conquest came an influx of settlers, many of whom also were anxious to make their fortunes. They came to develop Mexico rather than merely loot it. That required administrators and politicians rather than soldiers. As conquest gave way to settlement, Cortés was pushed aside. He faced constant challenges to his authority and was accused of hiding part of Montezuma's treasure and defrauding the Crown of its revenue. Under a cloud, Cortés was stripped of his governorship.

Playing on Cortés's love of conquest, Charles named him governor of the lands of the "Southern Sea"—the Pacific Ocean. Cortés outfitted several expeditions to explore the Pacific and search for a strait connecting it and the Caribbean. Little came of these voyages, although he did discover a sea between lower California and Mexico, which he named for himself. When he traveled to Spain to ask Charles to protect his remaining military power, he was met with indifference. Worn down by his struggle with Spanish authorities, he decided to stay in Spain and settle his "account with God." Although there is no evidence that he ever regretted his conquest of the Aztecs, he told Charles in 1544 that "it is better to lose my fortune than my soul." He never returned to the New World and in 1547 died at the age of sixty-two.

By then, other conquistadors had set off in search of more Native American empires. In 1531, Francisco Pizarro and several hundred Spanish soldiers marched into the Inca Empire high in the Andes mountains along the west coast of South America. Conquering and enslaving the Incas, Pizarro and his men seized a mother lode of gold and silver. A little later, other military expeditions probed north from New Spain. In the early 1540s, Francisco Coronado searched futilely for fabled cities of gold in what would later be the southwestern United States. At about the same time, Hernando de Soto traveled into the Mississippi Valley. Inspired by Cortés's success, these men helped Spain forge the richest European empire by the beginning of the seventeenth century. They also provided later English settlers in the New World a vivid example of the relationship between wealth and labor exploitation.

Cortés played a large role in defining the nature of the Spanish experience in the New World. By imposing the *encomienda* system on New Spain, he sealed the fate of millions of Indians. True, the passage of the New Laws—and Las Casas's successful efforts to keep them on the books—led to a decline of the *encomienda* system in the seventeenth century. But a new system of labor exploitation soon arose. Haciendas (large estates) came to be worked by Indians who were free and entitled to wages for their labor. In reality, these peons, or farm workers, quickly fell into debt and became debt slaves. The Catholic Church, New Spain's largest landowner by the seventeenth century, supported this system of debt peonage. As Indians became tied to the land, it was easier for clerics to see them as inferior dependents. Meanwhile, black slavery continued for several centuries as well, but only on a small scale compared to that in the West Indies and other areas of the New World. Most of New Spain's black slaves were imported in the sixteenth century and were absorbed into the larger Native American population. Indian debt peonage remained the dominant form of labor exploitation for generations.

Cortés's legacy was visible even in New Spain's remote borderlands. By the time the Spaniards settled Mexico's far northern frontier at the end of the sixteenth century, their attitudes toward the Indians were already fixed. The consequences for the Indians were much the same as they had been farther south. In New Mexico, colonized by Spaniards in 1598, the Pueblo Indians rose up in revolt in 1680 against the exploitation of their labor and efforts to wipe out their religion. When Spanish authorities regained control twelve years later, they were less zealous in fighting the Indians' culture. Nevertheless, the Indians remained in a subservient position. In California, colonized in 1769, the Indians were virtually enslaved by the missionaries there. In fact, wherever the Spaniards settled, their assumptions about the Indians' inferiority reinforced the basic Spanish need for labor. It was a powerful combination. The belief of Las Casas and a few other sixteenth-century clerics that Native Americans could be fully integrated into Spanish colonial society was no match for it.

Las Casas continued to struggle against Spanish policies in the New World for the rest of his life. Convinced that his most important work could be done at court in Spain, he resigned his New World bishopric in 1550 and moved to a Dominican monastery in his homeland. There he fought Spanish injustices against Native Americans and Africans with his pen. Las Casas had by then changed his views about African slavery. He knew that thousands of black slaves had been imported into the New World, but not one Indian had been freed as a result. He realized that the Africans' enslavement "was as unjust as the Indians'," but the Indians' fate still troubled him more. In 1552, he published his *Very Brief Account of the Destruction of the Indies* and two years later completed a sweeping *History of the Indies*. Both books recounted in gruesome detail Spanish atrocities in the West Indies and Cortés's brutal conquest of Mexico.

Eventually translated into many languages, these books had a huge impact on history. In particular, they laid the foundation for the long-standing "Black Legend" that the Spaniards had the bloodiest hands of all the Europeans in the New World. Often embraced by later English and American historians to exonerate English settlers, this legend was a gross distortion. The English, of course, amassed their own bloody record against the Indians. Moreover, the Spaniards often mixed with the Indians, as Cortés's union with Malinche demonstrates. By contrast, the English violently dispossessed the Indians of their land and pushed them away from areas of European settlement.

For all his work to save the Indians, Las Casas had a greater impact on Spain's image in the New World than on the native peoples themselves. In fact, he regretted until he died that he had not done more to affect their fate. Surely, he had had little influence on Cortés, who had established a colony with millions of Indians in bondage. Long after Las Casas died, though, his writings did have an influence on how later generations viewed Mexico's conqueror. Although Las Casas could not see the conquest of the New World as the native peoples did, he did see those events through sympathetic eyes. Thus he left enduring images that made it easier for later historians to question the more traditional views of the conquest. If Cortés prevailed over the Indians, Las Casas in the end prevailed over him.

PRIMARY SOURCES

SOURCE 1: *Cortés Describes the Aztecs* (1519, 1520)

In letters to King Charles I, Hernán Cortés described the religious practices of the Indians along the Gulf of Mexico and among the Aztecs. He also discussed the Aztec capital of Tenochtitlán. In this selection, how does Cortés portray Aztec civilization? What rationale does he offer for the conquest of the Indians?

One very horrible and abominable custom they have which should certainly be punished and which we have seen in no other part, and that is that whenever they wish to beg anything of their idols, in order that their petition may find more acceptance, they take large numbers of boys and girls and even of grown men and women and tear out their heart and bowels while still alive, burning them in the presence of those idols, and offering the smoke of such burning as a pleasant sacrifice. Some of us have actually seen this done and they say that it is the most terrible and frightful thing that they have ever seen. Yet the Indians perform this ceremony so frequently that, as we are informed and have in part seen from our own scanty experience since we have been in this land, there is no year passes in which they do not thus kill and sacrifice fifty souls in every such temple, and the practice is general from the island of Cozumel to the region in which we have now settled. Your Majesties can therefore be certain that since the land is large and they seem to have a large number of temples there can be no year (so far as we have been able up to the present to ascertain) in which they have not sacrificed in this manner some three or four thousand souls. Your Majesties may therefore perceive whether it is not their duty to prevent such loss and evil, and certainly it will be pleasing to God if by means of and under the protection of your royal Majesties these peoples are introduced into and instructed in the holy Catholic Faith, and the devotion, trust and hope which they now have in their idols turned so as to repose in the divine power of the true God; for it is certain that if they should serve God with that same faith, fervour and diligence they would work many miracles. And we believe that not without cause has God been pleased to allow this land to be discovered in the name of your royal Majesties, that your Majesties may reap great merit and reward from Him in sending the Gospel to these barbarian people who thus by your Majesties' hands will be received into the true faith. . . .

The images of the idols in which these people believed are many times greater than the body of a large man. They are made from pulp of all the cereals and greenstuffs which they eat, mixed and pounded together. This mass they moisten with blood from the hearts of human beings which they tear from their breasts while still alive, and thus make sufficient quantity of the pulp to mould into their huge statues: and after the idols have been set up still they offer them

SOURCE: Reprinted in J. Bayard Morris, *Five Letters of Cortés to the Emperor* (New York: W. W. Norton & Company, 1962?), pp. 23–24, 92–94. Copyright © 1969 by J. Bayard Morris. Used by permission of W. W. Norton & Company, Inc.

more living hearts which they sacrifice in like manner and anoint their faces with the blood. Each department of human affairs has its particular idol after the manner of the ancients who thus honoured their gods: so that there is one idol from whom they beg success in war, another for crops, and so on for all their needs.

The city contains many large and fine houses. . . . All the nobles of the land owing allegiance to Muteczuma [Montezuma] have their houses in the city and reside there for a certain portion of the year; and in addition there are a large number of rich citizens who likewise have very fine houses. All possess in addition to large and elegant apartments very delightful flower gardens of every kind, both on the ground level as on the upper storeys.

Along one of the causeways connecting this great city with the mainland two pipes are constructed of masonry, each two paces broad and about as high as a man, one of which conveys a stream of water very clear and fresh and about the thickness of a man's body right to the centre of the city, which all can use for drinking and other purposes. The other pipe which is empty is used when it is desired to clean the former. Moreover, on coming to the breaks in the causeway spanned by bridges under which the salt water flows through, the fresh water flows into a kind of trough as thick as an ox which occupies the whole width of the bridge, and thus the whole city is served. The water is sold from canoes in all the streets, the manner of their taking it from the pipes being in this wise: the canoes place themselves under the bridges where the troughs are to be found, and from above the canoes are filled by men who are especially paid for this work.

At all the entrances to the city and at those parts where canoes are unloaded, which is where the greatest amount of provisions enters the city, certain huts have been built, where there are official guards to exact so much on everything that enters. I know not whether this goes to the lord or to the city itself, and have not yet been able to ascertain, but I think that it is to the ruler, since in the markets of several other towns we have seen such a tax exacted on behalf of the ruler. Every day in all the markets and public places of the city there are a number of workmen and masters of all manner of crafts waiting to be hired by the day. The people of this city are nicer in their dress and manners than those of any other city or province, for since Muteczuma always holds his residence here and his vassals visit the city for lengthy periods, greater culture and politeness of manners in all things has been encouraged.

Finally, to avoid prolixity in telling all the wonders of this city, I will simply say that the manner of living among the people is very similar to that in Spain, and considering that this is a barbarous nation shut off from a knowledge of the true God or communication with enlightened nations, one may well marvel at the orderliness and government which is everywhere maintained.

Source 2:   *An Aztec View of the Temple Massacre*   (ca. 1550)

This picture is an adaptation of an Aztec rendering of the massacre of Aztec nobles by Pedro Alvarado in the temple at Tenochtitlán made shortly after the Spanish conquest. What does this Aztec view emphasize?

Source: Figure on p. 122 "Aztec view of temple massacre" from *The Conquest of America: The Question of the Other* by Tzvetan Todorov. Translated by Richard Howard. English translation copyright © 1984 by Harper & Row, Publishers, Inc. Reprinted by permission of HarperCollins Publishers, Inc.

SOURCE 3:   *Cortés Defends* Encomiendas   (1522)

In this letter to King Charles, Hernán Cortés defends holding the Indians in encomiendas. On what grounds does he do so?

I have likewise informed your Majesty that the natives of these parts are of much greater intelligence than those of the Islands; they seem to us indeed to possess sufficient intelligence to conduct themselves as average reasonable beings. On this account it seemed to me a very serious matter to compel them to serve the Spaniards in the same way as the natives in the Islands; yet without this service the conquerors and settlers of these parts would not be able to maintain themselves. In order, therefore, not to enslave the Indians at that time, and yet to assist the Spaniards to settle, it seemed to me that your Majesty might order a certain portion of the royal revenues accruing to your Majesty from these parts to be appropriated to the expenses and maintenance of the colonists, as I explained very fully to your Majesty. Since then, however, bearing in mind the many and continued expenses of your Majesty, and the fact that we should seek in every way to increase your Majesty's revenues rather than diminish them, and seeing, moreover, the long time that we have spent in fighting against the natives and the hardships and loss which we have been put to on that account, together with the delay which your Majesty might for that reason command; above all, on account of the many importunities of your Majesty's officials and all my men, which there was no means of resisting, I found myself practically forced to hand over the rulers and natives of these parts to the Spaniards, taking into consideration when doing so their estate and the services which they have rendered your Majesty in these parts, so that until your Majesty shall make some fresh arrangement or confirm this one, the aforesaid rulers and natives will serve and provide the Spaniards, to whom they were respectively allotted, with whatever they may need to sustain themselves. All this was done with the approval of persons who have great knowledge and experience of the country. No better course could have been taken, nor one which contributes more both to the proper maintenance of the Spaniards, and the conservation and good treatment of the Indians; of all this the procurators now proceeding to your Majesty from New Spain will give your Majesty a long and complete account. Your Majesty's farms and granaries have been placed in the best and most convenient cities and provinces. I beseech your Majesty to approve this and order in what way the royal interests may best be served.

SOURCE: Reprinted in J. Bayard Morris, *Five Letters of Cortés to the Emperor* (New York: W. W. Norton & Company, 1962), pp. 240–241. Copyright © 1969 by J. Bayard Morris. Used by permission of W. W. Norton & Company, Inc.

SOURCE 4: *Las Casas Attacks Conversion by Conquest* (1537)

In The Only Method of Attracting All People to the True Faith, *published in 1537, Bartolomé de Las Casas argues against the conquistadors' method of converting the Indians to Christianity through conquest. What assumptions does Las Casas make about the natives? How do they compare to Cortés's assumptions?*

The one and only method of teaching men the true religion was established by Divine Providence for the whole world, and for all times; that is, by persuading the understanding through reasons, and by gently attracting or exhorting the will. This method should be common to all men throughout the world, without any distinction made for sects, errors, or corrupt customs. . . .

A method contrary to the one we have been defending would be the following: that . . . the pagans should first be subjected, whether they wished to be or not, to the rule of the Christian people, and that once they were subjected, organized preaching would follow. In this case, the preachers would not compel them to believe but would convince them by arguments and also draw them gently, once the many impediments which preaching could encounter had been removed by the said subjection.

But since no pagan, above all no pagan kings, would wish voluntarily to submit to the rule of a Christian people, or of any prince, it would certainly be necessary to come to a war.

However, war brings with it these evils: the crash of arms; sudden attacks and invasions, impetuous and furious; violence and deadly confusion; licentiousness, deaths and massacres; rapine, pillage and plunder; parents deprived of their sons, and sons of their parents; captivities; kings and natural lords deprived of their estates and dominions; the devastation and desolation of innumerable towns and cities. And all these evils fill kingdoms . . . with sad laments. . . .

Laws are silent, humane feelings are mocked, nowhere is there rectitude, religion is an object of scorn, and there is absolutely no distinction made between the sacred and the profane. War also fills every place with highwaymen, thieves, ravishers, fires, and murders. Indeed, what is war but general murder and robbery among many? And the more widespread it is, the more criminal it is. Through war extreme misfortune is brought upon thousands of innocents who do not deserve the injury that is done them. To sum up, in war men lose their riches, their bodies, and their souls. . . .

But now we have to see how this method of preaching the faith is contrary to the one indicated above, and also that it is the most unsuitable method of all . . . for attracting and enticing peoples to the congregation of Christ. . . . This is proved first by the following argument. . . .

A rational creature has a natural capacity for being moved, directed and

SOURCE: Reprinted in George Sanderlin, ed., *Bartolomé de Las Casas: A Selection of His Writings* (New York: Alfred A. Knopf, 1971), pp. 158, 161–162. Copyright © 1971 by Alfred A. Knopf, a division of Random House, Inc. Used by permission of Alfred A. Knopf.

drawn to any good gently . . . because of his freedom of choice. But if pagans find themselves first injured, oppressed, saddened, and afflicted by the misfortunes of wars, through the loss of their children, their goods, and their own liberty . . . how can they be moved voluntarily to listen to what is proposed to them about faith, religion, justice, and truth?

Source 5:   *Las Casas Attacks* Encomiendas   (1542)

In this memorial delivered to King Charles, Las Casas calls for the elimination of the encomienda system. On what grounds does he attack the system?

Since the purpose of the dominion of Your Majesty over those peoples is the preaching and establishing of the faith among them, and their conversion and knowledge of Christ, this and no other . . . , Your Majesty is therefore obliged to remove all obstacles that can hinder the attainment of this purpose. . . . But one of the greatest obstacles and impediments that there has been until now . . . has been for the Christians to hold them in encomiendas. The same and much worse could be said if they were given to the Christians as vassals. As proof of this we give three reasons.

The first, which has been manifest to everyone, is the great greed and avarice of the Spaniards, because of which they neither wish nor permit the religious to enter the towns of Indians entrusted to them. For they say they receive chiefly two injuries from this. One, that . . . when the religious preach to the Indians, the Spaniards lose them . . . because of the Indians' being idle and not going to work on the estates. And it has happened that there were Indians in a church listening to a sermon and the religious preaching to them, and a Spaniard entered before all and took fifty or a hundred of them whom he needed to carry loads from his estate. And because they did not wish to go, he gave them kicks and blows with a stick in spite of them and the religious, scandalizing all the people there and hindering the salvation of both Spaniards and Indians.

The other injury which they say they receive is that after the Indians have been instructed and made Christians, they become babblers; they know more than they knew, and because of that the Spaniards cannot profit so much by them thenceforth as before. . . .

Spaniards who hold Indians in encomiendas and wish to keep them as vassals usually . . . say and argue . . . that if the Indians are taken away from them the Spaniards will be unable to live in the land. They say that if the Indians remain by themselves, Your Majesty's dominion over them and, consequently, the Catholic faith, would be endangered . . . and they would go to hell as they were accustomed to before the Christians entered among them, etc. . . .

But to be good Christians, all should feel that even though it were possible

Source: Reprinted in George Sanderlin, ed., *Bartolomé de Las Casas: A Selection of His Writings* (New York: Alfred A. Knopf, 1971), pp. 175–176, 180–181. Copyright © 1971 by Alfred A. Knopf, a division of Random House, Inc. Used by permission of Alfred A. Knopf.

for Your Majesty to lose his entire royal dominion and for the Indians never to become Christians, if the opposite could not take place without their death and total destruction, as has happened until now, it would not be unfitting for Your Majesty to cease to be their lord and for them never to become Christians.

The reason is what has been given, because the law of Christians forbids that evil be done in order that good may follow.

QUESTIONS TO CONSIDER

1. What do Bartolomé de Las Casas's writings reveal about his attitudes toward the Native Americans and their cultures? How do his reforms reflect his attitudes?

2. What does Las Casas's life reveal about the alternative possibilities regarding the fate of the Native Americans? What does it reveal about the forces working against the fulfillment of these possibilities?

3. What do Hernán Cortés's actions reveal about his attitudes toward the Native Americans and their cultures? How do his attitudes compare to those of Las Casas?

4. How does Cortés justify the Spanish conquest of the Indians? What does his life reveal about the forces behind the Spanish conquest and the factors shaping the fate of the Indians?

5. Both Cortés and Las Casas used their Christian faith to justify their views and actions regarding the Indians. What do the lives of these two men reveal about the competing impulses among the Christian Europeans who conquered and occupied the New World?

FOR FURTHER READING

Patricia de Fuentes, ed., *The Conquistadors* (New York: Orion Press, 1963), provides first-hand Spanish accounts of the conquest of Mexico.

Ross Hassig, *Mexico and the Spanish Conquest* (London: Longman, 1994), offers a concise treatment of Cortés's conquest of the Aztecs.

Peggy K. Liss, *Mexico Under Spain, 1521–1556* (Chicago: University of Chicago Press, 1975), is a brief analysis of the early years of Spanish rule in Mexico and the emergence of a new type of society there.

Richard Lee Marks, *Cortés: The Great Adventurer and the Fate of Aztec Mexico* (New York: Alfred A. Knopf, 1993), offers an engaging account of Cortés's life and his conquest of Mexico.

Henry Raup Wagner, *The Life and Writings of Bartolomé de Las Casas* (Albuquerque: University of New Mexico Press, 1967), is a thorough and carefully researched discussion of Las Casas's career as "Protector of the Indians."

Revolt on the Virginia Frontier:
Nathaniel Bacon and William Berkeley

Nathaniel Bacon   *William Berkeley*

As he paused just outside of Jamestown, Virginia, Nathaniel Bacon was in no mood to be denied. The twenty-nine-year-old planter had been accused by his own cousin, Governor William Berkeley, of slaughtering Indians. Declared an outlaw, Bacon was determined to fight back. He would wrest from Berkeley a military commission allowing him to wage indiscriminate war on the "savages." Backing Bacon were six hundred well-armed and angry colonists. Four hundred of them were on foot, too poor to afford a horse. At two o'clock in the afternoon on June 23, 1676, Bacon's men marched into Jamestown. Within a half hour, this "scum of the country," as one observer called them, had secured control of the capital.

Now Bacon would get what he wanted. Flanked by two musket-wielding columns, he marched up to the statehouse door. "God damn my blood, I came for my commission, and a commission I will have before I go," he shouted. Undaunted by Bacon's show of force, the seventy-year-old Berkeley flew out of the statehouse and confronted his young cousin. "Here! Shoot me . . . shoot," he screamed as he ripped open his shirt. Again Bacon demanded a commission as "general of all forces in Virginia against the Indians." When the enraged governor replied that he would rather see his own hand cut off, Bacon's men responded with shouts of "We will have it." Then they turned their guns on the legislators who had crowded at the windows to witness the confrontation out-side. "Damn my blood, I'll kill the governor, council[,] assembly[,] and all," Bacon shouted.

Bacon's threat had the desired effect. One frightened legislator waved a handkerchief and shouted back, "You shall have it. You shall have it." The as-sembly quickly persuaded Berkeley to grant Bacon his military command. Three days later, Bacon left Jamestown with his commission and his army. Yet the governor's problems with Bacon and his followers were not over. In the fol-lowing months, Bacon's men waged brutal war against the Indians, turned their guns on Berkeley's government and forced it to flee Jamestown, and burned the colony's capital to the ground. Not until early 1677 did Berkeley's forces stamp out the uprising that came to bear Bacon's name. But Bacon's Rebellion had vividly demonstrated that not all was well in Virginia.

"Ambitious and Arrogant"

Nathaniel Bacon and William Berkeley shared more than family ties—and hot blood. As sons of prominent English families, both had received an elite educa-tion and sought personal advancement in Virginia. Yet the two men arrived in the colony under very different circumstances: One brought the blessings of the king, while the other carried the burden of his own family's rejection.

William Berkeley was born in 1606 into a family with long influence at the English court. After receiving degrees from Oxford, he followed his family's footsteps to the Privy Council, a body of close advisers appointed by the monarch, where he became a favorite of Charles I.* As the author of several plays and pamphlets, the young courtier made a mark with his pen and polish. Eventually, however, the colonies came to play the key role in Berkeley's ad-vance, as they often did in the lives of younger sons whose older brothers in-herited family estates. (In William's family, John, first Lord Berkeley of Stratton, was the favored son.) He was appointed commissioner of Canadian affairs in 1632 and governor of Virginia nine years later.

When Berkeley arrived in Virginia in 1642, he promptly won the support of the colony's important planters, who were alarmed about talk in Parliament of reviving the defunct Virginia Company.* Such a move would jeopardize prop-erty titles established after the company's demise in 1624. When Berkeley landed with assurances that the company would not be restored, the grateful assembly presented him with two houses and an orchard. His reputation rose even higher when he met a threat to the colony from the Powhatan Indians, who had dealt the fatal blow to the Virginia Company when they attacked the colonists in 1622. In 1644, they struck again, leaving five hundred settlers dead. In response, Berkeley led a military force to the frontier, crushed the Powhatans' resistance, and extracted a treaty that ended hostilities on the frontier for a gen-eration.

Charles I: The king of England from 1625 to 1649.

Virginia Company: A joint-stock company founded by London merchants in 1606 to plant settlements in the New World. It was responsible for establishing Jamestown in 1607.

Berkeley proved no less popular with royal officials. A staunch supporter of the monarchy, he shared with other seventeenth-century aristocrats a disdain for commoners and once boasted that Virginia had neither free schools nor printing presses. Thus when the English civil war* broke out in 1642 between Oliver Cromwell's parliamentary forces and the supporters of King Charles, Berkeley stood behind the Crown and even provided refuge for royalists during the war. Although he had to surrender his power when Cromwell's fleet sailed up the James River to Jamestown, his loyalty to the king paid off. Living quietly for seven years at Green Spring Manor outside Jamestown, Berkeley watched from afar as Cromwell's government in England eventually collapsed. Then shortly after the monarchy was restored in 1660, he found himself back in the statehouse when Charles II named him governor.

With the support of other prominent planters, Berkeley quickly reestablished his political hold. Like the governor, many of his supporters were the second sons of wealthy English families. Often holding choice seats in the colony's government, they also were eager to claim what they regarded as their rightful inheritance. Some of them, such as Virginia secretary Thomas Ludwell, were related by marriage to the governor, who had solidified his own position through matrimony as well. (After arriving in Virginia, Berkeley had won the hand of Frances Culpeper, whose family owned vast tracts in the colony.) Once established in the colony, these members of Virginia's landed gentry expected to be treated with proper deference, and they recommended the colony enthusiastically to prospective settlers. As Berkeley himself noted, "A small sum of money will enable a younger brother to erect a flowering family in the New World."

Whereas Berkeley had found a place for himself in Virginia, newcomer Nathaniel Bacon found prospects there far less to his liking. Born in 1647, the only son of an English gentleman, Bacon grew up on his father's estate, Freestone Hall, surrounded by vast fields and woodlands. He attended Cambridge University and then continued his education back at home under the guidance of a private tutor. After a three-year grand tour of the continent, Bacon returned to Cambridge, where he was granted a master's degree in 1668. Following the path trod by numerous forebears, he read law at the Inns of Court.* By 1670, the young esquire had returned home and married Elizabeth Duke, the daughter of a Suffolk squire.

There seemed to be more to Bacon's makeup, however, than good breeding and a fancy education. In England, many who knew him came to doubt his character. His tutor acknowledged his "quick wit" but also concluded that he was "impatient of labor." Bacon's father-in-law was so dismayed at his daughter's choice that he disinherited her and would never speak to her again. Bacon also

---

English civil war: The war (1642–1649) fought between the Puritan-dominated forces raised by Parliament and the supporters of royal authority. It ended with the execution of Charles I, the triumph of Oliver Cromwell, and the establishment of a commonwealth.

Inns of Court: The London legal societies that had the exclusive right to allow individuals to practice law.

disappointed his own father, who had been forced to withdraw him from Cambridge for "having broken into some extravagances." Later, when the young spendthrift was caught defrauding another young man of his inheritance, Bacon's father gave him eighteen hundred pounds and packed him off to Virginia.

When the tall, thin, dark-haired Bacon arrived in Virginia in 1674, his youthful indiscretions were thousands of miles behind him. With Elizabeth, a daughter, and his father's largesse in hand, he was graciously received by Governor Berkeley and by another cousin, Nathaniel Bacon Sr. With the assistance of his namesake, who sat on the governor's council, Bacon was soon established as a frontier planter. Claiming that he had "always been delighted in solitude," Bacon used his endowment to purchase Curles Neck, a plantation forty miles up the James River in Henrico County. He took up residence there and began planting tobacco. He also bought another tract twenty miles farther upriver at the Fall Line,* which he placed in charge of an overseer. Altogether, Bacon owned more than twelve hundred acres. In addition, Berkeley granted him a seat on his council and a license to trade with the Indians. Though exiled in disgrace, Bacon had made an astonishing recovery in a remarkably short time.

Yet the frontier, which provided Bacon with solitude and a measure of prosperity, would bring him little peace. He was not there long before older residents began to accuse him of "despising the wisest of his neighbors for their ignorance." The young man, they said, was "ambitious and arrogant," possessing a "dangerous hidden pride of heart." In addition, festering social and economic problems were about to erupt, thrusting Bacon into a life-and-death struggle.

"A Sad Dilemma"

Relying on the labor of indentured servants, many of Virginia's planters had made handsome profits during the colony's early tobacco boom. By the time Bacon arrived, however, the days of getting rich quick by growing tobacco were over. After selling as high as twenty-seven cents a pound in 1618, tobacco had fallen in price to a penny a pound by 1630 and would never rise much above two and a half cents for the rest of the century. Virginians had been too successful in producing the leafy plant. Yet low prices had not stopped the colony's growth or, until the middle of the century, posed a threat to its stability. Even after the boom, immigrants continued to arrive, drawn by the dream of getting rich by planting tobacco. Many of these newcomers—mostly young men— arrived as servants, usually indentured for four years in exchange for passage across the Atlantic. Although approximately two thousand African slaves lived in Virginia by the 1670s, cheaper servants provided the main source of labor in the tobacco fields. With land easy to secure in the colony's early years, they could look forward to joining the ranks of the planters. In time, some former servants would even come to control the labor of others and begin to prosper.

Fall Line: The line marking the waterfalls of nearly parallel rivers. The falls limited navigation and thus posed a significant barrier to settlement for much of the seventeenth century. In this case, it refers specifically to the Appomattox, James, Rappahannock, and Potomac Rivers.

By the mid-seventeenth century, the number of servants who became freemen, set up their own households, and planted tobacco began to grow. Earlier, servants were lucky if they survived their terms of indenture. By the 1650s, however, Virginians began to live longer, thanks perhaps to healthier diets. Though still often overworked and abused by masters, more servants lived to become freemen. Mostly, of course, they planted tobacco, further depressing its price. They also competed for good tobacco land. Virginia had abundant uncultivated land, but prominent planters had secured much of the choice tidewater* land, often through their connections to the government. In fact, many were members of the "Green Spring faction," as Berkeley's influential supporters came to be known. By the 1660s, freemen who wished to plant found themselves facing a difficult choice. They could move to the frontier, where it was often impossible to ship tobacco to market and the danger of Indian attack was ever present. Or they could rent land from one of Virginia's big landowners. Many naturally chose the safety of settled areas. Though surrounded by vast stretches of uncultivated land, perhaps a third of the free adult males now worked as tenants for the colony's big planters or moved from place to place as vagrants. In 1670, the assembly declared these landless freemen ineligible to vote. In effect, an artificial scarcity of land had created a pool of poor—and powerless—workers.

Making matters worse, Virginians faced a crushing annual poll tax of as much as 200 pounds of tobacco, export taxes, and customs duties. The taxes helped fill the king's coffers, but they also paid for generous perquisites of office in Virginia. From the governor and legislators to clerks of the county courts, officeholders rewarded themselves handsomely. Governor Berkeley's salary was an astonishing twelve hundred pounds sterling—more than the average freeman could hope to see in a lifetime. In addition, he took 200 pounds of tobacco for every marriage license issued, 350 pounds annually from every tavern, and an annual tribute of beaver pelts from the colony's subject Indians, as well as payoffs from licensed fur traders. Meanwhile, the Speaker and clerk of the House of Burgesses were awarded as much as 20,000 pounds of tobacco each for every session of the legislature. As making money by planting tobacco grew more difficult, the colony's government became the way to wealth in Virginia. Yet participation in the government was beyond the reach of former servants. Not a single servant who arrived in Virginia after 1640 was elected to the House of Burgesses, much less appointed to the governor's council.

In the years before Bacon's Rebellion, discontent boiled to the surface of Virginia society. In 1661, servants rebelled in protest against their treatment. Though confined to one county and quickly suppressed, that uprising was followed two years later by the revelation of a plot among servants in another county. "Consider us," Berkeley told the king, "as a people press'd at our backes with Indians, [and] in our Bowills with our servants." Free Virginians, moreover, could be just as unruly, and the governor had to put down two small insurrections of freemen in 1674. To be sure, full-scale armed revolt was unlikely

---

Tidewater: The low, coastal areas east of the Fall Line whose rivers and streams were affected by tidal movements.

because settlers were spread over the land, separated by rivers and forests. Still, when war erupted, the colony mustered large numbers of armed men, and that could be dangerous. When the governor gathered a force in 1673 to prevent a Dutch invasion of the colony, he observed that one-third of the defenders were poor or indebted freemen who would just as soon join the Dutch "in hopes of bettering their condition by sharing the plunder of the country with them." As Berkeley would soon learn, an armed force raised to defend the colony from a different threat could be even more dangerous.

About the same time Bacon took up residence in Virginia, trouble was stirring on the colony's frontier. In the three decades following the Powhatans' failed uprising in 1644, the Pamunkey, Appomattox, Chickahominy, and other tribes lived peacefully under the sovereignty of the English king. The Indians, Berkeley boasted, "are absolutely subjected, so that there is no fear of them." The continuing growth of the English population in Virginia, however, threatened to change that. By 1670, maybe forty thousand English and four thousand subject Indians made Virginia their home. As the settlers' numbers grew, so did encroachment on Indian lands near the Fall Line.

The result by 1675 was rapidly escalating violence. In July of that year, some thirty Virginians responded with a violent outburst to the murder of a white settler by a Doeg Indian. First they killed eleven Doegs. Then they surrounded a cabin sheltering more frightened Indians and gunned them down when they attempted to flee. Fourteen bodies lay around the cabin by the time the men realized that the victims were friendly Susquehannas. Later that summer, a thousand armed Virginians descended on the Susquehannas. The Virginians were convinced that the Susquehannas, the most powerful tribe along the Fall Line, were sheltering other Indian marauders. The Susquehannas denied any involvement in the recent attacks. They blamed them on the Senecas, one of the Iroquois tribes that had squeezed the Susquehannas from the interior, just as the English now pressed them from the other direction. But their denials fell on deaf ears. Surrounding a fort sheltering about a hundred Susquehannas, the Virginians grabbed five chiefs who ventured out to ask the reason for the armed force. The Virginians led the chiefs away and murdered them. The rest of the Susquehannas eventually slipped out of the besieged fort at night, killing ten Virginians in their escape. In early 1676, the Susquehannas, still furious about the murder of their chiefs, launched a raid near the falls of the Potomac and Rappahannock Rivers, leaving sixty settlers dead. Confronted with rising danger on the frontier, white settlers demanded that the governor respond with armed force. [See Source 1.]

Berkeley was in a bind. As governor, he was responsible for maintaining order in the colony so that Virginians could continue to produce tobacco revenue for the Crown. He also was charged with overseeing the lucrative fur trade. Peaceful relations with the Indians were in both his and the colony's best interests, and he was livid about the murder of the Susquehanna chiefs. "If they had come to treat in peace," he declared, "they ought to have gone in peace." He was also well aware of the dangers of sending a force of armed Virginians to the frontier, given the recent indiscriminate attacks against the Indians. Thus the governor sought a solution that addressed the frontier dwellers' concerns without needlessly provoking the Indians.

Berkeley's answer became evident when he convened the assembly in

March 1676. The representatives promptly declared war on "all such Indians who . . . shall be discovered to have committed murders . . . and depredations." It also moved to restrain vigilante action on the frontier, passing a bill authorizing a string of forts to be built along the Fall Line. The forts would be manned not by frontiersmen, but by men from more secure parts of the colony. They would be commanded by officers reporting directly to the governor. In addition, the assembly forbade trade with the Indians, even by those with licenses. "Sad experience," it declared, had demonstrated that traders had broken the law by providing guns and powder to the Indians. From now on, commissions for trade with the Indians would be granted by the governor's appointees on the county courts. While issuing harsh words against the Indians, the legislature had actually exercised a restraining hand on white settlers.

Frontiersmen reacted angrily to the new laws. The forts would require new taxes at a time when tobacco prices were low and many planters were already in dire financial straits. Moreover, they charged, the forts would be placed too far apart to prevent Indian raids. The Indians could easily penetrate a stationary defense and attack exposed plantations at will. The frontier planters could not legally raise their own force to repel the Indian threat, but if they did not take action, they left themselves exposed to "the merciless power of a most bloody and barbarous enemy." It was, they protested, "a sad dilemma."

Fed by growing suspicion about Berkeley's motives and increasing doubts about the loyalty of any Indians, rumors spread up and down the Fall Line: Building forts was intended only to reward Berkeley's cronies with contracts. Berkeley's friends were selling arms to most hostile Indians. Virginia's Indians were paying tribute to other tribes two hundred to three hundred miles away to unite with them. And as the Indian uprising known as King Philip's War raged in New England, some Virginians even began to dread a "general combination of all [tribes] from New England hither."

In an atmosphere of growing fear and frustration, Bacon emerged to lead the fight against the Indians. The impetuous young planter had already run afoul of Berkeley's Indian policy. When Bacon saw fit to seize some Appomattox Indians the previous fall for allegedly stealing corn, the governor had condemned his "rash[,] heady action." Now Bacon, who had recently lost an overseer in a Susquehanna attack and had just begun a trading business, scorned Berkeley's plan for frontier defense. He accused the governor of excluding settlers from the Indian trade only to reward his "favorites." Although Bacon had little in common with Virginia's freemen, he shared with them a feeling that an inside group was reaping rewards at the expense of others.

He was not the only socially prominent newcomer to conclude that he had been treated unfairly. Richard Lawrence, an Oxford graduate; William Drummond, former governor of Carolina; and Giles Bland, whose family claimed extensive landholdings in Virginia, all had had run-ins with Berkeley or his officials. When Bland had arrived in 1671 to take over as customs collector, for instance, Berkeley's secretary Thomas Ludwell had dismissed him as a "puppy and Sonn of a whore." Feeling similarly excluded from Berkeley's ruling circle, Bacon paid a visit in April 1676 to a force of backcountry volunteers at the urging of several other planters. Denouncing the governor as "negligent, wicked, treacherous, and incapable," Bacon took unauthorized command of the force, promising to bear all the costs of the campaign against the Indians. The lives of the frontier inhabitants, he declared, had been "wretchedly sacrificed," and he resolved to risk his "life and fortune" in their defense.

Bacon's new position provoked a speedy response from Berkeley, who warned Bacon not to mutiny and ordered him to Jamestown. Bacon refused to go and instead requested that Berkeley entrust him "with the country's safety" by granting him a commission for command of the volunteers. When Berkeley denied the commission, Bacon issued his "Appeal of the Volunteers to all well minded and charitable people." Because "wrongs and violences" had been "cunningly" committed by several Indian tribes, he declared, it was very difficult to distinguish from which tribes "the said wrongs did proceed." As Bacon and his men mobilized for their first campaign, it would soon become clear just how little use they had for making distinctions between friendly and unfriendly Indians.

"So Glorious a Cause"

In May 1676, Bacon and several hundred of his followers set out to solve Virginia's Indian problem. In search of the Susquehannas, they marched about eighty miles southwest from the James River through thick forests to a fort belonging to the Occaneechees, a friendly tribe living near the present border of Virginia and North Carolina. Encamped near the Occaneechees, they found what they were looking for: a party of Susquehannas, refugees from the Virginians' attack on their fort to the north. When the Susquehannas sought the Occaneechees' aid, they instead alerted the Virginians to their new neighbors' whereabouts. After providing Bacon's exhausted force with food and shelter, the Occaneechees offered to attack the Susquehannas themselves. Bacon and his men were only too willing to have the Occaneechees do their fighting for them. When the Occaneechees returned victorious, however, the Virginians were far less willing to show their gratitude. Bacon demanded that they turn over their plunder, including Indians from other tribes who had been held prisoner by the Susquehannas. After the Occaneechees refused, Bacon's men turned their guns on them. In a fight that lasted through the night, the Virginians poured fire into the Occaneechee fort. They also fell upon men, women, and children left outside and, according to one of Bacon's men, "disarmed and destroyed them all." The next morning, Bacon's force headed home, leaving more than a hundred Indians dead.

By taking action against the Occaneechees, Bacon had openly defied the king's representative in Virginia. Governor Berkeley had more on his mind, though, than respect for royal authority. Bacon's command of an unauthorized army could have dangerous social consequences in the kind of society Virginia had become. In fact, Bacon's army looked a lot like the force of poor freemen that Berkeley had raised only three years earlier to defend the colony from a Dutch invasion. As Berkeley favorite Philip Ludwell said, Bacon's men were "Rabble of the basest sort." Thus while Bacon busied himself killing the Occaneechees, Berkeley moved swiftly to suppress growing discontent with his own policies. First he publicly denounced Bacon and removed him from his council. Then he moved to shore up his support by calling for the new assembly to be elected by all freemen, not just property holders. "All persons are to have liberty," declared Berkeley, "freely to present to [the assembly] all such complaints as they or any other have against me as governor." In addition, Berkeley demonstrated a newfound determination to kill Indians—or at least to make a show of it. Upon hearing reports that subject Indians had attacked colonists, he led a force to the frontier. On the way, he stopped at Curles Neck, where he told Elizabeth Bacon that her husband "would most certainly hang" upon his return from the Occaneechee campaign. In fact, Berkeley had no desire either to kill Indians or to execute Bacon. After several fruitless weeks on the upper James River, Berkeley and his men returned to Jamestown and awaited the convening of the new assembly. When Bacon's bedraggled force emerged from the forest, Berkeley hinted that he would pardon Bacon and offered to let him travel to England to state his case directly to King Charles II. [**See Source 2.**]

Bacon not only rejected Berkeley's offer but also refused to apologize for actions "in so glorious a cause as the country's defense." He was buoyed by his success against the Indians and by the fact that Henrico County voters had just elected him to the new assembly. In June 1676, he arrived in Jamestown to take his seat in the assembly and demand his military commission once again. When Bacon concluded that staying in the capital was too risky and headed back upriver, Berkeley sent an armed ship after him. The next time Bacon stepped ashore at Jamestown, he was a prisoner. "Now I behold the greatest rebel that ever was in Virginia," exclaimed the triumphant governor. After Bacon signed a written confession of his transgressions, Berkeley presented him to the assembly. In a show of public submission, the young rebel dropped to his knees before the governor, who proclaimed, "God forgive you! I forgive you!" Berkeley then took the further precaution of placing Bacon back on his council, removing a potentially troublesome voice from the assembly. Bacon had no choice but to head back to Curles Neck a few days later.

The governor had outmaneuvered Bacon. The conditions that had led to Bacon's rise, however, had not gone away. Nor had Bacon's popular support, which was reflected in the new assembly. What came to be known as Bacon's Assembly passed numerous laws to pacify disgruntled Virginians. [**See Source 3.**] It also abandoned Berkeley's plan for a string of frontier forts. Instead, it authorized a force of a thousand men, commanded by Bacon, to conduct war against hostile Indians. Soldiers would be paid up to 2,250 pounds of tobacco each and would "have benefit of all the plunder" taken from the Indians. To quell the possibility of open revolt, the assembly had handed Virginia's restless freemen a few reforms and the promise of greater action against the Indians.

At the same time, Berkeley moved to reinforce his own position by lecturing the assembly on the injustice of indiscriminate attacks on the Indians. As a result, the legislature refused to endorse an all-out war against the Indians. Rather, it declared that only Indians who left their lands without the permission of Virginia's authorities would be considered enemies. Berkeley challenged the representatives to find fault with him. Then he extracted a resolution from them that "humbly intreat[ed] and request[ed] his honor that he will please still to continue [as] our Governor."

Although the legislature had reiterated its support for the governor, it also had given Bacon the encouragement he needed to challenge Berkeley for a second time. Perhaps driven by a sense of power as champion of the people, Bacon was determined to claim the commission supported by the legislature. With it, he would lead the campaign against the Indians. For the second time in a month, he set out for Jamestown. This time, however, he was accompanied by a force of six hundred men.

"That Naked Country"

On June 23, 1676, Bacon and his army arrived in Jamestown. After the dramatic confrontation with the governor outside the assembly door, Bacon finally got his commission. He and his followers were no longer rebels but legitimate soldiers. The commander and his force, soon to number thirteen hundred men, quickly began to help themselves to supplies from plantations near Jamestown. Berkeley responded to Bacon's freebooting by rescinding his commission and raising a force of twelve hundred men to march against him. When the soldiers learned that they were marching against Bacon rather than the Indians, however, they refused to fight. Seizing the opportunity, Bacon led his men toward Jamestown. Berkeley once again declared Bacon a rebel—and then fled with five of his supporters across the Chesapeake to Virginia's Eastern Shore.

Setting up camp in the tiny settlement of Middle Plantation (later the site of Williamsburg), Bacon was joined by Richard Lawrence and William Drummond. At the end of July, he issued a "manifesto" defending his actions. **[See Source 4.]** He also summoned other prominent Virginians to Middle Plantation. At first, they balked when Bacon proposed that they swear an oath not to aid Berkeley and to fight any royal forces sent from England to assist the governor. That would be treason. In the end, though, they observed that "every magistrate that hath loyally declared his dissent against [Bacon's] . . . monstrous proceedings is threatened with the plundering and pulling down [of] their houses." Rather than be plundered, they hedged their bets and signed Bacon's oath. Meanwhile, other prominent planters abandoned their plantations and headed to Berkeley's refuge on the Eastern Shore.

Through the remainder of the summer and into the early fall, Virginia was plunged into civil war as Bacon's and Berkeley's forces clashed. Bacon saw to it that his men plundered the Indians as well. Marching a detachment of troops to the backcountry, he came across the peaceful Pamunkeys, killed some, and took forty-five others prisoner. Meanwhile, Giles Bland set out with three hundred men to capture Berkeley on the Eastern Shore, only to be taken prisoner himself. Heartened by this turn of events, Berkeley went on the offensive. To attract support, the governor offered the plunder from the plantations of those who signed Bacon's oath. He also offered freedom to servants who supported him. Though fearful of insurrection by the "rabble," Berkeley was desperate. When he sailed back to Jamestown in early September, however, few servants had rallied to his cause. By contrast, Bacon quickly gained volunteers as he marched toward Jamestown with his Indian captives in tow. He also offered freedom to the servants and slaves of Berkeley's loyalists, a move that led hundreds of blacks to join Bacon's ranks.

By the time he arrived in Jamestown, Bacon's force greatly outnumbered Berkeley's. Nonetheless, Bacon took the precaution of rounding up the wives of prominent Berkeley supporters from nearby plantations, including the wife of his cousin Nathaniel Bacon Sr. While his men dug in just outside Jamestown's palisade, Bacon placed the women on his fortifications to prevent a premature attack by Berkeley's men. When the governor's force launched an unsuccessful attack after Bacon had removed his female captives from danger, Bacon's men opened their guns on Jamestown. The next morning, after Berkeley and his force had retreated to nearby ships, Bacon and his men entered the deserted capital. Berkeley's forces still controlled the waters around Jamestown, however, and a loyalist force raised in Virginia's northern counties was marching south. Bacon realized that he could not hold the capital. Before withdrawing from Jamestown, he and his men torched twenty-five houses (five of them owned by Berkeley), the statehouse, the church, and outlying residences. After pillaging Berkeley's Green Spring plantation, they retreated across the York River to Gloucester County, not far from Yorktown. There Bacon continued to plunder plantations, try opponents, and imprison them.

By early October, the tide had turned against Bacon and his men. Berkeley had dispatched a message to the king, and Bacon and his men now faced the prospect of fighting royal reinforcements. When he asked his followers to swear an oath declaring Berkeley a traitor and vowing to fight the king's forces, they refused. When he delivered an appeal to the residents of the Eastern Shore to seize the "abominable Juggler" Berkeley and his "ring leaders," it had no impact. Meanwhile, Bacon had fallen ill. Weakened by his military exploits, he was afflicted with lice and dysentery. According to one witness, as Bacon lay near death at a Gloucester plantation, "the swarms of vermin that bred in his body he could not destroy but by throwing his shirts into the fire as often as he shifted himself." On October 26, 1676, he died. In the following months, the rebellious mood of Bacon's followers began to expire as well. Armed ships arrived from England, quashing resistance up and down the York and James Rivers. On the south bank of the York, Berkeley's rejuvenated troops found an armed force of four hundred black slaves and white freemen. Most were persuaded to surrender, but eighty blacks and twenty whites refused to lay down their arms until they were confronted with the thirty guns of the ship *Concord*. The slaves were quickly returned to their masters.

At the end of January 1677, a three-man royal commission sent to investigate the situation in the colony and to restore order arrived with a thousand troops. By the time it landed, Berkeley had already begun to crack down with trials of Bacon's prominent supporters. Giles Bland, William Drummond, and twenty-one others were convicted of treason and hanged. "That old fool," observed Charles II, "has hanged more men in that naked country than I did for the murder of my father." Berkeley regretted that he was unable to hang Bacon as well. Perhaps he found consolation in stripping the dead rebel's estate from Elizabeth Bacon. Under orders from Charles II, Berkeley returned to England in May to provide an account of Virginia's recent troubles. Two months later, he died.

By then, the royal commissioners had found much in Berkeley's Virginia to dismay them, especially the continued looting by the governor's forces. Noting the "sullen and obstinate" character of the colonists, the commissioners encouraged them to communicate their "pressures or grievances." Virginians responded in force. **[See Source 5.]** Yet the commissioners did not exonerate Bacon. Instead, they condemned the "inconsiderate sort of men who so rashly and causelessly cry up a war, and seem to wish and aim at an utter extirpation of the Indians." Like Charles II, the commissioners were mostly concerned that Virginians get back to the business of producing tobacco, which did so much to swell the royal coffers.

Bacon's Rebellion thus produced a new administration in Virginia but no major reforms in the colony's government or society. Nonetheless, this uprising was a crucial event in reshaping early Virginia. Prior to 1676, the colony was a social pressure cooker characterized by exploitation of the many and aggrandizement by the few. In 1676, the pressure cooker exploded. Bacon's Rebellion demonstrated to prominent Virginians the dangers of relying on laborers who could turn into unruly neighbors. In the years after the rebellion, these planters turned to another form of labor exploitation, relying increasingly on slaves rather than servants to wrest wealth from the land. Indeed, by the end of the seventeenth century, the place of Virginia's landed gentry had been firmly secured by its control of a growing slave-labor force that grew nearly sixfold from the eve of Bacon's Rebellion to the turn of the eighteenth century.

Moreover, Bacon clearly understood that conflicts among white colonists could be defused by rallying them against others. On the eve of the Occaneechee campaign, he informed Berkeley that the colonists' protest against taxes and the governor's plan for frontier forts had "been suppressed" because the "discourse and earnestness of the people [was] against the Indians." Hatred of an "inferior" race, in other words, was a powerful force to unite whites and subdue social discontent. Thus even before the colony's black population exploded at the end of the seventeenth century, Virginia's planter elite had learned how to unite freemen of all ranks against those at the bottom of society and thereby dampen resentment against those at the top. In the end, Bacon's Rebellion helped teach Virginia's ruling class how to keep poor whites and black slaves in their place.

PRIMARY SOURCES

SOURCE 1:　*Frontier Planters Appeal to Governor William Berkeley*　(Spring 1676)

What does this petition reveal about the attitude of Virginia's frontiersmen toward authority?

To the Right Honorable Sir William Berkeley Knight governor Capt. General of Virginia: The humble petition of the poor distressed subjects in the upper parts of [the] James River in Virginia humbly complain[s] that the Indians hath already

SOURCE: Reprinted in Warren M. Billings, ed., *The Old Dominion in the Seventeenth Century: A Documentary History of Virginia, 1606–1689* (Chapel Hill: University of North Carolina Press, 1975), p. 267; originally from Colonial Office 1/36, fol. 139, Public Record Office. On occasion, minor changes have been made to spelling and punctuation for the convenience of modern readers.

most barbarously and inhumanly taken and murdered several of our brethren and put them to most cruel torture by burning of them alive and by cruel torturing of them which makes our hearts ready to bleed to hear. And we the poor subjects are in daily danger of losing our lives by the heathen in so much that we are all afraid of going about our domestic affairs. Wherefore we most humbly request that your gracious Honor would be pleased to grant us a commission and to make choice of commissioned officers to lead this party now ready to take arms in defense of our lives and estates which without speedy prevention lie liable to the injury of such insulting enemies. Not that your petitioners desire to make any disturbance or put the country to any charge. Wherefore we humbly plead your Honor's speedy answer for we are informed that the Indians daily approach our habitations and we your petitioners as in duty bound shall ever pray.

Source 2: *William Berkeley, "Declaration and Remonstrance"* (May 1676)

Governor Berkeley issued this statement after Bacon's campaign against the Occaneeches. How does he try to gain Virginians' support against Bacon?

Now my friends I have lived amongst you four and thirty years as uncorrupt and diligent as ever [a] governor was. Bacon is a man of two years amongst you. His person and qualities [are] unknown to most of you. . . . This very action wherein he so much boasted was . . . foolishly and, as I am informed, treacherously carried to the dishonor of the English nation. Yet in it he lost more men than I did in three wars and by the Grace of God [I] will put myself to the same dangers and troubles again when I have brought Bacon to acknowledge the laws are above him. And I doubt not by the assistance of God to have better success than Mr. Bacon has had. The reason of my hopes are that I will take counsel of wiser men than myself. But Mr. Bacon has none about him but the lowest of the people.

Yet I must further enlarge that I cannot without your help do anything in this but die in the defense of my King, his laws, and subjects which I will cheerfully do though alone I do it. And considering my poor fortunes I cannot leave my poor wife and friends a better legacy than by dying for the King and you, for his sacred majesty will easily distinguish between Mr. Bacon's actions and mine. . . .

Now after all this, if Mr. Bacon can show me precedent or example where such actings in any nation whatsoever was approved of, I will mediate with the

Source: Reprinted in Warren M. Billings, ed., *The Old Dominion in the Seventeenth Century: A Documentary History of Virginia, 1606–1689* (Chapel Hill: University of North Carolina Press, 1975), pp. 271–272; originally from Henry Coventry Papers, LXXVII, fols. 157–158, Estate of the Marquis of Bath, Longleat, Warminster, Wiltshire, England. On occasion, minor changes have been made to spelling and punctuation for the convenience of modern readers.

King and you for a pardon and excuse for him. But I can show him a hundred examples where brave and great men have been put to death for gaining victories against the command of their superiors.

> Your incessant Servant
> William Berkeley

Source 3: *A Summary of the June Assembly's Laws* (1676)

The assembly of June 1676, often called Bacon's Assembly because most of the burgesses (representatives) were Bacon's supporters, passed a number of reforms. What do these laws reveal about the causes of their discontent? What changes did these laws make in the government?

ACT I. *An act for carrying on a warre against the barbarous Indians.*
Declared war against enemy Indians and ordered the raising of a thousand troops. Bacon was named "generall and commander in cheife of the force raised."

ACT II. *An act concerning Indian trade and traders.*
Prohibited all trade with the Indians, except for "friendly Indians."

ACT III. *An act concerning Indian lands deserted.*
Lands deserted by the Indians reverted to the colony; these lands were to "dispose to the use of the publique towards defraying the charge of this warr."

ACT IV. *An act for suppressing of tumults, routs, etc.*
Every officer and magistrate was authorized to suppress unlawfull "routs, riotts and tumults."

ACT V. *An act for the regulateing of officers and offices.*
Prohibited sheriffs from holding office "more than one year successively," abolished plural officeholding, regulated fees, and denied office to anyone not a resident of the colony for at least three years. . . .

ACT VII. *An act enabling freemen to vote for burgesses and preventing false returnes of burgesses.*
Repealed an act of 1670 that had restricted the franchise to freeholders and imposed a stiff fine on any sheriff who made a false election return. . . .

ACT XII. *Councellors and Ministers families to pay levies, and money allowed them.*
Removed tax exempt status of conciliar and ministerial families; gave councillors a fixed salary. . . .

SOURCE: Reprinted in Warren M. Billings, ed., *The Old Dominion in the Seventeenth Century: A Documentary History of Virginia, 1606–1689* (Chapel Hill: University of North Carolina Press, 1975), pp. 274–275; originally from William Waller Hening, ed., *The Statutes at Large: Being a Collection of All the Laws of Virginia from the First Session of the Legislature, in the Year 1619* (Richmond, New York, and Philadelphia, 1809–1823), II, 341–365.

ACT XIX. *An act of general pardon and oblivion.*

Pardoned all "treasons, misprison of treasons, murders, fellonies, offences, crimes, contempts and misdemeanors" committed between March 1 and June 25, 1676.

SOURCE 4:   *Bacon's Manifesto*   (July 1676)

How does the tone of Bacon's Manifesto differ from that of the frontier petition? How do you account for the difference? What does Bacon's attack on Governor Berkeley's government reveal about his motives? How does Bacon justify his attacks on the Indians?

[S]ince we cannot in our hearts find one single spot of rebellion or treason or that we have in any manner aimed at subverting the settled government . . . let truth be told and all the world know the real foundations of [our] pretended guilt. . . . [L]et us trace these men in authority and favor to whose hand the dispensation of the country's wealth has been committed. Let us observe the sudden rise of their estates compared with the quality in which they first entered this country or the reputation they have held here amongst wise and discerning men. . . . Let us consider their sudden advancement and let us also consider whether any public work for our safety and defense . . . [is] in any [way] adequate to our vast charge. Now let us compare these things together and see what sponges have sucked up the public treasure and whether it hath not been privately contrived away by unworthy favorites and juggling parasites whose tottering fortunes have been repaired and supported at the public charge. . . .

Another main article of our guilt is our open and manifest aversion of all, not only the foreign but the protected and darling Indians. This we are informed is rebellion . . . whereas we do declare and can prove that they have been for these many years enemies to the King and country, robbers and thieves and invaders of his Majesty's right and our interest and estates, but yet have by persons in authority been defended and protected even against his majesty's loyal subjects. . . .

Another main article of our guilt is our design not only to ruin and extirpate all Indians in general but all manner of trade and commerce with them. . . . Since the right honorable . . . Governor hath been pleased by his commission to warrant this trade, who dare oppose it?. . . .

Another article of our guilt is to assert all those neighbor Indians as well as others to be outlawed, wholly unqualified for the benefit and protection of the law, for the law does reciprocally protect and punish, and . . . all people offending must either in person or estate make equivalent satisfaction or restitution according to the manner and merit of the offenses, debts, or trespasses. Now

SOURCE: Reprinted in Warren M. Billings, ed., *The Old Dominion in the Seventeenth Century: A Documentary History of Virginia, 1606–1689* (Chapel Hill: University of North Carolina Press, 1975), pp. 277–279. On occasion, minor changes have been made to spelling and punctuation for the convenience of modern readers.

since the Indians cannot according to . . . any law to us known be prosecuted, seized, or complained against, their person being [with] difficulty distinguished or known, . . . such as makes them incapable to make us restitution or satisfaction, would it not be very guilty to say they have been unjustly defended and protected these many years.

SOURCE 5: *Grievances Submitted to the King's Commissioners* (1677)

What do these these grievances from one Virginia county reveal about the situation in the colony before Bacon's Rebellion? Do they reflect only a desire to complain about conditions in Virginia?

Whereas His Majesty's Commissioners . . . have commanded us the subscribers, in the behalf of Gloucester County to give in our grievances: in obedience thereunto, we have drawn up our Grievances, and they are as follows.

1. Whereas about 17 years since there was a tax laid upon tobacco shipped in this county of 2 shillings per hogshead by act of [the] assembly, under pretense of defraying the public charge of the county . . . in order to [prevent] other public taxes. . . . The county levies hath notwithstanding this tax been ever since as great or more than before. Therefore they humbly conceive the said tax of 2 shillings per hogshead to be a grievance, unless it may be employed as pretended when first raised. . . .

3. That within this 14 or 15 months, it is conceived [that] there hath been near 300 Christian persons barbarously murdered by the Indians. And after the murder of several numbers of the said persons, the assembly (called for that purpose) ordered 500 men to be raised against the said murderers, by whom forts were erected. We were informed that the commanders of the said soldiers had order not to molest an Indian unless they knew them to be the murderers or began to act in a hostile way first. [Such] leniency, we humbly conceive, gave the Indians encouragement to persist in their bloody practice and was occasion in part of the people arming themselves without command from their superiors in a rebellious manner, with whom the rebel Bacon, having before by extravagancy lost his fortunes, takes the opportunity and joins. And being amongst them reputed a wit, was adhered to by the rest . . . after he had illegally obtained a commission, which was published as legally obtained in the several counties by consent of the grand assembly. . . . Many people were ignorantly deluded and drawn into his party that thought of no other design than the

SOURCE: Reprinted in Warren M. Billings, ed., *The Old Dominion in the Seventeenth Century: A Documentary History of Virginia, 1606–1689* (Chapel Hill: University of North Carolina Press, 1975), pp. 280–282; originally from Colonial Office 1/39, 244, Public Record Office. On occasion, minor changes have been made to spelling and punctuation for the convenience of modern readers.

Indian war. Most of [these] persons, though never so innocent, are persecuted with rigor . . . which, with the ill-management of this war at first, we complain of as grievances.

4. That whereas there were several grievances presented to the assembly in June last, in order to prevent many exorbitant fees and other disorders in government, upon which many good laws were consented to, and agreed upon by that grand assembly before the rebel Bacon came to interrupt the said assembly. We beg that those good and wholesome laws may be confirmed by this assembly.

5. We complain that since the late rebellion the rebels have taken and plundered diverse good subjects' estates. We beg that this assembly will take some course that right owners may be empowered to be revested in all that was so taken from them. . . .

6. We complain that some particular persons near about the governor have obtained commission to plunder and destroy the rebels, which they have made use of to the imprisonment of the persons and rifling their estates, and converting them to their own uses. . . .

9. Whereas by the too frequent assemblies and high charges of the burgesses, the county is exposed to a great charge which we do complain [of] as a grievance.

Philip Lightfoot   James Taylor
John Buckner   John Rogers
Llewis Burwell   Thomas Kemp

Questions to Consider

1. One historian has remarked that Bacon's Rebellion was "a rebellion with abundant causes but without a cause." Do you agree? What were the causes of Bacon's Rebellion? Did Nathaniel Bacon have a cause? Did William Berkeley?

2. What do the essay and sources reveal about Bacon's motivation in challenging royal authority in Virginia? What do the actions of Bacon and Berkeley reveal about the difficulty of establishing the motives of people in the past?

3. In the early twentieth century, many historians saw Bacon's Rebellion as a precursor of the American Revolution: an attempt to overthrow a repressive royal government and establish a more democratic society. Later historians have argued that Bacon was no democrat and that this episode's significance is what it reveals about the evolution of Virginia society in the seventeenth century. What do you think is the significance of Bacon's Rebellion? What does it reveal about Virginia society? Did it bring changes to that society? What factors may have influenced historians' changing views of Bacon's Rebellion?

4. On the basis of the information in this chapter's sources, would you have moved to Virginia as an indentured servant in the third quarter of the seventeenth century? Would you have sided with Bacon's or Berkeley's forces in 1676?

For Further Reading

David W. Galenson, *White Servitude in Colonial America: An Economic Analysis* (Cambridge: Cambridge University Press, 1981), discusses the nature of indentured servitude in the colonies and its role in the colonial economy.

Edmund S. Morgan, *American Slavery American Freedom: The Ordeal of Colonial Virginia* (New York: W. W. Norton & Company, 1975), sees Bacon's Rebellion as a pivotal event in Virginia's evolution toward a society dominated by race-based slavery.

Wilcomb E. Washburn, *The Governor and the Rebel: A History of Bacon's Rebellion in Virginia* (Chapel Hill: University of North Carolina Press, 1957), offers a sympathetic view of Governor Berkeley as a defender of the Indians and portrays Bacon as their aggressive, ambitious, and unscrupulous enemy.

Stephen S. Webb, *1676: The End of American Independence* (New York: Alfred A Knopf, 1984), places Bacon against the backdrop of England's civil war and argues that his rebellion was a revolt against post-Restoration Stuart despotism.

Enthusiasm, Authority, and the Great Awakening: James Davenport and Charles Chauncy

A scene from the Great Awakening: James Davenport preached with fervor.

Charles Chauncy

As the sheriff marched in James Davenport to face the Connecticut legislature in June 1742, the crowd in the packed First Church of Hartford grew quiet. For a few minutes, Davenport stood motionless, and then he suddenly sprang to life. "We behold the very near approach of the end of the world," he shouted, as if stricken with terror. "Very soon, all things will be involved in a devouring flame." Flailing his arms, Davenport lifted his voice even higher. Many in the crowd, he cried out, "are dropping down to Hell!" When the sheriff grabbed his arm to stop his outburst, Davenport broke into prayer. "Lord! Thou knowest somebody's got hold of my sleeve. Strike them! Lord, strike them!"

Mayhem erupted in the church. According to one newspaper account, many in the crowd began "to sigh, groan, beat their breasts, cry out, and to be put into strange agitations of the body." The pandemonium soon spilled outside. Through the night, Hartford witnessed "shocking scenes of horror and confusion, under the name and pretext of religious devotion." Repulsed by these "wild outpourings," the legislature acted swiftly. It declared the contagion unleashed by Davenport a "bold and threatening insult" to the government. Then it summoned a forty-man armed force for protection.

After singing in jail all night, Davenport was hauled before the legislature again the next morning. Subdued now, he listened as one witness after another testified that he had encouraged people to break the law. Even Davenport's own witnesses were unable to say how a "different construction" could be put on his call for civil disobedience. Finally, in a calm voice, Davenport spoke. Most ministers in the land were unconverted, he declared. Not only had several of them confessed as much to him, but he had "strong impressions" that it was true.

The verdict was no surprise. The legislature found Davenport guilty of violating the colony's recently passed law against preaching by roving ministers. The statute was was intended to dampen the fervor unleashed by the Great Awakening, the religious revival that spread through the colonies during the 1730s and 1740s. The Awakening was characterized by widespread emotional outbursts ignited by the preaching of Davenport and others. Connecticut had been swept up in this religious "enthusiasm," but the assembly's punishment of Davenport was surprisingly lenient. It declared that he was "disturbed in the rational faculties of the mind" and ordered him deported from the colony.

Connecticut's authorities were mistaken if they thought they were done with Davenport and his wild preaching. In the coming months, he blazed a trail across New England. Its terminus was New London, Connecticut, where the most shocking event of the Great Awakening took place. Like no other preacher during the revival, Davenport demonstrated the dangerous and subversive directions that emotional religion could take.

"Our Religion Runs Low"

Reverend James Davenport of Southold, New York, found in neighboring Connecticut fertile soil for harvesting souls. It was a field he knew well, for his family's roots reached deep into the colony's past. In 1638, his Puritan great-grandfather John Davenport founded New Haven and served as pastor of its First Congregational* Church. James Davenport's father was a respected Congregational minister in Stamford, where Davenport was born in 1716. Davenport graduated from New Haven's Yale College at age sixteen, then continued his theological studies for several more years at this bastion of Puritan orthodoxy.* Licensed as a Congregational minister in 1735, he preached for a time in New Jersey. Then he accepted a call in 1738 from the First Church of Southold, a town founded in 1640 by New Haven Colony Puritans.

As a student at Yale, Davenport had fallen in with a small group that shared a pietistic* view of religious experience. David Ferris, a member of Davenport's

---

Congregational: The denomination of the New England Puritan church characterized by a form of organization in which individual congregations chose their own ministers and were not subject to the control of a higher church body.

Puritan orthodoxy: A set of beliefs conforming to the teachings of the sixteenth-century theologian John Calvin. Orthodox Puritans emphasized salvation at God's hand for only a few people and the doctrine of predestination—the belief that an individual's salvation is determined long before birth.

Pietistic: Relating to a religious faith characterized by a rejection of church ritual. Pietists emphasized simplicity of worship, inward devotion, and the individual's direct relationship with God.

circle, embraced the Quaker doctrine of the Inner Light—a belief that each individual is capable of receiving divine inspiration and guidance from within. Ferris insisted that the Holy Spirit, working within the heart, produced a sudden conversion. Evidently, other members of the group agreed. During the Great Awakening, several of them became itinerant preachers,* and two of them would be by Davenport's side as he cut his spectacular path through Connecticut. At Yale, though, their piety merely set them against the college and its teachers. As one student in Davenport's group said, he "WANTED NOT HUMAN LEARNING in order to declare the will of GOD to the world."

Davenport's great-grandfather John would have been appalled by claims of immediate and emotional religious experiences and such rejection of learning. Puritans of John Davenport's day understood God's will as much through their heads as through their hearts. Their conversion experience was not a sudden, emotionally wrenching rebirth, but a long gestation period that followed God's planting "the seed of grace." Thus early Puritans had no use for the likes of Anne Hutchinson,* whose assertion that "the person of the Holy Spirit dwells within" God's elect quickly attracted the attention of Massachusetts Bay Colony authorities. So did her claim that the elect could intuitively recognize whether others were among God's chosen or were merely seeking salvation by doing good works. Leading an upright life, Hutchinson argued, held no clue whatsoever to an individual's spiritual state. In effect, grace removed God's elect from the dictates of the law.

The dangers of Hutchinson's teaching were obvious, especially when she declared that only two ministers in Massachusetts were saved. Even more alarming was her later claim that God had spoken to her "by the voice of His own spirit to my soul." The Bible alone, Puritans believed, revealed God's will. The authority of ministers arose from their intellect and learning, which gave them the power to decipher the revealed Word. In short, Puritans placed their faith in education and reason. Hutchinson's heresy only proved how mere feelings could undermine the authority of both ministers and magistrates.

Massachusetts authorities banished Hutchinson from the colony in 1637. With its emphasis on the intellect, however, Puritanism was open to another threat. Whenever religion emphasizes the head over the heart, it runs the risk of becoming dull and sterile. As European Enlightenment* ideas began to percolate in the colonies by the early eighteenth century, that possibility seemed real to many colonists. Pointing to the scientific discoveries of Sir Isaac Newton, Enlightenment thinkers posited the existence of a rational, orderly universe. Benjamin Franklin, Thomas Jefferson, and other colonial intellectuals came to share

---

Itinerant preachers: Ministers who preach from place to place rather than at their own established parishes.

Anne Hutchinson: The wife of a prominent Puritan merchant in early-seventeenth-century Boston who challenged Puritan teachings while preaching in her home.

Enlightenment: A philosophical movement in the seventeenth and eighteenth centuries that assumed a universe governed by certain knowable laws. Enlightenment thinkers emphasized human reason rather than revelation as the source of knowledge and refused to accept ideas on faith alone.

their views by the middle of the eighteenth century. They embraced the Enlightenment faith in the ability of science to unravel the mysteries of the natural world. They also held that individuals should be guided by reason and restraint rather than emotion. God appeared to them as benign and remote, not the Puritans' fearsome ruler of the universe who had once revealed truth directly to biblical prophets. As Franklin admitted in his *Autobiography*, such divine "revelation" carried "no weight" with him.

Revelation, of course, was still a weighty matter for many colonists. They found it difficult to square the harsh doctrines of predestination and original sin* with the new Enlightenment view of the universe. As one clergyman observed, "Many men flatter themselves as if there is no Hell." Nonetheless, much evidence suggests that Enlightenment thought made God less immediate in the lives of many people and encouraged a more rational form of religious worship. In fact, by the eve of the Great Awakening, laments about uninspiring clergy and lifeless congregations rang throughout the region. As one minister put it in 1733, "Our Religion runs low."

Complaints about declining religious zeal were nothing new in Puritan New England. At Boston's First Church, known affectionately as "Old Brick," minister Charles Chauncy stood behind the pulpit for sixty years, from 1727 to 1787. There he fashioned a career as stable as James Davenport's was erratic. By all accounts, Chauncy was an unexciting preacher. Indeed, when he prayed that God would never grant him oratorical skills, one church member observed that the minister's prayer had been "unequivocally granted." Yet Chauncy's unimposing presence and uninspired preaching masked an incisive mind and a wellspring of energy. He committed both to a powerful attack on the Great Awakening in general and itinerant preachers like James Davenport in particular. In fact, it was frail Charles Chauncy who would prove to be the Great Awakening's most ferocious critic.

Chauncy's background prepared him perfectly for his prominent role. Born in 1705, he grew up in comfortable circumstances. His father was a successful Boston merchant and his mother the daughter of a Massachusetts Supreme Court judge. As a young man, he attended Harvard, where he exercised his considerable intellectual prowess. He impressed his teachers as a "hopeful, young scholar" and served as a tutor for six years before his ordination at First Church in 1727. There "Old Brick," as the stolid Chauncy also came to be known, was a model of self-control. The only hint of instability was in his domestic life. Chauncy married three times, first in 1738, and three times witnessed the death of his spouse.

All along, his preaching reflected both his training and his temperament. The cerebral Chauncy distrusted emotions as much as he valued reason and moderation. His self-restraint was reflected in his daily regimen, later recorded by a friend:

> At twelve o'clock he took one pinch of snuff, and only one in twenty-
> four hours. At one o'clock he dined on one dish of plain, wholesome

---

Original sin: The belief that individuals are inherently sinful because of Adam and Eve's fall from grace in the Garden of Eden.

food, and after dinner took one glass of wine, and one pipe of tobacco, and only one in twenty-four hours. And he was equally methodical in his exercise, which consisted chiefly or wholly of walking.

Chauncy's preaching also reflected broader influences. Exposed to Enlightenment ideas at Harvard, he came to reject predestination and instead believed in people's ability to decipher the truth. Thus Chauncy aimed at his parishioners' rational faculties rather than their "subjective" feelings. Religious understanding, he believed, grew primarily through study of the Bible. As he put it, the "work of the SPIRIT" lay in preparing individuals' minds to receive God's grace. Manipulating emotions only aroused passion and threatened to unseat the faculty of reason from its supreme position in the mind. "An enlightened Mind, not raised Affection," he declared, "ought always to be the Guide of those who call themselves Men."

"The Devil Incarnate"

At the same time that Chauncy was delivering dispassionate sermons to his Boston flock, some New England preachers set out to arouse their parishioners' "Affections." In 1734 in Northampton, Massachusetts, a young minister named Jonathan Edwards began preaching emotional sermons that had a remarkable impact. In one year, about three hundred converts joined his church. Even Edwards was amazed. Not only were people "seized with a deep concern about their eternal salvation," he said, but the fervor had ended "differences" between ministers and their parishioners. Although Edwards's revival spread out of Northhampton to some thirty towns in the Connecticut River Valley, it soon spent itself. By 1737, when he published his *Faithful Narrative of the Surprising Work of God,* an account of the remarkable awakening, it was already over.

Revival preaching was just getting started, however. The same year, a young English minister named George Whitefield (pronounced "Whitfield") arrived in Georgia. The son of an English tavern keeper, Whitefield was a slight, cross-eyed man with a booming voice and immense oratorical skill. An ordained Anglican* minister, he could leave crowds crying, weeping, and shouting. On his first trip to the colonies, Whitefield stayed in Georgia. In late 1739, however, he returned, preaching in Philadelphia and New York. In Philadelphia, the ever curious Benjamin Franklin turned out to get a glimpse of the sensational preacher, although he was more interested in the size of Whitefield's audience than his message. Franklin estimated that Whitefield could preach, without shouting, to thirty thousand souls. If the Great Awakening had a single catalyst, it was Whitefield's appearance in the middle colonies. "It seem'd," an amazed Franklin observed, "as if all the world were growing religious."

When word of Whitefield's success reached the Southold area, James Davenport gathered his congregation together and preached fervently for twenty-four hours straight before collapsing. When he recovered, he began to distinguish the saved from the unsaved in his flock. The redeemed he called "brothers"; the

---

Anglican: A member of the Church of England, which was established by Henry VIII in the sixteenth century as England's official church.

rest he addressed as "neighbors" and excluded from Communion. Soon Davenport also was preaching away from his church.

Davenport's enthusiasm was heightened in early 1740 when he traveled to Philadelphia and met Whitefield and Gilbert Tennent, another revival preacher whose intensity amazed even Whitefield. Tennent was the product of his father's seminary, housed in a Pennsylvania log cabin. This "Log College" graduate tagged along on Whitefield's tour of the middle colonies, then launched his own revival in New England in 1740. Betraying little formal education, he delivered fiery sermons that conveyed one central message: The heart should dominate the head. One observer noted that Tennent "roared more fiercely" than Whitefield "against Colleges, Human Reason and Good Works." The greatest danger in churches, Tennent said, was not slumbering parishioners, but "blind, unregenerate, carnal, lukewarm, and unskilled" ministers. By the time Tennent took his thunderous preaching on the road, the power of such attacks was obvious.

While Tennent prepared the soil of New England, Davenport concentrated his efforts in eastern Long Island. One target was East Hampton, where Davenport's preaching created "a great shaking commotion," according to one observer. By the end of the summer, he had converted about twenty people and was ready to extend his itinerant ministry. In the fall, Davenport joined Whitefield, who had just completed a tour of New England. "Shortly, I believe," Whitefield told him as they traveled together, "you will evangelize." He was right. Returning to Southold, Davenport tended his flock through the spring of 1741. By the summer, the man Whitefield called a "sweet, pious soul" was ready to launch an evangelical assault on New England.

Davenport's offensive began in July, when he landed at New London and preached his first sermon. It was difficult to distinguish between his praying and preaching, noted one witness, "for it was all Meer Confused medley." Confused or not, it had an immediate impact. As Davenport spoke, terrified women "cried out exceedingly." When he abandoned the pulpit and walked among the pews, female parishioners were left "fainting and in hysterics." Davenport departed this emotional scene and went off singing through the streets. Before leaving New London, he visited another parish, where he demanded that the minister relate his spiritual experience. Then Davenport judged him unconverted.

As Davenport pressed on, he reaped an ever larger and more diverse harvest. A few days later, in Groton, he preached for four or five days to crowds "attracted from all quarters"—that is, from all ranks of society. One meeting of nearly a thousand people lasted until two o'clock in the morning, although some people lingered all night outside the meetinghouse. At Stonington, his next stop, he scored a hundred conversions, while hundreds more "cryed out." One onlooker complained that his hay had not been cut because all his help had gone off to hear Davenport. Some were even moved to accompany Davenport on his crusade. As he left for Rhode Island, he headed a procession of singing followers. By the time he crossed back into Connecticut, he counted among his converts several Native Americans. At East Lyme, he saved twenty Niantic Indians and several Mohegans. One of the converts, a Mohegan named Samson Occam, would later proselytize the Indians.

When a Stonington minister refused to let Davenport preach in his church on Sunday, Davenport moved outside and attacked him so severely that some in the crowd retreated back into the church. Later, at Saybrook, he denounced the town's pastor as "a wolf in sheep's clothing" before preaching in the open air. In New Haven, the pastor did give him the pulpit. According to one onlooker, he then raised his voice "to the highest pitch" and exhibited "the most violent agitations of body." In the midst of this outburst, he called on the pastor to relate his spiritual experience and then pronounced him "an unconverted hypocrite and the devil incarnate."

As Davenport headed back to Southold for the winter, some Connecticut residents were reporting trances and visions. Others were simply alarmed. Although the Great Awakening had increased religious feeling, many observers' initial enthusiasm quickly evaporated. Unlike Jonathan Edwards's Northampton revival, which had lessened the bitterness between ministers and their flocks, the work of Whitefield, Tennent, and Davenport incited animosity. As they assaulted the authority of ministers, shepherds and flocks alike were dividing into two camps: "New Lights" (supporters of the Great Awakening) and "Old Lights" (opponents of it).

"Freaks of Madness"

In the face of this New Light onslaught, Old Lights mobilized. While Davenport stormed through Connecticut in the summer of 1741, fifteen Hartford ministers met to proclaim that no weight was to be given to the "cryings out, faintings and convulsions" that frequently accompanied revival preaching. Nor was it just ministers who counterattacked. Church and state were inseparable in most American colonies. Connecticut's Congregational Church, for instance, was sanctioned by the government and supported by taxes. Thus the next year, colonial authorities prepared for the inevitable summer assault by itinerant New Light preachers. That spring, the legislature passed a law designed to clamp down on the preaching of Davenport and others. Any minister preaching outside his parish without the consent of the local pastor could be fined one hundred pounds. Ministers from outside Connecticut who preached without consent were to be driven "out of the bounds of this Colony."

It did not take long for authorities to enforce the new statute. The next month, Davenport and the Reverend Benjamin Pomeroy were quickly charged with disturbing the peace when they began preaching. Then they were brought before the assembly. The result was Davenport's spectacular three-day trial in Hartford. After pointing to his "natural tendency to disturb & destroy the Peace & Order of this Government," the legislators judged him mentally disturbed and ordered that he be removed to Long Island. Upon hearing the verdict, Davenport remained defiant, proclaiming his hope that Christ would carry on his work in the face of "all the powers and malice of earth and hell." That afternoon, the sheriff and two columns of armed men took Davenport to the banks of the Connecticut River and loaded him and an armed escort on a boat bound for Southold. Pomeroy, who seemed "orderly and regular" by comparison, was simply let go.

Meanwhile, Charles Chauncy had already made his initial response to the

Great Awakening. In the summer of 1741, he stood before his parishioners at First Church and proclaimed, "There is nothing betwixt you and the place of darkness, but a poor frail, uncertain life. You hang, as it were, over the bottomless pit, by the slender thread of life, and the moment that snaps asunder, you sink down to perdition." Even "Old Brick" had been swept up in the evangelical fervor, but his flirtation with hellfire preaching did not last long. Soon he was warning his flock about criticism of ministers and the "itch" to follow other preachers, although he was not ready to condemn the Awakening itself. His temperament, of course, demanded restraint, and his parishioners, for the most part prosperous and content, were more comfortable with "rational" religion than with the emotional outbursts elicited by revivalists. Yet as Chauncy continued to observe the Awakening's spreading fires, his criticism in published sermons grew more forceful. In the spring of 1742, he denounced the tendency of people "to flock after every weak and illiterate EXHORTER." And when James Davenport came to Boston and brought evangelical religion to Chauncy's doorstep, "Old Brick" unequivocally condemned the Awakening as the work of madmen.

Davenport's trial and expulsion from Connecticut had temporarily saved the colony from his unsettling attacks. They did nothing, however, to dampen Davenport's enthusiasm. A few days after returning to Southold, he set out again, this time for Massachusetts. Toward the end of June, he arrived in Boston. With fifteen thousand residents, the town was a prime target for New England itinerants. As New England's commercial economy blossomed in the early eighteenth century, residents of the region's busiest port had not benefited equally. There was a widening gap between rich and poor and a growing pool of poor and propertyless people. Bostonians needed only to look at the new almshouses and workhouses, at the swelling numbers on relief rolls, and at the new mansions and carriages of prosperous merchants to see the uneven effects of commercial development. Even those who failed to notice the evidence of deepening social stratification would have found it difficult to ignore the grain shortage in 1741 and reports of mobs preparing to assault merchants' warehouses. They knew firsthand about severe shortages of hard money and heard the growing cries of cash-poor or indebted residents for paper money. And they likely realized that Boston's wealthy merchants opposed this solution, fearing that cheap currency would only reduce the value of the money owed them.

In short, Boston was highly flammable. It had already been heated up by George Whitefield, who had preached to enormous crowds in late 1741, including one gathered at First Church. Gilbert Tennent, whom Whitefield had instructed to "blow up the divine fire lately kindled there," soon followed. Tennent's preaching had ignited many of Boston's poorer residents. Whereas Whitefield had occasionally blasted aristocratic fashion and even suggested that Boston preachers were unconverted, Tennent had delivered an egalitarian message that led critics to call him "a monster! impudent & noisy."

Davenport's preaching touched off an emotional firestorm in Boston that made even Tennent's impact seem mild in comparison. On his first Sunday in Massachusetts, Davenport attended a morning church service in Charlestown. He stayed away in the afternoon because he concluded that the minister was unconverted. The next day, he was summoned to a meeting of Boston area ministers, where he was informed that the town's pulpits were closed to him. A couple of days later, when they issued a "declaration" condemning his preaching, Davenport declared the signers unconverted.

On Boston Common, he preached to huge crowds that, according to one newspaper, were composed mostly "of the idle or ignorant Persons, and those of the lowest Rank." He routinely led this noisy "Rabble of Men, Women, and Children" through the streets. Frequently, they sang—at night and loudly. **[See Source 1.]** More disturbing, though, was the preaching. Puritan minister Cotton Mather had advised ministers to "speak Deliberately" and to "avoid all Indecencies, everything that is Ridiculous." Davenport preached as if he belonged on the stage. As one onlooker put it, "His Gestures in preaching are theatrical, his Voice tumultuous, his whole Speech and Behavior discovering the Freaks of Madness." Worse, as usual, he attacked the ministers. People should drink rat poison, he declared, rather than listen to an "unconverted" and "carnal" clergy. They were "murdering . . . Souls by the Thousands and by Millions" and were themselves going to hell. To the same followers, he proclaimed that he was ready to die for the salvation "of but one soul." According to one shocked witness, Davenport's followers were "so red hot," they were ready to kill those who opposed them.

Thanks to Chauncy's published sermons, Davenport knew where to find his chief opponent in Boston. Early one morning, not long after he arrived in town, Davenport made his way to Chauncy's comfortable home. When "Old Brick" met him at the door, Davenport began to interrogate him about the state of his soul. Chauncy would have none of it. He accused Davenport of spreading the idea that religion is "wild, disorderly imaginary business." He was, Chauncy charged, out of his mind. If he ever regained it, he would beg God for forgiveness. Then Chauncy promptly ushered his visitor out. Not long after, the normally restrained "Old Brick" let loose a fusillade against the Great Awakening. In a published sermon titled *Enthusiasm Described and Caution'd Against*, he aimed squarely at the revival, enthusiasm, and Davenport—to whom he sent a copy. It might be useful, Chauncy informed him, in guarding "against the wilds of heated imagination." **[See Source 2.]**

"Strutt About Bare-Arsed"

By early August 1742, the authorities had had enough. Davenport was charged with making "many slanderous & reviling Speeches" against the colony's "worthy Ministers," whereupon the sheriff took him into custody. When Davenport refused either to post bail or to promise good behavior, he was thrown into jail. At his trial, Boston's ministers appealed to the court for leniency. The jury determined that although Davenport had made slanderous statements, he was non compos mentis (insane) and, therefore, not guilty. For the second time in two months, he was deported from a colony after being judged out of his mind.

Back in Southold, Davenport confronted another problem: a rebellious congregation. Unhappy about their minister's long absences and his activities, Davenport's flock requested that a council of ministers be called to investigate. The council found that the congregation had just cause to complain of his itinerant preaching. It also condemned his attacks on other ministers, "singing in the streets," and conduct guided by "immediate impulses." The council concluded that Davenport should continue as the First Church's minister, but only if he ceased these "irregularities."

Davenport was undaunted by the judgment. After staying in Southold through the winter, he set off for New London, Connecticut, in March 1743. Like Boston, New London had experienced the uneven economic effects of commercial development. It also had been visited by Gilbert Tennent and, of course, Davenport. As in other towns, their proselytizing encouraged a split between New Lights and Old Lights. On his earlier visit in 1741, Davenport had labeled the Congregational minister a "carnal Pharisee." By the next summer, a Separate church had begun to meet under the leadership of Timothy Allen, the member of Davenport's Yale group who had professed his lack of interest in "HUMAN LEARNING." Allen, his wife, and several other New Lights also had set up the Shepherd's Tent, a kind of seminary without walls. There they provided training for itinerant ministers, including several female students. Davenport enthusiastically supported the Shepherd's Tent, soliciting contributions as he traveled through New England. When he received a request in early 1743 to assist the little band more directly, he readily accepted.

Davenport quickly worked the New London Separatists into a frenzy. A few days after his arrival, townspeople ran to the wharf to see "if Murder or some mischief was not about to be done." There they found a bonfire. Gathered around were Davenport and his followers, who were tossing books into the flames as they sang "Hallelujah" and "Glory to God." The books were Puritan classics, including the works of such noteworthy writers as Increase Mather and Benjamin Colman. Two of the first items thrown into the fire were Chauncy's *Enthusiasm Described and Caution'd Against* and his letter to Davenport.

The next day, Davenport's followers ignited a second bonfire of books. Then they piled up "wigs, cloaks, and breeches, Hoods, Gowns, Rings, Jewels and Necklaces"—items representing "their idolatrous love of worldly things"—for yet another fire. Before the pile was lit, cooler heads prevailed. That was especially fortunate for Davenport, who had thrown his only pair of breeches into the pile. Without them, one witness said, he would have been "obliged to strutt about bare-arsed." **[See Source 3.]**

Shocked New England authorities quickly brought the Separatist leaders to trial. Even the area's pro-revival ministers condemned them. As newspapers carried news of the infernos well beyond Connecticut, Old and New Lights alike were stunned and quickly labeled the group's actions "wild," "indecent," and the work of "mad men." As the Shepherd's Tent folded, Davenport left for Southold complaining of fever, a sore leg, and a spirit "void of inward peace." He soon confessed that he was "full of impatience, pride and arrogance." The next year, in better health, he published his *Confession and Retractions*. **[See Source 4.]**

The timing of these events could not have been better for an Old Light like Chauncy, who composed a sweeping attack on the Great Awakening. When the 424-page *Seasonable Thoughts on the State of Religion in New-England* appeared later in 1743, it represented the most forceful assault on revival published during the Awakening. Chauncy had originally taken up his pen to refute Jonathan Edwards's treatise in defense of revival, *Some Thoughts Concerning the Present*

Revival of Religion in New-England. Yet it was impossible for most readers of *Seasonable Thoughts* not to think of Davenport. The "enthusiastical spirit," Chauncy declared, is the "Seed-Plot of Delusion," leading to "Tremblings and Agitations, Strugglings and Tumblings, which in some instances have been attended with Indecencies I shan't mention." **[See Source 5.]**

By the time *Seasonable Thoughts* appeared, "enthusiasm" in New England had already begun to wane. Although Baptists* in the South carried on the Great Awakening well into the 1750s, much of the revival's remaining support had gone up in the smoke of Davenport's New London bonfires. Nonetheless, the Great Awakening's broad impact was only then becoming clear. Old Lights continued to espouse a more rational approach to religion. They also carried on a fierce battle against New Light churches. In Connecticut, New Lights were forced to pay for Old Light churches and were even expelled from the colonial legislature. In the end, however, the New Lights prevailed, gaining control of the colony's legislature in 1757. New Light ranks continued to grow elsewhere as well, especially among Baptists and Presbyterians.* At the same time, the influence of Congregationalists and Anglicans steadily declined. Increasing religious diversity was soon reflected in the founding of such New Light colleges as Princeton, established by Presbyterians in 1746, and Brown, started by Baptists in 1764. Increasing diversity in turn led to growing pressure for religious tolerance throughout the colonies.

Equally important, the Great Awakening transformed the nature of Protestantism. Davenport and other revivalists promoted a less formal and more popular and emotional religious experience. By emphasizing the heart over the head and the individual's direct relationship with God, they helped make the individual, rather than traditional religious authorities, the ultimate source of religious truth. In other words, the Awakening promoted a potentially explosive religious egalitarianism. That spirit of equality was reflected in the many converts the revivals brought into the Protestant fold, including such "outsiders" as Native Americans and blacks. Revival preachers had made religion accessible and empowering for people "from all quarters" of society.

The Revolution's "Illustrious Agent"

As these effects emerged, Davenport and Chauncy continued down divergent paths. After publishing his *Confession and Retractions,* Davenport slipped back into obscurity. He resigned his position in Southold and for a time preached in Connecticut, New Jersey, and New York. In 1754, he was installed as a pastor in Hopewell, New Jersey, but in 1757, part of the congregation presented a petition for his removal. A couple of months later, Davenport died. He left a wife, whose feelings about her husband's stormy career are lost to history, and two children.

Long after the Great Awakening subsided, Chauncy continued to sound the alarm about the dangers of revival. Even as late as 1771, "Old Brick" was call-

Baptists: Members of a Protestant denomination with roots in early-seventeenth-century England. Baptists emphasize the individual's ability to accept or reject salvation.

Presbyterians: Members of a denomination that became the established church of Scotland and spread to the colonies in the seventeenth century.

ing revivalistic religion "worse than paganism" and warned that it would "undoe" Massachusetts. He also followed his rational religion to its logical conclusion. After the Awakening, he abandoned the belief in people's innate depravity, a position central to the hellfire preaching of Davenport and other itinerants. He also rejected another tenet of Calvinism—salvation only for God's "elect"—embracing instead the doctrine that salvation was open to all. Fearful of creating yet another schism, however, the ever cautious minister publicly revealed his Universalist* persuasion only in 1785.

Chauncy was far more open about the growing political crisis in the colonies. By the 1760s, Church of England officials pressed to have bishops for the colonies in an effort to exert more religious control at the same time the Crown had begun to impose stricter economic regulations on the colonies. Like many colonists, the staunchly anti-Anglican Chauncy saw political and religious controls as inseparable. Both needed to be opposed, he concluded, or the colonists would be "brought into a state of the most abject tyranny." Although he abhorred violence, he became an outspoken defender of American liberties by the 1770s. Indeed, years after his death in 1787, John Adams called him one of the "illustrious agents" of the American Revolution.

By contrast, even before the Revolution, James Davenport's name had become synonymous with fanaticism, and today some historians still dismiss him as insane. Yet there is no denying his appeal to many people who were not part of the religious establishment, nor the threat his "enthusiasm" posed to traditional ideas about authority. Few modern historians would argue that the Great Awakening caused the American Revolution; Chauncy's life alone undermines easy generalizations about that. Nonetheless, the growing colonial revolt had everything to do with American views about authority and equality. By promoting religious egalitarianism, New Lights like Davenport may have had more to do with a revolt against British authority than an Old Light patriot like Chauncy could ever have imagined.

PRIMARY SOURCES

SOURCE 1: *"A Song of Praise"* (1742)

Parishioners in New England's churches traditionally sang psalms, but singing was never an important part of worship. The Great Awakening in general, and James Davenport in particular, changed that for good. As one observer noted, Davenport "sing[s] as he goes to the places of worship, and returns from it." Often Davenport's songs were

SOURCE: Reprinted in Alan Heimert and Perry Miller, eds., *The Great Awakening: Documents Illustrating the Crisis and Its Consequences* (Indianapolis: Bobbs-Merrill Educational Publishing, 1967), pp. 202–203; originally from *A Song of Praise for Joy in the Holy Ghost* (Boston, 1742), pp. 1–2.

Universalist: A member of a Protestant religious denomination that rejects the Calvinist belief in God's salvation of only a few. Universalists emphasize that everyone is capable of receiving God's grace.

his own compositions, and they reflect the ecstatic nature of the religious experience unleashed by the Awakening. Why would such singing, and the message of this song in particular, have been threatening to opponents of revival?

My Soul doth magnify the Lord,
    My Spirit doth rejoice
In God my Saviour, and my God;
    I hear his joyful Voice.
I need not go abroad for Joy,
    Who have a Feast at home;
My Sighs are turned into Songs,
    The Comforter is come.

    Down from above the blessed Dove
    Is come into my Breast,
To witness God's eternal Love;
    This is my heavenly Feast.
This makes me *Abba* Father* cry,
    With Confidence of Soul;
It makes me cry, My Lord, my God,
    And that without Controul.

    There is a Stream which issues forth
    From God's eternal Throne,
And from the Lamb a living Stream,
    Clear as the Crystal Stone;
The Stream doth water Paradise,
    It makes the Angels sing:
One cordial Drop revives my Heart,
    Whence all my joys do spring.

Such Joys as are unspeakable,
    And full of Glory too;
Such hidden *Manna*, hidden Pearls,
    As Worldlings do not know.
Eye hath not seen, nor Ear hath heard,
    From Fancy 'tis conceal'd,
What thou Lord, hast laid up for thine,
    And hast to me reveal'd.

**Abba:* A New Testament name for God.

SOURCE 2:   Charles Chauncy, *Enthusiasm Described and Caution'd Against*   (1742)

After James Davenport's visit to Boston, few people had to guess the target of this attack by Charles Chauncy. What does Chauncy find so objectionable about what he calls "enthusiasm," or an emotional approach to religious devotion? What does his sermon reveal about the threat that itinerant preachers like Davenport posed to the ministerial establishment? What does it reveal about the social fears unleashed by the Awakening?

The cause of this *enthusiasm* is a bad temperament of the blood and spirits; 'tis properly a disease, a sort of madness: And there are few; perhaps none at all, but are subject to it, tho' none are so much in danger of it as those, in whom *melancholy* is the prevailing ingredient in their constitution. In these it often reigns; and sometimes to so great a degree, that they are really beside themselves, acting as truly by the blind impetus of a wild fancy, as tho' they had neither reason nor understanding.

And various are the ways in which their *enthusiasm* discovers itself. . . .

Sometimes, it affects their bodies, throws them into convulsions and distortions, into quakings and tremblings. . . .

But in nothing does the *enthusiasm* of these persons discover it self more, than in the disregard they express to the Dictates of *reason*. They are above the force of argument, beyond conviction from a calm and sober address to their understandings. . . .

This is the nature of *Enthusiasm*, and this its operation, in a less or greater degree, in all who are under the influence of it. 'Tis a kind of religious Phrenzy, and evidently discovers it self to be so, whenever it rises to any great height.

And much to be pitied are the persons who are seized with it. Our compassion commonly works towards those, who, while under distraction, fondly imagine themselves to be Kings and Emperors: And the like pity is really due to those, who, under the power of *enthusiasm*, fancy themselves to be *prophets; inspired of God,* and *immediately called and commissioned by him to deliver his messages to the world:* And tho' they should run into disorders, and act in a manner that cannot but be condemned, they should notwithstanding be treated with tenderness and lenity; and the rather, because they don't commonly act so much under the influence of a *bad mind,* as a *deluded imagination.* . . .

But no minister ought to be regarded, as tho' he was the author of our faith; nor, let his gifts and graces be what they will, is he to be so esteemed, as that others must be neglected, or treated in an unbecoming manner. . . .

Men may talk of their *impulses* and *impressions,* conceive of them as the call of GOD, and go about, as moved by them, from place to place, imagining they are sent of GOD, and immediately commissioned by him: But if they are censorious and uncharitable; if they harbour in their minds evil surmisings of their

SOURCE: Reprinted in Alan Heimert and Perry Miller, eds., *The Great Awakening: Documents Illustrating the Crisis and Its Consequences* (Indianapolis: Bobbs-Merrill Educational Publishing, 1967), pp. 230, 231–232, 234, 237, 238, 240, 241; originally from Charles Chauncy, *Enthusiasm described and caution'd against. A Sermon Preach'd . . . the Lord's Day After the Commencement . . .* (Boston, 1742), pp. 1–27.

brethren; if they slander and reproach them; if they claim a right to look into their hearts, make it their business to judge of their state, and proclaim them hypocrites, carnal unregenerate sinners, when at the same time they are visibly of a good conversation in CHRIST; I say, when this is the practice of any, they . . . are evidently under a spirit of delusion: And this is so obviously the case, that there is no reasonable room to doubt upon the matter. . . .

'Tis indeed a powerful argument with many, in favour of these persons, their pretending to *impulses,* and a call from GOD; together with their insatiable thirst to do good to souls. And 'tis owing to such pretences as these, that encouragement has been given to the rise of such numbers of *lay-exhorters and teachers,* in one place and another, all over the land. But if 'tis one of the things wrote by the apostle as the *commandment of* GOD, that there should be *officers* in the church, an *order of men* to whom it should belong, as their *proper, stated work,* to exhort and teach, this cannot be the business of others. . . .

And it deserves particular consideration, whether the suffering, much more the encouraging WOMEN, yea, GIRLS to speak in the assemblies for religious worship, is not a plain breach of that *commandment of the* LORD, wherein it is said, *Let your* WOMEN *keep silence in the churches; for it is not permitted to them to speak—It is a shame: for* WOMEN *to speak in the church.*

SOURCE 3: *"A Report on Religious Excess at New London"* (1743)

Why would eighteenth-century New Englanders have found James Davenport's assault on the written word especially shocking? Why might observers have concluded that the actions described here represented an assault on the social order?

SIR,

The Conduct of some of the People call'd N Lights, or Christians, as they please to call themselves, has been so extraordinary here the last Week, that 'tis desired by some that an Account of their wild, frantick and extravagant Management may be inserted in one of your next Prints; and therefore send you the following Sketch of some of their Transactions;

At the Beginning of the present Month came to this Place the famous Mr. *Davenport.* . . . [O]n the 6th [of this month], it being the Lord's Day, just before the Conclusion of the Publick Worship, and also as the People were returning from the House of GOD, they were surpriz'd with a great Noise and Out-cry; Multitudes hasten'd toward the Place of Rendezvous, directing themselves by the Clamor and Shouting, which together, with the ascending Smoak bro't them to one of the most public Places in the Town, and there found these good People encompassing a Fire which they had built up in the Street, into which they

SOURCE: Reprinted in Richard L. Bushman, ed., *The Great Awakening: Documents on the Revival of Religion, 1740–1745* (New York: Atheneum, 1970), pp. 51–53; originally from *Boston Weekly Post-Boy,* March 28, 1743.

were casting Numbers of Books, principally on Divinity, and those that were well-approved by *Protestant* Divines, *viz.* Bp. *Beveridge's* Thoughts, Mr. *Russel's* Seven Sermons, one of Dr. *Colman's,* and one of Dr. *Chauncy's* Books, and many others. Nothing can be more astonishing than their insolent Behaviour was during the Time of their Sacrifice, as 'tis said they call'd it: whilst the Books were in the Flames they cry'd out, *Thus the Souls of the Authors of those Books, those of them that are dead, are roasting in the Flames of Hell;* and that *the Fate of those surviving, would be the same, unless speedy Repentance prevented:* On the next Day they had at the same Place a second Bonfire of the like Materials, and manag'd in the same manner. Having given this fatal Stroke to *Heresy,* they made ready to attack *Idolatry,* and sought for Direction, as in the Case before; and then Mr. *D—p—t* told them to look at Home first, and that they themselves were guilty of idolizing their Apparel, and should therefore divest themselves of those Things especially which were for Ornament and let them be burnt: Some of them in the heighth of their Zeal . . . fell to stripping and cast their Cloaths down at their Apostle's Feet; one or two hesitated about the Matter, and were so bold as to tell him they had nothing on which they idoliz'd: He reply'd, that such and such a Thing was an Offence to him; and they must down with them: One of these being a Gentleman of Learning and Parts ventur'd to tell Mr. *D—p—t,* that he could scarce see how his disliking the Night-Gown that he had on his Back, should render him, guilty of Idolatry. However, This carnal Reasoning avail'd nothing; strip he must, and strip he did: By this Time the Pile had grown to a large Bulk, and almost ripe for Sacrifice; and . . . now the Oracle spake clear to the Point, without Ambiguity, and utter'd that *the Things must be burnt;* and to confirm the Truth of the Revelation, took his wearing Breeches, and hove them with Violence into the Pile, saying, *Go you with the Rest.* A young Sister, whose Modesty could not bear to see the Mixture of Cloaks, Petty Coats and Breeches, snatch'd up his Breeches, and sent them at him, with as much Indignation, as tho' they had been the Hire of a Wh—. . . . At this juncture came in a Brother from a neighbouring Town; a Man of more Sense than most of them have; and apply'd warmly to Mr. *D—p—t,* told him, He was *making a Calf,* and that he thot', *the D—l was in him:* Mr. *D—p—t* said, He *tho't* so too; and added, That he *was under the influence of an* evil Spirit, *and that God left Him.*

SOURCE 4:   James Davenport, *Confession and Retractions* (1744)

No copies of James Davenport's itinerant sermons exist. What may account for that? What does Davenport's defense of his confession in the postscript here reveal about the impact of the Great Awakening?

SOURCE: Reprinted in Richard L. Bushman, ed., *The Great Awakening: Documents on the Revival of Religion, 1740–1745* (New York: Atheneum, 1970), pp. 53–55; originally from James Davenport, *The Reverend James Davenport's Confession and Retractions* (Boston, 1744), pp. 3–8.

The *Articles,* which I especially refer to, and would in the most public Manner *retract,* and *warn others against,* are these which follow, *viz.*

I. The Method I us'd for a considerable Time, with Respect to some, yea many *Ministers* in several Parts, in openly *exposing such as I fear'd or thought unconverted, in public Prayer or otherwise:* herein making my private Judgment, (in which also I much suspect I was mistaken in several Instances, and I believe also that my Judgment concerning several, was formed rashly and upon very slender Grounds.) . . .

II. By my *advising and urging to such Separations* from *those Ministers,* whom I treated as above, as I believe may justly be called rash, unwarrantable, and of sad and awful Tendency and Consequence. And here I would ask the Forgiveness of those Ministers, whom I have injured in both these Articles.

III. I confess I have been much led astray by *following Impulses* or Impressions as a Rule of Conduct, whether they came with or without a Text of Scripture. . . .

IV. I believe further that I have done much Hurt to Religion by *encouraging private Persons to a ministerial and authoritative Kind or Method of exhorting;* which is particularly observable in many such being much puft up and *falling into the Snare of the Devil,* while many others are thus directly prejudic'd against the Work.

V. I have Reason to be deeply humbled that I have not been duly careful to endeavour to remove or prevent Prejudice, (where I now believe I might then have done it consistently with Duty) which appear'd remarkable in the Method I practis'd, of *singing with others in the Streets* in Societies frequently. . . .

July 28. 1744.

JAMES DAVENPORT.

P.S. In as much as a Number, who have fallen in with and promoted the *aforesaid Errors* and *Misconduct,* and are not alter'd in their Minds, may be prejudic'd against this *Recantation,* by a Supposition or Belief, that I came into it by Reason of Desertion or Dulness and Deadness in Religion: It seems needful therefore to signify, what I hope I may say without boasting, and what I am able thro' pure rich Grace to speak with Truth and Freedom; that for *some Months* in the Time of my coming to the *aboresaid Conclusions* and *Retractations,* and since I have come through Grace to them; I have been favoured a great Part of the Time, with a sweet *Calm and Serenity of Soul and Rest in God,* and sometimes with special and remarkable Refreshments of Soul, and these more free from corrupt Mixtures than formerly: *Glory to God alone.*

J.D.

Source 5: Charles Chauncy, *Seasonable Thoughts on the State of Religion in New England* (1743)

In this excerpt from his most famous work, Chauncy discusses what should be done with "enthusiastic" preachers. How does his position here compare to that in Source 2? How do you account for the difference? How does his position compare to that taken by Massachusetts authorities toward Anne Hutchinson in the early seventeenth century?

Civil Rulers may do a great deal, not only by their *good Example,* but a wise Use of their *Authority,* in their various Places, for the Suppression of every Thing hurtful to Society, and the Encouragement of whatever has a Tendency to make Men happy in the Enjoyment of their Rights, whether *natural* or *Christian.* And herein chiefly lies, (as I humbly conceive) the Duty of Rulers, at this Day. . . . Their *Duty* rather lies in keeping Peace between those, who unhappily differ in their Thoughts about the State of our religious Affairs: And their Care in this Matter ought to be *impartial.* Each Party, without Favour or Affection, should be equally restrain'd from Out-rage and Insult. Those, who may think themselves Friends to a *Work of GOD,* should be protected in the Exercise of all their *just Rights,* whether as *Men,* or *Christians:* So on the other Hand, those who may be Enemies to *Error* and *Confusion,* have the same Claim to be protected.

And if, on either Side, they invade the Rights of others, or throw out Slander, at Random, to the Hurt of their Neighbour's Reputation and Usefulness, and the bringing forward a State of Tumult and Disorder; I see not but the *civil Arm* may justly be stretched forth for the Chastisement of such Persons; and this, though their Abuses should be offered in the Name of the LORD, or under the Pretext of the most flaming Zeal for the Redeemer's Honour, and serving the Interest of *his Kingdom:* For it ought always be accounted an Aggravation of the Sin of *Slander,* rather than an Excuse for it, its being committed under the *Cloak of Religion,* and Pretence for the *Glory of GOD;* as it will, under these Circumstances, be of more pernicious Tendency. I am far from thinking, that any Man ought to suffer, either for his *religious Principles,* or *Conduct* arising from them, while he is no Disturber of the *civil Peace;* but when Men, under the Notion of appearing zealous for GOD and *his Truths,* insult their Betters, vilify their Neighbours, and spirit People to Strife and Faction, I know of no Persons more sutable to be taken in Hand by *Authority:* And if they suffer 'tis for their own Follies; nor can they reasonably blame any Body but themselves: Nor am I asham'd, or afraid, to profess it as my Opinion, that it would probably have been of good Service, if those, in these Times, who have been publickly and outragiously reviled, had, by their Complaints, put it properly in the *Magistrates* Power, to restrain some Men's *Tongues* with *Bit* and *Bridle.*

Source: Reprinted in Alan Heimert and Perry Miller, eds., *The Great Awakening: Documents Illustrating the Crisis and Its Consequences* (Indianapolis: Bobbs-Merrill Educational Publishing, 1967), pp. 299, 300–301; originally from Charles Chauncy, *Seasonable Thoughts on the State of Religion in New-England* (Boston, 1743).

QUESTIONS TO CONSIDER

1. Why did Charles Chauncy and other Old Lights find James Davenport's preaching and behavior so threatening? Why might the preaching of New Light ministers have been considered subversive in colonial society?

2. What does this chapter's evidence suggest about the types of people attracted to Davenport's revival preaching? What made his attacks on established churches and ministers like Chauncy so appealing to them?

3. What do the lives of Davenport and Chauncy reveal about the Great Awakening's impact on the attitudes of colonial Americans? What do they reveal about the connection between religion and the American Revolution?

4. Like the actions of Nathaniel Bacon (see Chapter 2), those of James Davenport were threatening to colonial authority. Yet compared to Bacon and his followers, Davenport was treated with leniency. How do you account for the authorities' responses in these two cases?

FOR FURTHER READING

Patricia U. Bonomi, *Under the Cope of Heaven: Religion, Society, and Politics in Colonial America* (New York: Oxford University Press, 1986), explores the connections between colonial religion and politics and the impact of the Great Awakening on the American Revolution.

Michael J. Crawford, *Seasons of Grace: Colonial New England's Revival Tradition in Its British Context* (New York: Oxford University Press, 1991), investigates the connection between revival in Great Britain and America in the eighteenth century.

Edward M. Griffin, *Old Brick: Charles Chauncy of Boston, 1705–1787* (Minneapolis: University of Minnesota Press, 1980), offers a sympathetic view of Chauncy as an opponent of the Great Awakening and an important eighteenth-century religious figure.

Frank Lambert, *Inventing the "Great Awakening"* (Princeton, N.J.: Princeton University Press, 1999), attempts to understand the Great Awakening as observers at the time saw it.

David S. Lovejoy, *Religious Enthusiasm in the New World: Heresy to Revolution* (Cambridge: Harvard University Press, 1985), is a sophisticated exploration of the connection between religious and revolutionary enthusiasm and the ways the Great Awakening subverted established institutions and ways of thinking.

Gary B. Nash, *The Urban Crucible: Social Change, Political Consciousness, and the Origins of the American Revolution* (Cambridge: Harvard University Press, 1979), relates the Great Awakening and the popularity of James Davenport to the social and economic strains in eighteenth-century colonial cities.

CHAPTER
4

The Price of Patriotism:
Jonathan Sewall and John Adams

The Boston Massacre: John Adams
A trial for Jonathan Sewall

As Jonathan Sewall strolled toward the hilltop overlooking Maine's sparkling Casco Bay, he had more on his mind than an early-morning view of the island-dotted Atlantic inlet. On this midsummer morning in 1774, he had asked John Adams to walk with him in a desperate attempt to save his friend from folly. Relations between Great Britain and the American colonies were approaching a dangerous point, and Adams had just been elected a delegate to the Continental Congress. Sewall was determined that he not serve. As they walked, Sewall reminded Adams that taking a seat in Philadelphia would be an act of rebellion against His Majesty's government. Adams's brilliant legal career would face certain ruin. "Great Britain is determined in her system," he declared. "Her power is irresistible and will be destructive to you if you persevere in opposition to her designs."

Adams considered Sewall his best friend but was unmoved by his pleas. "I will sink or swim, live or die, survive or perish with my country—that is my unalterable determination," he replied. When Sewall persisted, Adams declared, "I see we must part, and with bleeding heart I say, I fear forever." Adams was wrong. Thirteen years later, he met up with his old friend in London. By that time, the United States had won its independence from Britain and Adams had won the gratitude of the new nation for his service to it. He had sat in the First and Second Continental Congresses, negotiated the treaty ending the Revolution, and served as minister to Great Britain. The two men talked for several hours, and Sewall observed that their conversation was just what might be expected "at the meeting of two old sincere friends after a long separation."

Nonetheless, for Sewall the meeting could not have been easy. Adams had already secured an honored place as one of his country's founding fathers, while Sewall remained an outcast. He longed for his beloved Massachusetts, his brilliant legal career was over, and his mental state had deteriorated along with his fortunes. To be sure, Adams had made great personal sacrifices to serve his nation. Yet he also had led a full and rewarding life—a testament to the possibilities presented by his country's creation. Like Adams, Sewall had made an irrevocable commitment to *his* country. He chose to "sink or swim" with Great Britain, becoming at once an articulate defender of the Loyalist position and a prominent target of patriot wrath. As a result, he enjoyed neither honor nor fame, and he stands today as a reminder of the hopes and fears that motivated the Loyalists and the enormous toll this position exacted.

"A Brilliant Imagination"

"The childhood shows that man, as morning shows the day," wrote the Puritan poet John Milton. Jonathan Sewall was not born a Loyalist, but his sympathies seemed to arise naturally from his early years. The product of an old and distinguished New England family, he would be well served by family and social connections. When his merchant father died bankrupt in 1731, three years after Jonathan was born, young Sewall would be provided for by more successful relatives. The pastor of Sewall's exclusive Brattle Street Church in Boston saw to it that his wealthy parishioners opened their pocketbooks to pay for the boy's schooling. His uncle Stephen Sewall, chief justice of the Massachusetts Supreme Court, also helped out. When Jonathan turned fifteen, Justice Sewall reached into his purse and sent Jonathan to Harvard. After he graduated and took up teaching, a distant relative opened his Salem home and library to the young schoolmaster, and there he studied law. Several years later, his benefactor introduced him to Chambers Russell, a judge and colleague of Stephen Sewall's. Russell took the young man into his Charlestown home and tutored him further in the law. Russell was wealthy and well connected, sat in the Massachusetts assembly, and commanded the deference and respect of his fellow citizens. Sewall could not have found a better mentor.

By the time Russell died in 1766, Sewall had already taken over his Charlestown law practice. The next year, he was sworn in before the Massachusetts bar and set up his own practice. For much of the next decade, Sewall busied himself with petty squabbles over land, livestock, debts, and thefts. To secure additional cases, he followed the superior court as it sat in various counties throughout the year. The frequent travel was compensated by the opportunity to mix with other attorneys, including a fellow Harvard graduate named John Adams.

Although Sewall was lighthearted and Adams serious and introspective, the two men struck up a friendship sustained by the frequent exchange of letters. Adams found much to like in his friend: "a lively wit, a pleasing humor, a brilliant imagination, [and] great subtlety of reasoning." The mundane cases in both the superior and lower courts also gave Sewall the opportunity to master the intricacies of the law and hone his courtroom manner. He had "a soft, smooth, insinuating eloquence," Adams noted, "which . . . gave him as much power over [a jury] as any lawyer ought ever to have." Sewall's talents were also noticed by Edmund Trowbridge, the attorney general of Massachusetts. Eventually, Trowbridge made Sewall his junior partner, passing along wealthy clients to his young protégé. Through him, Sewall gained entry into the highest circles in the colony.

In time, personal loyalty led to service for men in power. Sewall's attachments were evident when an influenza epidemic swept Boston in 1760, claiming the life of Stephen Sewall. A battle for the justice's empty court seat between Speaker of the assembly James Otis Jr. and Lieutenant Governor Thomas Hutchinson quickly ensued. When Governor Francis Bernard chose Hutchinson, prominent merchants saw the appointment as an attempt by Bernard to gain control of the court at a crucial time. Several years earlier, the royal governor had introduced writs of assistance, which allowed customs officials to board ships and enter buildings and merchants' houses to search for smuggled goods, even without evidence that contraband might be held there. Smuggling was widespread on Boston's wharves, but the writs gave customs officials sweeping power. Outraged Massachusetts merchants had hired Otis to defend them against rummaging officials. Otis had denounced the warrants as an assault on the traditional rights of privacy guaranteed by the British constitution. Hutchinson's elevation to the supreme court, however, ensured that the issue would be decided in favor of the administration.

Although many Massachusetts lawyers sided with Otis, Jonathan Sewall did not. Chambers Russell and Edmund Trowbridge were friends of Hutchinson and supporters of Governor Bernard, who had just named Sewall justice of the peace for Middlesex County. In addition, when Sewall turned to Otis for assistance in settling his uncle's debt-ridden estate, the legislature refused to help. When the divide between Governor Bernard and the legislature deepened after the supreme court decided in favor of the writs, Sewall took up his pen in defense of the administration. In 1763, he blasted Otis in newspaper essays defending the governor's appropriation of provincial funds without the assembly's consent. Later, when the Otis faction launched an attack on Hutchinson for holding offices in all three branches of government, Sewall countered by declaring that citizens should not "give implicit credit to the turbulent harangues of every bold, disaffected, popular disclaimer." He could not have predicted how events in coming years would lead increasing numbers of Americans, including his friend John Adams, to do just that.

"Just Getting Under Sail"

John Adams was hardly an impetuous rebel but instead, like Sewall, exhibited an inbred conservatism. In fact, the two men may have been drawn to each other because they had so much in common. Both came from families of modest resources, graduated from Harvard, and pursued legal careers after unhappy stints as schoolteachers. Both developed a deep respect for British institutions and a reverence for the law. Both were ambitious and sought the recognition that each felt was his due.

Born in 1735, the son of a respectable Braintree farmer and shoemaker, Adams grew up on the family farm twelve miles south of Boston. His parents decided that their firstborn son would receive the best education their middling circumstances could provide. After progressing through two private academies, young Adams enrolled at Harvard. A reluctant student, he instead aspired to be a farmer, preferring hunting, fishing, and exploring the outdoors to the drudgery of study. At Harvard, however, he discovered a love of books. Upon graduation, he became a schoolmaster in Worcester, fifty miles west of Boston. Teaching "a large number of little runtlings" did not agree with him, so he turned to law. Here was a profession of growing importance in the colony's expanding commercial economy, one that could provide him the "Honor or Reputation" he sought. He was taken in by Worcester's leading attorney and two years later returned to Braintree to practice law.

Adams admired such prominent lawyers as James Otis and the up-and-coming Jonathan Sewall. Yet he had no family connections and lived at home to cut expenses. "[I]t is my Destiny to dig Treasures with my own fingers," he lamented. "No Body will lend me or Sell me an axe." Nor would polish or social graces pave the way. A lingering Puritan ethic had a deep impact on Adams, who was content to hole up in his study for hours on end. Reserved and serious, he was far too stiff to backslap his way to success. Instead, he imposed on himself a harsh discipline of study and hard work.

Gradually, his client list grew. In 1761, he was admitted to practice before the Massachusetts Superior Court. At about the same time, his personal life improved. He courted Hannah Quincy at the same time that Jonathan Sewall wooed her sister Esther, and the two lawyers frequently met at the Quincys' Braintree home. Hannah married another man, but Adams soon recovered after he met Abigail Smith, the daughter of a minister from nearby Weymouth. By 1763, John and the "prudent, modest, delicate, soft, [and] sensible" Abigail were inseparable, and the next year they were married. He was twenty-eight; she was nineteen. The couple moved into a cottage next door to the house where John had been born and raised. Although court cases frequently took him away from Abigail, it was a happy time, and the next summer Abigail gave birth to a daughter.

Events far from Adams's fireside, however, were about to disrupt his world. After the French and Indian War (1754–1763), the colonists entered a new relationship with Great Britain when Parliament sought additional revenue from them. In 1764, it passed the Sugar Act, which levied new duties on molasses and placed a heavy burden on New England shippers. The next year, Parliament passed the Stamp Act, which placed duties on various paper products already in the colonies. It was met with loud protests and riots up and down the colonies. In Massachusetts, John Adams's cousin Samuel Adams aroused popular sentiment by arguing that the act was part of a plot to destroy the colonists' liberties. Samuel had close contact with Boston's artisans and laborers, many of whom were facing diminished prospects. His ability to rally them was unsurpassed. Even John noticed that the "lowest ranks" had become "more attentive to their liberties . . . and more determined to defend them." If so, it was due in large part to the work of his cousin.

Samuel encouraged John to play a more active role in the Stamp Act crisis, but John held back. It "is very unfortunate for me," he wrote, for "[I am] just getting under Sail." Writing newspaper essays under a pen name, he attacked the Stamp Act as misguided. He also wrote the town of Braintree's instructions regarding the crisis to its representative in the legislature. **[See Source 1.]** Yet his participation was limited and reluctant. He did not want to be seen as irresponsible, and he was skeptical about the motives of the "designing persons" who were leading the popular protests, including his cousin. John found mob action frightening and distasteful. "That way madness lies," he told James Otis, who had asked Adams to "harangue" colonists in 1765. Even a decade later, he declared that "breaking open Houses by rude and insolent Rabbles, must be discountenanced." For the time being, he stayed home with his family, "thinking, reading, searching, concerning Taxation without Consent."

"Rendered Himself Quite Subservient"

Jonathan Sewall's life was also going well. The same year the colonies entered their new relationship with Britain—and John Adams with Abigail—Sewall married Esther Quincy. According to Adams, Esther was "celebrated for her beauty, her vivacity, and spirit," and when Sewall first set eyes on her, he "viewed her with . . . unruffled pleasure." Other rewards soon followed, especially after Sewall voiced his views about the growing popular unrest. Like Adams, Sewall opposed the Stamp Act. But whereas Adams believed that royal officials were a "restless grasping turbulent Crew," Sewall feared turbulence from another quarter. To him, the great danger was not the tax, but Samuel Adams and other rabble-rousers who defied the British government's authority. Submission to a bad law was far better than unlawful resistance to it, he argued. In the growing colonial crisis, such arguments would not go unnoticed. When Samuel Adams and James Otis continued to challenge Governor Bernard's authority after the Stamp Act was repealed in 1766, Sewall defended the governor in newspaper essays. Those in power had to be obeyed, he insisted, as long as they "steadily pursue[d] the sole end of their creation, the good of the community." Bernard liked what he read and quickly named Sewall advocate general of the Massachusetts vice-admiralty court,* which had been established by Parliament to take smuggling cases out of the hands of sympathetic colonial juries. A short time later, Bernard named him attorney general of the colony. At age forty, he had arrived.

Before long, however, Sewall found himself in the midst of a growing struggle between the Crown and Massachusetts's merchant class. His problems started with the Townshend Acts* of 1767, which imposed new import duties and set up an American Board of Customs Commissioners in Boston. As attorney

---

Vice-admiralty court: A special British court that heard cases involving shipping and maritime disputes.

Townshend Acts: Laws passed by Parliament that placed taxes on certain colonial imports, including glass, paper, paint, and tea.

general and advocate general of the vice-admiralty court, Sewall was responsible for enforcing the customs laws and prosecuting violators. He had no problem with the laws, but he often disagreed with their application by customs commissioners, who routinely engaged in racketeering. Nowhere was Sewall's conflict with the commissioners more evident than in their treatment of John Hancock, the colonies' richest merchant. When a customs man without a writ of assistance rummaged below deck on Hancock's ship *Lydia* in 1768, Hancock had him forcibly removed. Sewall believed that Hancock had acted within the law and refused to prosecute him. When Hancock's ship *Liberty* docked in Boston later that year, customs officials seized the ship, claiming that it had smuggled in wine. Hancock had already become a symbol of a growing struggle between imperial interests and colonial rights. Now the seizure of the *Liberty* set off a riot in which customs officers were attacked and driven from Boston. Undaunted, the commissioners proceeded with their case against Hancock, which was a reluctant Sewall's responsibility to prosecute. Hancock and five others faced fines of nine thousand pounds each for allegedly avoiding seven hundred pounds in duties. Hancock's lawyer was an equally reluctant John Adams. Concerned about the effect that political activism might have on his career, Adams looked with "disgust" at his duties in defending the imperial authorities' prime target. The commissioners' case was weak, however, and they had Sewall drop the charges the next year.

The case made Hancock a hero and sullied Sewall's reputation. Samuel Adams declared that Sewall was nothing more than a "little creature of the court" who had betrayed the colony's interests. Sewall had just been appointed to the Halifax vice-admiralty court at the considerable salary of six hundred pounds a year. He now held seats on the Massachusetts and Halifax vice-admiralty courts and as Massachusetts attorney general. Sewall, concluded Samuel Adams, had "rendered himself quite subservient" by accepting so many "favors" from the governor. Certainly, he had learned all about the perquisites of power. In response to these accusations, Sewall urged John Adams to succeed him as attorney general. Though still fearful of an association with radicals, Adams felt a growing disdain for royal officials such as Lieutenant Governor Thomas Hutchinson, whose death, he concluded, "would have been a Smile of Providence." Thus he quickly turned Sewall down.

Sewall's troubles only mounted. In 1770, guards outside the customshouse opened fire on an angry mob, killing five civilians. It was Sewall's job to prosecute the soldiers involved in what came to be known as the Boston Massacre. He believed that the troops were innocent. He was also convinced that James Otis and Samuel Adams had orchestrated the mob. Prosecuting the case vigorously would violate Sewall's sense of justice, but a weak prosecution would surely raise charges of conspiracy. Only one reasonable course seemed open to him. Sewall drew up the indictment against the soldiers and then returned to his country home in Middlesex, where he stayed in personal exile for a year.

While Sewall ran, John Adams stepped into the fray by agreeing to defend the soldiers. Adams later claimed that he accepted their defense because he thought they deserved a fair trial. Yet Samuel Adams and other radicals may have pushed him into it, convinced that the propaganda value of a guilty verdict would be greater if one of the province's best lawyers defended the soldiers. The promise of a seat in the Massachusetts legislature may have been an-other inducement. Whatever his motives, John Adams waged a brilliant de-fense. He argued that the soldiers were following orders and had the right to shoot in self-defense against a "motley rab[b]le of saucy boys, Negroes and Mu-lattoes, Irish teagues and outlandish jacktars." The commander and six redcoats were acquitted, while two soldiers were convicted of manslaughter and pun-ished lightly. Remarkably, Adams emerged unscathed from the controversy. In fact, the trial enhanced his reputation as a gifted lawyer, and within months he won a seat in the legislature. A couple of years later, John and Abigail moved into a handsome brick home in Boston. Adams could easily have concluded that he had followed a wiser course than the timid Sewall, whom he accused of "desertion."

At the same time, Sewall could believe that *he* had made the correct deci-sion. As the hysteria surrounding the incident died down, Sewall looked opti-mistically to a stable future. Most Americans had no thought of revolution in 1771. Only a few radicals were thinking about independence. Like many colonists, Sewall felt secure in the assumption that the status quo would be pre-served and that he would enjoy the rewards of a successful career. About this time, he moved his family into a large house on Cambridge's fashionable Brat-tle Street. There and at their country retreat outside Boston, the Sewalls enjoyed the perquisites of their position atop Massachusetts society: servants, an elegant coach, fine wine, and the company of others who shared their small and secure world. From that position, Sewall soon took up his pen in defense of the British government. [See Source 2.]

"Atlas of American Independence"

John Adams would not have disagreed with Sewall's assessment of the future. He also had good reason to believe that the colonial crisis was over. After Par-liament repealed all but one of the Townshend duties—the tax on tea—in 1770, colonial protests had died down. Resigning his seat in the Massachusetts legis-lature after one term, Adams declared that he had served his country "at an im-mense Expense . . . of Time, Peace, Health, Money, and Preferment." He was determined to avoid "Politicks, Political Clubs, Town Meetings, [or] General Court," confessing that his "Heart" was "at Home." In fact, Adams had long been reluctant to commit himself fully to the colonial cause. As late as 1772, James Otis accused him of "moaping about the Streets of this Town" and caring about little more than money. Otis's "Rant" obviously stung Adams, who protested that he had sacrificed as much to "the public Cause" as had his accuser.

Soon, however, few would doubt Adams's commitment. In 1773, Parlia-ment required that judges' salaries be paid by the Crown rather than the colony's legislature, a move Adams believed was intended to destroy the inde-pendence of the judiciary. In addition, Thomas Hutchinson, who had replaced Bernard as governor, declared that Parliament's power over the colonies was unlimited. The legislature's reply, drafted by John and Samuel Adams, argued that colonial legislatures had sovereign power. When Parliament passed the Tea Act later in 1773, it was clear to John that the colonial crisis was not over. Many colonists saw the measure, which reduced the price of East India Company tea in the colonies, as a plot to make it easier to pay the remaining Townshend tax on it. When fifty men slipped onto the company's ships in Boston Harbor and threw overboard forty-five tons of tea, thousands cheered, including John Adams. The Boston Tea Party, he declared, was the "grandest event" since the beginning of the controversy with Britain.

Parliament quickly cracked down on Massachusetts with the Intolerable Acts. These drastic measures closed Boston's port, limited town meetings, strengthened the power of the royally appointed governor at the expense of the popularly elected legislature, and replaced Hutchinson with a military governor, General Thomas Gage. When the colonists responded to the growing crisis by calling the First Continental Congress,* the Massachusetts legislature selected four delegates. One of them was John Adams. Like other Whigs (opponents of Britain's policies) and Tories (supporters of the policies), Adams and Sewall were now divided as never before. Like many colonists, Adams believed that British actions reflected more than a desire to raise revenue from the colonies. Rather, he thought, Britain's government was engaged in a plot to rob colonists of their cherished liberties. If it succeeded, they would be reduced to abject slavery. Sewall, an appointee of the royal governor, saw no such danger, and he continued to defend the British government and its right to tax the colonies. By the summer of 1774, friends could no longer set aside their political differences. When Sewall and Adams met in Falmouth, Maine, in July to conduct business before the court, the two men bade each other farewell.

After Sewall returned home from Maine, his circumstances quickly deteriorated. A mob surrounded the Sewalls' Cambridge home, smashed the windows, and threatened the family. Jonathan was in Boston at the time, and a terrified Esther finally dispersed the attackers by offering up the contents of the wine cellar. When Sewall returned to Cambridge the next day, he and his family decided to join the growing number of Tories seeking refuge in Boston. Conditions in the besieged city were abysmal. Prices skyrocketed, food was scarce, and people died daily as a result of dysentery. Sewall continued as attorney general and also served as Gage's personal secretary and adviser. Although he found time to record his ideas on the rebellion **[see Source 3]**, mostly he despaired. "Everything I see is laughable, cursable, and damnable," he wrote. "My pew in church is converted into a pork tub; my house into a den of rebels, thieves, & lice; [and] my farm in possession of the very worst of all god's creations." By the summer of 1775, in the face of "musketry, bombs, great guns, . . . battles, sieges, murder, plague, pestilence, famine, rebellion, and the Devil," he was ready to leave. Before the end of the summer, Sewall and his family boarded a ship bound for England. He would never see Boston again.

Adams, too, was quickly caught up in the rush of events. After attending the Philadelphia convention, he returned home to a loud counteroffensive launched by Tories in provincial newspapers. He responded in twelve essays in which he laid out the nature of the threat posed by the British government. **[See**

First Continental Congress: A meeting of delegates from twelve colonies in Philadelphia held in the fall of 1774.

Source 4.] He finished his last essay shortly before Gage dispatched troops to Concord in April 1775 to seize the colonists' weapons. Bloodshed at Lexington and Concord was on Adams's mind as he left for the Second Continental Congress the next month, still hopeful that peace could be restored. For the next two years, Adams sat in Congress, his influence growing as he gradually impressed the other delegates with his intellect and his immense capacity for work.

By early 1776, a swift series of events made Adams realize that independence was inevitable. First, the crisis had descended into open warfare. The previous year, when Congress had expressed its hope for reconciliation with its Olive Branch Petition, King George III had rejected it outright. Then Thomas Paine's *Common Sense,* a devastating attack on monarchy, had radicalized many colonists. When the delegates named Adams to a committee to draft a declaration of independence, he declined the task, leaving the job to Thomas Jefferson instead. It was Adams, though, who took to the floor in early July to defend the move for independence. His speech was so masterful that Jefferson called him "our Colossus on the Floor." Another awed delegate commented that "the man to whom the country is most indebted for the great measure of independency is Mr. John Adams of Boston. I call him the Atlas of American Independence."

"Ungrateful Sons of Bitches"

By July 1776, Jonathan Sewall had been in London for a year and had found much to encourage him. He was greeted by Thomas Hutchinson and other prominent Loyalists from Massachusetts who had already established a refugee colony in the British capital, and he looked to an appointment to high office. And then there was London itself. Everything in the city was on such a grand scale that Sewall was "lost and confounded." Surely, the colonies would not be able to withstand Britain's greatness.

As the war dragged on, however, his mood changed. Only a few refugees secured offices, and he was not among them. Although Sewall found Britain's wealth "truly astonishing," he discovered that his six-hundred-pound vice-admiralty court salary was now "as a Drop in the Ocean." "Everything I have seen in my own Country," he wrote, "is all Miniature, yankee-puppet-show." Britain's inability to crush the rebellious colonists made matters worse. Sewall yearned for Massachusetts, and his homesickness only increased his hatred of the rebels. He longed for "one peep at my house," but the "damned, fanatical, republican, New England, rebellious, ungenerous, ungrateful sons of bitches" had confiscated and sold his property and banned him from the state. News of the stunning British defeat at Saratoga in 1777 dashed Sewall's hopes for a speedy return home, and the following spring he left London for less expensive Bristol.

Even when Americans won their independence, Sewall consoled himself with the belief that they still faced certain ruin. "Poor Beasts," he wrote, "I pity them from my soul." In fact, Sewall himself was defeated. Suffering from debt and depression, he moved into a room detached from his family's main house, where his only company was a cat and two goldfinches. Blaming Esther for his circumstances, he told a friend that he wished she was out of his life forever. Meanwhile, his financial difficulties mounted. The Royal Commission on Losses and Services of American Loyalists, established to settle Loyalists' claims for service and loss of property in the Revolution, awarded only a portion of his six-thousand-pound claim. He was forced to move again to more economical accommodations. Complaining of headaches, stomachaches, and dizziness, he retreated to his bedroom, where for eighteen months he slept for up to ten hours a day. "I was mad as the Devil the whole time," he later observed. Only the desire to be reunited with his son in Canada finally drew him out of his isolation. In 1787, Jonathan, Esther, and their other son departed Britain.

They settled in St. John, New Brunswick. Shortly after their arrival, the royal treasury abolished the Halifax vice-admiralty court, depriving Sewall of his remaining official position. He was left with a pension of only two hundred pounds. "I have sacrificed to my Duty, my property in America," he protested in a letter to treasury officials. It did no good, although within a couple of years, Sewall did receive a settlement from the Royal Commission on Losses, as well as another pension for his "loss of profession." By the standards of his new home, he was well off, but he never escaped the belief that he had been wronged. Sewall's bitterness found numerous targets, including the freed slaves he saw arriving in St. John after the Revolution. "I believe the Maker of all never intended Indians, Negroes or Monkeys, for Civilization," he told a friend. He never rid himself of his anger or melancholy. In the last six years of his life, he was confined to bed. Esther nursed him even as he complained that she denied him peace and solitude. He died in 1796. John Adams later concluded that the cause of death was a "broken heart."

By that time, Adams had also paid a price for his "unalterable" commitment to his country. Two years before the start of the Revolution, he had written Abigail that he longed for his Braintree farm, where his family again lived. There, he said, a "Hoe and Spade, would do for [his] Remaining Days." He could not know how long it would be before he was able to enjoy his farm and the uninterrupted pleasure of Abigail's company. In the meantime, he found life as a delegate to the Continental Congress "solitary" and "gloomy." He returned home in late 1777, but early the next year he accepted an assignment as emissary to France. He shared quarters with Benjamin Franklin, who Adams thought got by with guile and charm rather than substance. Adams was shocked by Franklin's extravagant tastes and excessive socializing. Franklin would "come home at all hours," noted a dismayed Adams, who found his own skills lacking for a diplomatic assignment "in highly polished society." He also realized that Abigail, back home in charge of the farm and family, was growing distant. Her letters now contained "a Strain of Unhappiness and Complaint."

Nonetheless, after Adams returned home from Paris in 1779, he soon departed again, this time as a delegate to the state constitutional convention. There he drafted the document that became the Massachusetts Constitution. Later that fall, Congress appointed him to negotiate an end to the war with Britain. He headed back to Paris with sons John Quincy and Charles in tow. Not long after his arrival, he traveled to Amsterdam, where he spent nearly two years working to secure from the Dutch desperately needed financial support for the American cause. Then he was back in Paris to help negotiate the treaty ending the Revolution. Not until 1784 were John and Abigail reunited in London. For the next three years, he served as American minister to Britain, with Abigail at his side.

When they returned to Massachusetts in 1788, John and Abigail bought a new home in Quincy, near the Adams homestead. They had just gotten settled when he was elected the first vice president of the United States. In 1797, he succeeded George Washington as president. Finally, in 1801, he returned permanently to his farm and family.

As a young man, Adams had feared that he would die in obscurity. Before he died on July 4, 1826—fifty years after the signing of the Declaration of Independence and within hours of Thomas Jefferson's death—he knew that his early fears would not be realized. Yet he was also convinced that Americans would never place him in the same category as Washington, Franklin, or even Jefferson. "I am not, never was, & never shall be a great man," he declared. Still, his long public service, often at tremendous personal sacrifice, had done much to launch the new nation.

"As Ardent an American . . . as I"

When the Revolution divided Whigs and Tories, both sides were quick to assign petty motives to the other. Although John Adams asserted that his old friend Jonathan Sewall was "as ardent an American . . . as I ever had been," Adams saw in Sewall a personal flaw. He believed that when James Otis had not supported Sewall's petition in the legislature regarding his deceased uncle's estate "with as much zeal as he wished," Sewall became bitter and resentful. "Hutchinson, Trowbridge, and Bernard soon perceived his ill humor, and immediately held out to him prospects of honor, promotion, and wealth," Adams concluded.

Sewall was unquestionably interested in "honor, promotion, and wealth," but Adams's explanation for his friend's loyalism was unfair. Sewall was not manipulated by powerful royal officials such as Bernard and Hutchinson. Rather, his sympathies sprang from a long pattern of experience. Sewall's life was a testament to the importance of paternalistic relationships. Older, well-connected patrons repeatedly took an interest in his education and career and helped him achieve a measure of wealth. He learned that status and comfort were to be found in loyalty to men who served established institutions. His desire to establish his rightful place through attachment to men in power led Sewall to value authority, deference, and order. Whig fears about the destruction of liberty at the hands of powerful and corrupt rulers never gripped him. Rather, he embraced an ideology that emphasized the fragility of established institutions and the inherent dangers of disobedience and disorder.

Adams was just as interested as Sewall in "honor, promotion, and wealth" and just as concerned about the effect of his political commitments on his career. In addition, he shared Sewall's concerns about social order and the rule of law. Forced to "dig Treasures with [his] own fingers," however, Adams never hitched personal ambition to powerful men who served imperial interests. On the contrary, as the crisis with Britain deepened, service to the colonial cause became Adams's means to achieve recognition and honor. Even so, his patriotism sprang from more than his own ambition. He had grown up in a town of freeholders—independent and upright, if not rich. Government was conducted with their consent. Moreover, in his society, someone like himself could rise above his inherited station through hard work. Finally, as his Puritan forebears could have told him, America was to be a place of virtuous inhabitants ever vigilant against the enervating effects of luxury, corruption, and self-indulgence. As naturally as Sewall embraced royal administrators and loyalism, Adams accepted the Whig argument that Americans' liberties and very way of life were threatened by the policies of a tyrannical government in a corrupt mother country. Although these two sons of Massachusetts had much in common, their personal histories were different, and thus only one would risk his position to oppose the "conduct of Britain toward America."

PRIMARY SOURCES

SOURCE 1:   *"Instructions of the Town of Braintree to the Representative"*   (1765)

During the Stamp Act crisis in 1765, the town of Braintree turned to John Adams to draft instructions to its representative in the Massachusetts legislature. In this document, what does Adams see as the important issues raised by the British government's actions?

[Braintree, ante 24 September 1765]

To Ebenezer Thayer Esqr
Sir

In all the Calamities, which have ever befallen this our dear native Country, *[since our the first settlement]*[1] within the Memory of the oldest of Us all, We have never felt So *[great and]* sincere a Grief, and Concern or So many Allarming Fears and Apprehensions, as at the present Time. We have many of Us lived to see, both Pestilence and Scarcity, and the Encroachments And *[Depredations,]* Hostilities of *[French and Indian]* bitter, subtle and powerful Enemies, but We never yet apprehended, our Liberties and Fortunes and our very Being, in any real Danger, till now. It was the Saying of a great Statesman that "Britain, could never be undone but by a British Parliament." In the same Manner We may truly say, that such is our affectionate and dutiful Loyalty *[to our King]* and Devotion to our most gracious King, such our profound Reverence and Veneration for both Houses of Parliament, and such our Love, Esteem, and Friendship to all our fellow subjects in Britain, that it is that Country and that Parliament only, *[that and by means of our]* that could enslave and destroy us. And We can no

SOURCE: Reprinted by permission of the publisher from *The Adams Papers: Papers of John Adams*, Volume 1, edited by Robert J. Taylor, pp. 132–134, Cambridge: The Belknap Press of Harvard University Press. Copyright © 1977 by the Massachusetts Historical Society.

1. Words in brackets were crossed out in the original manuscript.

longer forbear complaining, that, to our infinite astonishment We Apprehend we have Reason to fear, that [*Designs*] Plans have been formed in that Country, and Measures pursued with a direct and formal Intention to enslave Us. We apprehend that great Evidence of such a Design may be deduced from the late Acts of Parliament restricting, and burdening and embarrassing our Trade: but We shall confine ourselves at present chiefly to the Evidence that Results, from what is called the stamp Act.

By this Act a very burdensome, and in our apprehension, unconstitutional Tax is to be laid upon us all.—and by the same Act we are all of Us subjected to numerous and enormous Penalties and Forfeitures, for Violations of that Act, seventy shillings to fifty Pounds Sterlg. which are at the option of an Informer to be prosecuted, sued for and recovered in a Court of Admiralty, without a Jury. . . .

We further apprehend this Tax to be unconstitutional. . . .—And We have always understood it to be a grand and fundamental Principle of the British Constitution that no Freeman should be subjected to any Tax to which he has not given his own Consent in Person or by Proxy. And indeed, the Maxims of the Common Law, as we have hitherto received them, are to the same Effect that a Man and his Property cannot be seperated but by his own Act or fault.

Source 2:   *Jonathan Sewall Offers a Defense of British Authority*   (1771)

Sewall defended the British government in a series of newspaper essays published after the Boston Massacre verdict. On what important premises does he base his argument? What does he see as the real danger of recent events?

Man is a social Animal—a Being whose wants, whose natural powers of Reason and whole capacity of improving those powers continually demonstrate to him that he was made for a social life. . . . Reason and experience soon convince him that the advantages of society cannot be enjoyed without the establishment of certain rules, to which he and all of the community must conform[.] [T]hese rules, so long as he takes Reason for his guide, he will always hold sacred, notwithstanding they abridge him of a part of . . . unlimited freedom of action. . . . [B]ecause he sees the necessity of them, in order to his obtaining and enjoying the more valuable blessings and benefits of society[,] he no longer considers himself as an individual, absolutely unaccountable and uncontrol[l]able, but as one of a community, every member of which is bound to consult and promote the general good. . . . [H]e sees that . . . the publick good and his own are so intimately connected and interwoven together that whatever is inconsistent with the former is equally incompatible with the latter; and therefore, from the most

SOURCE: *Boston Evening Post*, January 14, 1771. On occasion, minor changes have been made to spelling and punctuation for the convenience of modern readers.

forceable principle in human nature, will be, at all times, a true Patriot[.] [H]ence 'the publick peace and happiness will be the principal object of his care and attention. . . . [H]e will hold his right of private judgment as subordinate to that of the public, and of those in whom the society have placed the right of judging; and of consequence he will be very cautious in charging with want of ability or integrity those to whom any of the powers of government are intrusted[.] [H]e will honor the King as supreme, and will upon no pretence, however plausible, presume to revile or speak evil of the Rulers of the people[.] [I]f it happens that from the enacting unpopular laws or from any untoward accident the minds of the multitude are disturbed and inflamed, he will consider their passions as a flood which knows no bounds when once the dikes are broken, and will carefully avoid every thing which may encourage them in breaking thro' that essential subordination upon which the well being and happiness of the whole absolutely depends. . . . [I]f he should judge that a wrong step has been taken in one department of government, he will by no means take occasion from thence to persuade himself or others that . . . all in authority are traiterously combined in plotting the slavery, misery and ruin of the society[.] [H]e will consider human fallibility and integrity of intention as being perfectly consistent and will therefore be disposed to conclude either that he himself is mistaken in his judgment, or that those whose conduct he disapproves will see their error and reform the grievance[.] [H]e will not weaken the pillars of the state by arraigning, accusing and condemning those in the important stations, whose inflexible virtue has been proved and confirmed by long experience. . . .

Slavery I detest, and would be foremost in execrating the sordid unnatural wretch, who, for a kingdom, could stoop to enslave the lowest peasant, in the meanest village of his country—but wide, infinitely wide is the difference between social liberty, and savage licentiousness. . . . [L]et us consider where is the danger of slavery[.] [T]hro' the favor of an indulgent providence, we have a good King, whom God Almighty bless & long preserve, who is, and who glories in being, the father of a free people[.] [W]e are his children and while George the third sits on the British throne, I never can be made to believe his American subjects can be slaves, unless by their own madness and folly they enslave themselves[.] [U]nder the best of Kings, we are chiefly govern'd in our several internal departments, by men who are not only accountable to him, but who are bone of our bone, and flesh of our flesh—men born & bred among us. . . . [C]an we be duped into a belief, because we cannot see the good policy of some of the publick measures, that therefore, in such a government, under such a King, a design is formed of enslaving us? No, reason and common sense forbid the thought.

SOURCE 3: *Jonathan Sewall on the Revolutionary Threat* (1775)

Shortly before Sewall departed for Britain, he analyzed the nature of the patriots' challenge to British authority. What threats to society does he see in their actions? What is his view of his fellow Americans? What is his solution to the crisis?

It is now become too plain to be any longer doubted, that a Union is formed by a great Majority, almost throughout this whole Continent, for opposing the Supremacy, and even the lowest Degree of legislative Jurisdiction, of the British Parliament, over the British Colonies—that an absolute unlimited Independence, is the Object in View—and that, to obtain this End preparations for War are made, and making, with a Vigor, which the most imminent Dangers from a foreign Enemy, could never inspire. It should seem astonishing, that a Country of Husbandmen, possessed every one, almost, of a sufficient Share of landed property, in one of the finest Climates in the World; living under the mildest Government, enjoying the highest portion of civil and religious Liberty that the Nature of human Society admits, and protected in the Enjoyment of these, and every other desirable Blessing in Life, upon the easiest Terms, by the only Power on Earth capable of affording that protection—that a people so scituated for Happiness, should throw off their rural Simplicity, quit the peaceful Sweets and Labours of Husbandry, bid open Defiance to the gentle Intreaties and the angry Threats of that powerful parent State which nursed their tender Years, and rush to Arms with the Ferocity of Savages, and with the fiery Zeal of Crusaders!—and all this, for the Redress of Chimerical Grievances—to oppose a claim of Parliament, made explicitly, exercised uniformly over, and quietly acquiesced in by, the Colonies from their earliest Origin! It is, I say, so truly astonishing, so entirely out of the Course of Nature, so repugnant, to the known principles which most forceably actuate the human mind, that we must search deeper for the grand and more hidden Spring which causes so wonderful a movement in the Machine. . . . [B]y the help of the single Word, *Liberty*, they conjured up the most horrid Phantoms in the Minds of the common people, ever, an easy prey to such specious Betrayers—the Merchants, from a Desire of a free and unrestrained Trade, the sure and easy Means of arriving at a Superiority in Wealth, joined in Bubbling the undiscerning Multitude—the Clergy, from that restless Spirit and Lust of Dominion, which, with a melancholy Notoriety, mark the Character of the priesthood in all Ages and Nations; from a genuine republican Temper, and from a rooted Enmity against the Church of England, opined, as Leaders of the pack, upon those never failing Topics of Tyranny and Popery—the simple unmeaning Mechanics, peasants and Labourers, who had really no Interest in the Matters of Controversy, hoodwinked, inflamed and goaded on by their Spiritual Drivers, fancied they saw civil and

SOURCE: Reprinted in Jack P. Greene, *Colonies to Nation: 1763–1789* (New York: McGraw-Hill Book Company, 1967), pp. 266–268; originally from Dartmouth Papers, William Salt Library, Stafford, England.

religious Tyranny advancing with hasty Strides; and by the Help of kindred Spirits on the other Side [of] the Atlantic it has at length spread through the Continent. . . .

It is in vain to think any longer of drawing them—to such a pitch is the Frenzy now raised, that the Colonists will never yield Obedience to the Laws of the parent State, till, by Experience, they are taught to fear her power. Such is the Infatuation, that, like madmen, they are totally incapable of attending to the Dictates of reason, and will remain so till the passion of Fear is awakened; this will never be effected by Threats, or by the Appearance of a Force with which they imagine themselves able to contend. . . . I am so well convinced that my Countrymen, at least a Majority of them, act under the power of mere Delusion, rather than from positive vicious Intentions, that I most ardently wish to see them brought back to a Sense of their Duty, with as little Havock and Bloodshed as may be; to this End, I wish to see Great Britain rise with a power that shall strike Terror through the Continent, and leave it no longer problematical whether she is in earnest or not.

Source 4:   John Adams, *"Novanglus"*   (1775)

Writing as "Novanglus" (New England), John Adams responded to the Tory newspaper offensive in 1775. What does he see as the threat posed by Britain? What is his position on independence?

"The whigs were sensible that there was no oppression that could be seen or felt." The tories have so often said and wrote this to one another, that I some-times suspect they believe it to be true. But it is quite otherwise. The castle of the province was taken out of their hands and garrisoned by regular soldiers; this they could see, and they thought it indicated an hostile intention and disposi-tion towards them. They continually paid their money to collectors of duties, this they could both see and feel. An host of placemen, whose whole business it was to collect a revenue, were continually rolling before them in their chariots. These they saw. Their governor was no longer paid by themselves according to their charter, but out of the new revenue, in order to render their assemblies useless and indeed contemptible. The judges salaries were threat[e]ned every day to be paid in the same unconstitutional manner. The dullest eye-sight could not but see to what all this tended, viz. to prepare the way for greater innova-tions and oppressions. They knew a minister would never spend his money in this way, if he had not some end to answer by it. Another thing they both saw and felt. Every man, of every character, who by voting, writing, speaking, or otherwise, had favoured the stamp act, the tea act, and every other measure of

Source: Reprinted in Robert J. Taylor, ed., *The Adams Papers: Papers of John Adams* (Cambridge: Harvard University Press, 1977), Volume 2, 265–266, 268, 307, 336; originally from *Boston Gazette*, February 13, 1775; March 6, 1775; March 13, 1775.

a minister or governor, who they knew was aiming at the destruction of their form of government, and introducing parliamentary taxation, was uniformly, in some department or other, promoted to some place of honour and profit for ten years together; and on the other hand, every man who favoured the people in their opposition to those innovations, was depressed, degraded and persecuted as far as it was in the power of the government to do it.

This they considered as a systematical means of encouraging every man of abilities to espouse the cause of parliamentary taxation, and the plan of destroying their charter privileges, and to discourage all from exerting themselves, in opposition to them. This they thought a plan to enslave them, for they uniformly think that the destruction of their charter, making the council and judges wholly dependent on the crown, and the people subject to the unlimited power of parliament as their supreme legislative, is slavery. They were certainly rightly told then that the ministry and their governors together had formed a design to enslave them, and that when once this was done, they had the highest reason to expect window taxes, hearth taxes, land taxes and all others. And that these were only paving the way for reducing the country to lordships. . . .

America has all along consented, still consents, and ever will consent, that parliament being the most powerful legislature in the dominions, should regulate the trade of the dominions. This is founding the authority of parliament to regulate our trade, upon *compact* and *consent* of the colonies, not upon any principle of common or statute law, not upon any original principle of the English constitution, not upon the principle that parliament is the supream and sovereign legislature over them in all cases whatsoever. . . .

That there are any who pant after "independence," (meaning by this word a new plan of government over all America, unconnected with the crown of England, or meaning by it an exemption from the power of parliament to regulate trade) is as great a slander upon the province as ever was committed to writing. The patriots of this province desire nothing new—they wish only to keep their old privileges. They were for 150 years allowed to tax themselves, and govern their internal concerns, as they tho't best. Parliament governed their trade as they tho't fit. This plan, they wish may continue forever. But it is honestly confessed, rather than become subject to the absolute authority of parliament, in all cases of taxation and internal polity, they will be driven to throw off that of regulating trade.

QUESTIONS TO CONSIDER

1. How would you compare Jonathan Sewall's defense of British policies and John Adams's argument against them? What threats did Sewall see in the colonial challenge to British authority? What threats did Adams see in that authority? What did each see as the cause of the crisis?

2. One historian has written that Loyalists reveal "the interrelationship of public and private experience" and that the key to understanding their commitment during the American Revolution may be found in their childhood experiences. How do Sewall's and Adams's positions in the revolutionary crisis reveal a link between "public and private experience"? Do you think the key to understanding their loyalties in the Revolution is to be found in their early lives or elsewhere?

3. Sewall's biographer concluded that he was "a man at odds with his times." Considering Sewall's and Adams's political and social views, do you agree? How were Adams's ideas in step with the times?

4. One exiled Loyalist complained about the "shameless partiality" of late-eighteenth-century historians of the Revolution toward the patriots. From your understanding of Sewall, Adams, and the colonial crisis, what defense can you offer for loyalism?

5. If you had been at the London reunion of Adams and Sewall in 1787, what question would you have asked each?

FOR FURTHER READING

Bernard Bailyn, *Faces of Revolution: Personalities and Themes in the Struggle for American Independence* (New York: Vintage Books, 1992), examines the central themes of the Revolution and the personalities and ideas of Loyalists and Whigs.

Carol Berkin, *Jonathan Sewall: Odyssey of an American Loyalist* (New York: Columbia University Press, 1974), is the only full-length biography of Sewall.

Joseph J. Ellis, *Passionate Sage: The Character and Legacy of John Adams* (New York: W. W. Norton & Company, 1993), is a study of Adams in his later years, but it offers great insight into the way his ideas shaped his actions throughout his life.

David McCullough, *John Adams* (New York: Simon & Schuster, 2001), offers an engaging account of Adam's public and private lives.

William H. Nelson, *The American Tory* (London: Oxford University Press, 1961), remains perhaps the best brief introduction to the Loyalists and their ideas.

The Conflict over the Constitution:
Patrick Henry and James Madison

Patrick Henry   James Madison

In the summer of 1788, Patrick Henry was desperate. Just the previous year, the Federalist enemies of liberty had proposed a new Constitution to replace the Articles of Confederation. Henry was sure that the Federalists' plan for a new central government would concentrate enormous power in the hands of the few. In fact, it would establish the very kind of government that Americans had rebelled against during the Revolution. Under the Constitution, an elite would promote their own interests and rob ordinary citizens of their freedoms. If approved, it would surely bring tyranny once again. Yet Henry also realized that the Federalists were vulnerable. To go into effect, the Constitution had to be ratified by nine states in special conventions. Right here in Virginia, the Constitution could be stopped. After all, Virginia was the most populous state in the nation. If the Federalists did not win here, they stood little chance of success. Buoyed by the thought, Henry rose to speak at the ratifying convention. With unmatched eloquence, he tore into the Constitution, raised the specter of government run roughshod over the people, and reminded the delegates of the Revolution so recently won.

Across the room sat an angry and frustrated James Madison. The principal architect of the Constitution, Madison was just as convinced that a far more powerful central government was necessary for the country to survive. He had heard enough of Henry's demagoguery, however, to think that the situation was hopeless. Henry had roused the convention with his eloquence and presented a formidable attack on the Constitution. He had to be countered. But to whom could the Federalists turn? None of them could hope to match Henry's rhetorical skill. Moreover, the opposition to the Constitution might well have the majority of the convention. Madison had listened long enough as Federalists argued back and forth about what to do. The time had come, he decided, for him to lead the fight.

Madison was an unlikely champion for the Federalist cause. To be sure, he was brilliant and possessed a fine education and breadth of knowledge. Perhaps no one in the nation had thought more deeply about government than Madison. Yet he was so shy and timid that most of his public speeches ended in disaster. Usually, no one in the audience could even hear what he said. Only slightly over five feet tall, he was referred to by some as "Little Jemmy Madison." And although he was a member of the Virginia gentry who disdained the common people, he was plagued with doubts about his own abilities. In fact, he often preferred the company of books to people. As one disappointed belle concluded, he was "the most unsociable creature in existence."

Nonetheless, Madison would lead the Federalist counterattack at the Virginia Ratifying Convention. In the debates that raged through the summer of 1788, he and Henry squared off again and again. While Henry moved the convention with his eloquence, Madison responded with calm logic. Quietly, he disputed his opponent's arguments as the audience strained to hear his voice. Hanging in the balance was the fate of the Constitution and the future of the nation.

"I Speak the Language of Thousands"

Patrick Henry was almost a failure. Throughout his early adult years, he tried to find a career, but each attempt fell short. His father was a planter, a member of the "back country gentry," which traced its roots to England's lesser nobility. In the 1600s, this group had established its dominance over the colony. The planters made fortunes growing tobacco and built vast plantations that sometimes stretched for miles along Virginia's rivers. Those who lived in the more settled eastern low country, or tidewater, became the elite of the colony. In succeeding generations, some of their offspring moved west and continued to assert their social dominance. John Henry, Patrick's father, had migrated to Virginia from his native Scotland in 1727. He married a wealthy widow and through her attached himself to the gentry. "Marrying up" was one route to wealth and status, and widows of good fortune were much sought after. With his marriage, John Henry gained the status of gentleman.

Patrick, born in 1736, and his older brother, William, grew up in comfortable circumstances. Patrick received little more than a common-school education, instead spending much of his time roaming the woods with an uncle, who taught him how to hunt and survive in the wilderness. Unlike the sons of many tidewater aristocrats, he was neither polished nor well read. His eloquent oratory was honed by listening to another uncle, a Presbyterian minister, preach on

Sundays. Young Patrick would memorize the sermon and then recite it from memory, complete with appropriate gestures, during the carriage ride home.

John Henry proved to be a poor businessman and planter, and his wife's fortune was tied to her family. John hoped to secure his sons' future by setting them up as shopkeepers. When Patrick was fifteen, his father gave him and William money to invest in a supply of goods and establish a general store. The boys had inherited their father's poor business sense, however, and the store failed. Patrick's fortune seemed to take a turn for the better when he married Sarah Shelton in 1754 and received her dowry, which consisted of a three-hundred-acre farm and six slaves. But he proved to be as poor a planter as he was a storekeeper. His tobacco crop was destroyed by worms, drought, and an early frost. His father-in-law then offered him the opportunity to operate a tavern at Hanover Court House. For the next several years, he eked out a living as a tavern keeper, but it was barely enough to keep the family fed.

Henry then decided to study law. After passing the bar, he served as a circuit-riding lawyer for several years. He earned his reputation in a case involving religious freedom. Under the practice of established religion, the government of Virginia was supported by the Anglican Church* and the church by the civil authorities. The question in this case was whether a clergyman had to be paid by the local officials. Henry's eloquence carried the day, and the jury decided against payment. From that day forward, Henry was associated with the cause of religious liberty.

During the decade leading up to the Revolution, few colonists were more radical or outspoken for the American cause than Henry. His oratory during the Stamp Act crisis of 1765 electrified the colonies. His "Give Me Liberty or Give Me Death" speech in 1775 helped unite and mobilize Britain's opponents. During the Revolution, he served as governor of Virginia, compiling a mediocre record. When he left office, he returned to his law practice, but he remained an important political figure—a man who could be counted on to have an opinion on nearly every issue. Even before the end of the war, he was elected to the Virginia legislature.

Late in the Revolution, Henry moved his family to a newly settled area of Virginia near the North Carolina border. He established a ten-thousand-acre plantation, Leatherwood, and eventually acquired seventy-five slaves to work the land. Despite his newfound wealth, Henry was not a full-fledged member of Virginia's planter aristocracy, and he did not share its social and political outlook. Removed from the tidewater, he was surrounded by yeomen farmers with whom he could easily identify. He did not believe in a natural order that made some superior and others inferior. His own roots were too humble for that.

Ironically, Henry claimed to be a "democrat" and self-appointed watchdog of the people's rights, even though he held many slaves. In his world, only property-holding white males could vote and participate in politics, and his fears regarding tyranny extended only to these citizens, not black slaves. He

---

Anglican Church: Also known as the Church of England, it was the official, or established, church in England and in several of the colonies, including Virginia.

believed that unchecked government power was a big threat to ordinary people, whose rights as property holders and freemen were always in jeopardy. The recent colonial past had taught Henry and many other Americans about the dangers of a powerful central government too far removed from the people. In fact, those concerns were reflected in the central government Americans created during the Revolution. The one-house Congress under the Articles of Confederation had no power to tax, regulate domestic or foreign commerce, or compel citizens to obey its laws. The states, not the central government, were clearly sovereign.

After the Revolution, however, the serious problems facing the nation left some Americans wondering whether the central government had too little power. Many of those problems were economic. Before the war, the colonists had been dependent on manufactured goods imported from Britain. During the war, British imports had been cut off, and Americans had done without. In fact, wearing homespun was a patriotic act. After the war, Americans rushed to import long-denied goods, often on credit. What little gold and other hard money they possessed quickly slipped out of their hands and into the pockets of British merchants. Yet there was little the government could do to stem the flow. When Congress attempted to pass a 5 percent tax on imports, it was voted down.

Unable to tax, the central government attempted to pay for the Revolutionary War effort by borrowing and issuing paper money. It printed so much paper currency and Americans had so little faith in the government, however, that the money had little value. Many Americans refused to accept it as payment. The states only added to the problem by issuing their own currency. Meanwhile, Americans' postwar spending spree created another problem. Drowning in a sea of worthless currency, they quickly found themselves without any money of real value to buy goods. Before long, the country slid into a severe and prolonged depression.

Hard times in turn raised the threat of class conflict. Once again, debt was the catalyst. State governments had borrowed money to finance the Revolution. With little money to pay their debts, they were often forced to raise taxes. At the same time, poor farmers often owed money to rich creditors. With little money to pay their debts, small farmers now faced the prospect of higher taxes and the foreclosure of their farms. Many were literally up in arms. In 1786 and 1787, no less than six states experienced rebellions against legal authority.

The most shocking was Shays's Rebellion in Massachusetts. Captain Daniel Shays had served with distinction in the Revolutionary War but had returned home to his farm in western Massachusetts without receiving the land or money promised him for his service. During the economic crisis following the Revolution, the Massachusetts legislature took steps to support the merchants and bankers. They owed money to England but were creditors within the state. To help bail out these wealthy men, the legislature raised taxes but provided no relief for the poor artisans and farmers in debt to the merchants. Underrepresented in the legislature, farmers in the western areas of the state began to protest. Shays stepped up to lead them. They tarred and feathered tax collectors, shouted "no taxation without representation," and stockpiled arms and ammunition. Finally, in early 1787, the governor sent out the state militia to crush the rebellion.

To many Americans, Shays's Rebellion demonstrated the central government's weakness. The government was not even able to ensure domestic tranquillity. In the words of George Washington, the country seemed to be moving toward "anarchy and confusion." There were other problems, too. After the Revolution, Britain had maintained a string of forts from upstate New York through the Great Lakes region. Americans knew that these forts were on their soil, but their weak central government could do nothing about them. Meanwhile, Spain closed the Mississippi River to Americans, preventing farmers on the western side of the Appalachians from shipping their products to market. As if that were not enough, the Spaniards signed an agreement with the Creek Indians in the Southeast to supply the Indians with guns and powder.

Henry was well aware of these problems, but he believed that they were solvable under the existing government. In fact, he had quietly supported Shays's Rebellion and the other uprisings. He knew that the small backcountry farmers often involved in these disturbances were underrepresented in their state legislatures. He also knew firsthand the crisis that farmers faced as markets dried up and agricultural prices slumped. Their only hope, he believed, was debt relief. That, not the use of armed force against them, would solve the problem. Likewise, Henry was worried about securing the country's western boundaries. He saw the frontier as a land of opportunity for common people. In an agricultural society, ownership of land was the primary form of property holding. It was the principal means by which individuals attained economic independence—and the right as property holders to participate in the political life of their society. Land was the key to creating independent republican citizens. These were the people for whom Henry spoke when he said, "I speak the language of thousands."

"To Control the Governed"

James Madison assumed that he spoke for everyone. By the time of the Revolution, his father and uncle had accumulated more than ten thousand acres of land and owned more than one hundred slaves. Already wealthy when James was born in 1751, they continued to add more land and more slaves to their holdings. From his early childhood, James was taught that he was to be master of his universe, to have control over himself, his family, and his neighbors. It was his birthright.

Naturally, he had a first-rate education, attending the College of New Jersey (later Princeton University). An excellent student, he quickly mastered philosophy, science, languages, and history. He studied Greek and Roman politics and political philosophy and learned about the short histories of the ancient republics. Returning to Virginia after graduation, he began to study law, although he was unsure what he wanted to do with his life. He was still pondering his future when the American Revolution began, presenting him with the prospect of a career in politics.

Excited by the tumultuous events of the Revolution, Madison ran for office and won election to the Virginia legislature in 1776. He allied himself with Patrick Henry, a distant relative, on the issue of religious toleration, defeating those who wanted to continue an established church. Nonetheless, Madison lost his bid for reelection in 1777. His opponent was a man named Charles Porter, a tavern keeper. Madison refused to campaign in the acceptable manner—stumping and treating voters to whiskey during the campaign. He deplored this practice, and his shyness made him reluctant to engage in debates or public speaking. Instead, he hoped to win on his merits. After all, the people had a clear choice: Madison, the born statesman, or Porter, a rude tavern keeper. So he stayed home. On Election Day, Madison was appalled to learn that he had lost.

From that day forward, Madison began to doubt the ability of the people to govern themselves. He was committed to a republican form of government—that is, one in which the people govern through elected representatives. Yet he worried that too much democracy was dangerous. He had read John Locke, the English political philosopher who argued that government was a social contract. Madison accepted Locke's view that in society, people agreed to limit their rights and freedoms for security. Yet he disagreed with Locke's belief that human beings were basically good. Instead, he sympathized with Thomas Hobbes's view of human nature. In his classic *Leviathan* (1651), the English social philosopher defended absolute monarchy and argued that humans would be overcome by their grasping self-interest if left to themselves. Madison did not agree with Hobbes's preference for monarchy, however. Instead, he preferred a republic with the power divided among and shared by different governing bodies. This made the concentration and abuse of power more difficult. A republic, though, was not a democracy. Certain rights and powers, Madison believed, should not be subject to majority rule. A republic was the best form of government because it allowed the citizens to express their concerns through representatives and set up checks and balances against the accumulation of power. Furthermore, Madison agreed with David Hume, the eighteenth-century Scottish philosopher who believed that people were naturally governed by their passions. Far from being rational beings, the masses were a mob of unthinking creatures. In a democracy, passions ruled because the mob voted emotionally and without regard to the long-term welfare of the nation. In a republic, government helped people control their passions for the good of the country.

With these lessons driven home by his election defeat, Madison returned to his family's plantation and took up the duties of a planter. Unlucky in love, he did not take a wife until 1794, when he married a wealthy young widow named Dolley Payne Todd. Until then, politics had been his mistress. He returned to the assembly in 1778 and two years later was elected to the Continental Congress, where he emerged as a national leader. Other representatives recognized the power of the young Virginian's mind and turned to him for advice on matters ranging from diplomacy to finance. He also strengthened his relationship with Thomas Jefferson, a fellow Virginian, with whom he had already forged a friendship.

While in Congress, Madison concluded that the Articles of Confederation were fatally flawed. This was especially true during the dark days of the war. He feared that the new national government, unable even to raise adequate supplies, was not up to the task of winning the war. His fears were heightened after the Revolution, especially as the country slipped into a depression and many Americans clamored for debt relief. Although Madison himself was not a major creditor, he believed that debts had to be repaid in order to strengthen the economy. Hard work and money saved were the bases of a sound financial future.

Loans received with real money should not be paid back with worthless currency. Madison thus insisted that the money system had to be based on specie—gold or silver money. This stance placed him in opposition to the poor and indebted, and he was naturally opposed to the poor farmers who joined in such armed uprisings as Shays's Rebellion. He always claimed, however, that he was not insensitive to the poor. He simply wanted a sound currency to prevent economic chaos, stabilize the economy, and promote domestic and foreign trade.

Like Patrick Henry, Madison was concerned about securing the country's western boundaries. Unlike Henry, he believed that only a stronger government could protect the territory of the United States. Negotiations with Great Britain, Spain, and France were critical to keep the frontier open. If the national government lacked the military power to back up its will, those foreign powers might simply take what they wanted. A strong government would not only secure what already belonged to the nation but also add new territory to it.

Others, such as the young nationalist Alexander Hamilton from New York, felt the same way. In 1786, they had already moved to reform the Articles of Confederation with a meeting at Annapolis, Maryland. Delegates from only six states showed up, and Hamilton had insisted that another meeting take place. The next year, fifty-five men from twelve states arrived in Philadelphia to revise the Articles. The existing Congress had given its blessing to the meeting. The Federalists dominated the gathering, and early on they voted to scrap the Articles and start over. When they did, Madison was ready. Through fellow Virginian Edmund Randolph, he presented his Virginia Plan to the convention, which quickly adopted it as the basis for debate. Working behind locked doors throughout the sweltering summer, the delegates debated and revised Madison's plan. When they were finished, it remained the foundation of the new Constitution.

The Constitution created a central government with vast powers, including the power to tax, regulate domestic and foreign commerce, and compel citizens to obey its laws. Yet as it increased power, it also divided it among three branches of government and devised a system of checks and balances to prevent one branch from tyrannizing the others. And although the people would be directly represented in the House of Representatives, those sitting in every other part of the new government—the Senate, the presidency, and the Supreme Court—would be chosen only indirectly by more qualified people sitting in state legislatures, the Electoral College, or the new federal government itself. Madison noted, "You must enable the government to control the governed; and in the next place oblige it to control itself." His plan, he believed, had done that by removing the people from too much direct say in the government, separating the government's powers, and establishing checks and balances. Madison was confident that the new framework would alleviate the country's problems while preserving the republic.

"Overpowered in a Good Cause"

Submitted to the states in the fall of 1787, the Constitution sparked a fierce debate as voters elected delegates to state ratifying conventions. The Antifederalists (as those who opposed the Constitution came to be called) attacked the document immediately. They were no radical fringe. Indeed, their fears about government were widely shared. The loyalty of most Americans was to their states, not the new nation. Most, too, were farmers, rooted in a particular place and fearful of concentrated power too far removed from them. As they examined the Constitution, the Antifederalists feared that a national government would replace a confederation of sovereign states. They also saw an undemocratic government. As Henry's fellow Virginian Richard Henry Lee observed, the country was too big and the national legislature too small to fairly represent all interests. **[See Source 1.]**

In response, the Federalists fired back. Many of their arguments were contained in newspaper essays, collectively known as *The Federalist Papers,* written by James Madison, Alexander Hamilton, and John Jay. Perhaps Madison's most important essay was "The Federalist No. 10," in which he countered the Antifederalists' fear that a large republic would inevitably place power in the hands of better-represented factions and thus lead to oppression by a minority. In fact, he turned this argument on its head. Rather than deny that factions would exist in the national government, Madison argued that the very size and diversity of the country would prevent the influence of special interests over the government. Moreover, fewer representatives speaking for more people would actually "refine and enlarge the public views." **[See Source 2.]**

For Patrick Henry, such arguments were proof that the new Constitution was dangerous. It was the work of a small group of men who wanted to gain power for themselves at the expense of the people. The Federalists, he argued, were the rich and the elite. They wanted to keep the people down and ensure that their own power and wealth were protected and extended. Only a few men had attended the convention, and most of them were wealthy and powerful members of society. Leaving the comforts of Leatherwood, he returned to the Virginia legislature and in 1788 took his place as a delegate to the Virginia Ratifying Convention that June. By then, eight states had already voted to ratify, and Henry was alarmed. He was sure that the Federalists' desire for order and strong government threatened the liberties only recently won in the Revolution. Thus, from the opening moments, he went on the attack. Reading the Preamble to the Constitution, Henry found the opening phrase objectionable. "What right had they to say, *We, the People?*" he asked. "My political curiosity . . . leads me to ask: Who authorized them to speak the language of, *We, the People,* instead of, *We, the states?*" He argued that the "states are the characteristics and the soul of a confederation." **[See Source 3.]**

Here were two of his major arguments against the Constitution. First, the Philadelphia convention had overstepped its bounds by doing more than revising the Articles. Second, the republic was a confederacy of sovereign states. The Constitution established what he called a "consolidated government"—a centralized, national government that had all the power. This would jeopardize state sovereignty and, along with it, the rights and liberty of the people. When the planter-aristocrat George Mason argued that he could not support the new Constitution because it did not contain a Bill of Rights specifically protecting the liberties of the people, Henry became even more convinced that the Constitution would lead to tyranny. He attacked the Constitution on other points as well. He opposed the power to levy taxes and feared a standing army. He argued that the power of Congress would eventually destroy the right of suffrage to the point that elections would not really matter. And he objected that "there is no true responsibility," since the Congress would not make laws to govern itself. Those in power would not have to obey the laws they forced the people to obey. [**See Source 4.**]

Each time the Antifederalists attacked the Constitution, the Federalists looked to Madison to lead the defense. Each time he followed his set plan of action: He rose very calmly, took his notes from his hat, and responded point by point. Despite his anger and frustration, he did not interrupt Henry and the other Antifederalists during their long orations. Instead, he sat and took careful notes. When he rose to respond, he did so with quiet grace. Doing so, he hoped, would defuse Henry's oratory and restore a sense of civility, rationality, and levelheaded discourse to the convention.

Often Madison's remarks could barely be heard. Yet his frustration with Henry gradually warmed him to his topic, and his voice grew stronger as he responded to each challenge. He urged the convention to consider the Constitution "on its own merits solely." Then he turned to the specifics of Henry's arguments. Far from being held by a tiny minority, the Federalist position was widely popular, since all the states had acknowledged their problems and wanted change. As for standing armies, they would preserve, not threaten, liberty. He outlined the "various means whereby nations lost their liberties" and concluded that an army was necessary to make the nation respectable and secure. He chided Henry for his objections to taxation, since the right to tax was not for direct taxation on citizens, but for tariffs and other indirect taxes. These taxes were necessary to address the problems confronting the republic, such as the Indian wars on the frontier and the instability of the currency system. The notion that the national government would destroy all other levels of government was absurd, because the national body derived its power from the state and local governments and the people. Furthermore, the checks and balances of the new system would prevent any single branch or individual from taking complete control and abusing the power of the Constitution. Refuting Henry's charges about the creation of a "consolidated" government, he pointed out that the new system was a federal one, with the states maintaining powers and rights. [**See Source 5.**]

Madison threw all his energies into the defense. In fact, he wore himself out physically and emotionally. When he became so ill that he could not speak, his friends and allies rallied to carry on the debate. They knew by late June that the Constitution had been ratified when the ninth state—New Hampshire—approved the document. Yet they also realized that the new government had little chance of success without the support of large states such as Virginia and New York. And in Virginia, the Antifederalists had a majority. The Federalists grew desperate. They went to George Mason and asked him what changes he required to support the Constitution. He told them a Bill of Rights needed to be attached to the Constitution. When they promised to do that, he agreed to ratify, bringing some of his allies with him. Henry and his supporters, however, still had enough votes to reject the Constitution. Finally, the Federalists played their trump card. They called on George Washington to publicly support the Constitution. Washington had been president of the Philadelphia convention

and supported the new framework, but he wanted to stay out of the controversy. He believed that he might be the first president under the new government and wanted to be able to heal the wounds inflicted by the battles over
ratification. Now realizing how desperate the situation was, Washington announced his position, swinging more votes. In the end, Virginia ratified the
Constitution by ten votes, 89 to 79. Backcountry delegates interested in a more
powerful government able to stop Indian attacks ultimately tipped the balance
for the Federalists.

The battle over ratification was close in other states as well. In New York, an
Antifederalist majority was led by the promising young attorney Aaron Burr.
Only the deft political maneuvering of Alexander Hamilton saved the day.
Hamilton wisely delayed the vote until it was clear that the Constitution would
be adopted by other states like Virginia. By a slim margin of three votes, New
York then ratified. Resistance to the new government was strong in other areas,
especially in more isolated counties. Once the largest and most influential states
voted to support it, though, the Federalists had their victory.

Henry left the battlefield gracefully, and although he retained "a conviction
of being overpowered in a good cause," he pledged his allegiance to the new
government. Soon thereafter, he retired from politics and returned to his career
as a lawyer.

The Federalist victory came at a price. After the Constitution was ratified in
1788 and national elections were held the following year, the Federalists carried
out their promise to enact a Bill of Rights. Yet bitter divisions remained between
them and their Antifederalist opponents. The Federalists' exercise of power in
the new national government only made matters worse. (See Chapter 6.) President Washington tried to cool partisan passions, but he was not successful. In
1799, he even urged Henry to run for the Virginia legislature in an effort to
lessen partisan bickering. Henry agreed to help Washington for the good of the
country and easily won the election. The old Antifederalist's health, however,
had been growing steadily worse, and shortly after making his dramatic return
to the legislature, he died.

By then, the rift between the Federalists and their opponents, led by
Thomas Jefferson, was complete. Ironically, Henry's old adversary had joined
the Jeffersonian opposition long before. Earlier in the 1790s, Madison had become convinced that the Federalist administrations of Washington and his successor, John Adams, were going too far in consolidating and centralizing power
in the national government. When the Jeffersonian Republicans swept the Federalists from power in 1800, Madison served under Jefferson as secretary of
state. Then in 1808, he was elected to the first of two consecutive terms as president. After retiring from politics in 1817, Madison came to be known as the
"Last of the Fathers." As the last of the revolutionary generation's dominant
figures, he frequently offered advice to younger politicians. He continued to
emphasize the dangers of democracy and the necessity of protecting the rights
of those in the minority. And even though he had left the Federalist Party, he
made clear his continued faith in the new government that he had helped create. Two years before he died in 1836, Madison drafted a brief essay titled "Advice to My Country." In it, he urged that "the union of states be cherished and
perpetuated" by his fellow Americans.

PRIMARY SOURCES

SOURCE 1: *An Antifederalist Attacks the Constitution*
(1787)

In this selection, Antifederalist Richard Henry Lee attacks several features of the proposed government. What are his fears? Why might many Americans in the late eighteenth century have shared them?

The essential parts of a free and good government are a full and equal representation of the people in the legislature, and the jury trial of the vicinage* in the administration of justice—a full and equal representation, is that which possesses the same interests, feelings, opinions, and views the people themselves would were they all assembled—a fair representation, therefore, should be so regulated, that every order of men in the community, according to the common course of elections, can have a share in it—in order to allow professional men, merchants, traders, farmers, mechanics, &c. to bring a just proportion of their best informed men respectively into the legislature, the representation must be considerably numerous—We have about 200 state senators in the United States, and a less number than that of federal representatives cannot, clearly, be a full representation of this people, in the affairs of internal taxation and police, were there but one legislature for the whole union. The representation cannot be equal, or the situation of the people proper for one government only—if the extreme parts of the society cannot be represented as fully as the central—It is apparently impracticable that this should be the case in this extensive country—it would be impossible to collect a representation of the parts of the country five, six, and seven hundred miles from the seat of government. . . .

In examining the proposed constitution carefully, we must clearly perceive an unnatural separation of these powers from the substantial representation of the people. The state government will exist, with all their governors, senators, representatives, officers and expences; in these will be nineteen twentieths of the representatives of the people; they will have a near connection, and their members an immediate intercourse with the people; and the probability is, that the state governments will possess the confidence of the people, and be considered generally as their immediate guardians.

The general government will consist of a new species of executive, a small senate, and a very small house of representatives. . . . Thus will stand the state and the general governments, should the constitution be adopted without any alterations in their organization; but as to powers, the general government will possess all essential ones, at least on paper, and those of the states a mere shadow of power. And therefore, unless the people shall make some great exertions to

SOURCE: Reprinted in Cecelia M. Kenyon, ed., *The Antifederalists* (Indianapolis: Bobbs-Merrill, 1966), pp. 208–209, 212–213.
*Vicinage: People living in the same neighborhood.

restore to the state governments their powers in matters of internal police; as the powers to lay and collect, exclusively, internal taxes, to govern the militia, and to hold the decisions of their own judicial courts upon their own laws final, the balance cannot possibly continue long; but the state governments must be annihilated, or continue to exist for no purpose.

SOURCE 2:   James Madison, "The Federalist No. 10"   (1788)

James Madison defends the Constitution in this essay. How does he attempt to allay the concerns raised by Richard Henry Lee, Patrick Henry, and other Antifederalists about the proposed government's undemocratic nature?

By a faction I understand a number of citizens, whether amounting to a majority or minority of the whole, who are united and actuated by some common impulse of passion, or of interest, adverse to the rights of other citizens, or to the permanent and aggregate interests of the community. . . .

[T]he most common and durable source of factions has ever been the unequal distribution of property. Those who hold as opposed to those who are without property have ever formed distinct interests in society. Those who are creditors, and those who are debtors, likewise share different concerns. A landed interest, a manufacturing interest, a mercantile interest, a moneyed interest, with many lesser interests, grow up of necessity in civilized nations, and divide them into different classes, actuated by different sentiments and views. The regulation of these various and interfering interests forms the principal task of modern legislation, and involves the spirit of party and faction in the necessary and ordinary operations of government. . . .

A common passion or interest will, in almost every case, be felt by a majority of the whole; and there is nothing to check the inducements to sacrifice the weaker party or individual. Hence it is that such pure democracies have ever been spectacles of turbulence and contention; have ever been found incompatible with personal security or the rights of property; and have in general been as short in their lives as they have been violent in their deaths. . . .

A republic, on the other hand, by which I mean a government in which a scheme of representation takes place, opens a different prospect and promises the cure for which we are seeking. Let us examine the points in which it varies from pure democracy, and we shall comprehend both the nature of the cure and the efficacy it must derive from the Union.

The two great points of difference between a pure democracy and a republic are: first, the delegation of the government in a republic to a smaller number of citizens elected by the rest; secondly, the greater number of citizens and greater sphere of country over which the republic may be thus extended.

The effect of the first difference is, on the one hand, to refine and enlarge the

SOURCE: Reprinted in Forrest McDonald and Ellen Shapiro McDonald, eds., *Confederation and Constitution, 1781–1789* (New York: Harper & Row, 1968), pp. 205, 206, 208–209.

public views by passing them through the medium of a chosen body of citizens, whose wisdom may best discern the true interest of their country and whose patriotism and love of justice will be least likely to sacrifice it to temporary or partial considerations. Under such conditions it may well happen that the public voice, pronounced by the representatives of the people, will be more consonant to the public good than if pronounced by the people themselves. It is possible, of course, that the effect may unhappily be inverted. Men of factious tempers, of local prejudices or of sinister designs, may, by intrigue, by corruption, or by other means, first obtain the votes and then betray the interests of the people. The question resulting is, then, whether small or extensive republics are most favorable to the election of proper guardians of the public weal; and it is clearly decided in favor of the larger.

SOURCE 3: ## Patrick Henry, *Speech to the Virginia Convention* (June 4, 1788)

In his opening speech to the Virginia Ratifying Convention, Patrick Henry charged that the Federalists had no authority to create the Constitution. What does this speech reveal about Henry's fears?

Make the best of this new government—say it is composed of any thing but inspiration—you ought to be extremely cautious, watchful, jealous of your liberty; for, instead of securing your rights, you may lose them forever. If a wrong step be now made, the republic may be lost forever. If this new government will not come up to the expectation of the people, and they shall be disappointed, their liberty will be lost, and tyranny must and will arise. I repeat it again, and I beg gentlemen to consider, that a wrong step, made now, will plunge us into misery, and our republic will be lost. It will be necessary for this [Virginia Ratifying] Convention to have a faithful historical detail of the facts that preceded the session of the federal Convention, and the reasons that actuated its members in proposing an entire alteration of government, and to demonstrate the dangers that awaited us. If they were of such awful magnitude as to warrant a proposal so extremely perilous as this, I must assert, that this Convention has an absolute right to a thorough discovery of every circumstance relative to this great event. And here I would make this inquiry of those worthy characters who composed a part of the late federal Convention. I am sure they were fully impressed with the necessity of forming a great consolidated government, instead of a confederation. That this is a consolidated government is demonstrably clear; and the danger of such a government is, to my mind, very striking, I have the highest veneration for those gentlemen; but, sir, give me leave to demand: What right had they to say, *We, the people?* My political curiosity,

SOURCE: Reprinted in Morton Borden, ed., *The Antifederalist Papers* (East Lansing: Michigan State University Press, 1965), pp. 109–110.

exclusive of my anxious solicitude for the public welfare, leads me to ask: Who authorized them to speak the language of, *We, the people,* instead of, *We, the states?* States are the characteristics and the soul of a confederation. If the states be not the agents of this compact, it must be one great, consolidated, national government, of the people of all the states. I have the highest respect for those gentlemen who formed the Convention, and, were some of them not here, I would express some testimonial of esteem for them. America had, on a former occasion, put the utmost confidence in them—a confidence which was well placed; and I am sure, sir, I would give up any thing to them; I would cheerfully confide in them as my representatives. But, sir, on this great occasion, I would demand the cause of their conduct. Even from that illustrious man who saved us by his valor [George Washington], I would have a reason for his conduct. . . . That they exceeded their power is perfectly clear. . . . The federal Convention ought to have amended the old system; for this purpose they were solely delegated; the object of their mission extended to no other consideration. You must, therefore, forgive the solicitation of one unworthy member to know what danger could have arisen under the present Confederation, and what are the causes of this proposal to change our government.

Source 4:   Patrick Henry, *Speech to the Virginia Convention*   (June 5, 1788)

In another speech before the Virginia Ratifying Convention, Henry raised numerous objections to the Constitution. What are they? Are they reasonable?

Having premised these things, I shall, with the aid of my judgment and information, which, I confess, are not extensive, go into the discussion of this system more minutely. . . .

Let me here call your attention to that part which gives the Congress power "to provide for organizing, arming, and disciplining the militia, and for governing such part of them as may be employed in the service of the United States—reserving to the states, respectively, the appointment of the officers, and the authority of training the militia according to the discipline prescribed by Congress." By this, sir, you see that their control over our last and best defence is unlimited. If they neglect or refuse to discipline or arm our militia, they will be useless: the states can do neither—this power being exclusively given to Congress. . . .

If you make the citizens of this country agree to become the subjects of one great consolidated empire of America, your government will not have sufficient

Source: Reprinted in Cecelia Kenyon, ed., *The Antifederalists* (Indianapolis: Bobbs-Merrill, 1966), pp. 240, 248–249, 251–252, 255–256, 258–260.

energy to keep them together. Such a government is incompatible with the genius of republicanism. There will be no checks, no real balances, in this government. What can avail your specious, imaginary balances, your rope-dancing, chain-rattling, ridiculous ideal checks and contrivances? . . .

Consider our situation, sir: go to the poor man, and ask him what he does. He will inform you that he enjoys the fruits of his labor, under his own fig-tree, with his wife and children around him, in peace and security. Go to every other member of society,—you will find the same tranquil ease and content; you will find no alarms or disturbances. Why, then, tell us of danger, to terrify us into an adoption of this new form of government? And yet who knows the dangers that this new system may produce? They are out of the sight of the common people: they cannot foresee latent consequences. I dread the operation of it on the middling and lower classes of people: it is for them I fear the adoption of this system. . . .

In this scheme of energetic government, the people will find two sets of tax-gatherers—the state and the federal sheriffs. This, it seems to me, will produce such dreadful oppression as the people cannot possibly bear. The federal sheriff may commit what oppression, make what distresses, he pleases, and ruin you with impunity; for how are you to tie his hands? Have you any sufficiently decided means of preventing him from sucking your blood by speculations, commissions, and fees? Thus thousands of your people will be most shamefully robbed. . . .

What can be more defective than the clause concerning the elections? The control given to Congress over the time, place, and manner of holding elections, will totally destroy the end of suffrage. The elections may be held at one place, and the most inconvenient in the state; or they may be at remote distances from those who have a right of suffrage: hence nine out of ten must either not vote at all, or vote for strangers; for the most influential characters will be applied to, to know who are the most proper to be chosen. I repeat, that the control of Congress over the *manner*, &c., of electing, well warrants this idea. The natural consequence will be, that this democratic branch will possess none of the public confidence; the people will be prejudiced against representatives chosen in such an injudicious manner. The proceedings in the northern conclave will be hidden from the yeomanry of this country. . . .

Where is the responsibility—that leading principle in the British government? In that government, a punishment certain and inevitable is provided; but in this, there is no real, actual punishment for the grossest mal-administration. They may go without punishment, though they commit the most outrageous violation on our immunities. That paper may tell me they will be punished. I ask, By what law? They must make the law, for there is no existing law to do it. What! will they make a law to punish themselves?

This, sir, is my great objection to the Constitution, that there is no true responsibility and that the preservation of our liberty depends on the single chance of men being virtuous enough to make laws to punish themselves.

SOURCE 5:   James Madison, *"The Federalist No. 39"*   (1788)

In this selection from The Federalist Papers, *James Madison discusses the structure of the new government and its relationship to the people. How does he answer the concerns raised by Patrick Henry in Sources 3 and 4? How does he use the nature of the ratification processs to bolster the Federalist case?*

What, then, are the distinctive characters of the republican form? . . . [W]e may define a republic to be, or at least may bestow that name on, a government which derives all its powers directly or indirectly from the great body of the people, and is administered by persons holding their offices during pleasure, for a limited period, or during good behavior. It is essential to such a government that it be derived from the great body of the society, not from an inconsiderable proportion, or a favored class of it; otherwise a handful of tyrannical nobles, exercising their oppressions by a delegation of their powers, might aspire to the rank of republicans, and claim for their government the honorable title of republic. It is sufficient for such a government that the persons administering it be appointed, either directly or indirectly, by the people; and that they hold their appointments by either of the tenures just specified; otherwise every government in the United States, as well as every other popular government that has been or can be well organized or well executed, would be degraded from the republican character. . . .

On comparing the Constitution planned by the convention with the standard here fixed, we perceive at once that it is, in the most rigid sense, conformable to it. The House of Representatives, like that of one branch at least of all the State legislatures, is elected immediately by the great body of the people. The Senate, like the present Congress, and the Senate of Maryland, derives its appointment indirectly from the people. The President is indirectly derived from the choice of the people, according to the example in most of the States. Even the judges with all other officers of the Union, will, as in the several States, be the choice, though a remote choice, of the people themselves. . . .

Could any further proof be required of the republican complexion of this system, the most decisive one might be found in its absolute prohibition of titles of nobility, both under the federal and the State governments; and in its express guaranty of the republican form to each of the latter.

But it was not sufficient, say the adversaries of the proposed Constitution, for the convention to adhere to the republican form. They ought, with equal care, to have preserved the federal form, which regards the Union as a Confederacy of sovereign states; instead of which, they have framed a national government, which regards the Union as a consolidation of the States. And it is asked by what authority this bold and radical innovation was undertaken? The

SOURCE: Reprinted in Jacob E. Cooke, *The Federalist* (Middletown, Conn.: Wesleyan University Press, 1961), pp. 250–257; originally from James Madison, "The Federalist No. 39," *Independent Journal,* January 16, 1788.

handle which has been made of this objection requires that it should be examined with some precision. . . .

[I]t appears, on the one hand, that the Constitution is to be founded on the assent and ratification of the people of America, given by deputies elected for the special purpose; but, on the other, that this assent and ratification is to be given by the people, not as individuals composing one entire nation, but as composing the distinct and independent States to which they respectively belong. It is to be the assent and ratification of the several States, derived from the supreme authority in each State,—the authority of the people themselves. The act, therefore, establishing the Constitution, will not be a national, but a federal act.

That it will be a federal and not a national act, as these terms are understood by the objectors; the act of the people, as forming so many independent States, not as forming one aggregate nation, is obvious from this single consideration, that it is to result neither from the decision of a majority of the people of the Union, nor from that of a majority of the States. It must result from the unanimous assent of the several States that are parties to it, differing no otherwise from their ordinary assent than in its being expressed, not by the legislative authority, but by that of the people themselves. Were the people regarded in this transaction as forming one nation, the will of the majority of the whole people of the United States would bind the minority, in the same manner as the majority in each State must bind the minority. . . . Each State, in ratifying the Constitution, is considered as a sovereign body independent of all others, and only to be bound by its own voluntary act. In this relation, then, the new Constitution will, if established, be a federal, and not a national constitution.

. . . The House of Representatives will derive its powers from the people of America; and the people will be represented in the same proportion, and on the same principle, as they are in the legislature of a particular State. So far the government is national, not federal. The Senate, on the other hand, will derive its powers from the States, as political and coequal societies; and these will be represented on the principle of equality in the Senate, as they now are in the existing Congress. So far the government is federal, not national. The executive power will be derived from a very compound source. The immediate election of the President is to be made by the States in their political characters. The votes allotted to them are in a compound ratio, which considers them partly as distinct and coequal societies, partly as unequal members of the same society. The eventual election, again, is to be made by that branch of the legislature which consists of the national representatives; but in this particular act they are to be thrown into the form of individual delegations, from so many distinct and coequal bodies politic. From this aspect of the government, it appears to be of a mixed character, presenting at least as many federal as national features. . . .

The proposed Constitution, therefore, is, in strictness, neither a national nor a federal Constitution, but a composition of both. In its foundation it is federal, not national; in the sources from which the ordinary powers of the government are drawn, it is partly federal and partly national; in the operation of these powers, it is national, not federal; in the extent of them, again, it is federal, not national.

QUESTIONS TO CONSIDER

1. Both Patrick Henry and James Madison were part of the Virginia planter class, but they disagreed on the Constitution. How do you account for that? What important ideas, experiences, or events influenced them to take opposite sides?

2. What were Madison's principal arguments for the Constitution? What were Henry's principal arguments against it? Whose do you find more compelling? Why?

3. You are an undecided delegate to the Virginia Ratifying Convention. You are unhappy about the conditions under the Articles of Confederation but uncertain about the changes proposed by the Constitution. What one question do you wish to ask Henry? Madison?

4. If Madison and Henry were alive today, which one do you think would feel more vindicated? Were Madison's hopes justified? Were Henry's fears justified?

FOR FURTHER READING

Thornton Anderson, *Creating the Constitution: The Convention of 1787 and the First Congress* (University Park: Pennsylvania State University Press, 1993), is a recent study of the Constitutional Convention.

Lance Banning, *The Sacred Fire of Liberty: James Madison and the Founding of the Federal Republic* (Ithaca, N.Y.: Cornell University Press, 1995), is a revisionist view arguing that Madison was not a pragmatic politician but a consistent ideologue who was committed to democracy and only reluctantly supported the Federalists.

Saul Cornell, *The Other Founders: Anti-Federalism and the Dissenting Tradition in America, 1788–1828* (Chapel Hill: University of North Carolina Press, 1999), offers a sophisticated study of Antifederalist thought.

Christopher Duncan, *The Anti-Federalists and Early American Political Thought* (De Kalb: Northern Illinois University Press, 1993), is a recent study of the Antifederalists and their contributions to political philosophy.

Henry Mayer, *A Son of Thunder: Patrick Henry and the American Republic* (New York: Franklin Watts, 1986), is an accessible biography of Henry.

Jack Rakove, *James Madison and the Creation of the American Republic* (New York: Harper-Collins, 1990), is a short, readable biography of Madison.

CHAPTER
6

Agrarians and Capitalists in the Early Republic: John Taylor and Alexander Hamilton

John Taylor

Alexander Hamilton

John Taylor loved manure. Walking though the fields of his Virginia plantation, he breathed deeply, taking in the smells of fertilizer and moist soil. Stooping to pick up a clod of dirt, crumbling it, and letting it fall through his fingers, he could inhale the life-giving aroma of the earth. He could almost taste the productive potential of the land, the liberating power it contained. Here in the fields lay the future of the United States. As an agrarian, Taylor believed that farming was a morally superior way of life. He was sure that farms and plantations were the only firm foundation on which to build a great nation. And he was just as sure that government had to promote agriculture. Planting crops and reaping the harvest meant freedom for sturdy planters and independent yeomen farmers. Their ownership of land made them subservient to no one.

Faraway, in the bustling port city of New York, Alexander Hamilton envisioned a very different future for the nation—a commercial one. It could be fulfilled, he knew, only with the help of the new federal government. The Constitution gave the central government far more power than did the Articles of Confederation. Yet he also knew that this power was only on paper. The challenge now was to make it real. Hamilton had a plan to do just that. First, he would attach the "rich and well-born" to the government. Then with the

93

investing class on its side, the government could promote commercial and manufacturing enterprise. Only by moving America away from its dependence on farming could the nation hope to achieve wealth and power. One influential group, however, stood in the way: farmers like John Taylor, who romanticized agriculture and clung to the past. A threat to the very future of the nation, these misguided agrarians would have to be overcome with bold action and persuasive arguments. They could not deny the nation its greatness.

"John Taylor of Caroline"

John Taylor was a true Virginian, born in 1753 in Caroline County to a family of tobacco planters. His father was not very wealthy but did claim the status of gentleman. At age six, John went to live with an uncle, Edmund Pendleton, a leading member of the Virginia gentry. Through him, John was able to claim a position in the highest ranks of Virginia society. Pendleton also helped him prepare for a career by providing him with a solid education that culminated at the College of William and Mary. After graduation, Pendleton tutored Taylor in law and saw him admitted to the bar in 1774.

When the Revolution broke out soon after, Taylor volunteered for the American cause. He often clashed with his superior officers in the Continental Army, especially those he considered unqualified, and he even testified against his commanding officer in an official inquiry following several defeats. Disgusted with the corruption and personal ambition he saw, Taylor grew increasingly disillusioned with the army and resigned his commission. He returned to Caroline County, where he served in the Virginia militia. Although he was still dedicated to the cause of independence, his main loyalty was to Virginia.

Back home, he was elected during the war to the Virginia legislature, where he began using the name "John Taylor of Caroline" to distinguish himself from another politician of the same name. Forever after, he would be associated with his home county. To Taylor, this was appropriate, for he believed that it was a man's land, county, and state that gave him his identity. Appropriately, much of his service in the assembly revolved around land issues, especially the legal standing of colonial land grants. For instance, both he and Pendleton owned land in North Carolina that they had purchased as English grants to Virginia. North Carolina politicians hoped to nullify those grants and take the land for the citizens of their state. After pushing a bill recognizing the legal authority of colonial land grants through the Virginia assembly, he convinced the North Carolina legislature to do the same.

After the Revolution, Taylor practiced law and continued to serve in the assembly. He was not active in the debates over the new Constitution, but he agreed with Antifederalists such as Patrick Henry, George Mason, and Richard Henry Lee, who opposed ratification. At the moment, his personal destiny seemed more pressing. Taylor's plan was to become a full-time planter and return to the land he loved. His marriage to Lucy Penn, the daughter of a wealthy North Carolina planter, added to his wealth. So did a lucrative legal practice. By 1787, he had purchased more than a thousand acres of land and more than forty slaves. After amassing a huge fortune, he retired from the legal profession in 1789. At age thirty-four, he was one of the hundred wealthiest planters in Virginia, with an estimated fortune of $100,000. Taking up residence on his plantation, Hazelwood, he raised a family of six sons and two daughters and occasionally fired off written salvos on the issues of the day.

His foremost concern was farming. Like many Virginia planters, Taylor discovered that he was in the midst of an agricultural crisis. By 1789, the land he cherished had been depleted of nutrients. It was no longer able to produce enough tobacco for him to make a living. If the land could not be revived, Taylor's plans for his future were doomed. He threw himself into the study of agricultural science, experimenting with manures and other fertilizers that might replenish the soil. For years, Taylor immersed himself in mundane matters such as crop rotation, irrigation, imported seeds, the condition of slaves, and overseers. In time, he would turn Hazelwood into a model plantation and become one of the nation's leading agricultural experts.

Taylor believed that more than his own property was at risk. So was the very future of Virginia and even the nation. Like many eighteenth-century republicans, Taylor believed that the preservation of self-government depended on the character of the citizenry, not external forces. Virtuous citizens were guided by reason rather than passion. They were self-controlled, able to restrain their own passions and withstand the debilitating and corrupting effects of luxury. They were motivated by public-spiritedness rather than selfishness and greed. And they were independent, beholden to no one. Thus public virtue was possible only if citizens owned their own means of production. In addition to Taylor, agrarians such as Thomas Jefferson and Richard Henry Lee assumed that widespread property ownership was possible only in an agrarian society. Of course, that was no guarantee of good behavior. Planters could easily fall prey to debt, greed, selfishness, and laziness, slipping from virtue to decadence amid rivers of red ink and piles of worthless paper money.

Still, an agrarian society was the best bet to preserve a republican government. Farming, Taylor declared, "offered the strongest invitations to the practice of morality." Agrarians needed to look no further than the cities for proof of that. In these urban "sores," as Jefferson called them, could be found mobs of propertyless, dependent citizens who labored for others. There, too, wealthy people lived in luxury and dissipation. Surely, this was no foundation on which to build a self-governing society. It would be better to keep the factories in Europe and leave most Americans as simple tillers of the soil, thus preserving the nation's virtue. **[See Source 1.]**

For agriculture to thrive, the land had to be nurtured. Farmers and planters could not exhaust the soil with irresponsible and wasteful practices. Just as surely as soil depletion, policies favoring manufacturing, commerce, and cities could doom the republic. Yet that was exactly what the new secretary of the Treasury proposed. Alexander Hamilton envisioned a powerful central government that promoted manufacturing, commerce, and their associated evils: cities festering with passionate mobs of propertyless people and an idle, luxury-loving elite. Hamilton would destroy everything that Taylor had worked for at Hazelwood, along with the moral foundation of the republic itself.

"Bastard Brat"

If John Taylor's birth into a family of gentlemen farmers determined his course in life, so did the circumstances of Alexander Hamilton's birth in 1757. As John Adams so bluntly expressed it, Hamilton was a "bastard brat of a Scottish pedlar." Throughout his life, Hamilton suffered from an inferiority complex. Plagued by self-doubts, he was convinced that others held his illegitimate birth against him. Hamilton's mother, Rachel, was married to a planter named John Lavien and started a family with him on the island of St. Croix in the West Indies. They had a tumultuous relationship, however, and Rachel was jailed for refusing to live with her husband. Upon her release, she moved to the neighboring island of Nevis, where she lived as the wife of James Hamilton and bore him two sons, including Alexander, without getting a divorce from Lavien. Although Lavien finally divorced her in 1759, when the Hamilton family moved to St. Croix and James learned the truth about Rachel, he left her and his children, never to return.

During his childhood, Alexander learned that to overcome his illegitimacy, he had to work hard and cultivate friendships with powerful men. The islands were the center of a thriving merchant trade, and he grew up in the midst of it. When he moved to the mainland colonies, Hamilton was an outsider, unattached to any particular region or state. This allowed him to view the country as a whole—to love the nation rather than some locality. Thus he approached politics and economics from a national and a capitalist perspective. His position put him squarely opposite that of John Taylor.

Hamilton was exposed early to the world of commerce. At age nine, he went to work as a clerk in a merchant house in Christiansted on St. Croix. Ships from all over the world passed through the bustling port. Most of his employer's transactions were with businessmen from New York, and Alexander grew curious about that British colony. After his mother died in 1768, Alexander attached himself to two important men in Christiansted—his employer and a Presbyterian minister. Both were impressed with his intellect and abilities as a clerk, and they decided that he should pursue an education. They urged him to attend the College of New Jersey (now Princeton University). After a year in a preparatory school, he passed the strenuous entrance exams and went off to New Jersey with his benefactors' help. When the faculty at the College of New Jersey refused to let him study at his own pace, he transferred to King's College (now Columbia University) in New York City. Thus, when the American Revolution began, he was in one of the colonies' biggest cities and a hotbed of patriot agitation.

Hamilton was right in the thick of it. He made speeches, passed out pamphlets, and published numerous letters in support of the American cause. He also studied artillery, preparing himself for military service. When the war broke out in 1775, he organized an artillery company and was commissioned as a captain in the Continental Army. He lusted for military glory, believing that heroism on the battlefield would help him overcome his lowly roots. Seeing action repeatedly in the early months of the conflict, he performed boldly. His accomplishments as a soldier, however, were not as impressive as his abilities as an administrator. Before long, he received numerous offers to serve as a staff officer. He refused them all, until General George Washington approached him.

Hamilton jumped at the opportunity, hoping that attaching himself to the head of the Continental Army would bring more rewards when independence was won. As Washington's aide, he became indispensable to the general, who relied more and more on his advice and abilities as the war wore on.

The Revolution also brought Hamilton military glory. In 1781, Washington gave his young aide a field command. As a lieutenant colonel, Hamilton led a heroic attack at Yorktown, contributing to Washington's greatest battlefield victory. His thirst for military glory quenched, he was now convinced that his lasting fame would be ensured by serving his country in politics. In 1782, he turned to the study of law, passed the bar, and became an attorney. About the same time, he married Elizabeth Schuyler, the daughter of an old and very wealthy New York family. Through marriage, Hamilton continued his habit of attaching himself to others as a means to obtain power. Given his political aspirations, the Schuylers' political connections would prove invaluable to a man with no roots in New York and no birthright of his own. The union was significant in another way, too. Although Hamilton's money came mostly from his own ambition and hard work, his marriage placed him near the highest ranks of American society. With the zeal of a convert, he would have little difficulty embracing the view that the rich were, as he later put it, "generally speaking, enlightened men." An unabashed elitist, he believed that the common people should not have too much say in government. It was far better, he thought, to leave the affairs of state to the "rich and well-born," who took a broader view of the nation's interests.

Such assumptions would guide Hamilton's thinking about politics and economics. The Revolution, meanwhile, provided him with ample opportunities to expand his thoughts in both areas. Throughout the war, he had to balance the needs of the army with a shortage of funds. Furthermore, the army had to contend with disputes between Congress and the states. This experience convinced him that the country's future depended on a sound economy. Only prosperity could guarantee that future wars would not end in defeat. And prosperity required a powerful national government. With the impatience of youth, Hamilton became involved in a plot to bring it about. It was hatched after the war by former military officers who planned to raise an army that would force Congress to revise the Articles of Confederation. Among their demands was a plan for national taxation that would provide revenue so that war veterans could be paid. Washington put a quick end to this plot, and Hamilton returned to the legal profession.

Within a few years, however, Hamilton would have a chance to shape the nation's future. Convinced that the Articles of Confederation were far too weak, he played a key role in persuading Congress to sanction a meeting to strengthen them. Later, he attended the Constitutional Convention as a delegate from New York. At the convention, he was one of the most vocal supporters of the new framework for a national government, even though he believed that the Constitution did not give the new government enough power. He also played a key role in the ratification process as one of the most outspoken Federalists, contributing dozens of letters and pamphlets in defense of the Constitution. When elections in early 1789 swept the Federalists into power, President George Washington turned to Hamilton as a trusted and dependable adviser. When Hamilton became the nation's first secretary of the Treasury, he took up the problems of the nation's finance with an almost religious zeal. The result was a bold plan designed to assert the new government's power and dramatically transform the country. The details were contained in three reports to Congress in which he proposed a national banking system and developed ways to pay the nation's Revolutionary War debt.

In his *First Report on Public Credit,* issued in 1790, Hamilton insisted that all of the national debt be paid back. The national government owed more than fifty million dollars to foreign and domestic lenders, and the states owed about half as much. Hamilton realized that the government would need to borrow money in the future. Repaying all of the national government's debt would make it easier and cheaper to do so. Furthermore, rich investors, who held much of the debt, would be tied through their pocketbooks to the new government. They would be quick to support a government that paid them back their money and all the interest due. The certificates issued to the government's creditors would provide a sound medium of exchange, thereby expanding the nation's supply of badly needed sound money. [**See Source 2.**] For the same reasons, Hamilton also called for the national government to assume all the Revolutionary War debts of the state governments. This would further tie the investing class to the national regime and help establish its sovereignty over the states.

In the *Second Report on Public Credit,* also issued in 1790, Hamilton proposed that Congress establish a national bank to be headquartered in Philadelphia. The Bank of the United States, he argued, would perform a number of useful services. It would be able to issue payments for the public debt, serve as a repository for government funds, and print bank notes that would stabilize the nation's currency. In addition, it could also make loans to businesses. To fund the bank, the national government would borrow money from the bank to purchase one-fifth of its stock. The remainder of the stock would be sold to citizens. Because private citizens would be able to purchase stock in the bank, their interests would be further tied to the government. Here was another marriage of the investing classes and the government.

Finally, Hamilton's *Report on Manufactures* in 1791 called for a diverse economy based on agriculture, commerce, and manufacturing. The American economy continued to rely on the export of agricultural surpluses, just as in the colonial period. The role of the colonies in the empire had been to produce low-value farm products. The British realized that the real wealth was in making high-value finished products. Now Hamilton wanted the United States to emulate Britain, a wealthy nation with a powerful central government that promoted manufacturing and commerce. Wealth, Hamilton realized, was in making goods, not growing them. The government, therefore, had to stimulate private commercial and manufacturing enterprises. Hamilton thus called for government subsidies to help promote the construction of factories. He also proposed protective tariffs—taxes on imported goods—to help domestic manufacturing compete against foreign imports. This would raise prices, but he believed that such tariffs were necessary in the short term. Industry, after all, would make the economy stronger and would encourage hard work among the populace. [**See Source 3.**]

In Congress, Hamilton got most of what he wanted, but his programs sparked a bitter fight. The opposition was led by Antifederalists such as George

Mason and Richard Henry Lee, who had opposed a stronger government all along. Especially odious to many was the assumption of the state debts because Virginia and several other states had already retired their debts. Now they would have to share the burden of paying those of the states that had not. Congress narrowly passed Hamilton's proposal to fund, or pay back, the national debt, but assumption was defeated by two votes. In desperation, Hamilton and his Federalist supporters played politics. According to legend, Secretary of State Thomas Jefferson and Representative James Madison, leading opponents of assumption, hosted a dinner party during which they struck a deal with Hamilton. The Virginians wanted the new national capital located along the Potomac River. Hamilton wanted assumption. The two parties came to an agreement: Washington, D.C., would be the capital, and Hamilton's assumption plan was enacted in 1790.

Meanwhile, Hamilton's proposal to create the Bank of the United States received more support in Congress. Most politicians thought that the bank would quickly prove profitable and the government's credit would become all the more sound. But some leaders were skeptical. Foremost among them was Madison, who argued that chartering a private corporation was beyond the constitutional scope of the national government. Congress approved the bank, but opposition to it remained fierce. President Washington turned to Hamilton to demonstrate its constitutionality. Hamilton argued that chartering a bank was covered under the implied powers given to Congress in the Constitution, specifically the closing clause of Article I, Section 8. That clause empowers Congress to "make all laws which shall be necessary and proper for carrying into execution the foregoing powers." Hamilton argued that this clause applied to the bank, which was both "necessary and proper" for executing Congress's power to regulate commerce. His opponents disagreed. They argued for a "strict construction" of the Constitution. Hamilton's argument for a "loose construction," which interprets the Constitution more broadly, became the foundation of a long tradition in American politics.

Only the *Report on Manufactures* failed. Madison and other southern planters rallied to defeat this report in Congress. The Tariff of 1792 provided more protection to agricultural interests than to the few American factories in existence. The bulk of Hamilton's other programs were ignored. Hamilton was disappointed, but the facts were against him. According to the 1790 Census, 95 percent of Americans lived in rural areas. Even in the cities, merchants and artisans outnumbered manufacturers and factory workers. Hamilton had gone too far in attempting to move America away from its agricultural roots. Meanwhile, the fight over his plan revealed how far his vision for America was from that of his agrarian opponents. Among them, no one was more alarmed at the implications of the Treasury secretary's proposals than John Taylor.

"Crying in the Wilderness"

By the time Taylor publicly joined the battle against Hamilton's financial plan, Congress had already approved funding of the national debt, assumption of the state debts, and the national bank. After he joined the U.S. Senate in 1792 to finish the term of another Virginia senator, however, Taylor launched a frontal assault on Hamilton's economic policies. Writing under the pseudonym "Franklin," he published a series of letters and pamphlets over the next three years criticizing nearly all of Hamilton's plans: funding, assumption, the bank, tariffs, excise taxes, and standing army. The entire Hamiltonian system, he believed, was an attempt to create an artificial financial aristocracy attached to the new government. Through his program, northern finance capital had placed its foot squarely on the necks of farmers.

The bank was a case in point. It was, Taylor charged, the "master key" of Hamilton's system. Devised to cheat Americans with exorbitant interest rates and paper money of dubious value, the bank was a fraud. So was Hamilton's excise tax on whiskey. Authorized by Congress in 1791 at Hamilton's request, it was intended to raise revenue for the government. The tax fell on backcountry farmers, who frequently distilled their grain into whiskey. The revenue it raised, however, flowed right into the pockets of the rich bondholders who were receiving interest on the national debt. Hamilton's tax only made the rich richer and the poor poorer. Worse, when farmers in western Pennsylvania rebelled against the tax in 1794, President Washington followed Hamilton's advice and sent a large army to put it down. The Federalist response to the so-called Whiskey Rebellion sent a clear message that the national government would use force if necessary to enforce laws passed by Congress. To Taylor, it was a frightening example of Federalist tyranny.

Taylor continued to attack Hamilton and the Federalists throughout the 1790s, but his full-scale assault on Hamilton's "capitalist" system was not published until much later. In his books *Arator* (1813) and *An Inquiry into the Principles and Policy of the Government of the United States* (1814), Taylor took on the special interests that threatened to destroy the republic. These "artificial" interests included banks, corporations, paper currency, and all the other trappings of Hamilton's "paper system." Arrayed against these parasites was the "common interest"—that is, farms and plantations. The farming majority would never form an aristocracy, nor would they oppress a minority. As Taylor wrote, "The many have no motive to oppress the few." But now the few were oppressing the many. "I do not recollect," he wrote, "a single law . . . passed in favour of agriculture." The explanation was simple: An "aristocratical order" had seized power. [See Source 4.]

A planter aristocracy, of course, stood atop Taylor's own society. Indeed, Hazelwood's master was part of it. Yet his agrarian philosophy, which saw all farmers as opponents of northern capital, made it easy to ignore. Taylor also conveniently overlooked the servile dependents who lay at the invisible heart of his agrarian vision: black slaves. The fact was not lost on some Federalists who, like Hamilton, abhorred slavery. As one Federalist congressman declared, "These high priests of liberty are zealously proclaiming freedom on the one hand while on the other they are rivetting the chains of slavery." Yet Taylor knew that by keeping blacks in bondage, slavery provided the basis for the liberty of whites. In an agrarian society, the ownership of slaves was the basis for economic independence. Poor whites would be able to own land and perhaps even slaves. They would not form a mass of propertyless dependents. In Hamilton's world, however, the sturdy yeoman farmer would be turned into a wage slave, dependent and oppressed. For Taylor, the personal (black) slavery of the plantation system was preferable to the impersonal (white) slavery of a capital-ist economic system.

Unwilling to recognize the legitimacy of capital as opposed to landed wealth, Taylor concluded that the only legitimate interests served by govern-ment were related to farming. And if government needed to serve the soil, so did those working it. To that end, Taylor's *Arator* returned inevitably to the is-sue of improving the land. No problem related to healthy agriculture was too small: crop rotation, fertilizers, the best fencing, the proper care of slaves, the raising of livestock. The stakes, Taylor knew, were huge. Commercial and in-dustrial sectors could coexist, but only if the agrarian society were dominant. Otherwise, commerce would corrupt the political system. Good horticultural practices were thus imperative. If agriculture could not thrive, it would be eas-ier for "paper" interests to get their way, and the republic would be doomed.

Refusing to seek reelection, Taylor served only two years in the Senate. Meanwhile, his essays on horticulture failed to spark an agricultural revolution in the South. They did, however, have a significant political impact. As one prominent Virginia politician wrote to George Washington, "It would astonish you, sir, to learn the success which has attended [Taylor's] efforts to rouse the cool and substantial planters." In fact, Hamilton's policies—and Taylor's de-nunciation of them—played an important role in stirring the organized Repub-lican opposition that began to coalesce around Thomas Jefferson. As fears about Hamilton's policies mounted, Republican strength grew in the 1790s, especially in the agricultural South and West. Yet Taylor remained pessimistic, as he con-tinued to see only vile and selfish motives in Hamilton and the Federalists. He feared that Hamilton's aristocracy of capital had gotten its way. In 1798, he told Jefferson, "I give up all for lost."

All was not lost, though, at least not for the Republicans. Ironically, many Federalists never understood that Hamilton's enemies had their own princi-ples. Indeed, Hamilton was so convinced of the correctness of his position that he believed he could win over the worst enemies through logical argument. When that failed, he was sure that they had stooped to the lowest personal and political attacks. That attitude did not serve him or the Federalists well. When Republicans engaged in mounting criticism of the Federalist administration of President John Adams, Hamilton joined other Federalists in support of the Alien and Sedition Acts. Passed in Congress in 1798, these acts were merely an attempt to muzzle the increasingly vocal Republican opposition. The Sedition Act, for instance, provided jail sentences for critics of Adams and other high ad-ministration officials. Hamilton's inability to see political conflict in other than personal terms may have contributed to his own demise a few years later. After resigning as Treasury secretary in 1795, he returned to his law practice in New York. There he resumed a feud with longtime political foe Aaron Burr. Hamil-ton played a key role in denying Burr the presidency in 1800, while Burr op-posed Hamilton's election as governor of New York. In 1804, their political and personal animosity led the two men to a dueling field in New Jersey. There the vice president of the United States shot and killed the former secretary of the Treasury.

By then, Jefferson and the Republicans had swept the Federalists from power. Still, Taylor found much to criticize in his fellow Republicans. Within a few years, he concluded that Jefferson and other Republicans had compromised their principles. Not only had they left in place Hamilton's Bank of the United States, but during the War of 1812, many of them had even reconsidered their opposition to manufacturing. As Britain brought its enormous power to bear against the United States, Jefferson declared, "We must now place the manufacturer by the side of the agriculturalist." Jefferson was alarmed by the extent to which Americans were dependent on British goods. That dependence was clear during the economic embargoes against Britain that Jefferson and his Republican successor, James Madison, instituted. The shortage of manufactured goods during the war drove the point home further. Only by encouraging domestic industry could the nation be truly independent of foreign nations. Those who opposed manufacturing, Jefferson said, would condemn Americans "to be clothed in skins, and to live like wild beasts in dens and caverns."

Meanwhile, from the quiet of Hazelwood, Taylor carried on his fight. One visitor reported, "I found an old grey-headed gentleman in an old fashioned dress [and] plain in his manners." In his writings, he continued to blast away at capitalism and defend agriculture. Increasingly, he also assaulted free labor and defended slavery. Few developments in national life pleased him. In the early nineteenth century, manufacturing would begin to play an increasingly important role in the economy. **[See Source 5.]** The War of 1812 only furthered the manufacturing revolution, especially in the North. After the war, Taylor watched as Republicans embraced Hamilton's philosophy with a vengeance. In 1816, they created the Second Bank of the United States—a bigger and more powerful version of Hamilton's bank—passed higher tariffs than any Federalist Congress ever had, and even supported the use of federal money for major transportation projects. With the Federalists literally swept from the political field after the War of 1812, it was the Republicans who now advocated a strong, interventionist government that promoted commerce and industry. In 1824, Jefferson noted that Taylor was "the voice of one crying in the wilderness."

But the agrarian vision was not dead, and Americans would struggle over the competing visions of Hamilton and Taylor for a long time. Although few may remember Taylor today, the conflict between advocates of a powerful interventionist government and those of a limited government still goes on. Meanwhile, throughout the nineteenth century, the fight between manufacturing and agrarian interests would continue, as would the suspicion of banks and paper money. Finally, a defense of slavery and states' rights would become increasingly intertwined in the minds of southerners, as they had in Taylor's. In fact, in 1823, Taylor predicted that a conflict between states' rights and an all-powerful central government would eventually lead to war, probably between the North and the South. Ironically, as Taylor looked back longingly at the lost dominance of an agrarian society, he had an uncanny sense of what lay ahead.

![PRIMARY SOURCES banner]

PRIMARY SOURCES

SOURCE 1: Thomas Jefferson, *Notes on the State of Virginia* (1787)

Thomas Jefferson was one of the most important agrarians, and he often joined with John Taylor in defending agriculture and attacking Alexander Hamilton's policies. In this excerpt, he expresses his view of manufacturing and agriculture. How does Jefferson defend the agrarian tradition? What are his views on manufacturing?

We [Virginia] never had an interior trade of any importance. Our exterior commerce has suffered very much from the beginning of the present contest. During this time we have manufactured within our families the most necessary articles of cloathing. Those of cotton will bear some comparison with the same kinds of manufacture in Europe; but those of wool, flax and hemp are very coarse, unsightly, and unpleasant: and such is our attachment to agriculture, and such our preference for foreign manufactures, that be it wise or unwise, our people will certainly return as soon as they can, to the raising raw materials, and exchanging them for finer manufactures than they are able to execute themselves.

The political œconomists of Europe have established it as a principle that every state should endeavour to manufacture for itself: and this principle, like many others, we transfer to America, without calculating the difference of circumstance which should often produce a difference of result. In Europe the lands are either cultivated, or locked up against the cultivator. Manufacture must therefore be resorted to of necessity not of choice, to support the surplus of their people. But we have an immensity of land courting the industry of the husbandman. Is it best then that all our citizens should be employed in its improvement, or that one half should be called off from that to exercise manufactures and handicraft arts for the other? Those who labour in the earth are the chosen people of God, if ever he had a chosen people, whose breasts he has made his peculiar deposit for substantial and genuine virtue. It is the focus in which he keeps alive that sacred fire, which otherwise might escape from the face of the earth. Corruption of morals in the mass of cultivators is a phænomenon of which no age nor nation has furnished an example. It is the mark set on those, who not looking up to heaven, to their own soil and industry, as does the husbandman, for their subsistance, depend for it on the casualties and caprice of customers. Dependance begets subservience and venality, suffocates the germ of virtue, and prepares fit tools for the designs of ambition. This, the natural progress and consequence of the arts, has sometimes perhaps been retarded by accidental circumstances: but, generally speaking, the proportion which the aggregate of the other classes of citizens bears in any state to that of its husband-

SOURCE: Reprinted in Thomas Jefferson, *Writings* (New York: Library of America, 1984), pp. 290–291; originally from Thomas Jefferson, *Notes on the State of Virginia* (London: John Stockdale, 1787).

men, is the proportion of its unsound to its healthy parts, and is a good-enough barometer whereby to measure its degree of corruption. While we have land to labour then, let us never wish to see our citizens occupied at a work-bench, or twirling a distaff. Carpenters, masons, smiths, are wanting in husbandry: but, for the general operations of manufacture, let our work-shops remain in Europe. It is better to carry provisions and materials to workmen there, than bring them to the provisions and materials, and with them their manners and principles. The loss by the transportation of commodities across the Atlantic will be made up in happiness and permanence of government. The mobs of great cities add just so much to the support of pure government, as sores do to the strength of the human body. It is the manners and spirit of a people which preserve a republic in vigour. A degeneracy in these is a canker which soon eats to the heart of its laws and constitution.

SOURCE 2:   Alexander Hamilton, *First Report on Public Credit* (1790)

John Taylor, Thomas Jefferson, James Madison, and other opponents of Alexander Hamilton's financial proposals argued that their benefits would not be distributed equally through American society. How does Hamilton address that concern here?

It cannot but merit particular attention, that, among ourselves, the most enlightened friends of good government are those whose expectations are the highest.

To justify and preserve their confidence; to promote the increasing respectability of the American name; to answer the calls of justice; to restore landed property to its due value; to furnish new resources, both to agriculture and commerce; to cement more closely the union of the States; to add to their security against foreign attack; to establish public order on the basis of an upright and liberal policy;—these are the great and invaluable ends to be secured by a proper and adequate provision, at the present period, for the support of public credit.

To this provision we are invited, not only by the general considerations which have been noticed, but by others of a more particular nature. It will procure, to every class of the community, some important advantages, and remove some no less important disadvantages.

The advantage to the public creditors, from the increased value of that part of their property which constitutes the public debt, needs no explanation.

But there is a consequence of this, less obvious, though not less true, in which every other citizen is interested. It is a well-known fact, that, in countries in which the national debt is properly funded, and an object of established confidence, it answers most of the purposes of money. Transfers of stock or public

SOURCE: Reprinted in Henry Cabot Lodge, ed., *The Works of Alexander Hamilton* (New York: G. P. Putnam's Sons, 1904), II, 232–233, 235.

debt are there equivalent to payments in specie; . . . . The same thing would, in all probability, happen here under the like circumstances.

The benefits of this are various and obvious:

First.—Trade is extended by it, because there is a larger capital to carry it on. . . .

Secondly.—Agriculture and manufactures are also promoted by it, for the like reason, that more capital can be commanded to be employed in both; and because the merchant, whose enterprise in foreign trade give to them activity and extension, has greater means for enterprise.

Thirdly.—The interest of money will be lowered by it; for this is always in a ratio to the quantity of money, and to the quickness of circulation. This circumstance will enable both the public and individuals to borrow on easier and cheaper terms. . . .

The proprietors of lands would not only feel the benefit of this increase in the value of their property, and of a more prompt and better sale, when they had occasion to sell, but the necessity of selling would be itself greatly diminished.

SOURCE 3:   Alexander Hamilton, *Report on Manufactures* (1791)

Hamilton's Report on Manufactures *calls for the expansion of domestic manufacturing and commercial enterprises. Much of the report is devoted to countering the objections of agrarians such as Thomas Jefferson and John Taylor. What arguments does Hamilton offer in support of manufacturing? How, specifically, does he attempt to refute the idea that only some Americans would benefit from it?*

[T]wo important references are to be drawn, one, that there is always a higher probability of a favorable balance of Trade, in regard to countries in which manufactures founded on the basis of a thriving Agriculture flourish, than in regard to those, which are confined wholly or almost wholly to Agriculture; the other (which is also a consequence of the first) that countries of the former description are likely to possess more pecuniary wealth, or money, than those of the latter.

Facts appear to correspond with this conclusion. The importations of manufactured supplies seem invariably to drain the merely Agricultural people of their wealth. Let the situation of the manufacturing countries of Europe be compared in this particular, with that of Countries which only cultivate, and the disparity will be striking. Other causes, it is true, help to Account for this disparity between some of them; and among these causes, the relative state of Agriculture; but between others of them, the most prominent circumstance of dissimilitude arises from the Comparative state of Manufactures. In corroboration of

SOURCE: Reprinted in Morton J. Frisch, ed., *Selected Writings and Speeches of Alexander Hamilton* (Washington, D.C.: American Enterprise Institute, 1985), pp. 312, 313–314, 315–317. On occasion, minor changes have been made to spelling and punctuation for the convenience of modern readers.

the same idea, it ought not to escape remark, that the West India Islands, the soils of which are the most fertile, and the Nation, which in the greatest degree supplies the rest of the world, with the precious metals, exchange to a loss with almost every other Country. . . .

Not only the wealth; but the independence and security of a Country, appear to be materially connected with the prosperity of manufactures. Every nation, with a view to those great objects, ought to endeavour to possess within itself all the essentials of national supply. These comprise the means of *Subsistence habitation clothing* and *defence*.

The possession of these is necessary to the perfection of the body politic, to the safety as well as to the welfare of the society; the want of either, is the want of an important organ of political life and Motion; and in the various crises which await a state, it must severely feel the effects of any such deficiency. The extreme embarrassments of the United States during the late War, from an incapacity of supplying themselves, are still matter of keen recollection: A future war might be expected again to exemplify the mischiefs and dangers of a situation, to which that incapacity is still in too great a degree applicable, unless changed by timely and vigorous exertion. To effect this change as fast as shall be prudent, merits all the attention and all the Zeal of our Public Councils; 'tis the next great work to be accomplished. . . .

One more point of view only remains in which to Consider the expediency of encouraging manufactures in the United states.

It is not uncommon to meet with an opin[ion] that though the promoting of manufactures may be the interest of a part of the Union, it is contrary to that of another part. The Northern & southern regions are sometimes represented as having adverse interests in this respect. Those are called Manufacturing, these Agricultural states; and a species of opposition is imagined to subsist between the Manufacturing a[nd] Agricultural interests.

This idea of an opposition between those two interests is the common error of the early periods of every country, but experience gradually dissipates it. Indeed they are perceived so often to succour and to befriend each other, that they come at length to be considered as one: a supposition which has been frequently abused and is not universally true. Particular encouragements of particular manufactures may be of a Nature to sacrifice the interests of landholders to those of manufacturers; But it is nevertheless a maxim well established by experience, and generally acknowledged, where there has been sufficient experience, that the *aggregate* prosperity of manufactures, and the *aggregate* prosperty of Agriculture are intimately connected. . . .

But there are more particular considerations which serve to fortify the idea, that the encouragement of manufactures is the interest of all parts of the Union. If the Northern and middle states should be the principal scenes of such establishments, they would immediately benefit the more southern, by creating a demand for productions; some of which they have in common with the other states, and others of which are either peculiar to them, or more abundant, or of better quality, than elsewhere. These productions, principally are Timber, flax, Hemp, Cotton, Wool, raw silk, Indigo, iron, lead, furs, hides, skins and coals. Of these articles Cotton & Indigo are peculiar to the southern states; as are hitherto *Lead & Coal*. Flax and Hemp are or may be raised in greater abundance there, than in the More Northern states; and the Wool of Virginia is said to be of better quality than that of any other state: a Circumstance rendered the more probable by the reflection that Virginia embraces the same latitudes with the finest Wool Countries of Europe. The Climate of the south is also better adapted to the production of silk.

SOURCE 4: John Taylor, *Arator* (1813)

In his 1813 book Arator, *a collection of essays originally published in a local Virginia newspaper, Taylor relates the sad state of agriculture to the policies of "an aristocratical order." How does Taylor make that connection? Do you think this was an effective argument at the time?*

A patient must know that he is sick, before he will take physick. A collection of a few facts, to ascertain the ill health of agriculture, is necessary to invigorate our efforts towards a cure. One, apparent to the most superficial observer, is, that our land has diminished in fertility. Arts improve the work of nature—when they injure it, they are not arts, but barbarous customs. It is the office of agriculture, as an art, not to impoverish, but to fertilize the soil, and make it more useful than in its natural state. Such is the effect of every species of agriculture, which can aspire to the character of an art. Its object being to furnish man with articles of the first necessity, whatever defeats that object, is a crime of the first magnitude. . . .

In collecting the causes which have contributed to the miserable agricultural state of the country, as it is a national calamity of the highest magnitude, we should be careful not to be blinded by partiality for our customs or institutions, nor corrupted by a disposition to flatter ourselves or others. I shall begin with those of a political nature. These are a secondary providence, which govern unseen the great interests of society; and if agriculture is bad and languishing in a country and climate, where it may be good and prosperous, no doubt remains with me, that political institutions have chiefly perpetrated the evil; just as they decide the fate of commerce.

The device of subjecting it to the payment of bounties to manufacturing, is an institution of this kind. This device is one item in every system for rendering governments too strong for nations. Such an object never was and never can be effected, except by factions legally created at the public expense. The wealth transferred from the nation to such factions, devotes them to the will of the government, by which it is bestowed. They must render the service for which it was given, or it would be taken away. It is unexceptionably given to support a government against a nation, or one faction against another. Armies, loaning, banking, and an intricate treasury system, endowing a government with the absolute power of applying public money, under the cover of nominal checks, are other

SOURCE: Reprinted in John Taylor, *Arator: Being a Series of Agricultural Essays, Practical and Political: In Sixty-Four Numbers* (Indianapolis: Liberty Classics, 1977), pp. 68, 73–75, 79–80.

devices of this kind. Whatever strength or wealth a government and its legal factions acquire by law, is taken from a nation; and whatever is taken from a nation, weakens and impoverishes that interest, which composes the majority. There, political oppression in every form must finally fall. . . . Agriculture being the interest covering a great majority of the people of the United States, every device for getting money or power, hatched by a fellow-feeling or common interest, between a government and its legal creatures, must of course weaken and impoverish it. Desertion, for the sake of reaping without labour, a share in the harvest of wealth and power, bestowed by laws at its expense, thins its ranks; an annual tribute to these legal factions, empties its purse; and poverty debilitates both its soil and understanding.

The device of protecting duties, under the pretext of encouraging manufactures, operates like its kindred, by creating a capitalist interest, which instantly seizes upon the bounty taken by law from agriculture; and instead of doing any good to the actual workers in wood, metals, cotton or other substances, it helps to rear up an aristocratical order, at the expense of the workers in earth, to unite with governments in oppressing every species of useful industry. . . .

Still more hopeless is the promise of the manufacturing mania, "that it will make us independent of foreign nations," when combined with its other promise of providing a market for agriculture. The promise of a market, as we see in the experience of England, can only be made good, by reducing the agricultural class to a tenth part of the nation, and increasing manufacturers by great manufactural exportations. This reduction can only be accomplished by driving or seducing above nine-tenths of the agricultural class, into other classes, and the increase by a brave and patriotic navy. Discontent and misery will be the fruits of the first operation, and these would constitute the most forlorn hope for success in the second. By exchanging hardy, honest and free husbandmen for the classes necessary to reduce the number of agriculturists, low enough to raise the prices of their products, shall we become more independent of foreign nations? What! Secure our independence by bankers and capitalists? Secure our independence by impoverishing, discouraging and annihilating nine-tenths of our sound yeomanry? By turning them into swindlers, and dependents on a master capitalist for daily bread.

SOURCE 5:   *Values of the Manufactures of the United States, Exclusive of Doubtful Articles*   (1810)

Alexander Hamilton and John Taylor were engaged in a fierce debate about the economic future of the country. This table lists the values of American manufacturing in 1810. What kinds of goods did the nation produce? How many were related to agriculture? Does this vindicate Hamilton's argument in Source 3? Or does it support Taylor's view?

SOURCE: Curtis P. Nettels, *The Emergence of a National Economy, 1775–1815* (New York: Holt, Rinehart, and Winston, 1962), p. 390.

1. Goods manufactured by the loom, of cotton, wool,
   flax, hemp, and silk, with stockings .... $ 39,497,000
2. Other goods of these five materials, spun 2,052,000
3. Instruments and machinery manufactured—
   value $186,650, carding, fulling, and floor cloth,
   stamping by machinery—value $5,957,816 6,144,466
4. Hats of wool, fur, etc., and mixtures of them 4,323,000
5. Manufactures of iron 14,364,000
6. Manufactures of gold, silver, set work, mixed metals 2,483,000
7. Manufactures of lead 325,000
8. Soap, tallow, candles, and spermaceti, spring oil,
   and whale oil 1,766,000
9. Manufactures of hides and skins 17,935,000
10. Manufactures from seeds 858,000
11. Grain, fruit, and case liquors, distilled and fermented 16,528,000
12. Dry manufactures from grain, exclusively of flour, meal 75,000
13. Manufactures of wood 5,554,000
14. Manufactures of essences of oils, of and from wood 179,000
15. Refined or manufactured sugars 1,415,000
16. Manufactures of paper, pasteboard, cards, etc. 1,939,000
17. Manufactures of marble, stone, and slate 462,000
18. Glass manufactures 1,047,000
19. Earthen manufactures 259,000
20. Manufactures of tobacco 1,260,000
21. Drugs, dyestuffs, paints, etc., and dyeing 500,000
22. Cables and cordage 4,243,000
23. Manufactures of hair 129,000
24. Various and miscellaneous manufactures 4,347,000

$127,694,000[1]

QUESTIONS TO CONSIDER

1. How would you compare Alexander Hamilton's and John Taylor's visions for American society, the economy, and the role of government? Who made the better argument for his vision?

2. How did Hamilton's and Taylor's backgrounds and lives influence their political and economic views? What were the most important factors shaping their philosophies?

3. Hamilton, born in obscurity, became a champion of the "rich and well-born." Taylor, a planter-aristocrat, denounced the influence of a selfish elite within the government. How do you account for that?

4. Does modern American society more resemble Hamilton's vision or Taylor's? Or neither?

---

1. Rounded off.

For Further Reading

Joyce Appleby, *Capitalism and a New Social Order: The Republican Vision of the 1790s* (New York: New York University Press, 1984), is a revisionist view of Jefferson and his allies, which argues that they were not as anticapitalist as older interpretations made them out to be.

Richard Brookhiser, *Alexander Hamilton: American* (New York: Free Press, 1999), is a short, readable biography that attempts to dispel many of the myths surrounding Hamilton's politics and life.

John F. Kasson, *Civilizing the Machine: Technology and Republican Values in America, 1776–1900* (New York: Grossman Publishers, 1976), traces the development of economic and political traditions in early American history, including the early Republic.

Allan Kulikoff, *The Agrarian Origins of American Capitalism* (Charlottesville: University Press of Virginia, 1992), is a useful study that argues for the development of the market economy in agricultural areas.

Robert E. Shalhope, *John Taylor of Caroline: Pastoral Republican* (Columbia: University of South Carolina Press, 1980), sets Taylor and his philosophy within the context of his times.

Resistance and Western Expansion: Tecumseh and William Henry Harrison

Tecumseh　　　　　　　　*William Henry Harrison*

The negotiations had gone nowhere. Tempers had flared, and now William Henry Harrison drew his sword to kill Tecumseh. The governor of Indiana Territory viewed the Shawnee chief as a dangerous enemy. His movement to unify Native Americans in armed resistance to whites was a frightening obstacle in the path of American progress. The United States had bought this land from other tribes. Now settlers were pouring into the territory to carve farms, homes, and towns out of the wilderness. No Indian leader was going to stand in the way of that. Harrison would eliminate Tecumseh's threat to the country in hand-to-hand combat. This was politics on the frontier in 1810: nation versus nation, Native American versus European American, man versus man. It was political, and it was personal.

Harrison and Tecumseh had two very different visions of the future. For Harrison, the area west of the Appalachian Mountains, east of the Mississippi River, and north of the Ohio River represented an unrivaled opportunity for the expansion of the nation. The Ohio country, or Northwest Territory as it was often called, could support millions of Americans in future generations. Settlers would build a vast commercial empire there. At the same time, they would prevent European powers such as Great Britain and Spain from blocking the westward growth of the United States. Whoever ensured that American civilization advanced into this area would be a hero.

For Tecumseh, the land along the Spaylaywitheepi (Ohio River) was sacred. The Shawnees were one of the most warlike Indian nations in North America. For generations, they had battled their traditional enemies, the Cherokees and Iroquois. The Shawnees had lived in what is now Pennsylvania, Tennessee, and other areas before finally coming to the Ohio country. In about 1725, another powerful tribe, the Miamis, had invited the Shawnees to live on the lands to their east. The Shawnees would serve as a buffer between the Miamis and the Iroquois. For the first time in tribal history, the Shawnees had a defined homeland. They thanked Waashaa Monetoo (the Great Spirit, who had created the world) for this land. Here they could live in peace, grow crops and hunt game, and follow the ways of their ancestors.

To the east, though, the Long Knives (Americans) had begun to push westward into the Ohio country. The end of the Revolutionary War had brought a small stream of them. But now it flowed continuously, bringing thousands across the Appalachians. Watching the white settlers tramp into the Ohio country, Tecumseh had done his best to avoid warfare. Yet he longed for the day when the Shawnees would drive the Americans out and restore their former power and glory. In 1810, Harrison and Tecumseh met at Vincennes, on the Wabash River north of the Ohio River. In a long tirade, Tecumseh taunted the governor. He shouted so angrily that one of the officers standing nearby ordered his men to seize the Indians in front of them. As the soldiers started forward, the Indians produced their tomahawks. Harrison pulled his sword, convinced that the time had come to kill the Indian leader, but cooler heads prevailed. Tecumseh spun on his heels and stalked away. Both leaders now knew that only bloodshed would resolve their differences.

"Panther Passing Across"

Tecumseh (Panther Passing Across, or Shooting Star) was born in 1768 as a huge meteor streaked across the sky. His father, Pukeshinwau (Something That Falls), named his son after Panther, a spirit who traveled like a powerful meteor. From the first, Tecumseh's family thought that he had the blessing of the spirit world. His father was a great warrior who had become one of the most important chiefs in the tribe. He had married an attractive woman named Methoataaskee (Turtle Laying Her Eggs in the Sand), and they had begun to raise a family. Tecumseh was their fourth child. He far surpassed the other boys in the tribe and showed an uncommon skill with weapons. Attentive and intelligent, he spent hours listening to the elders of the village as they passed on the tribe's history and customs. By the time he was ten, Tecumseh was a successful hunter and a tribal historian. When he brought home a deer, he shared it with the elderly members of the village, earning their respect. Such generosity was expected of a great hunter and warrior.

The young man also learned the religious rites that governed Shawnee life. The Shawnees organized every aspect of day-to-day living around rituals. Social relations, war, trade, hunting, and planting crops all required rituals that summoned or appeased the spirits. Tecumseh had great respect for these rites, but he learned that many young people did not. Some older members of the tribe feared that the spirits would someday punish the Shawnees for this. They blamed the loss of interest in old ways on the whites who were encroaching on Shawnee land. The whites' trade goods, they said, created among the Indians a growing dependency on the Long Knives. They also blamed the Christian missionaries, who brought new ideas and a new religion to challenge the old. And they blamed the whites' "firewater" (usually rum and brandy), to which so many young warriors were addicted.

Even before the American Revolution, many Shawnee leaders were ready to take up arms. Hokolesqua (Cornstalk), the principal chief of the tribe, opposed war. He argued that fighting the Long Knives would do far more harm than good. Eventually, however, the push to fight was too strong, and he reluctantly agreed to lead the Shawnees on the warpath. When an army of Virginia militia threatened to invade Shawnee territory in 1774, Cornstalk struck first. The result was the Battle of Point Pleasant. Both sides claimed victory, but the Indians had inflicted many more casualties than the whites. One of the Indians who died was Tecumseh's father. The family was adopted by Chiungalla (Black Fish), a respected chief and longtime family friend, who became Tecumseh's foster father.

The war with the Long Knives raged on after the Revolution. It also split the Shawnee tribe. More than half had chosen not to fight in a war they believed they could not win. They did not want to risk their lives and the children's futures and had instead moved farther west, beyond the Mississippi. The rest of the tribe had stayed behind, fighting desperately for their land as allies of the British. Tecumseh and his family were among those who stayed. Accompanied by his older brother Chiksika, Tecumseh led raids on the Americans and in time became an accomplished warrior.

The Indian style of warfare was personal. Face-to-face relations in peace became hand-to-hand combat in war. Adversaries often knew and had great respect for each other. The Shawnees and their allies won many great victories. The Miami chief, Mishikiniqua (Little Turtle), joined Chiungalla and other great chiefs in leading the warriors. They ambushed entire armies and humiliated the young United States with devastating defeats. But in the end, it was a losing effort. In 1794, twenty years of warfare came to an end when General "Mad Anthony" Wayne defeated the allied tribes at the Battle of Fallen Timbers. The following year, Wayne forced the chiefs to sign the Treaty of Greenville, which turned over half of what is now the state of Ohio to the United States. Included in the treaty was most of the land the Shawnees had called home for two generations. Wayne also forced the Indians to accept the conditions of previous treaties. Some of those treaties involved fraudulent land sales, including the sale to whites of Shawnee land by the Iroquois. Some Shawnee chiefs refused to sign Wayne's treaty and argued that those who did sign lacked the authority to do so. Many warriors, including Tecumseh, followed the lead of these chiefs.

"A Most Desirable Object"

William Henry Harrison was not born under a celestial sign. He did enter the world in 1773, however, under very favorable circumstances. Harrison's father was a prominent planter and politician, a member of the Virginia gentry, a delegate to the Continental Congress, and a signer of the Declaration of Independence. His mother also hailed from the gentry. The Harrisons lived on a sprawling plantation along the James River called Berkeley. William was well educated and attended Hampden-Sydney College, although he did not graduate. Instead, he went off to Philadelphia, where he studied medicine under the renowned Dr. Benjamin Rush, a leading man of medicine and hero of the American Revolution. Yet Harrison was not cut out for a career in medicine. Military glory was what he sought. When his father died, he expressed his displeasure with the medical field, left his studies, and was commissioned as an officer in the U.S. Army.

Harrison served as a lieutenant in the infantry and was posted to the Northwest Territory. By the time he arrived there in 1792, the area was aflame with the Indian wars. He served as General Wayne's aide and distinguished himself in the campaign that ended the long conflict with the allied tribes in 1795. Military service suited Harrison. Although he did not like the long periods of inactivity and boredom between battles, his thirst for combat allowed him to endure the slow times, and he flourished under military discipline. He came to admire Wayne, whose decisiveness led to victory on the battlefield. A bold fighter, Wayne once told Harrison that his standing battle order was "Charge the damned rascals with the bayonets!" Emulating his commanding officer, Harrison never shied away from a fight. Still, the boredom of military life wore on him. During the long hours in camp, he began to study theology, thinking that he might pursue a career as a minister. He soon gave that up and turned instead to the art of distilling spirits, thinking he might open his own distillery. Then he began studying the law, but he gave that up as well.

Following Wayne's successful campaign in 1794–1795, Harrison went to Lexington, Kentucky, where he met Anna Symmes. Lovely, graceful, and well educated, she was the daughter of Judge John Cleves Symmes, who had large claims in Ohio. Symmes headed up a grand real estate scheme called the Symmes Purchase. Along with other investors, Symmes proposed to buy a vast tract in Ohio and then sell it off to settlers. Harrison cut a dashing figure as he courted Anna. He rode well, looked handsome in uniform, and projected ruggedness as a result of his long military service.

Judge Symmes, however, was unimpressed. When he asked young Harrison how he expected to support his daughter, the soldier replied with a flourish, "By my sword and my own right arm." The answer impressed Symmes, but he found the match distasteful nonetheless. Referring to Harrison's inability to decide on a profession, Symmes wrote to a friend that his daughter's suitor "can neither bleed, plead, nor preach." Eventually, though, he came to accept Harrison's military career. "His best prospect is in the army," Symmes said, "he has talents, and if [he] can dodge [bullets] a few years, it is probable he may become conspicuous."

After marrying Anna in secret in 1795, Harrison settled near what is today Cincinnati. He was promoted to captain, but the boredom of garrison duty proved too much, and he resigned his commission in 1798. Then, using his family connections, he obtained a position as territorial secretary of the Northwest

Territory. The following year, the territorial legislature elected him its delegate to Congress. As territorial representative, Harrison served on a committee to oversee the sale of public lands. The position enabled him to solidify friendships and political connections. In 1800, President John Adams appointed him governor of Indiana Territory, one of two territories carved out of the original Northwest Territory.

Convinced that the residents of Indiana wanted slavery, Harrison attempted to introduce the institution there, even though it was prohibited under the Northwest Ordinance.* His family had owned slaves in Virginia, and he faced a labor shortage on his own farm near Vincennes. He managed to push a bill through Congress that allowed slavery under another name, but when this was later repealed, he did not object. Still, Harrison tried several temporary slavery experiments on his farm and continued privately to support the "peculiar institution." As governor and superintendent for Indian affairs, he efficiently carried out President Thomas Jefferson's Indian policy. Jefferson urged him to acquire all Indian land within the territory for the United States and even suggested loaning the tribes money so that their land could later be taken away by way of collection. Harrison agreed that doing away with Indian titles to the land was "a most desirable object." **[See Sources 1 and 2.]**

All the while, Harrison saw himself as a moderate when it came to dealing with the Indians. He sincerely believed that friendly relations should be developed with the tribes. He claimed to respect the Native Americans and acknowledged that many of their arguments about the land were correct. He also believed that he understood their culture. In fact, he arrogantly claimed to have a better understanding of the Indians than did some of their own chiefs. After all, he had traded with them, practiced some of their rituals, and negotiated and fought with them many times. And he certainly felt qualified to expound on them in print. Later, he would write a book about the tribes titled *A Discourse on the Aborigines of the Ohio Valley*. In this short tract, Harrison argued that the tribes who had sold their territory to the United States had never owned the land and had no right to do so. Of course, this was long after Harrison had already carried out the policies that took the Indians' land away from them. **[See Source 3.]**

In fact, Harrison had few qualms about enforcing Indian land sales. As an officer of the U.S. government, his duty was to implement the policies that its leaders devised. Yet there was more to his actions than that. He also had personal ambitions and knew that opening up Indian land for white settlement could win him fame and fortune. Furthermore, he knew that the land in question rightfully belonged to the United States by the laws of nature, politics, and conquest. And he suspected that the British were behind recent Indian attacks on the frontier. The British had fought with the Indians in the American Revolution and had maintained a string of forts on American soil in the Great Lakes

---

Northwest Ordinance: This 1787 law organized the Northwest Territory and established the process by which territories could become states. It also prohibited slavery, a measure that Harrison and other proponents of slavery opposed.

region after the war. Now operating from Canada, they were deeply involved in the fur trade around the Great Lakes. Harrison believed that they had designs on the entire Northwest, and he was determined to keep it from them.

"The Open Door"

Sometime in the fall of 1803, Tecumseh's younger brother Lalawethika (Loud Mouth) underwent a religious transformation. Lalawethika was generally regarded as a failure among the Shawnees. Unlike Tecumseh, he had not become a successful hunter and warrior. In fact, he had lost an eye in a hunting accident and in other ways had fallen short of the expectations of Shawnee manhood. Instead of hunting with the men, he preferred to sit around camp and converse with the women. In addition, he was surly, arrogant, and disliked by nearly everyone. Only Tecumseh showed him any respect. Lalawethika had become an alcoholic in his early teens and depended on Tecumseh to keep him supplied with whiskey bought or stolen from the whites. He had married a woman with a strong personality, and she constantly nagged him and humiliated him in front of the other men of the tribe. He spent most of his days and nights in a drunken stupor.

In 1803, Lalawethika fell into a drunken coma, and his family thought that he had died. While they were making preparations for his funeral, he suddenly awoke and announced that he had been in a religious trance. He had been transported to the spirit world, had had a vision of the future, and had been given a new name. He insisted that he now be called Tenskwatawa—"The Open Door." He called for the Shawnee people to avoid the whites, to give up their trade goods and be independent of them. He predicted that the dwindling game would return in great numbers, that long-dead ancestors would come back to life, and that the whites would eventually be driven out of the Indians' land forever. He claimed that the Great Spirit had ordered him to destroy those Indians who practiced witchcraft or prayed to the Christian God. Such individuals, he declared, should be burned at the stake.

Many suspected that it was Tecumseh who had had this vision. Perhaps he had simply asked his younger brother to convey the vision for him. Whatever the case, Tenskwatawa, aided by Tecumseh, attracted a following of young warriors from the Shawnees and other tribes. This Indian religious revival spread quickly. In fact, it resembled the series of Christian revivals known as the Second Great Awakening* that were sweeping the country at the time. Before long, hundreds of Indians were moving to live near Tenskwatawa, who came to be called "the Prophet." The movement was a cultural revitalization, a return to traditional values, and a promise that the Indians' lost greatness would be restored.

When word of Tenskwatawa reached Governor Harrison, he suspected that this was all part of a plan devised by Tecumseh to stir up trouble with the whites. He challenged Tenskwatawa to prove himself. The Prophet agreed to do so, saying that he would blot out the sun. Hundreds of skeptical Indians joined

---

Second Great Awakening: The Protestant religious revival in the first decades of the nineteenth century. Often characterized by tremendous emotional outpourings, this revival spread from the frontier to urban areas and resulted in thousands of conversions.

his devoted followers to see what would happen. On the appointed day, the Prophet chanted and prayed to the spirits. As high noon approached, he spread out his hands, and the sun was darkened by a full solar eclipse. The onlookers were amazed, and the religious awakening became even more widespread.

In 1808, Tecumseh and Tenskwatawa moved their followers from the area around Greenville, Ohio, and established a new Indian town in central Indiana. Called Prophet's Town, it was soon home to several thousand Indians. To keep their followers fed, the leaders of the movement depended on the annual food supplies and trade goods that the U.S. government gave the conquered tribes. These annuities had been part of the hated Treaty of Greenville. Harrison used these supplies to his advantage and tried to bargain with Tecumseh by threatening to withhold them if he did not contain his movement. Realizing the advantage the trade goods gave the whites, Tecumseh now refused to accept the supplies on principle.

The two men met on several occasions. There were heated arguments and threats from both sides. As mentioned earlier, during one meeting in 1810, Harrison nearly physically attacked Tecumseh. [**See Source 4.**] At another meeting, Tecumseh told Harrison that there was nothing he could do to stop the Indians. He also told the governor that he was going south to bring the southern tribes into the movement. He would build a pan-Indian movement, uniting all the tribes between the Appalachian Mountains and the Mississippi River. He would persuade them to set aside their differences and accept the leadership of those the Great Spirit had appointed to restore them to greatness. Once united, the Indians would be in a position of strength and would set the terms for future treaties with the whites. If the Americans refused to negotiate and accept the Indians' position, then the great alliance would attack all across the frontier, from the Great Lakes to the Gulf of Mexico. It would drive the whites east of the Appalachians.

In the 1670s, the Wampanoag leader Metacom (also called Philip) had forged an alliance that had killed thousands of whites in New England in King Philip's War. At the conclusion of the French and Indian War,* the Ottawa leader Pontiac had tried to unite all of the Great Lakes tribes against the British. Pontiac's confederation had nearly destroyed all of the British posts on the frontier, but in the end his plans had failed. Now, as Tecumseh and Tenskwatawa hatched a similar plan, Harrison was alarmed. He had great respect for Tecumseh, and he feared the young leader's influence. He heard reports that the Prophet's followers accused Christian Indians of witchcraft and burned them at the stake. His spies brought news of large numbers of warriors coming to Prophet's Town, supposedly to hear Tenskwatawa's religious message. He viewed the religious awakening among the Indians as a serious threat to the United States and was convinced that he had to act.

In 1811, Tecumseh toured the camps of the southern tribes. He spoke before the gathered councils of the Cherokee, Creek, Chickasaw, and Choctaw Nations. He implored them to set aside their differences and join his pan-Indian

---

French and Indian War: The war fought in North America from 1754 to 1763. It pitted Britain and its colonial allies against France and its Indian allies.

confederation. He asked them give up their tribal identities and become brothers with all other children of the Great Spirit. He called for them to give up
white culture and return to their own traditional ways. He pleaded for them to
take up the hatchet and join the northern tribes in an all-out war against the
Americans the following year. **[See Source 5.]**

Although war appealed to many young warriors, Tecumseh was unable to
rally all the tribes. He failed to overcome the Cherokees' traditional hatred of
the Shawnees. The Choctaws also refused to join the confederacy, although for
a time it seemed that they were inclined to do so. In the end, an influential chief,
Pushmataha, single-handedly opposed Tecumseh in debate and convinced his
people to remain at peace with the whites. Tecumseh was more successful
among the Creeks, persuading nearly half of them to join the northern tribes
on the warpath the following summer. A small number of warriors from the
other southern tribes also agreed to fight. Some even started north to join the
movement at Prophet's Town. Tecumseh left the southern tribes, telling those
who would listen to him to look for a great sign—a trembling of the earth—
that would demonstrate his power and signal the beginning of the war against
the whites.

While Tecumseh was in the South pleading his case, Harrison decided to
strike. In November 1811, he mustered his troops and led them toward Prophet's
Town. Before leaving, Tecumseh had instructed Tenskwatawa to avoid conflict.
The time for battle, he said, had not yet come. The Indians were not quite ready.
When reports of Harrison's march reached Tenskwatawa, however, he insisted
that he had had a vision. The spirits, he said, were telling him that the time for
war was at hand. The Indians would attack in the predawn darkness, and Tenskwatawa predicted that the spirits would enable the warriors to see in the dark
as if it were the middle of the day. The whites, he declared, would be blinded.
And so Tenskwatawa ordered the attack that started the Battle of Tippecanoe.
The result was a devastating defeat for the Indians. Harrison and his army
killed nearly two hundred warriors, burned Prophet's Town, and in one fell
swoop destroyed the Prophet's power.

Tecumseh returned after the defeat. He saved his disgraced brother from
execution at the hands of his disillusioned followers. Then, as Tecumseh had
predicted, came a great earthquake that shook the entire Midwest and much of
the South. He became the Indians' religious leader, but they could not overcome
the military defeat at Tippecanoe. Many of the warriors who had dedicated
themselves to the cause went home disgusted. Only Tecumseh's forceful leadership and suddenly evident prophetic abilities managed to keep the movement alive.

By the following year, the rising Indian unrest on the frontier symbolized
by Tecumseh and Prophet's Town helped foment anti-British sentiment in
many Americans. Like Harrison, they were convinced that the British had instigated Tecumseh's movement. Unable to see that their troubles with Native
Americans were of their own making, they were looking for a scapegoat. British
agents operating from Canada did have relations with the Indians, and the
British navy, locked in a war with France, had been harassing neutral American
commercial vessels for years. In the minds of many Americans, the United
States was under assault on land and sea. The result was a rising chorus for war,

and in 1812 President James Madison succumbed. When the War of 1812 began, Tecumseh's followers joined with the British to fight the Americans.

Tecumseh fought bravely, even recklessly, during the war, especially in battles against his old foe Harrison. His ferocious attacks thwarted American plans to conquer Canada at the Battle of the Raisin River, and Canadians would later praise Tecumseh for saving their country. The final battle with Harrison was the last of Tecumseh's life. They met in October 1813 at the Battle of the Thames along Canada's Thames River north of Lake Erie. The day before the conflict, Tecumseh had another vision. This time, it was a premonition of his death. When he told his fellow warriors, they protested. Surely, he must be mistaken, for he had never suffered even a slight wound in battle. They all believed that he enjoyed the special blessing of the spirits and could not be hurt in battle. Tecumseh insisted that his vision was accurate and told them that when they saw him fall, they should strike his body four times with a ramrod. Then, he said, he would rise from the dead and lead them to victory. After that, Tecumseh prophesied, all that Tenskwatawa had preached would come true: The game would return, their long-dead ancestors would join them, and the whites would be driven out forever. The following day, the Indians went into battle against Harrison and his troops. In the heat of the fray, Tecumseh was killed. A warrior, ramrod in hand, rushed forward to carry out his instructions. He struck his fallen leader's body once, twice, three times—then was shot and killed himself. Tecumseh did not rise from the dead. The Indians did not win a great victory.

By the time the British and Americans signed the treaty ending the War of 1812, Tecumseh's Indian confederation was smashed. In the coming years, Andrew Jackson would carry out mopping-up actions against the Creeks and other hostile tribes. Even the Choctaws, Cherokees, and other Indians who had fought with the United States in the war were removed to the trans-Mississippi West. The door was now wide open to a flood of white settlers. Within five years, two more new states would enter the union from the Northwest Territory. By 1820, the surge of settlers would cross the Mississippi into territory acquired in the Louisiana Purchase. By 1830, more Americans lived west of the Appalachians than had lived in the original thirteen states in 1790. Many of them had settled on land taken from Indians in treaties negotiated after the War of 1812.

Harrison's vision for the Northwest Territory became a reality as thousands, and eventually millions, of whites settled on old tribal lands. His role in defeating the Indians in the War of 1812 made him a hero. His career in politics carried him to the House of Representatives, the U.S. Senate, and eventually the White House. When he ran for the presidency with John Tyler in 1840, it was as a military hero and Indian fighter. Their slogan "Tippecanoe and Tyler Too" was a powerful reminder of Harrison's military feats. Harrison served as president for only one month, however, before dying of pneumonia.

His death, of course, did the Indians little good. By 1841, the Indians between the Appalachians and the Mississippi had been defeated. Their game had been depleted, and the old traditions and rituals had fallen by the wayside. They had lost the battle, the war, their land, and their culture. In Tecumseh, they had also lost a great leader. In helping to kill Tecumseh, Harrison had extended the domain of the United States.

PRIMARY SOURCES

Source 1:   Thomas Jefferson, *Letter to William Henry Harrison*   (1803)

Thomas Jefferson wrote this letter to William Henry Harrison when Harrison was governor of Indiana Territory. What changes does Jefferson propose in the Indians' way of life? What means does he suggest for bringing these changes about?

[T]his letter being unofficial and private, I may with safety give you a more extensive view of our policy respecting the Indians, that you may the better comprehend the parts dealt out to you in detail through the official channel, and observing the system of which they make a part, conduct yourself in unison with it in cases where you are obliged to act without instruction. Our system is to live in perpetual peace with the Indians, to cultivate an affectionate attachment from them, by everything just and liberal which we can do for them within the bounds of reason, and by giving them effectual protection against wrongs from our own people. The decrease of game rendering their subsistence by hunting insufficient, we wish to draw them to agriculture, to spinning and weaving. The latter branches they take up with great readiness, because they fall to the women, who gain by quitting the labors of the field for those which are exercised within doors. When they withdraw themselves to the culture of a small piece of land, they will perceive how useless to them are their extensive forests, and will be willing to pare them off from time to time in exchange for necessaries for their farms and families. To promote this disposition to exchange lands, which they have to spare and we want, for necessaries, which we have to spare and they want, we shall push our trading uses, and be glad to see the good and influential individuals among them run in debt, because we observe that when these debts get beyond what the individuals can pay, they become willing to lop them off by a cession of lands. At our trading houses, too, we mean to sell so low as merely to repay us cost and charges, so as neither to lessen or enlarge our capital. This is what private traders cannot do, for they must gain; they will consequently retire from the competition, and we shall thus get clear of this pest without giving offence or umbrage to the Indians. In this way our settlements will gradually circumscribe and approach the Indians, and they will in time either incorporate with us as citizens of the United States, or remove beyond the Mississippi. The former is certainly the termination of their history most happy for themselves; but, in the whole course of this, it is essential to cultivate their love. As to their fear, we presume that our strength and their weakness is now so visible that they must see we have only to shut our hand to crush them, and that all our liberalities to them proceed from motives of pure humanity only. Should any tribe be fool-hardy enough to take up the

Source: Reprinted in Merrill C. Peterson, *Thomas Jefferson: Writings* (New York: Literary Classics of the United States, 1984), pp. 1117–1119.

hatchet at any time, the seizing the whole country of that tribe, and driving them across the Mississippi, as the only condition of peace, would be an example to others, and a furtherance of our final consolidation.

SOURCE 2:   William Henry Harrison, *Letter to William Eustis, Secretary of War*   (1809)

William Henry Harrison negotiated a number of treaties with the Indian tribes of the Ohio country while serving as governor of Indiana Territory. In this letter, Harrison reports on the actions of the Prophet and discusses his own plans for buying more land in Indiana. At the time, he believed that the Prophet had been unable to unify the tribes and hoped to use that failure as an opportunity to purchase more land. Why did Harrison think that he had to acquire more territory in yet another treaty?

I have great pleasure in being enabled to inform you that there no longer exists the least probability of a rupture with any of the Indian tribes of this frontier. The party which the Prophet had assembled have dispersed with manifest indications of terror and alarm. Whether this is to be attributed to the military preparations which were made here, [t]o the want of provisions, disappointment upon the part of the Prophet as to the force he expected to raise, or to the combination of all these causes, or whether indeed he had ever any design of attacking us I cannot at present determine. Whatever I shall be able to discover on this subject shall form the matter of another communication. I have engaged a confidential Frenchman who speaks the Indian languages to reside at the Prophet's Town for a few weeks to watch his movements and discover his politics.

I have for several years considered a further extinguishment of Indian title to the North East of this and extending from the Wabash to the purchase made at the Treaty of Grouseland as a most desirable object. And it appears to me that the time has arrived when the purchase may be attempted with a considerable prospect of success. Our settlements here are much cramped by the vicinity of the Indian lands, which in the direction above mentioned is not more than twenty-one miles. The country on the Wabash below this is sunken and wet, that to the north and west almost entirely Prairie and not of such a quality to be settled for many years. These circumstances must necessarily render the settlements here feeble for a considerable time unless a further extinguishment of title is effected in the direction I have mentioned.

The effecting of this purchase will come within the scope of the Instructions hitherto received, but I shall conclude no bargain until I am honored with the President's further direction.

SOURCE: Reprinted in Logan Esarey, ed., *Governors Messages and Letters: Messages and Letters of William Henry Harrison, 1800–1811* (Indianapolis: Indiana Historical Commission, 1922), I, pp. 346–347.

SOURCE 3:   William Henry Harrison, *A Discourse on the Aborigines of the Ohio Valley*   (1839)

In the following excerpt from his pamphlet, Harrison describes several Indian leaders including Tecumseh (Tecumthey). What does Harrison think of these Indians? In his view, what kind of men are they?

As it regards their moral and intellectual qualities, the difference between the tribes was still greater. The Shawanees, Delawares, and Miamis, were much superior to the other members of the confederacy. I have known individuals among them of very high order of talents, but these were not generally to be relied upon for sincerity. The Little Turtle, of the Miami tribe, was one of this description, as was the Blue Jacket, a Shawanee chief. I think it probable that Tecumthey possessed more integrity than any other of the chiefs, who attained to much distinction; but he violated a solemn engagement, which he had freely contracted,—and there are strong suspicions of his having formed a treacherous design, which an accident only prevented him from accomplishing. Sinister instances are, however, to be found in the conduct of great men, in the history of almost all civilized nations. But these instances are more than counterbalanced by the number of individuals of high moral character, which were to be found amongst the principal, and secondary chiefs, of the . . . tribes above mentioned. This was particularly the case with Tarhe, or the Crane, the grand sachem of the Wyandots, and Black Hoof, the chief of the Shawanees. Many instances might be adduced, to show the possession on the part of these men, of an uncommon degree of disinterestedness and magnanimity, and strict performance of their engagements, under circumstances—which would be considered by many as justifying evasion. But one of the brightest parts of the character of those Indians, is their sound regard to the obligations of friendship. A pledge of this kind, once given by an Indian of any character, becomes the ruling passion of his soul, to which every other was made to yield—He regards it as superior to every other obligation. And the life of his friend would be required at the hands of him, (or his tribe,) who had taken it, even if it had occurred in a fair field of battle, and in the performance of his duty as a warrior. . . .

Every Indian family has one or more of the skins or images above mentioned, which is called in the Miamie [sic] language Corpenohor Corpenyomer. It is those instruments that they consider sacred, and accordingly worship them. They say when the Great Spirit formed them, that he placed those things in their possession and told them if they would worship them that they would live to an immense age, and always remain happy, consequently, some one member of each respective family pays reverence to those divine images monthly. After singing all night such songs as he has been instructed to do on such occasions by his ancestors, which may be called religious songs; he then prepares a kettle of victuals and a few pipes of tobacco, and invites his neigh-

SOURCE: William Henry Harrison, *A Discourse on the Aborigines of the Ohio Valley* (1839; reprint, Chicago: Fergus Printing Company, 1883), pp. 39–40, 91–92.

bors to come and partake of what he has prepared for the occasion. When the company has collected, he tells them the cause of his calling them together. The company then proceeds to eating; with a great deal of ceremony too tedious to mention. Each person will throw a small piece of the victuals in the fire before he puts any in his mouth.

There are but few Indians that will give an opinion respecting a future state. They say that those things are only enquired after by fools and the white people. Some of them have told me that they believed there were two other worlds. One was intended as the place of residence for the spirits of the good people on this earth; and the other for the spirits of those that were bad, and that the bad ones were always assisting the evil spirit to do ill, while the good ones resided with the good spirit and remained in peace and quietness.

I once asked a very distinguished chief what he supposed was necessary to constitute a good and a great man. He replied, that a good father, a good husband, a good neighbor, a good warrior, and a lover of his nation, was all in his opinion that was necessary for a man to possess, to fulfill the expectations of the Great Spirit, who placed us on this earth; though, the Indians generally appear to care but little about a future state. They are only anxious to live to an old age in this world.

Source 4: Tecumseh, *Speech to Harrison at Vincennes* (1810)

In 1810, William Henry Harrison and Tecumseh met, and their negotiations nearly culminated in violence. In the following excerpt, Tecumseh argues that the Treaty of Greenville was not legitimate and speaks of Indian relations with the British. At the close of this speech, Harrison stood and drew his sword, preparing to attack Tecumseh. Why do you think Harrison was so upset by this speech?

Brother. This land that was sold and the goods that was given for it was only done by a few. The treaty was afterwards brought here and the Weas [a subtribe of the Miamis] were induced to give their consent because of their small numbers. The treaty at Fort Wayne was made through the threats of Winamac but in future we are prepared to punish those chiefs who may come forward to propose to sell their land. If you continue to purchase of them it will produce war among the different tribes and at last I do not know what will be the consequence to the white people.

Brother. I was glad to hear your speech you said if we could show that the land was sold by persons that had no right to sell you would restore it. . . . These tribes set up a claim but the tribes with me will not agree to their claim, if the land is not restored to us you will soon see when we return to our homes

Source: Reprinted in Logan Esarey, ed., *Governors Messages and Letters: Messages and Letters of William Henry Harrison, 1800–1811* (Indianapolis: Indiana Historical Commission, 1922), I, pp. 463–469.

how it will be settled. We shall have a great council at which all the tribes shall be present when we will show to those who sold that they had no right to sell the claim they set up and we will know what will be done with those Chiefs that did sell the land to you. I am not alone in this determination it is the determination of all the warriors and red people that listen to me.

I now wish you to listen to me. If you do not it will appear as if you wished me to kill all the chiefs that sold you this land. I tell you so because I am authorised by all the tribes to do so. I am at the head of them all. I am a Warrior and all the Warriors will meet together in two or three moons from this. Then I will call for those chiefs that sold you the land and shall know what to do with them. If you do not restore the land you will have a hand in killing them.

Do not believe that I came here to get presents from you[.] [I]f you offer us anything we will not take it. By taking goods from you you will hereafter say that with them you purchased another piece of land from us. If we want anything we are able to buy it, from your traders. Since the land was sold to you no traders come among us. I now wish you would clear all the roads and let the traders come among us. Then perhaps some of our young men will occasionally call upon you to get their guns repaired. This is all the assistance we ask of you. . . .

If you think proper to give us any presents and we can be convinced that they are given through friendship alone we will accept them. As we intend to hold our council at the Huron village that is near the British we may probably make them a visit. Should they offer us any presents of goods we will not take them but should they offer us powder and the tom[a]hawk we will take the powder and refuse the Tom[a]hawk.

I wish you *Brother* to consider everything I have said is true and that it is the sentiment of all the red people who listen to me.

By your giving goods to the Kickapoos you killed many they were seized with the smallpox by which many died.

Source 5:   Tecumseh, *"Sleep Not Longer, O Choctaws and Chickasaws"*   (1811)

In 1811, Tecumseh went to the southern tribes and tried to convince them to join his confederacy against the whites. How does he appeal to the Choctaws and Chickasaws? What reasons does he give them for uniting with the northern tribes?

[H]ave we not courage enough remaining to defend our country and maintain our ancient independence? Will we calmly suffer the white intruders and tyrants to enslave us? Shall it be said of our race that we knew not how to extricate ourselves from the three most dreadful calamities—folly, inactivity and cowardice?

Source: Reprinted in W. C. Vanderwerth, *Indian Oratory: Famous Speeches by Noted Indian Chieftains* (Norman: University of Oklahoma Press, 1971), pp. 62–65.

But what need is there to speak of the past? It speaks for itself and asks, Where today is the Pequod? Where the Narragansetts, the Mohawks, Pocanokets, and many other once powerful tribes of our race? They have vanished before the avarice and oppression of the white men, as snow before a summer sun. In the vain hope of alone defending their ancient possessions, they have fallen in the wars with the white men. Look abroad over their once beautiful country, and what see you now? Naught but the ravages of the pale face destroyers meet our eyes. So it will be with you Choctaws and Chickasaws! Soon your mighty forest trees, under the shade of whose wide spreading branches you have played in infancy, sported in boyhood, and now rest your wearied limbs after the fatigue of the chase, will be cut down to fence in the land which the white intruders dare to call their own. Soon their broad roads will pass over the grave of your fathers, and the place of their rest will be blotted out forever. The annihilation of our race is at hand unless we unite in one common cause against the common foe. Think not, brave Choctaws and Chickasaws, that you can remain passive and indifferent to the common danger, and thus escape the common fate. Your people, too, will soon be as falling leaves and scattering clouds before their blighting breath. You, too, will be driven away from your native land and ancient domains as leaves are driven before the wintry storms.

Sleep not longer, O Choctaws and Chickasaws, in false security and delusive hopes. Our broad domains are fast escaping from our grasp. Every year our white intruders become more greedy, exacting, oppressive and overbearing. Every year contentions spring up between them and our people and when blood is shed we have to make atonement whether right or wrong, at the cost of the lives of our greatest chiefs, and the yielding up of large tracts of our lands. Before the palefaces came among us, we enjoyed the happiness of unbounded freedom, and were acquainted with neither riches, wants nor oppression. How is it now? Wants and oppression are our lot; for are we not controlled in everything, and dare we move without asking, by your leave? Are we not being stripped day by day of the little that remains of our ancient liberty? Do they not even kick and strike us as they do their black-faces? How long will it be before they will tie us to a post and whip us, and make us work for them in their corn fields as they do them? Shall we wait for that moment or shall we die fighting before submitting to such ignominy?

. . . Shall we give up our homes, our country, bequeathed to us by the Great Spirit, the graves of our dead, and everything that is dear and sacred to us, without a struggle? I know you will cry with me: Never! Never! Then let us by unity of action destroy them all, which we now can do, or drive them back whence they came. War or extermination is now our only choice. Which do you choose? I know your answer. Therefore, I now call on you, brave Choctaws and Chickasaws, to assist in the just cause of liberating our race from the grasp of our faithless invaders and heartless oppressors. The white usurpation in our common country must be stopped, or we, its rightful owners, be forever destroyed and wiped out as a race of people. I am now at the head of many warriors backed by the strong arm of English soldiers. Choctaws and Chickasaws, you have too long borne with grievous usurpation inflicted by the arrogant Americans. Be no longer their dupes. If there be one here tonight who believes that his rights will not sooner or later be taken from him by the avaricious

American pale faces, his ignorance ought to excite pity, for he knows little of the character of our common foe.

QUESTIONS TO CONSIDER

1. How would you compare the visions of the Northwest Territory held by Tecumseh and William Henry Harrison?

2. Harrison and Tecumseh met many times to negotiate. They ultimately failed to reach a compromise. Was there any way their competing visions for the territory could have been reconciled and allowed to coexist? Why or why not?

3. What does the conflict between Harrison and Tecumseh show you about the westward expansion of the United States in the early nineteenth century? Were individual personalities, government policy, or conflicting values most important in explaining the conflict between these two men?

4. If Tecumseh had survived and the Indians had won at the Thames or Tippecanoe, do you think his vision for the future would have become reality? Why or why not?

FOR FURTHER READING

Gregory Evans Dowd, *A Spirited Resistance: The North American Indian Struggle for Unity* (Baltimore: Johns Hopkins University Press, 1992), offers an intriguing study that concentrates on Tenskwatawa, the Prophet.

James A. Green, *William Henry Harrison: His Life and Times* (Richmond, Va.: Garrett and Massie, 1941), is a reliable, if dated, biography of Harrison.

Francis Paul Prucha, *American Indian Policy in the Formative Years: The Indian Trade and Intercourse Acts, 1780–1834* (Cambridge: Harvard University Press, 1970), provides an overview of early American Indian policy.

John Sugden, *Tecumseh: A Life* (New York: Henry Holt and Company, 1997), is the most reliable biography of the Shawnee leader.

CHAPTER
8

Gradualism, Colonization, and Militant Abolitionism: Benjamin Lundy and David Walker

Benjamin Lundy

Frontispiece from
David Walker's Appeal

Rumors flew as word of David Walker's death spread across the northern states in 1830. Some observers claimed that the black abolitionist leader had been lynched. Others believed that he had been poisoned. Southern slaveholders, they said, had struck back at the man who had launched a bold challenge to their "peculiar institution." To slavery's opponents, rumors of Walker's violent death were not that far-fetched. After all, his intemperate attacks on slavery had been met with alarm in the South. Moreover, many people in the North believed that southern slaveholders were bent on spreading slavery everywhere. These northerners could easily believe that slaveholders wanted to strike at the very heart of the small but growing northern abolitionist movement—and that Walker would have been a prime target.

Abolitionists could not be faulted for wondering whether Walker's ideas had cost him his life. Nor could they be blamed for concluding that the ideas of moderates such as Benjamin Lundy were more feasible—and more prudent. Walker had challenged slavery in a direct manner. He not only had decried the evils of slavery but also had suggested that slaves needed to rise up in bloody revolt against it. Lundy hated slavery every bit as much as Walker. He had even been threatened and attacked by slavery's defenders. Compared to Walker, though, he approached the fight with a practical mind. He wanted slavery to end, but he was willing to admit that achieving that goal would be neither quick nor easy. The key was to find a peaceful and smooth transition from slavery to freedom that whites in the South *and* North could accept.

Like most movements, abolitionism was divided over the best means to achieve its goal. Some opponents of slavery sought to achieve freedom for slaves little by little and were willing to compromise. Others would accept no halfhearted measures, delays, or compromises. Walker and Lundy agitated against slavery in the years before abolitionism became a powerful force in northern society. Yet in the history of American abolitionism, few individuals better illustrate the outlooks and temperaments of moderate and radical opponents of slavery. None worked harder for practical, moderate solutions than Benjamin Lundy. Few were more uncompromising or impatient than David Walker.

"Every Inch of Him Is Alive with Power"

Benjamin Lundy was born into a Quaker farming family in New Jersey in 1789. The Lundys had been Quakers for generations, and Benjamin's religious upbringing had an important influence on his life and career. The Quakers were a Protestant Christian demonination founded in England in the mid-1600s. They were pacifists who sought to dedicate their lives to God and find the Inner Light of holiness that God had instilled in the human soul. Embracing the doctrine of the equality of all believers, the Quakers were among the most radical churches in the nineteenth century. They called for religious liberty, toleration, and equality for women and nonwhites in the spiritual and secular realms. Some Quakers were among the first to oppose slavery in England and the United States. Thus it was no accident that Lundy came to be an antislavery activist.

Raised on the family farm, Lundy had little formal education. When he was nineteen, he went to Wheeling, Virginia (now West Virginia), to work as an apprentice in a saddler's shop. There he learned the craft of leatherworking, a trade he would return to throughout his life. Although he had strayed from the Quaker faith during a period of youthful rebellion, he returned to the fold in young adulthood. He gave up frivolous behavior, wore plain clothing, refused to indulge in worldly amusements, read only those books that provided instruction, and concentrated on learning his craft. While working in Wheeling, he saw slavery for the first time. The sight of chained and handcuffed slaves sickened him and offended his Quaker principles. The violence and cruelty he witnessed against slaves repulsed him. It also spurred him to vow that he "would break at least one link of that ponderous chain of oppression." While in his early twenties, he moved to Ohio and hired himself out as a journeyman saddler. Shortly after he married, Lundy and his wife moved to St. Clairsville, in southeastern Ohio. There he opened a saddle and harness shop and built a prosperous business.

Lundy could not forget about slavery, though. As he sat working at his bench, stitching harnesses and reins and making saddles, his mind turned again and again to the evil and injustice he had seen. Soon his thoughts became actions. In 1816, he helped found the Union Humane Society, based in nearby Mount Pleasant, Ohio. The society's members pledged to work for gradual abolition. They vowed, for instance, to vote only for politicians who opposed slavery and to help free blacks in the North. Few white northerners, however, viewed blacks as equal, and few relished the prospect of competing with free blacks for jobs and land. Thus, although the Union Humane Society grew quickly at first, Lundy and his friends found little interest in their cause. With resources to help only a few people, the organization began to decline within months.

Undeterred by the failure of the Union Humane Society, Lundy sought other ways to energize what now seemed to him to be a dying abolitionist movement. In the late eighteenth century, abolitionism had been a much more powerful force in the United States, thanks in part to the American Revolution. Underlying the Revolution, of course, were the concepts of natural rights and equality. In a society characterized by hierarchy and inequality, these were potentially explosive ideas. Many Americans, especially blacks, understood their implications for slavery and racial inequality. So did many whites. Thus it was no accident that the northern states began to pass laws doing away with slavery in the years after the Revolution. Nor was it an accident that thousands of slaves were freed in the South, due to the individual acts of emancipation by slaveholders. In fact, the period from the 1780s to the early 1820s came to be known as the Age of Manumission because so many slaves were emancipated or allowed to buy their freedom. True, most individual acts of emancipation occurred around Chesapeake Bay, where generations of tobacco cultivation had devastated the soil. Whereas John Taylor of Caroline and other plantation owners sought ways to rejuvenate the land, other planters began to plant less labor-intensive crops. (See Chapter 6.) As that happened, many planters began to view their slaves as a liability rather than an asset. Their revolutionary ideology may have given them pangs of conscience about slavery, but their pocketbooks no doubt made such feelings easier to act on.

Whatever their motives, southerners in Maryland and Virginia and Quakers in the North came together to champion abolition. These early opponents of slavery called for gradual, rather than immediate, abolition. The final end of slavery, they believed, might not be achieved for generations. More important, they believed that emancipation must be accompanied by the colonization of free blacks outside the country. For many Americans, this was an appealing solution to both slavery and the race "problem." It allayed their fears that emancipation would lead to interracial marriage and increased labor competition. That was especially true for many southerners who professed antislavery sentiments. Thomas Jefferson, for instance, did not believe that blacks were fit to become citizens and spent much time pondering various colonization schemes. He was not alone. In the early nineteenth century, Virginia and other southern states passed harsh laws against free blacks that made it difficult if not impossible for them to stay in the South. Colonization's popularity was also reflected in the founding of the American Colonization Society in 1817. Based in Washington, D.C., the organization brought together northerners and southerners interested in promoting the removal of freed slaves from American society. In the coming years, the American Colonization Society would provide funds for the transportation of several thousand free blacks to the west coast of Africa. It also came to symbolize early abolitionism. **[See Source 1.]**

The founding of the American Colonization Society was the high point of early abolitionism. In fact, the unity of northerners and southerners in opposition to slavery ended only a couple of years later. In 1819, Congress took up a bill to admit Missouri as a slave state. As southerners rushed to defend slavery's expansion and northerners to oppose it, Congress and the nation immediately divided along regional lines. Americans suddenly found themselves in the midst of a serious sectional crisis, eventually resolved by the Missouri Compromise of 1820. It admitted Missouri as a slave state and Maine as a free state and established 36°30' north latitude as the boundary between free and slave territory in the rest of the Louisiana Purchase. The controversy, however, had only engendered hatred and bitterness. Southerners were now less willing to consider an end to slavery and more likely to perceive a growing northern assault on the institution. Northerners perceived an increasing proslavery militance in the South.

In fact, many southerners did become more aggressive in defending slavery. The opening of fertile lands in the Deep South after the War of 1812 sparked a tremendous cotton boom—and an increased demand for slave labor. The South's fortunes were more and more tied to cotton—and the expansion of slavery. As the Missouri crisis demonstrated, many white southerners now considered limits on slavery's westward expansion a challenge to slavery itself. Unable to withstand these dramatic developments, a unified abolitionist movement fell apart. In the early 1820s, the Age of Manumission came to an end. The American Colonization Society continued on, but the southern flank, long the leadership of the movement, fell away.

Watching these developments from his workbench in southern Ohio, Benjamin Lundy was even more convinced that a moderate abolitionist course was wisest. Emancipation could not occur overnight without causing a backlash against whites in the South and North. No plan for ending slavery, he believed, could ignore deep white racism and widespread white fears about economic security. To be sure, he opposed the *extension* of slavery, and during the crisis in 1819, he had gone to Missouri to campaign for an antislavery state constitution. Later, he championed a free produce movement, which called for the boycott of all goods produced by slave labor. Most of all, though, he believed that whites, especially in the upper South, could be persuaded to move against slavery. When enough of them saw the light, states such as Kentucky and Tennessee might use political means to end slavery. Even with the abolitionist movement in retreat, the tide could be turned against slaveholders.

First, though, they had to be persuaded. The printed word, Lundy concluded, was the best way to begin this work. In 1821, he began publishing an antislavery newspaper, the *Genius of Universal Emancipation*, in Mount Pleasant. Lundy addressed his paper to nonslaveholding whites in the South. To be closer to his audience, he moved the paper to Greenville, Tennessee, the following year. There he preached that small farmers, or yeomen, made up "the bone and sinew, the strength and support of the nation." Unfortunately, he argued, slavery had contributed to the economic decline of the yeoman class. At the very least, this decline inhibited the economic progress of the South; at worst, it threatened the republic. Two years later, Lundy moved the *Genius* to Baltimore, then in 1830 he moved it again to nearby Washington, D.C.

Wherever it was published, the *Genius* was harsh and insulting to slaveholders, calling them "the most disgraceful whoremongers upon earth." These "remorseless 'SOUL SELLERS' with horsewhips and bludgeons in their hands" made "a *business* of raising bastards and selling them for money" and drove barefooted slaves through mud and snow. **[See Source 2.]** Many Southerners did not react kindly to such rhetoric. In 1827, for instance, one irate Maryland slave trader, upset by Lundy's attacks, assaulted him on a Baltimore street. The man beat Lundy so badly that he was confined to his room for a week. Although Lundy's attacker was found guilty, he was fined only one dollar. The judge declared that he "had never seen a case in which the provocation for a battery was greater."

Even after this assault, Lundy's attacks on slavery continued. By then, they had attracted the attention of William Lloyd Garrison, one of the many younger abolitionists who would come of age in the 1830s. Garrison's burning hatred of slavery was fueled by evangelical Protestant Christianity. Like thousands of Americans, Garrison had found religion during the Second Great Awakening. After his conversion, he took up abolition as a righteous crusade against evil. Filled with evangelical fervor, he was soon drawn to Lundy's highly charged attacks on slavery. When he met Lundy for the first time in 1828, Garrison found a small, slender, meek man who certainly did not fit Garrison's image of him. He quickly realized, however, that Lundy's appearance was deceiving. "Every inch of him," Garrison concluded, "is alive with power." In fact, Garrison was so convinced that Lundy would "yet free our land" that he joined him in Baltimore and became coeditor of the *Genius*. Garrison's first editorial declared that Lundy's paper was "the bravest and best attempt in the history of newspaper publication" and praised its publisher's heroism and "untiring benevolence." For his part, Lundy intended to groom Garrison as his protégé to carry the antislavery banner. Yet their cooperation would not last. Garrison adamantly opposed colonization and called for immediate emancipation. For all of his harsh rhetoric, Lundy was still a moderate and supported gradual emancipation.

Throughout his career, Lundy had been drawn to the idea of colonization. Although he was never a leader of the American Colonization Society and was repulsed by the racism that underlay it, he endorsed the organization's approach. Lundy believed that thousands of slaves would be freed when their masters were persuaded that they would be transported out of the United States. Colonization appealed to Lundy for yet another reason. He assumed that slavery would not end for at least a century. By that time, he calculated, three million blacks would live in the United States. With so many people in bondage, a slave rebellion was inevitable. Prudence alone dictated that the number of slaves be reduced.

Thus Lundy worked persistently for colonization. Unlike many members of the American Colonization Society, he did not think that Africa offered the most practical or principled location for colonization. He believed that Americans could have more control over colonization projects in the Western Hemisphere, where it would be easier to defend and pay for them. He was particularly interested in Canada and Haiti, and he would help start colonies for former slaves in both countries. Lundy could overlook colonization's racist implications because he believed that an important end would be served. As he said, colonization would "pave the way for the completion of that grand and benevolent work, the Abolition of slavery." **[See Source 3.]**

"Your Destruction Is at Hand"

David Walker may have shared Lundy's belief that abolition was "grand" work. Yet he could not have disagreed more with Lundy's benevolent brand of abolitionism. To Walker, abolition was no charitable act. It would occur when slaves seized freedom for themselves. If anything, it meant waging war.

Walker's view of abolition, like Lundy's, was a product of his background. Walker was born in 1796 in Wilmington, North Carolina. He was probably the son of a free black woman. His father may have been a slave. Like many other cities in the South, Wilmington had an African-American majority. Black laborers dominated a number of the area's crafts and industries: carpentry, shipping, and the production of naval supplies and rice. Unlike Walker, most of these workers were slaves, although many of them labored under the "hiring-out" system, in which they worked for an employer who paid them wages. Their masters received a significant portion of their earnings, but those hired out achieved relative autonomy, lived apart from their masters, and enjoyed some discretionary income. The slaves on the rice plantations often had their own garden plots in which they grew vegetables to supplement the rations provided by their masters, and they sometimes sold surplus produce to whites in the area. Because of their large numbers, blacks were able to sustain their own institutions. The most obvious example was the Methodist* church in Wilmington, which was composed largely of blacks. They made up a vast majority of the church's membership and played an important part in its governance.

In this setting, Walker could have seen considerable evidence of African Americans' talents and abilities. He was also no doubt aware of the efforts of Wilmington's whites to restrict them. White workers regularly petitioned for restrictions on black employment. City leaders also passed laws attempting to stop or regulate commerce between whites and blacks. Even slaves who managed to achieve some autonomy were subject to the lash and the temper of the master. Free blacks such as Walker lived in a tenuous world. On the very edge of slavery, they could never escape the fear of falling into bondage on the whim of hostile whites.

Perhaps to escape such conditions, Walker moved to Charleston, South Carolina, where he had more opportunities to better himself. Few cities in the South had a larger free black population. In Charleston, blacks had access to more jobs and professions. Greater numbers also made it possible for them to join together in social, religious, and benevolent societies. Although the details of

---

Methodist: A member of an evangelical Protestant church founded in the 1700s by Englishman John Wesley. Emphasizing the doctrine of free will (as opposed to predestination) and individual conversion in revival services, the Methodist Church became the country's largest denomination by the time of the Civil War.

Walker's life in Charleston are unknown, his later activities reveal that he must have already secured a basic education. He probably moved in the social circles created by free blacks, including the new African Methodist Episcopal Church, the first separate black denomination in the United States. The church was founded in 1816 in Philadelphia by Richard Allen, and Charleston's free blacks formed a branch of the church the following year. Walker would later acknowledge his admiration for Allen, and he also likely was aware of whites' resentment of the church and their efforts to suppress it.

More important, in Charleston Walker no doubt witnessed for the first time the power of slave resistance. In 1822, the Denmark Vesey conspiracy disrupted Charleston and the surrounding area. This conspiracy was led by a free black carpenter, Denmark Vesey. With the help of several members of the A.M.E. church, Vesey coordinated the efforts of blacks in the city with those on nearby rice plantations. He called for the rebels to set portions of the city on fire, seize weapons, and murder whites. The appeal of Vesey's Christian rhetoric was powerful. Their actions, he claimed, were moral and sanctioned by God. Soon dozens of people were involved, but as they prepared for the revolt, an informer revealed the plot. White authorities quickly arrested, tried, and executed the leaders. Walker was probably still living in Charleston at the time and certainly knew about the conspiracy. Thus it was no accident that he would later combine religion with slave resistance.

Sometime after the discovery of the Vesey conspiracy, Walker left Charleston, along with a number of other free blacks, including leaders in the A.M.E. church. By the mid-1820s, Walker had moved to Boston, where he found a free black community comprising some fifteen hundred residents—about one-third the size of Charleston's. In a relatively short time, Walker had become a leader in the community. Soon after his arrival, he opened a used-clothing store, one of the few businesses open to blacks at the time. In 1826, he married a local woman and joined the city's black Masonic lodge, a key institution among the city's African Americans. He was also a member of the Methodist church, and he joined the most exclusive group within Boston's African-American community: homeowners.

Living in a free state, free blacks like Walker could at least take comfort in knowing that they would not be forced into slavery. In other ways, though, it was no place of refuge, especially by the time Walker arrived in Boston. As elsewhere in the North, virulent racism had emerged in the 1820s. Most northern states had begun to pass laws designed to keep their small but growing free black populations in their place. As a result, most northern blacks lacked political rights, including the right to vote. They were barred from hotels and restaurants and excluded from public schools—or forced to attend poorly funded segregated ones. Ironically, this heightened racism emerged at a time of greater *political* equality. In the 1820s, for example, all white males enjoyed equal access to the ballot box. But at the same time, rapid urban, industrial, and commercial growth had created greater *social and economic* inequality. Expecting to "make it" in a growing commercial economy, many northern whites found their economic and social aspirations unfulfilled. As the number of free blacks grew, they had an obvious scapegoat. By debasing free blacks, they reaffirmed the idea that whites of all ranks were equal after all.

Boston was no exception to these trends. As one member of the city's black community put it in 1827, "We are an oppressed and degraded race." In fact, no blacks escaped what David Walker himself called "derision, violence, and oppression." As elsewhere in the North, blacks were segregated into separate institutions and neighborhoods and largely confined to menial jobs. They also faced vicious racial stereotyping and rising violence. On the streets of Boston, they were subjected to frequent taunts regarding their physical features and "inferior" intellectual abilities. One of Walker's associates noted, "Placards descriptive of the negroe's deformity, are everywhere displayed." Blacks who entered Boston Common were routinely harassed and even beaten by groups of white toughs. Even African-American celebrations, such as the one marking the end of American involvement in the Atlantic slave trade, were often disrupted by whites.

Although Walker and other free blacks managed to achieved some success in Boston, the racism they confronted only increased their alienation from the larger white society. Thus in 1827, Walker's Masonic lodge cut its ties with all white lodges. Walker himself helped organize meetings, rallies, and parades in the black community. In the mid-1820s, he joined with a number of other leaders in Boston's black community to form the Massachusetts General Colored Association, which promoted the interests of the state's blacks. In 1827, Walker became involved in the distribution of *Freedom's Journal,* the first national black newspaper and an outgrowth of growing anticolonization sentiment among free blacks. Colonization had provided a powerful incentive for the rise of black abolitionism, and free blacks in the North had reacted swiftly to the formation of the American Colonization Society. **[See Source 4.]** Like blacks elsewhere in the North, Walker and others in Boston could not help feeling that they were under assault not only by white thugs but also by white abolitionists. It was no accident, then, that the meeting to consider "giving aid and support" to *Freedom's Journal* was held at Walker's home.

Walker's commitment to fight black oppression led him to an extraordinary action. In 1829, he published a pamphlet titled *Appeal to the Coloured Citizens of the World.* No other published work had attacked slavery in such vivid terms or with greater fervency. The institution, Walker charged, was savage and un-Christian. It robbed blacks of their history and culture. It deprived them of education, religion, and civil liberty. "We, (coloured people of these United States of America)," he declared, "are the *most wretched, degraded* and *abject* set of beings that *ever lived* since the world began. . . ."

The *Appeal* was intended as more than a diatribe against slavery. Rather, Walker hoped that it would be a trumpet call for blacks themselves. Its message would lift them up and encourage them to begin resisting slavery. The failure to resist was a sin, for God would no longer tolerate apathy on the part of slaves. Not just freedom but eternity was at stake. "[Y]our full glory and happiness . . . under Heaven, shall never be fully consummated," Walker told them, "but with *the entire emancipation of your enslaved brethren all over the world."* Although his *Appeal* was written for blacks, he also condemned white Americans for their sins. Indeed, the nation as a whole was damned by the evil of slavery. "O Americans! Americans!" he wrote, "I call God—I call angels—I call men, to witness, that your DESTRUCTION *is at hand,* and will be speedily consummated unless you REPENT." Walker went further. He was not opposed to joining whites in the fight for racial justice and even sent white abolitionists such as Benjamin Lundy a copy of the *Appeal*. Yet Walker believed that blacks themselves had to end slavery. He knew that there had never been a successful slave rebellion in the United States, but it was clear that the *Appeal* was calling for one. [**See Source 5.**]

Walker failed to lay out a precise plan of action in the *Appeal*. He did, however, have a very clear plan of action to spread his message in the South. To incite a revolution to throw off slavery, he enlisted the help of black and white sailors to distribute his *Appeal* in southern port cities. He also sent copies of it by mail to black church and business leaders, hoping they would help him reach the masses of slaves in their areas. White southerners, however, were appalled and frightened. By late 1830, they had virtually halted the circulation of the *Appeal* in the South. By that time, of course, Walker was dead—the victim of a respiratory disease that also struck other members of his family. Contrary to rumor, he had not been murdered. Depending on one's sympathies, however, his death could not have been more timely—or untimely.

"To No Man Is the Country So Deeply Indebted"

Benjamin Lundy's sympathies were decidedly against Walker and his *Appeal*. "I can do no less than set the broadest seal of reprobation upon it," Lundy wrote. "It is a laboured attempt to rouse the worst passions of human nature, and inflame the minds of those to whom it is addressed." In fact, the next year Lundy's worst fears seemed to be confirmed. In late August 1831, a slave named Nat Turner started an uprising in Southampton County, Virginia, which resulted in the largest slave revolt in American history. Starting in the early-morning hours of August 21, Turner and some seventy followers killed at least fifty-five whites in a matter of thirty-six hours. Like the Vesey conspiracy many years before and Walker's recent call for rebellion, the Turner revolt had a religious foundation. Turner, a Baptist preacher, had used the Bible to justify his plan.

Many people were convinced that Walker's *Appeal* had helped incite this bloodbath. Lundy was quick to add his voice to the chorus. He even declared that Turner "had probably seen" the *Appeal*. It also was "probable," Lundy added, that the revolt was "instigated chiefly" by it. In fact, Lundy probably had his own motive for pointing his finger at Walker. After the Turner revolt, many white southerners were pointing their fingers at him and his fellow abolitionist William Lloyd Garrison. The same year as the Turner revolt, Garrison had started his own abolitionist newspaper, the *Liberator*, based in Boston. The paper denounced colonization and gradual emancipation, but it saved its harshest rhetoric for southern slaveholders. They were, Garrison charged, vile sinners who had to give up slavery immediately to save themselves. Now many white southerners were convinced that the *Genius* and the *Liberator* were responsible for inciting Turner and his followers. To salvage any influence he had left in the South, Lundy quickly pointed to Walker as the real culprit.

Modern historians have found no evidence to back up Lundy's charges. The damage, however, had been done. The Turner rebellion and the rise of a new, militant abolitionism symbolized by the *Liberator* set off a reaction across the South. Fearful slaveholders called for action, and state legislatures began to pass new laws and strengthen old ones to prevent slave literacy, stop abolition-ist propaganda in the mail, curb the free assembly of blacks, and head off possi-ble slave rebellions. Separate black churches were forced to go underground to survive, as slaves were now required to attend churches dominated by their masters. White southerners also took steps to muzzle public dissent on slavery in the South. In fact, the last serious public debate about ending slavery oc-curred in the Virginia legislature in 1831. After that, white southerners rarely discussed the desirability of abolition in a public forum.

As the white South closed ranks and dug in its heels, Lundy continued his assault on slavery. Yet the middle ground quickly dropped out from under him. By the early 1830s, reformers fired by the evangelical zeal of the Second Great Awakening began to espouse numerous reform causes promoting social im-provement and moral uplift. Suddenly, the abolitionist movement in the North was rejuvenated. Led by Garrison, Theodore Dwight Weld, Wendell Phillips, Harriet Jacobs, Frederick Douglass, and others, it would enlist thousands of whites and blacks in numerous organizations. Symbolized by the formation of the American Anti-Slavery Society in 1833, this new movement rejected gradual emancipation and denounced colonization.

Throughout the 1830s, Lundy denied that "modern abolitionism," as con-temporaries called the new movement, differed in any significant way from the movement of the 1820s. "They have taken no new ground, " he said in 1835. "They have denounced the system of slavery in no stronger terms than many others have done before them." In a way, he was correct, for there were conti-nuities between the movements in the 1820s and 1830s. Lundy himself could take credit for keeping the antislavery cause alive in the difficult years after the Missouri controversy. If nothing else, he had served as a mentor to Garrison, the most influential of the new abolitionists. Indeed, Garrison would declare that "to no man is the country so deeply indebted for the mighty impulse it has received on the subject of abolition." Moreover, none of the new abolitionists would de-nounce slavery more vociferously than Lundy. Like Lundy and others in the 1820s, the new abolitionists flooded the mail with abolitionist literature, took to the lecture circuit to decry the evils of slavery, published newspapers, and wrote emotional books presenting slavery's evils in personal terms. Like earlier aboli-tionists, they also faced threats to their own safety. And although their numbers grew in the 1830s, they remained a minority in the North. Most northerners, even those increasingly concerned about the impact of slavery's spread on their future, were opposed to emancipation right up to the start of the Civil War.

Yet the abolitionist movement had changed by the early 1830s. Garrison and other proponents of immediate emancipation now dominated the cause. Although the American Colonization Society continued its work, it had little ef-fect. For a time, Lundy continued his work, too. In 1836, three years before his death, he wrote a pamphlet titled *The War in Texas*. In it, he argued that the war for independence fought that year by Sam Houston and other Texans against Mexico was part of a southern conspiracy to extend and protect slavery. Even though later historians would dismiss Lundy's theory, abolitionists accepted it as truth. *The War in Texas* thus played an important role in spreading the in-creasingly popular northern belief that they faced a dangerous plot by southern planters to take over the government and spread slavery everywhere. Still, if the new abolitionists agreed with Lundy's analysis of the slavery problem, they rejected his solution. Garrison and the others were not about to negotiate with slaveholders or preserve their evil institution.

At the same time, most of the new abolitionists also rejected David Walker's violent solution to the slavery problem. Nonetheless, they shared his uncompromising stand against slavery itself. In fact, in the generation following Lundy's death, the nation would discover that there was no middle ground on slavery. Walker, of course, had contributed to the erosion of that ground. By feeding panic in the white South, he had reinforced slaveholders' uncompromising stand on slavery. The author of the *Appeal* had been correct: The only way to destroy slavery would be by shedding blood.

PRIMARY SOURCES

SOURCE 1: Elias B. Caldwell, *"A Call for Colonization"* (1816)

Elias B. Caldwell was one of the founders of the American Colonization Society. This is an excerpt from his address at the founding meeting of the organization in Washington, D.C., which took place in late 1816 and led to the formal establishment of the American Colonization Society in 1817. What is his rationale for colonization?

"The expediency of colonizing the free people of colour in the United States, may be considered in reference to its influence on our civil institutions, on the morals and habits of the people, and on the future happiness of the free people of colour. It has been a subject of unceasing regret and anxious solicitude among many of our best patriots and wisest statesmen, from the first establishment of our independence, that this class of people should remain a monument of reproach to those sacred principles of civil liberty which constitute the foundations of all our constitutions. We say in the Declaration of Independence, "that all men are created equal," and have certain "unalienable rights." Yet it is considered impossible, consistently with the safety of the State, and it is certainly impossible with the present feelings towards these people, that they can ever be placed upon this equality, or admitted to the enjoyment of these "[u]nalienable rights" while they remain mixed with us. Some persons may declaim and call it prejudice. No matter. Prejudice is as powerful a motive, and will as certainly exclude them as [would] the soundest reason. Others may say they are free enough. If this is a matter of opinion let them judge. . . . This state of society [slavery] unquestionably tends, in various ways, to injure the morals and destroy the habits of industry among our people. This will be acknowledged by every person who has paid any attention to the subject, and it seems to be so

SOURCE: Reprinted in Archibald Alexander, *A History of Colonization on the Western Coast of Africa* (New York: Negro Universities Press, 1969), pp. 82–83; originally published in 1846.

generally admitted that it would promote the happiness of the people, and the interest of the people, to provide a place where these people might be settled by themselves, that it is unnecessary to dwell on this branch of the subject.

SOURCE 2:   Benjamin Lundy, *"United States' Internal Slave Trade"*   (1823)

Starting in the early 1820s, Benjamin Lundy's Genius of Universal Emancipation *attacked slavery ferociously. What does this attack on the slave trade from an early edition of the* Genius *reveal about Lundy's tactics in the battle against slavery?*

UNITED STATES' INTERNAL SLAVE TRADE.

"Hail Columbia, Happy Land!"

"SHALL THY FAIR BANNERS O'ER OPPRESSION WAVE?"

TO THE AMERICAN PEOPLE.

The above is a faint picture of the *detestable traffic in human flesh*, carried on by citizens of this Republic in the open face of day, and in violation of the fundamental principles of our government, the maxims and precepts of Christianity, and the eternal rules of justice and equity. LOOK AT IT, *again and again;* and then say whether you will permit so disgraceful, so inhuman, and so wicked a practice to continue in our country, which has been emphatically termed THE HOME OF THE FREE.

SOURCE: *Genius of Universal Emancipation*, January 1823, p. 97.

SOURCE 3:   Benjamin Lundy, *"Proposal for the Abolition of Slavery"* (1823)

In his Genius of Universal Emancipation, *Lundy offered this detailed proposal for the abolition of slavery. What role does colonization play in it? What future does he envision in the United States for free blacks?*

For the purpose of effecting a gradual Abolition of Slavery in the Unite[d] States, I would propose—

First, That the General government totally prohibit it in the districts over which Congress possesses the exclusive controul to prevent its spreading over a greater extent of the country, and consequently increasing in magnitude: and for the purpose of guarding more effectually against its extension, let a positive injunction be issued against the admission of any new state into the Union, hereafter, without an express provision against slavery in its Constitution.

Secondly—to prevent smuggling slavery into the country from abroad, to put a stop to the domestic or internal "slave trade," and also to prevent the atrocious crime of kidnapping free negroes, &c. let the transportation of them from one state to another be prohibited under the severest penalties, in all cases except the actual removal of their owners for the purpose of settlement.

Thirdly—Let the free states all agree to receive free coloured persons upon the footing of aliens, without imposing any other restraints than white persons of that description are subject to.

Fourthly—Let all the blacks that may be willing to go to Hayti, or elsewhere, be sent out at the public expense, or rather the joint expense of the general and state governments, societies, &c. &c.

Proposition 1st. It may be laid down as an incontrovertible axiom, that a further extension of the system of slavery over the territory of the United States will inevitably tend to increase the magnitude of the evil, and augment the difficulties already existing in the promotion of the work of emancipation. . . .

Proposition 2nd. In those sections of the country where sugar and cotton cannot be raised to advantage, there would be but little inducement to employ the labor of slaves, provided, the breeding of them for the purpose of sale, should not be considered an object worthy of attention. It is notorious that in those districts of Maryland, Virginia, &c. &c. where the slaves are comparatively few in number, the country improves much more rapidly, and the people accumulate wealth with greater facility than where the labor is chiefly performed by slaves; and it is in those parts of the country where slave labor is the least profitable; that the abominable practice of kidnapping and purchasing of negroes for the purpose of carrying on the internal *slave trade*, is most generally known. This scandalous and outrageous business which has no paralel in the black catalogue of human crimes, save and except that of the foreign "slave trade," with its attendant barbarities, is so aggravating in its nature, so demoralizing in its tendency, and so cruel and unjust in its operations, that it is doubtful whether

SOURCE: *Genius of Universal Emancipation,* January 1823, pp. 97–98, 99, 100.

any government can long exist that is weak or wicked enough to tolerate it. The corruption of morals, and the declension of republican principles will invariably follow in its train. . . .

Proposition 3rd. In order to assist the southern people in carrying on the work of emancipation, let the free states open their doors for the reception of free coloured people upon the same terms that *foreigners* are admitted into the United States;—Or, otherwise, let a proper system of regulations relative to naturalization, pauperism, &c. be adopted expressly for the purpose of guaranteeing the rights and privileges which it may be expedient to grant them. Such limitations and restrictions as may comport with the welfare of all should be defined by law, and a due regard should be paid to the improvement of their minds, to qualify them for citizenship. This, indeed, is a prime object which should be kept constantly in view—without it, the hopes of the philanthropist can never be realized, neither will his labors be of any avail.

All such as choose to remove to the free States, should have the privilege of locomotion, be protected in person and property, and admitted to the enjoyment of all rights and immunities of citizens, except the elective franchise—As to the latter, justice would depend that they should have it as soon as expediency would permit; but it might be impolitic to grant it to them immediately, as some time must necessarily be allowed for them to acquire a knowledge of the art of exercising it properly. . . .

Proposition 4th. For the same reasons that it would be necessary to admit the free people of colour into the free States, it would also be politic to send as many as possible to the Republic of Hayti, and other places beyond the limits of the U. States.

Should Congress & the State Legislatures make a few liberal appropriations for this purpose, its beneficial effects would soon be visible: and should societies and wealthy individuals also set about the work in good earnest, thousands would soon be released from a state of degredation, and permitted to assume their wonted dignity.

A portion of the blacks might be *colonized* in some remote part of the territory of the U. States. These might be taken from the western part of Virginia and from Kentucky and Tennessee. Some might also be sent to Africa. If a colony should be established there *under proper regulations* they might furnish facilities to the powers of America and Europe in crippling the Slave Trade. But nothing of *very great importance* could be expected to result from this, for I repeat it as my decided opinion, that IT WILL BE UTTERLY IMPOSSIBLE TO PUT A STOP TO THE FOREIGN TRAFFIC IN SLAVES, WHILE A MARKET CONTINUES OPEN FOR THEM ON THE AMERICAN CONTINENT & ISLANDS.

SOURCE 4:   *A Black Response to Colonization*   (1817)

Shortly after the formation of the American Colonization Society, a meeting of free blacks in Philadelphia wrote a protest against the aim of the organization to remove freed slaves from American society. On what grounds do they argue against it?

Whereas our ancestors (not of choice) were the first successful cultivators of the wilds of America, we their descendants feel ourselves entitled to participate in the blessings of her luxuriant soil, which their blood and sweat manured; and that any measure or system of measures, having a tendency to banish us from her bosom, would not only be cruel, but in direct violation of those principles, which have been the boast of this republic.

Resolved, That we view with deep abhorrence the unmerited stigma attempted to be cast upon the reputation of the free people of color, by the promoters of this measure, "that they are a dangerous and useless part of the community," when in the state of disfranchisement in which they live, in the hour of danger they ceased to remember their wrongs, and rallied around the standard of their country.

Resolved, That we never will separate ourselves voluntarily from the slave population in this country; they are our brethren by the ties of consanguinity, of suffering, and of wrong; and we feel that there is more virtue in suffering privations with them, than fancied advantages for a season.

Resolved, That without arts, without science, without a proper knowledge of government, to cast into the savage wilds of Africa the free people of color, seems to us the circuitous route through which they must return to perpetual bondage.

Resolved, That having the strongest confidence in the justice of God, and philanthropy of the free states, we cheerfully submit our destinies to the guidance of Him who suffers not a sparrow to fall, without his special providence.

Resolved, That a committee of eleven persons be appointed to open a correspondence with the honorable Joseph Hopkinson, member of Congress from this city, and likewise to inform him of the sentiments of this meeting, when they in their judgment may deem it proper.

SOURCE: Reprinted in Herbert Aptheker, ed., *A Documentary History of the Negro People in the United States: From Colonial Times Through the Civil War* (Secaucus, N.J.: Citadel Press, 1973), pp. 71–72.

SOURCE 5:   David Walker, *Appeal to the Coloured Citizens of the World*   (1829)

David Walker's Appeal to the Coloured Citizens of the World *stands as one of the most important pieces of abolitionist literature. What does this excerpt reveal about Walker's approach to the problem of slavery? Why do you think his* Appeal *stirred so much controversy?*

[We], (coloured people of these United States of America) are the *most wretched, degraded* and *abject* set of beings that *ever lived* since the world began, and . . . the white Americans having reduced us to the wretched state of *slavery*, treat us in that condition more cruel (they being an enlightened and Christian people,) than any heathen nation did any people whom it had reduced to our condition. These affirmations are so well confirmed in the minds of all unprejudiced men, who have taken the trouble to read histories, that they need no elucidation from me. . . .

[T]hose enemies who have for hundreds of years, stolen our *rights*, and kept us ignorant of Him and His divine worship, he will remove. Millions of whom, are this day, so ignorant and avaricious, that they cannot conceive how God can have an attribute of justice, and show mercy to us because it pleased Him to make us black—which colour, Mr. Jefferson calls unfortunate!!!!!! As though we are not as thankful to our God, for having made us as it pleased himself, as they, (the whites,) are for having made them white. They think because they hold us in their infernal chains of slavery, that we wish to be white, or of their color— but they are dreadfully deceived—we wish to be just as it pleased our Creator to have made us, and no avaricious and unmerciful wretches, have any business to make slaves of, or hold us in slavery. How would they like for us to make slaves of, and hold them in cruel slavery, and murder them as they do us?—But [are] Mr. Jefferson's assertions true? viz. "that it is unfortunate for us that our Creator has been pleased to make us *black*." We will not take his say so, for the fact. The world will have an opportunity to see whether it is unfortunate for us, that our Creator *has made us*, darker than the *whites*. . . .

The man who would not fight under our Lord and Master Jesus Christ, in the glorious and heavenly cause of freedom and of God—to be delivered from the most wretched, abject and servile slavery, that ever a people was afflicted with since the foundation of the world, to the present day—ought to be kept with all of his children or family, in slavery, or in chains, to be butchered by his *cruel enemies*. . . .

—Here let me ask Mr. Jefferson, (but he is gone to answer at the bar of God, for the deeds done in his body while living,) I therefore ask the whole American people, had I not rather die, or be put to death, than to be a slave to any tyrant, who takes not only my own, but my wife and children's lives by the inches? . . .

Are WE MEN!!—I ask you, O my brethren! are we MEN? Did our Creator

SOURCE: Reprinted in Sean Wilentz, ed., *David Walker's Appeal to the Coloured Citizens of the World* (New York: Hill and Wang, 1995), pp. 7, 12, 14, 16, 69–70, 71–72, 75.

make us to be slaves to dust and ashes like ourselves? Are they not dying worms as well as we? Have they not to make their appearance before the tribunal of Heaven, to answer for the deeds done in the body, as well as we? Have we any other Master but Jesus Christ alone? Is he not their Master as well as ours?—What right then, have we to obey and call any other Master, but Himself? How we could be so *submissive* to a gang of men, whom we cannot tell whether they are *as good* as ourselves or not, I never could conceive. However, this is shut up with the Lord, and we cannot precisely tell—but I declare, we judge men by their works. . . .

Remember Americans, that we must and shall be free and enlightened as you are, will you wait until we shall, under God, obtain our liberty by the crushing arm of power? Will it not be dreadful for you? I speak Americans for your good. We must and shall be free I say, in spite of you. You may do your best to keep us in wretchedness and misery, to enrich you and your children; but God will deliver us from under you. And wo, wo, will be to you if we have to obtain our freedom by fighting. Throw away your fears and prejudices then, and enlighten us and treat us like men, and we will like you more than we do now hate you, and tell us now no more about colonization, for America is as much our country, as it is yours. Treat us like men, and there is no danger but we will all live in peace and happiness together. For we are not like you, hard hearted, unmerciful, and unforgiving. What a happy country this will be, if the whites will listen. . . .

If any are anxious to ascertain who I am, know the world, that I am one of the oppressed, degraded and wretched sons of Africa, rendered so by the avaricious and unmerciful, among the whites.—If any wish to plunge me into the wretched incapacity of a slave, or murder me for the truth, know ye, that I am in the hand of God, and at your disposal. I count my life not dear unto me, but I am ready to be offered at any moment. For what is the use of living, when in fact I am dead. But remember, Americans, that as miserable, wretched, degraded and abject as you have made us in preceding, and in this generation, to support you and your families, that some of you, (whites) on the continent of America, will yet curse the day that you ever were born. You want slaves, and want us for your slaves!!! My colour will yet, root some of you out of the very face of the earth!!!!!! . . .

See your Declaration Americans!!! Do you understand your own language? Hear your language, proclaimed to the world, July 4th, 1776 "We hold these truths to be self evident—that ALL MEN ARE CREATED EQUAL!! that they *are endowed by their Creator with certain unalienable rights; that among these are life, liberty,* and the pursuit of happiness!!"

QUESTIONS TO CONSIDER

1. How would you compare Benjamin Lundy's and David Walker's approaches to ending slavery? How do those approaches reflect the two men's backgrounds? What role did religion play in each?

2. What was colonization's appeal for many Americans? What were black abolitionists' views toward it? Why did Lundy think it was practical?

3. What impact did Lundy and Walker have? Who had the better plan for ending slavery? Whose plan was more realistic?

4. The division between abolitionists willing to compromise for small gains and those unwilling to compromise is characteristic of many movements. What modern movement or cause do you think best reflects such a division?

For Further Reading

Merton L. Dillon, *Benjamin Lundy and the Struggle for Negro Freedom* (Urbana: University of Illinois Press, 1966), is the standard biography of Lundy.

Peter P. Hinks, *To Awaken My Afflicted Brethren: David Walker and the Problem of Antebellum Slave Resistance* (University Park: University of Pennsylvania Press, 1997), is a recent and well-researched biography of Walker that explores his world and the extent of his influence.

Henry Mayer, *All on Fire: William Lloyd Garrison and the Abolition of Slavery* (New York: St. Martin's Press, 1998), is an excellent biography of the famous abolitionist, who was influenced by Lundy and Walker.

Benjamin Quarles, *Black Abolitionists* (New York: Oxford University Press, 1969), offers an overview of black abolitionism and deals briefly with Walker.

Sean Wilentz, ed., *David Walker's Appeal to the Coloured Citizens of the World* (New York: Hill and Wang, 1995), is a recent edition of the *Appeal* with an insightful introduction by the editor.

CHAPTER
9

Liberation and Control in Antebellum Culture: Fanny Wright and Catharine Beecher

Fanny Wright   *Catharine Beecher*

atharine Beecher had watched Fanny Wright's antics long enough. As she traveled the country, Wright attracted large audiences of men and women. After making shocking speeches on topics such as abolition and religion, she left many places in pandemonium. Worst of all, she launched an unseemly and dangerous challenge to proper roles for women. In the early 1830s, Wright advocated nothing less than complete equality between men and women. Beecher was appalled by such thinking. She believed that the position of women in society had to be elevated. Yet she also knew that women could have their greatest impact in their own feminine sphere, not in the masculine world of business and politics. In fact, Wright's physical appearance demonstrated what was wrong with her ideas. She dressed, spoke, and acted like a man. With her "brazen front and brawny arms," Beecher said in 1836, Wright attacked all that was dear and sacred.

Beecher and Wright were not alone in their desire to change the position of women in American society in the 1830s and 1840s. The early-nineteenth-century revival known as the Second Great Awakening aroused in many Americans an intense desire not only to save themselves but also to remake society. By the 1830s, reformers were busy promoting temperance, abolition, school reform, penal and asylum reform, and even utopian communities. Many of these reforms were intended to liberate Americans from old customs and institutions.

145

Often, though, reform could be a means of control. Disturbed by rapid economic and social changes, many reformers feared social disorder and sought new ways to restrain behavior. Perhaps nowhere were the rival impulses behind reform more evident than in the struggle over the position of women in American society. Denied equal rights and excluded from the world of business and the professions, women had little power within the household and no power outside it. In an age of increasing political equality for white men, the status of women posed a glaring contradiction to the ideology of natural rights and equality that underlay the American Revolution. Some reformers responded to this situation by arguing that women needed to be liberated from the home. Others argued that women needed to be elevated within their domestic sphere. Only then would they be able to do the work for which they were uniquely suited: guarding moral virtue. For these reformers, uplifting women and ensuring social order were one and the same.

Few early-nineteenth-century women better exemplified these competing ideas than Beecher and Wright. Beecher wanted to elevate the position of women in the private world. Because women were by their very nature more virtuous, their role was to instruct and uplift. Their greatest influence was in the feminine, household sphere, although they could do more outside the home to civilize the nation and protect its morals. By contrast, Wright believed that the ideals of the Declaration of Independence applied to women as well as men. Thus women's proper role was in the public sphere, right alongside men.

"The Subordinate Station"

Catharine Beecher was a member of one of the most illustrious families in the early American Republic. Her father, Lyman Beecher, was a clergyman who became one of the most famous ministers in the country. Her brothers Edward and Henry Ward followed their father into the ministry. Edward became an important theologian, and Henry Ward became a leading preacher in the second half of the century. Her abolitionist sister, Harriet Beecher Stowe, wrote *Uncle Tom's Cabin* (1852), an abolitionist novel that caused an outcry in both the North and the South prior to the Civil War.

Born in 1800 in East Hampton on the eastern tip of New York's Long Island, Catharine Beecher grew up in isolated but comfortable circumstances. Although her father sprang from humble beginnings, her mother was from a well-to-do and socially secure Connecticut family. After Catharine was born, her father's reputation as a revivalist preacher spread. By the time she was nine, he had moved to a pulpit in prosperous and socially conservative Litchfield, Connecticut, where he gained a powerful influence in the community by preaching the need for personal salvation and obedience to established authority. He was also a powerful force in Catharine's life. Lyman instilled in his daughter an abiding desire for moral leadership, and she would share his concerns about social order and morality throughout her life. Indeed, Lyman and Catharine Beecher were living examples of the link between evangelism, which demanded individual regeneration, and reform, which demanded moral regeneration of society.

At the same time, Catharine resisted Lyman's encouragement that she assume a traditionally dependent female role. The Beecher family's circumstances no doubt contributed to her growing sense of independence. When their mother died in 1816, Harriet took up the responsibility of raising her younger siblings. Her maternal role continued when Lyman remarried. Catharine did not like her father's second wife, nor did she approve of his third choice after his second wife died. These feelings may have made it easier for her to reject her father's urgent message of repentance and salvation. Young people in evangelical Christian families were expected to undergo a conversion experience, something Catharine would not—or could not—do. She further asserted her independence when her fiancé, a young Yale College professor, died in a shipwreck in 1822. After her fiancé's death, Lyman increased his pressure on her to convert. "And now, my dear child," he asked her, "what will you do? Will you turn at length to God, and set your affections on things above, or cling to the shipwrecked hopes of earthly good?" Such pleading did little good. Catharine did not have her conversion experience, nor did she ever marry. Freed from the obligations of marriage, she would concentrate instead on doing "earthly good."

For the rest of her life, most of Catharine Beecher's efforts were directed at helping women achieve their proper place in society and the family. Education, she believed, was the key to that. Since the eighteenth century, education for females beyond the primary grades was limited to daughters of well-off families who had the opportunity to attend private academies. There they received an "ornamental" education, designed to prepare them for their roles in the private, domestic sphere. The curriculum emphasized sewing, music, and art—subjects designed to provide young women with polish. The goal was to make them more acceptable companions for men, not to help them enter the masculine sphere of politics and business.

Beecher rejected education designed only to make women shining ornaments. She believed that girls should receive the same curriculum as boys: mathematics, science, history, literature, rhetoric, and logic. The year after her fiancé's death, she acted on her belief by founding the Hartford Female Seminary. Like a number of other female academies opened in the 1820s, Beecher's seminary went beyond the "ornamental" subjects and soon became one of the most rigorous girls' schools in the country. She did not reject the idea of separate spheres for men and women but instead sought to elevate women within their sphere. Like other advocates of female seminaries, Beecher argued that an "advanced" education would actually make women better housekeepers and mothers. Thus, at the Hartford Female Seminary, domestic economy replaced "ornamental" subjects as the chief course of study. As Beecher noted in 1827, "A lady should study, not to *shine*, but to *act*." Educated women, she insisted, could exert a powerful influence "upon the general interest of society."

The belief that women could have an impact on society even in the domestic sphere was not new. In the decades after the American Revolution, many Americans saw a connection between women's activities at home and the "general interests of society." The Republic, they argued, rested on the character of the citizenry. Child rearing took on new importance, as virtuous republican mothers were necessary to raise good republican citizens. Beecher's views about society's "general interests," however, revealed more than eighteenth-century concerns. They also reflected broad economic and social changes during the early nineteenth century. These changes dramatically affected middle-class families, especially in the North. They also helped transform many Americans' views about women

By the 1820s, what historians now call a market revolution* drew more and more Americans into a commercial capitalist economy characterized by cash transactions, occupational specialization, and economic fluctuations. As commercial capitalism spread, trade and manufacturing expanded, cities grew, and more work was performed outside the home. More and more families ceased to be productive units. While women remained within the home, husbands more often left it to "make a living." As production was removed from the home, the household became a social rather than an economic unit. Women in urban, middle-class families now had more time to devote to child rearing and house-keeping. As the functions of husbands and wives began to be differentiated in a conscious way as never before, domestic life became an exclusively feminine domain. New publications directed at middle-class female readers reinforced this view. Publications such as *Godey's Lady's Book* and *Ladies Magazine* held up the home as a feminine retreat isolated from the harsh outside world of politics and business.

Embedded in this view was the assumption that the masculine and feminine spheres reflected distinctive character traits. Men were naturally individualistic, competitive, and materialistic. Women were passive, affectionate, and pure. They were expected to exhibit distinctly "feminine" traits, such as submission, piety, self-sacrifice, and humility, which would naturally counteract the "masculine" traits so important for success in the emerging market economy. Related to female piety was the idea of purity. Because women were morally superior to men, naturally they were less physical. Unlike men, women lacked lust. Indeed, their very lack of passion gave them influence over their weaker-willed male counterparts. Because these "feminine" traits were also Christian virtues, ministers such as Lyman Beecher played an important role in fostering the idea of female moral superiority. For the same reason, religion was one of the few activities outside the home that women could safely engage in without leaving their sphere.

By the 1820s, Catharine Beecher and some other women began to argue that women's "natural" traits made them better qualified than men for another activity: teaching. In fact, Beecher's seminary was designed to prepare women to become teachers. To that end, its curriculum also emphasized instruction in "moral philosophy"—in a course taught by Beecher herself. Here was a career for women outside the home, but one related to the feminine sphere. Schools,

---

Market revolution: An economic transformation revolving around the dominance of a free market—that is, the production and sale of goods for profit. In the early nineteenth century, it was associated with the increasing use of cash, rather than barter, and the growing importance of impersonal rather than face-to-face transactions.

like families, were incubators of character. And women far more than men were suited to the task of character formation, whether in the family or the school. Harriet Beecher Stowe, who taught at her sister's seminary, put it well: Men did not have the "patience, the long-suffering, and gentleness necessary to superintend the formation of character."

In one way, Beecher's timing was perfect. During the 1820s, public schools expanded across the nation, especially in the North. At the same time, men, who had traditionally dominated the teaching profession, began to find new opportunities in factories and offices. As school boards discovered by the 1830s, many women were eager to serve in these low-paying positions. Better yet, they were willing to serve at half the salaries received by male teachers. Starting in New England in the 1830s, female teachers began to make significant inroads in the profession, and by 1860 one-quarter of the nation's teachers were female.

Despite these long-term changes, after operating for eight years, the Hartford Female Seminary failed in 1831 for lack of funds. The school was dependent on financial assistance from the community, which was not ready to embrace Beecher's curriculum or the idea of women working outside the home—even in a role related to natural feminine traits. As the editor of the *Connecticut Courant* said, "I had rather my daughters would go to school and sit down and do nothing, than to study Philosophy, etc. These branches fill young Misses with *vanity* to a degree that they are above attending to the more useful parts of an education."

Beecher was not about to give up, though. Instead, she decided to accompany her father when he moved to Cincinnati in 1832. Lyman Beecher had accepted the position of president of the Lane Theological Seminary, where he would direct the education of ministerial students, many of whom would go on to serve in the reform movements of the coming decades. For Catharine Beecher, the move west represented an opportunity not only to start over but also to apply her ideas on an even grander scale. In the years after the War of 1812, a flood of settlers had moved into the Old Northwest. Many of them had come from New England. Others, however, were European immigrants, especially Germans, or southerners who had moved north across the Ohio River. Like many New England Protestants, Beecher was convinced that these non-Yankee westerners were in urgent need of civilization and uplift. For one thing, the area lacked churches and schools. Even worse, too many of the newcomers were "uncivilized." Many of them were Roman Catholics, who many Protestants feared did not share their own middle-class values of self-restraint and sobriety. As Beecher put it, "Thousands and thousands of degraded foreigners, and their ignorant families, are pouring into this nation at every avenue." These growing hordes of uneducated, unrestrained, lower-class people represented a crisis for American democracy. The West, she believed, was a battleground between morality and degeneration. Here, she declared, "it shall be decided whether disenthralled intellect and liberty shall voluntarily submit to the laws of virtue and of Heaven, or run wild to insubordination, anarchy and crime."

The remedy was clear. Beecher estimated that one-third of the children in the West were without schools. Ninety thousand teachers, she believed, were needed immediately in the name of civilization and democracy. And male teachers alone could not address the problem. In short, the nation needed a corps of female teachers "who have the highest estimate of the value of moral and religious influence." To fill that need, Beecher started another female seminary in 1832. Located in Cincinnati, it was called the Western Female Institute. The school would teach Protestant, middle-class values and, she hoped, serve as a model for the nation. It also would give women an opportunity to be an "all-pervading" influence in American society.

Beecher traveled from Cincinnati to New England to champion her new seminary. Yet she was careful not to challenge traditional ideas about women's roles. In lectures and essays, she always insisted that female teachers would uphold rather than challenge traditional relations between the sexes. "Heaven has appointed to one sex the superior, and to the other the subordinate station," she declared. In fact, women's method of gaining influence and exercising power had nothing to do with their similarity to men. "Let every woman become so cultivated and refined in intellect, that her taste and judgment will be respected; so benevolent in feeling and action, that her motives will be reverenced," Beecher declared in 1837. Then, she concluded, "the fathers, the husbands, and the sons, will find an influence thrown around them, to which they will yield not only willingly but proudly." [See Source 1.]

It was a prudent argument. Beecher knew that her first seminary had failed because of the widespread fears that it undermined traditional roles. She also knew that upholding such roles was more important than ever because of a danger from another quarter. About the same time that Beecher began her plans for a female assault on ignorance and immorality, Fanny Wright appeared on the scene. An infamous woman who had already become a symbol of female deviance, Wright threatened to undermine all of Beecher's work.

"Sentenced to Mental Imbecility"

In 1836, a steamboat churned its way up the Ohio River toward Cincinnati. On board was Fanny Wright. Wright was already well-known in the "Queen City of the West" and elsewhere. During the 1830s, her name had become synonymous with numerous causes, from abolition and communal living to women's rights. In fact, her enemies attached her name to causes they wished to ridicule. They called various reforms "Fanny Wrightism" and their supporters "Fanny Wrightists." They believed that Wright was a symbol of female deviance, and they knew that such labels would discredit those who sought changes in American society.

Born in 1795 in Dundee, Scotland, Frances Wright learned independence at an early age. Her father was a linen merchant and offered his family a comfortable life. But "Fanny" was orphaned when she was not yet three, and she and her siblings were sent to live with various relatives. Fanny and one of her sisters were reunited under the roof of an aunt and maternal grandfather, but soon after, her grandfather and one of her brothers died. These early tragedies may have given Fanny the ability to empathize with the plight of others.

Although Fanny's grandfather had told her that the beggars living on the streets of London were too lazy to work, she soon learned differently. After moving in with an aunt who lived in a twenty-room mansion above the English Channel, Fanny watched the proprietors of large estates forcibly turn the peasants off the land so that the landowners could raise sheep. Fanny lived in a world of servants, governesses, and tutors, but she knew that social injustice was the cause of much human suffering. Even as a child, she disdained the idleness of the English gentry, later writing, "How little was to be learned in drawing-rooms." Inspired by a "disgust of frivolous reading, conversation, and occupation," Wright developed a seriousness and sense of purpose. She committed herself to righting "the grievous wrongs which seemed to prevail in society."

In 1813, Fanny and her sister went to live with their uncle James Mylne, a professor at the University of Glasgow. Mylne was an admirer of the American Revolution and especially Thomas Paine. An English immigrant to the colonies, Paine had helped spark the Revolution with the publication in early 1776 of *Common Sense,* a republican propaganda pamphlet attacking the very idea of monarchy. Fanny's uncle also possessed a hatred of the slave trade and slavery itself. He espoused a utilitarian philosophy, which valued those things leading to the greatest good for the greatest number of people. He also encouraged Fanny's growing interest in the United States, checking books on America out of the university library for her.

In 1815, Parliament passed a new corn law, which placed a high tax on imported grain. By making bread more expensive, this measure devastated the poor. Fanny began to invest her hopes for a better society in America. In contrast to Britain, it seemed to provide a much greater good for a greater number of people. Soon she was ready to see for herself whether life there was as good as it seemed. In 1818, when she was twenty-two, she set sail for New York.

Wright immediately fell in love with the United States. Like many European visitors, she was impressed with the country's seeming lack of class distinctions. Further, she was pleased by the American reception of a play she had written in Scotland. It revolved around the Swiss struggle for independence from Austrian tyranny, and crowds in New York and Philadelphia flocked to see it. As she traveled around the country, she kept a journal and wrote letters to a Scottish friend. The letters provided the basis for a memoir titled *Views of Society and Manners in America,* published in England in 1823. In it, Wright recognized the evil of slavery and criticized the condition of American women, declaring that they needed to be "invigorated" in body and mind. Nonetheless, the book offered an idealized and romantic view of the country. "What other country before," she asked, "was ever rid of so many evils?"

Wright's book caught the attention of reformers in Europe. It also won her many friends, including the marquis de Lafayette, the French commander who had provided Americans with invaluable assistance during the Revolution. Lafayette, who had become a symbol of liberty and equality in France, was smitten with Wright, and their relationship scandalized high society. When Lafayette toured the United States in 1824, Wright was part of his entourage, and rumors that they were lovers spread quickly. He alternately called her "my daughter" and "my adored Fanny." Eventually, she told him that he should either marry her or adopt her. He did neither. When he returned to France in 1825, she stayed in America.

By that time, Wright was immersed in the work of perfecting her adopted land. In 1825, she visited New Harmony, Indiana, where the British cotton mill owner and social reformer Robert Owen had purchased several thousand acres of farmland to build a utopian community. There cooperation and communal property would replace competition and private property. Wright was overwhelmed by the community's equality and idealism. Inspired to perfect the land that was already "rid of so many evils," she decided to apply Owen's methods to rid it of yet another—slavery. In 1826, she bought 640 acres in Tennessee and with the help of several other reformers founded the Owenite "plantation" of Nashoba. Then she bought several slaves and began educating them. Slavery, she argued, was not profitable. Thus she offered the slaves their freedom and parcels of land in exchange for five years of labor on her plantation. This would increase production, allow her to make a profit from their emancipation, and prove that slaves would work for freedom if given an incentive.

Nashoba caused a stir. Initially, it had widespread support, even from some southern slaveholders such as Thomas Jefferson and James Monroe. Soon, though, the community was the subject of scandal. In 1827, Benjamin Lundy's antislavery newspaper, the *Genius of Universal Emancipation* (see Chapter 8), published portions of a Nashoba trustee's journal. The journal described the practice of sexual relations between unmarried partners. Even worse, Wright herself admitted that interracial sexual relations had occurred at Nashoba and that she had even encouraged such behavior. Wright had simultaneously assaulted the ideal of female purity and raised the specter of racial mixing. Few Americans were ready for her argument that only through sexual relations between the races and the birth of interracial children could racism be erased. Already suffering from poor harvests and mounting debt, Nashoba could not withstand this controversy and fell into ruin.

With her radical antislavery experiment finished, Wright turned to publishing. She served as coeditor of the *New Harmony Gazette* with Robert Dale Owen, the son of New Harmony's founder. Thus she became one of the first women to edit a newspaper. She also became one of the first women to speak in public to a mixed audience of men and women, again shocking society. In 1829, Wright and Owen went on the lecture circuit, touring the country to debate numerous controversial subjects. Everywhere they traveled, they were accompanied by public outcries, offended mobs, and even riots. Wright vociferously attacked organized religion, decried capital punishment, and argued for racial equality. **[See Source 2.]** In several cities, mobs interrupted her lectures and violence closed down her meetings. She made even more enemies by calling for equality for the poor and rights for the lower classes. Wright believed that the increasing disparity between rich and poor threatened American democracy. To offset this threat, she called for public education, paid for by graduated property taxes.* Her interest in education reform led her to New York's Working Men's Party.

Graduated property taxes: Taxes structured so that those with more property pay at a higher rate than those with less.

Composed mostly of skilled workers, the Working Men's Party was advocating a ten-hour workday, public schools, and more equal property distribution. Opponents, however, quickly dubbed it the "Fanny Wright party."

Wright also became more adamant in her support for women's rights. Like Catharine Beecher, Wright believed that education was essential for women. But she went beyond Beecher's domestic ideal by calling for women to pursue whatever career they chose. They should be able to take an active part in politics and become full-fledged citizens. Jefferson's words "all men are created equal" in the Declaration of Independence, she insisted, applied to women, too. So, for that matter, did the "pursuit of happiness." Thus she even called for birth control to be used as a means of empowering women and their partners to enjoy sex.

Wright wanted America to live up to its egalitarian ideals. Britain had no such ideals, she believed, as was evidenced by the Corn Laws, which reinforced inequality and human misery. Wright called for laws that reflected America's professed commitment to equality. Under the current laws, women had few rights. Men had legal control of all property, and even land inherited by a woman from her father came under her husband's authority. Furthermore, the rights that women did have were restricted by social norms and male juries that were sympathetic to men. Wright called for full equality with men, including property rights, legal rights, economic rights, political rights, and sexual rights. Half of the population "is left in civil bondage," she declared, "and . . . sentenced to mental imbecility." [**See Source 3.**]

By 1829, Wright's radical opinions and defiance of social convention had made her infamous. The *Journal of Commerce* summed up the feelings of many observers when it declared that she posed "the singular spectacle of a female, publicly and ostentatiously proclaiming doctrines of atheistical fanaticism, and even the most abandoned lewdness." Many of Wright's enemies were no doubt pleased when she left for England the next year. If they had known that the unmarried Wright was pregnant, their worst fears about her would have been confirmed. Fanny carried the child of Phiquepal D'Arusmont, a French physician who had accompanied her to Haiti after the failure of the Nashoba community. Wright had kept her promise to the slaves she had purchased by securing their freedom and personally directing their move to the former French colony in the Caribbean. If that trip was a personal triumph, this one was a retreat. "I have done what I could to make myself forgotten," she wrote Lafayette. By the time she gave birth to a daughter and married D'Arusmont the next year, she had succeeded. Most Americans had already forgotten about Fanny Wright.

Wright lived a quiet life in Paris for five years, but in 1835 she was ready to return to the United States. She and her husband landed in New Orleans and immediately headed up the Mississippi and Ohio Rivers to Cincinnati. It was the first stop on a speaking tour similar to the one she had conducted with Robert Dale Owen in 1829. Six years earlier, she was met with riots and mob violence. This time it was different. In fact, on this tour, Wright changed her position on a number of issues, including slavery. Northerners, she declared, should not attack southerners until they had rid their region of its own forms of slavery. She even expressed support for Andrew Jackson's Democratic Party, which was hostile to abolitionists and reform in general. Wright's baffling reversal sprang in part from her acceptance of the Democrats' egalitarian rhetoric and perhaps from the animosity she still felt toward ministers and organized religion, especially revivalism. Wright believe that Protestant ministers such as Lyman Beecher upheld domestic ideals that subjugated women. She also knew that these evangelical ministers were Whigs* almost to a man.

Whatever the cause of Wright's condemnation of abolition, Catharine Beecher was horrified by her reappearance in Cincinnati. Beecher herself was a "moderate" on slavery. In favor of colonization, she readily denounced William Lloyd Garrison and other "radical" abolitionists. Moreover, she believed that female abolitionist activity represented a trespass into the masculine sphere of public issues. Yet Beecher still believed that Wright was dangerous. By snubbing convention, Wright gave conservatives powerful ammunition against any change in the status of women. Beecher saw this as a threat to her own cause for the elevation of women within the domestic sphere. "There she stands," Beecher wrote, "with brazen front and brawny arms, attacking the safeguards of all that is venerable and sacred in religion, all that is safe and wise in law, all that is pure and lovely in domestic virtue." [**See Source 4.**]

"Dignity of Domestic Knowledge"

Catharine Beecher had good reason to loathe Fanny Wright. Whether Beecher realized it or not, though, Wright's argument for full equality for women made Beecher's call for elevating women within the domestic sphere seem sensible and moderate in comparison. By defining the proper role for women in personal and moral terms, Beecher continued to acknowledge that there were some areas in which women should not to be involved, such as politics. Women, she insisted, should protect and extend morality. Entering the political world would only stain their virtue and prevent them from fulfilling their own unique duties. Unlike Wright, who wanted women to have power in the public sphere, Beecher wanted them to have influence. She was satisfied in knowing that behind every good citizen was a woman's domestic power. In contrast to the anarchy and riotous behavior sparked by Wright, Beecher held out the image of social harmony. This, in fact, was Beecher's primary appeal as she continued to drum up support for her Western Female Institute. She envisioned the school as the first in a national system of female seminaries designed to train teachers who would help create a "virtuous democracy." Like Lyman Beecher and other evangelical preachers, Catharine Beecher called for a moral crusade to battle national corruption and moral decline. Hers, however, would be led by women.

Beecher pinned her high hopes for women and the nation on her Cincinnati school. Her fundraising activities, however, fell short, and the school closed in 1837. Beecher continued to campaign for a corps of teachers to elevate western society, and she gradually emerged as the nation's leading authority on domestic life. In a stream of articles and books, she called for more power for women within the domestic arena and in related functions outside the home. Her views

---

Whigs: The political party organized in 1834 in opposition to Andrew Jackson's Democratic Party. The Whigs favored a strong government committed to the moral improvement of the nation. (See Chapter 14.)

were fully developed in her best-known work, *A Treatise on Domestic Economy*. First published in 1841 and reprinted annually well into the 1850s, the book was a phenomenal success. With it, Beecher joined a growing number of women writers who quietly entered the masculine world of the marketplace. Meanwhile, by elevating what Beecher called "the importance and dignity of domestic knowledge," *A Treatise on Domestic Economy* helped transform housekeeping into a profession comparable to any filled by men. **[See Source 5.]**

Beecher's argument echoed that made by the defenders of "republican womanhood" in the late eighteenth century. "The success of democratic institutions," she maintained, depended on the "intellectual and moral character of . . . the people." The formation of that character, she went on, "is committed mainly to the female hand." Proper education was essential if women were to have a positive impact on the men who entered the public sphere. As the guardians of moral virtue and the bearers of culture, women were responsible for instilling values and ethics in their children. This would be done by developing in each child a conscience, or internalized sense of right and wrong. Mothers and teachers should appeal to each child's heart with emotional reactions. They should teach valuable lessons with Bible reading and proper correction. In similar ways, women would have influence over men. Women could encourage their husbands to work and behave properly. They could give their husbands valuable advice and moral perspective. Thus, she advised, women should have more power over finances, work, and child rearing. Men should acknowledge the important role women played in domestic life. Marriage, in short, should be based not on male authority, but on mutual love and respect.

By evangelizing for the elevation of women through moral influence, Beecher became the leading advocate of the domestic ideal. Meanwhile, Wright grew despondent. By the late 1830s, she was discouraged by what she perceived as the public's lack of interest in equality, especially between men and women. Disillusioned with her adopted country, she concluded that Americans were not ready for her. Far from pushing them toward the realization of their ideals, her radicalism had turned them away. Like Beecher, they were disgusted and shocked by her words, ideas, and actions. One of her last lectures in the United States, delivered in an abandoned Philadelphia factory, was met with a hail of stones from bystanders. One newspaper reported, "Terror predominated both in the bosom of the lecturer and the lectured, the latter enduring the twofold pain of being assailed by Fanny within and the stones without."

In 1839, Wright left the United States again. Over the next decade, she traveled between Europe and America numerous times, although she struggled with debt and financial crisis. When she and D'Arusmont divorced in 1850, he fought her for control of their property, almost all of which had derived from her income. After a long and complicated battle in the Ohio courts, Wright was awarded her property—a major victory for the time. But her triumph was offset by her estrangement from her daughter, who sided with D'Arusmont in the divorce. Wright spent much of her time writing letters in hopes of regaining her daughter's affection, but the two never reconciled. Wright died in Cincinnati in 1852, discouraged and disillusioned by the failure of her work and the public humiliation caused by her family's betrayal.

Ironically, the idea of female quality was just then taking hold in America.

By the 1840s, a relatively small but vocal women's rights movement had emerged to push for the legal equality of women, including the right of women to own property, to sue in court, to own and operate businesses, to speak in public, and even to vote. Many of its participants, including Sarah and Angelina Grimké and Elizabeth Cady Stanton, were abolitionists who had been drawn into the public sphere by their reform efforts. Confronting discrimination at the hands of male reformers, many female abolitionists concluded that they could not free the slaves without first freeing themselves. In 1848, the Grimkés and Stanton joined other women's rights advocates and their male sympathizers at the Seneca Falls Convention in upstate New York. The convention called for equality for women in the Declaration of Sentiments, which parallels the language of the Declaration of Independence. By the 1850s, a growing women's rights movement succeeded in getting new laws passed in some states allowing, for example, married women to own property. Nonetheless, it did not seriously challenge the domestic ideal championed so effectively by Catharine Beecher. Indeed, women did not win the vote nationwide until the ratification of the Nineteenth Amendment in 1920. They would wait even longer for full legal equality.

Meanwhile, the woman most responsible for broadcasting the domestic ideal would never have a home of her own. As was usually the case with "respectable" unmarried women in the nineteenth century, Beecher lived with her siblings' families until her death in 1878. Yet she never stopped promoting the domestic ideal in her writings. She also went on to found several more schools for women, and she continued to oppose woman suffrage, which she believed would only undermine women's moral influence. Ironically, by continuing to participate in the public world of education and publishing, Beecher gave credence to the radical egalitarian ideas of Fanny Wright. Nonetheless, she could take satisfaction in knowing that her views had triumphed. **[See Source 6.]** By the middle of the nineteenth century, middle-class women had broader powers within the home. Thanks in part to Beecher's work, Americans' consciousness about women and families was transformed. Men now idealized families. They accepted the nurturing hand of the mother and the role of education and religious faith in the development of good citizens. They embraced the idea that mothers were responsible for imparting morality in the form of a conscience. They did not question that the task of raising good citizens was women's responsibility. In the end, Beecher's persistent claim to female moral virtue helped promote some of the most important changes affecting women in nineteenth-century America.

PRIMARY SOURCES

SOURCE 1:   *Catharine Beecher on Women's Proper Place*
            (1837)

In this essay from 1837, Catharine Beecher explains her views about women's "subordinate" place in society. How does she define and justify that position? How does she justify the call for female teachers?

It is Christianity that has given to woman her true place in society. And it is the peculiar trait of Christianity alone that can sustain her therein. "Peace on earth and good will to men" is the character of all the rights and privileges, the influence, and the power of woman. A man may act on society by the collision of intellect, in public debate; he may urge his measures by a sense of shame, by fear and by personal interest; he may coerce by the combination of public sentiment; he may drive by physical force, and he does not outstep the boundaries of his sphere. But all the power, and all the conquests that are lawful to woman, are those only which appeal to the kindly, generous, peaceful and benevolent principles.

Woman is to win every thing by peace and love; by making herself so much respected, esteemed and loved, that to yield to her opinions and to gratify her wishes, will be the free-will offering of the heart. But this is to be all accomplished in the domestic and social circle. There let every woman become so cultivated and refined in intellect, that her taste and judgment will be respected; so benevolent in feeling and action; that her motives will be reverenced;—so unassuming and unambitious, that collision and competition will be banished;—so "gentle and easy to be entreated," as that every heart will repose in her presence; then, the fathers, the husbands, and the sons, will find an influence thrown around them, to which they will yield not only willingly but proudly. A man is never ashamed to own such influences, but feels dignified and ennobled in acknowledging them. But the moment woman begins to feel the promptings of ambition, or the thirst for power, her ægis of defence is gone. All the sacred protection of religion, all the generous promptings of chivalry, all the poetry of romantic gallantry, depend upon woman's retaining her place as dependent and defenceless, and making no claims, and maintaining no right but what are the gifts of honour, rectitude and love. . . .

It is allowed by all reflecting minds, that the safety and happiness of this nation depends upon having the *children* educated, and not only intellectually, but morally and religiously. There are now nearly two millions of children and adults in this country who cannot read, and who have no schools of any kind. To give only a small supply of teachers to these destitute children, who are generally where the population is sparse, will demand *thirty thousand teachers*; and

SOURCE: Catharine Beecher, *An Essay on Slavery and Abolitionism, with Reference to the Duty of American Females* (Philadelphia: Henry Perkins, 1837), pp. 100–102, 105–108.

six thousand more will be needed every year, barely to meet the increase of juvenile population. But if we allow that we need not reach this point, in order to save ourselves from that destruction which awaits a people, when governed by an ignorant and unprincipled democracy; if we can weather the storms of democratic liberty with only one-third of our ignorant children properly educated, still we need *ten thousand* teachers at this moment, and an addition of *two thousand every year*. Where is this army of teachers to be found? Is it at all probable that the other sex will afford even a moderate portion of this supply? The field for enterprise and excitement in the political arena, in the arts, the sciences, the liberal professions, in agriculture, manufactures, and commerce, is opening with such temptations, as never yet bore upon the mind of any nation. Will men turn aside from these high and exciting objects to become the patient labourers in the school-room, and for only the small pittance that rewards such toil? No, they will not do it. Men will be educators in the college, in the high school, in some of the most honourable and lucrative common schools, but the *children*, the *little children* of this nation must, to a wide extent, be taught by females, or remain untaught. The drudgery of education, as it is now too generally regarded, in this country, will be given to the female hand. And as the value of education rises in the public mind, and the importance of a teacher's office is more highly estimated, women will more and more be furnished with those intellectual advantages which they need to fit them for such duties.

The result will be, that America will be distinguished above all other nations, for well-educated females, and for the influence they will exert on the general interests of society. But if females, as they approach the other sex, in intellectual elevation, begin to claim, or to exercise in any manner, the peculiar prerogatives of that sex, education will prove a doubtful and dangerous blessing. But this will never be the result. For the more intelligent a woman becomes, the more she can appreciate the wisdom of that ordinance that appointed her subordinate station, and the more her taste will conform to the graceful and dignified retirement and submission it involves.

Source 2: *Fanny Wright on Her Lectures in Cincinnati* (1829)

Fanny Wright's first trip to Cincinnati in 1829 set off a violent reaction. In this passage, Wright sets forth her view of the cause. What is it? What does this passage reveal about Wright? What does it reveal about the reasons many Americans found her objectionable?

The city of Cincinnati had stood for some time conspicuous for the enterprise and liberal spirit of her citizens, when, last summer, by the sudden combination of the clergy of three orthodox sects, a *revival*, as such scenes of distraction are

Source: Frances Wright, *Course of Popular Lectures* (New York: Office of the *Free Enquirer*, 1829), pp. 9–10.

wont to be styled, was opened in houses, churches, and even on the Ohio river. The victims of this odious experiment on human credulity and nervous weakness, were invariably women. Helpless age was made a public spectacle, innocent youth driven to raving insanity, mothers and daughters carried lifeless from the presence of the ghostly expounders of damnation; all ranks shared the contagion, until the despair of Calvin's* hell itself seemed to have fallen upon every heart, and discord to have taken possession of every mansion.

A circumstantial account of the distress and disturbance on the public mind in the Ohio metropolis led me to visit the afflicted city; and, since all were dumb, to take up the cause of insulted reason and outraged humanity.

The consequences of the course of lectures I then first delivered, on three successive Sundays, in the Cincinnati courthouse, and re-delivered in the theatre, were similar to those which have been witnessed elsewhere;—a kindling of wrath among the clergy, a reaction in favor of common sense on the part of their followers, an explosion of public sentiment in favor of liberty, liberality, and instructional reform, and a complete exposure of the nothingness of the press, which, at a time when the popular mind was engrossed by questions of the first magnitude, sullenly evaded their discussion, betraying alike ignorance the most gross, and servility the most shameless. All that I then observed, conspired to fix me in the determination of devoting my time and labour to the investigation and exposure of existing evils and abuses, and to the gradual developement of the first principles of all moral and physical truth, every where so perplexed and confounded by the sophistry of false learning, the craft of designing knavery, and the blunders of conceited ignorance.

SOURCE 3:   Fanny Wright, *Course of Popular Lectures*
(1829)

In lectures delivered on her speaking tour of the United States in 1829, Fanny Wright frequently addressed the question of women's place in American society. How does she describe the condition of women? How do her views of education compare to Catharine Beecher's?

It is with delight that I have distinguished, at each successive meeting, the increasing ranks of my own sex. Were the vital principle of human equality universally acknowledged, it would be to my fellow beings without regard to nation, class, sect, or sex, that I should delight to address myself. But until equality prevail in condition, opportunity, and instruction, it is every where to the least favored in these advantages, that I most especially and anxiously incline.

SOURCE: Frances Wright, *Course of Popular Lectures* (New York: Office of the *Free Enquirer,* 1829), pp. 38–39, 44–46.

Calvin: John Calvin, the sixteenth-century theologian who believed that God, rather than any human action, determined who would be saved.

Nor is the ignorance of our sex [a] matter of surprise, when efforts, as violent as unrelaxed, are every where made for its continuance.

It is not as of yore. Eve puts not forth her hand to gather the fair fruit of knowledge. The wily serpent now hath better learned his lesson; and, to secure his reign in the garden, beguileth her *not* to eat. Promises, entreaties, threats, tales of wonder, and, alas! tales of horror, are all poured in her tender ears. Above, her agitated fancy hears the voice of a god in thunders; below, she sees the yawning pit; and, before, behind, around, a thousand phantoms, conjured from the prolific brain of insatiate priestcraft, confound, alarm, and overwhelm her reason!

Oh! were that worst evil withdrawn which now weighs upon our race, how rapid were its progress in knowledge! Oh! were men—and, yet more, women, absolved from fear, how easily and speedily and gloriously would they hold on their course in improvement! The difficulty is not to convince, it is to *win attention*. Could truth only be heard, the conversion of the ignorant were easy. And well do the hired supporters of error understand this fact. Well do they *know*, that if the daughters of the present, and mothers of the future generation, were to drink of the living waters of knowledge, their reign would be ended—"their occupation gone." So well do they know it, that, far from obeying to the letter the command of their spiritual leader, "Be ye fishers of men;" we find them every where *fishers of women*. Their own sex, old and young, they see with indifference swim by their nets; but closely and warily are their meshes laid, to entangle the female of every age.

Fathers and husbands! do ye not also understand this fact? Do ye not see how, in the mental bondage of your wives and fair companions, ye yourselves are bound? Will ye fondly sport yourselves in your imagined liberty, and say, "it matters not if our women be mental slaves?" . . .

However novel it may appear, I shall venture the assertion, that, until women assume the place in society which good sense and good feeling alike assign to them, human improvement must advance but feebly. It is in vain that we would circumscribe the power of one half of our race, and that half by far the most important and influential. If they exert it not for good, they will for evil; if they advance not knowledge, they will perpetuate ignorance. Let women stand where they may in the scale of improvement, their position decides that of the race. Are they cultivated?—so is society polished and enlightened. Are they ignorant?—so is it gross and insipid. Are they wise?—so is the human condition prosperous. Are they foolish?—so is it unstable and unpromising. Are they free?—so is the human character elevated. Are they enslaved?—so is the whole race degraded. Oh! that we could learn the advantage of just practice and consistent principles! that we could understand, that every departure from principle, how speciously soever it may appear to administer to our selfish interests, invariably saps their very foundation! that we could learn that what is ruinous to some is injurious to all; and that whenever we establish our own pretensions upon the sacrificed rights of others, we do in fact impeach our own liberties, and lower ourselves in the scale of being!

But to return. It is my object to show, that, before we can engage successfully in the work of enquiry, we must engage in a body; we must engage collectively; as human beings desirous of attaining the highest excellence of which our nature is capable; as children of one family, anxious to discover the true and the useful for the common advantage of all. It is my farther object to show that no co-operation in this matter can be effective which does not embrace the two sexes on a footing of equality; and, again, that no co-operation in this matter can be effective, which does not embrace human beings on a footing of equality. Is this a republic—a country whose affairs are governed by the public voice— while the public mind is unequally enlightened? Is this a republic, where the interests of the many keep in check those of the few—while the few hold possession of the courts of knowledge, and the many stand as suitors at the door? Is this a republic, where the rights of all are equally respected, the interests of all equally secured, the ambitions of all equally regulated, the services of all equally rendered? Is this such a republic—while we see endowed colleges for the rich, and barely *common schools* for the poor; while but one drop of colored blood shall stamp a fellow creature for a slave, or, at the least, degrade him below sympathy; and while one half of the whole population is left in civil bondage, and, as it were, sentenced to mental imbecility?

Let us pause to enquire if this be consistent with the being of a republic. Without knowledge, could your fathers have conquered liberty? and without knowledge, can you retain it? Equality! where is it, if not in education? Equal rights! they cannot exist without equality of instruction. "All men are born free and equal!" they are indeed so *born,* but they do so *live?* Are they educated as equals? and, if not, can they *be* equal? and, if not equal, can they be free?

Source 4: *Catharine Beecher on Fanny Wright* (1836)

Catharine Beecher criticized Fanny Wright on several occasions. In this excerpt from a letter that Beecher wrote in 1836, she attacks Wright's character and appearance. Why does she find Wright so disgusting? Why would her description have been an effective attack?

Who can look without disgust and abhorrence upon such an one as Fanny Wright, with her great masculine person, her loud voice, her untasteful attire, going about unprotected, and feeling no need of protection, mingling with men in stormy debate, and standing up with bare-faced impudence, to lecture to a public assembly. . . . There she stands, with brazen front and brawny arms, attacking the safeguards of all that is venerable and sacred in religion, all that is safe and wise in law, all that is pure and lovely in domestic virtue. Her talents only make the more conspicuous and offensive . . . her amiable disposition and sincerity, only make her folly and want of common sense the more pitiable, her freedom from private vices, if she is free, only indicates, that without delicacy,

Source: Reprinted in Celia Morris Eckhardt, *Fanny Wright: Rebel in America* (Cambridge: Harvard University Press, 1984), pp. 249–250; originally from Catharine Beecher, *Letters on the Difficulties of Religion* (Hartford: Belknap & Hamersley, 1836).

and without principles, she has so thrown off all feminine attractions, that freedom from temptation is her only, and shameful palladium. I cannot conceive any thing in the shape of a woman, more intolerably offensive and disgusting.

SOURCE 5:   Catharine Beecher, *A Treatise on Domestic Economy*   (1841)

Catharine Beecher's most famous book, A Treatise on Domestic Economy, *became the standard text for teaching the domestic arts. In these excerpts, Beecher argues for the study of domestic economy as an essential part of the curriculum for women. What logic does she use to make her case?*

The success of democratic institutions, as is conceded by all, depends upon the intellectual and moral character of the mass of the people. If they are intelligent and virtuous, democracy is a blessing; but if they are ignorant and wicked, it is only a curse, and as much more dreadful than any other form of civil government, as a thousand tyrants are more to be dreaded than one. It is equally conceded, that the formation of the moral and intellectual character of the young is committed mainly to the female hand. The mother writes the character of the future man; the sister bends the fibres that hereafter are the forest tree; the wife sways the heart, whose energies may turn for good or for evil the destinies of a nation. Let the women of a country be made virtuous and intelligent, and the men will certainly be the same. The proper education of a man decides the welfare of an individual; but educate a woman, and the interests of a whole family are secured. . . .

Another reason for introducing [the study of Domestic Economy], as a distinct branch of school education, is, that, as a general fact, young ladies *will not* be taught these things in any other way. In reply to the thousand-time-repeated remark, that girls must be taught their domestic duties by their mothers, at home, it may be inquired, in the first place, What proportion of mothers are qualified to teach a *proper* and *complete* system of Domestic Economy? When this is answered, it may be asked, What proportion of those who are qualified, have that sense of the importance of such instructions, and that energy and perseverance which would enable them actually to teach their daughters, in all the branches of Domestic Economy presented in this work?

When this is answered, it may be asked, How many mothers *actually do* give their daughters instruction in the various branches of Domestic Economy? Is it not the case, that, owing to ill health, deficiency of domestics, and multiplied cares and perplexities, a large portion of the most intelligent mothers, and those, too, who most realize the importance of this instruction, actually cannot

SOURCE: Catharine Beecher, *A Treatise on Domestic Economy* (Boston: Marsh, Capen, Lyon, and Webb, 1841), pp. 13, 41–46.

find the time, and have not the energy, necessary to properly perform the duty? They are taxed to the full amount of both their mental and physical energies, and cannot attempt any thing more. Almost every woman knows, that it is easier to do the work, herself, than it is to teach an awkward and careless novice; and the great majority of women, in this Country, are obliged to do almost every thing in the shortest and easiest way. This is one reason why the daughters of very energetic and accomplished housekeepers often are the most deficient in these respects; while the daughters of ignorant or inefficient mothers, driven to the exercise of their own energies, often become the most systematic and expert.

It may be objected, that such things cannot be taught by books. This position may fairly be questioned. Do not young ladies learn, from books, how to make hydrogen and oxygen? Do they not have pictures of furnaces, alembics, and the various utensils employed in *cooking* the chemical agents? Do they not study the various processes of mechanics, and learn to understand and to do many as difficult operations as any that belong to housekeeping? All these things are studied, explained, and recited in classes, when every one knows that little practical use can ever be made of this knowledge. Why, then, should not that science and art, which a woman is to practise during her whole life, be studied and recited?

It may be urged, that, even if it is studied, it will soon be forgotten. And so will much of every thing studied at school. But why should that knowledge, most needful for daily comfort, most liable to be in demand, be the only study omitted, because it may be forgotten?

It may also be objected, that young ladies can get such books and attend to them out of school. And so they can get books on Chemistry and Philosophy, and study them out of school, but *will* they do it? And why ought we not to make sure the most necessary knowledge and let the less needful be omitted? If young ladies study such a work as this, in school, they will remember a great part of it; and, when they forget, in any emergency, they will know where to resort for instruction. But if such books are not put into schools, probably not one in twenty will see or hear of them, especially in those retired places where they are most needed. So deeply is the Writer impressed with the importance of this, as a branch of female education, at school, that she would deem it far safer and wiser to omit any other, rather than this.

Another reason, for introducing such a branch of study into female schools, is, the influence it would exert, in leading young ladies more correctly to estimate the importance and dignity of domestic knowledge. It is now often the case, that young ladies rather pride themselves on their ignorance of such subjects; and seem to imagine that it is vulgar and ungenteel to know how to work. This is one of the relics of an aristocratic state of society, which is fast passing away. Here the tendency of every thing is to the equalisation of labor, so that all classes are feeling, more and more, that indolence is disreputable.

Source 6:   *The Woman's Sphere*   (1844)

This frontispiece from The Housekeeper's Annual and Lady's Register, *published in 1844, shows a homemaker devoted to numerous tasks. What are they? What does this illustration reveal about the hold of Catharine Beecher's domestic ideal by the middle of the nineteenth century?*

Source: Caroline Howard Gilman, *The Housekeeper's Annual and Lady's Register* (Boston: Redding & Co., 1844), frontispiece.

QUESTIONS TO CONSIDER

1. How would you compare the ideas of Catharine Beecher and Fanny Wright regarding the proper position of women in American society? What were the most important influences in shaping their ideas?

2. What do the lives and careers of Beecher and Wright reveal about the limits imposed on women in early-nineteenth-century America? Why was Wright considered so radical? Why was Beecher more successful in getting her ideas accepted?

3. Some historians have argued that early-nineteenth-century reformers were motivated by the desire to impose order on society. Others take the opposite view, suggesting that they were interested in liberating individuals from old institutions, ideas, and practices. What do the ideas of Beecher and Wright reveal about these interpretations?

4. How would you compare the ideas and tactics of Beecher and Wright for changing the status of women in American society to those of Benjamin Lundy and David Walker (see Chapter 8) for changing the status of slaves? Was Beecher's or Wright's approach more effective in elevating the position of women?

FOR FURTHER READING

Nancy Cott, *The Bonds of Womanhood: "Women's Sphere" in New England, 1780–1835* (New Haven, Conn.: Yale University Press, 1977), studies the emergence of domesticity and separate spheres for men and women in the early American republic.

Celia Morris Eckhardt, *Fanny Wright: Rebel in America* (Cambridge: Harvard University Press, 1984), is a comprehensive biography of Wright.

Lori Ginzberg, *Women and the Work of Benevolence: Morality, Politics, and Class in the Nineteenth-Century United States* (New Haven, Conn.: Yale University Press, 1991), explores the social divisions among women involved in various reform movements.

Nancy Isenberg, *Sex and Citizenship in Antebellum America* (Chapel Hill: University of North Carolina Press, 1998), focuses on various forms of female political activity in the early nineteenth century.

Kathryn Kish Sklar, *Catharine Beecher: A Study in American Domesticity* (New Haven, Conn.: Yale University Press, 1973), is the most comprehensive and interpretive biography of Beecher to date.

CHAPTER
10

The Fruits of the Factory System:
Sarah Bagley and Nathan Appleton

Women tending power looms:
Sarah Bagley's first job at Lowell

Nathan Appleton

Nathan Appleton had every reason to be happy. The father of the Massachusetts mill town of Lowell had just traveled with thirteen other cotton mill
owners from Boston to New Hampshire's Lake Winnipesaukee. There they had
scouted out a site for another textile mill complex. Confident that it would eventually rival Lowell, the men decided to celebrate with a dinner at the plush Merrimack Hotel. Appleton and the other mill owners had built the Merrimack to
accommodate them on their periodic trips from Boston to Lowell. Now, on this
late March evening in 1845, they could bask in their good fortune over a fine
dinner prepared by the hotel's cooks.

It was a perfect occasion for Appleton to reflect on his own success. At age
sixty-five, he was the central figure among the Boston Associates, the group of
merchants-turned-manufacturers who controlled dozens of New England textile mills. His stake in those properties at Lowell and elsewhere had made him
a rich man. In the past fifteen years, his income from five textile companies
alone had amounted to $336,000—enough to provide a fine home in Boston, ser-
vants, trips to Europe, and expensive schooling for his seven children. No wonder this "lord of the loom" had become one of the nation's leading spokesmen
for an emerging industrial order.

As he dined with his companions, Appleton also could take satisfaction in
knowing that he had done well by doing good. He and his associates had not
enriched themselves at the expense of their employees. Rather, they had built

Lowell as a model factory town where workers would be uplifted, not degraded as in England's wretched mills. And although his profits had been great, Appleton had a reputation as a scrupulously honest man and one of the nation's leading philanthropists. In fact, what he called an "enlightened public spirit" had guided all of his activities.

Yet not everyone in Lowell was happy. Only a few weeks earlier, Appleton could have joined another social gathering in a reading room just a few blocks from the Merrimack Hotel. This one featured various comic performances, including one by a "Reformed Drunkard Player." Appleton might have been amused by the entertainment, but he would not have appreciated its purpose. Sponsored by the Lowell Female Labor Reform Association (LFLRA), the gathering was intended to raise funds for this organization of female mill workers. Appleton would have learned that the LFLRA, founded only three months before, already claimed nearly three hundred members. And he could have met its president, a thirty-nine-year-old worker named Sarah Bagley.

If Appleton was a leading spokesman for the emerging industrial system, Bagley was quickly becoming one of its most outspoken critics. Brought face-to-face with the mill owner, she would have given him an earful regarding the conditions at Lowell. At a time when women were supposed to remain silent on controversial subjects, Bagley founded the LFLRA to fight for a ten-hour workday and to show the *"driveling* cotton lords" that "our rights cannot be trampled upon with impunity." She would go on to serve as an officer in a male-dominated labor organization and as an editor of the *Voice of Industry*, a newspaper that printed articles critical of conditions in the mills. She even took her case for shorter hours of labor to the Massachusetts legislature. Although Bagley never faced off against Appleton, by the time her brief career as a labor leader was over, she had called into question the beneficence of the new industrial system and left Americans with a competing image of it that survives to this day.

"Like the Setting at an Opera"

Born in 1779 to a prosperous New Hampshire farmer, Nathan Appleton was fifteen when he arrived in Boston to begin his career in business. He had just turned down a chance to attend Dartmouth College for the opportunity to join his brother's trading firm. Working as a clerk for Samuel Appleton, a retailer of goods, Nathan applied himself diligently. In his spare hours, he studied French and taught himself double-entry bookkeeping. Soon Samuel expanded into imports and gave Nathan the job of managing them. When Nathan turned twenty-one, his brother made him a partner in the firm. They were no longer just shopkeepers but merchants—that is, importers and wholesalers as well as retailers. They also were well connected. Related to several prominent Boston merchants, including the Cabots, Jacksons, and Lowells, the Appletons were able to secure space on Boston ships. With Samuel based in England to supervise purchases, Nathan was left in charge of S. & N. Appleton's Boston countinghouse. There he oversaw the sale of various dry goods, cutlery, notions, and luxury items.

It was a profitable business, and the Appletons gradually established contacts in French and Dutch ports and even as far away as Calcutta. Often handling shipments of ten thousand dollars or more, they soon began to buy and sell southern cotton and rice and West Indian sugar and coffee. Nathan often supervised those purchases and proved to be an astute trader. On one trip to the South, he recorded markups of up to 120 percent over his purchase price for goods. No wonder he could write to Samuel that if the shipments arrived safely in England, they would bring "handsome profits."

By 1807, however, safe passage of the Appletons' goods was a problem. Britain and France were at war, and both sides struck hard at American neutral shipping. Before Thomas Jefferson responded to these attacks in 1807 with an embargo on all American exports, the Appletons had already severely curtailed their business. It was a sound decision. Jefferson's embargo resulted in a drastic decline in American commerce that sparked a severe nationwide depression. The Appletons found other goods to sell in the American market, including Turkish opium. Nonetheless, the Republicans' attempt to coerce Britain and France to respect American neutral shipping proved ruinous to many merchants. Although Congress replaced the embargo in 1809 with a prohibition on trade only with Britain and France, the Appletons decided "by mutual consent" to dissolve their partnership in the face of continued disruption of their trade.

Yet Nathan Appleton had no intention of leaving the trading business. With a fortune standing at $200,000, he quickly formed his own wholesale import firm to take advantage of new trading opportunities after the United States lifted the embargo on Britain and France in 1810. Still, turning a profit was not easy. New England markets were slow to recover from the embargoes, forcing Appleton to expand to New York City, Philadelphia, and even the South. Then, in 1811, Madison reimposed the embargo on Britain after France promised to respect American neutral rights. Normally restrained, Appleton was furious. These trade restrictions, he fumed, fell "on the most meritorious part of society." When growing anti-British sentiment finally provoked an American declaration of war on Britain the next year, Appleton declared it the work of "madmen." During the War of 1812, he refused to support some fellow New England Federalists' calls for secession. By importing stockpiled goods from Canada and using vessels of foreign registry, however, he aggressively took advantage of loopholes in the law. Nonetheless, by 1814 his business was at a standstill. Conditions did not improve much after the war either. Resuming trade as an importer of British goods in 1815, he battled high American tariffs* and a glutted domestic market. By then, however, he was interested in another business.

Five years earlier, in 1810, Appleton and his wife, Maria, had left Boston for a year of travel in Britain. Maria suffered from tuberculosis, and Nathan hoped the trip would improve her health. While there, Appleton met his distant cousin Francis Cabot Lowell. In Britain ostensibly for *his* health, Lowell had visited numerous textile mills, where he saw new power looms—machinery using waterpower to convert thread into finished cloth—in operation. The two men spoke repeatedly, and for the remainder of Appleton's trip, textile factories captured

---

Tariffs: Taxes placed on foreign imports to protect domestic producers of competing items.

his attention. As a merchant, he could surely sense that conditions were favorable for textile manufacturing in America. Ever since Samuel Slater had opened his Pawtucket, Rhode Island, yarn mill in 1793, the number of spindles operating in New England had grown steadily. By cutting British imports, the embargoes and the War of 1812 had increased domestic yarn production further. Dozens of spinning mills had sprung up in New England to meet the demand for thread. But nobody had yet combined spinning and weaving under one roof.

After meeting with Appleton, Lowell returned home and began work on a loom to produce finished cloth. The British guarded their textile technology closely, and Lowell was forced to steal the design for the loom by making mental notes while in their mills. Like looms in Britain, his would harness waterpower to weave cloth. But Lowell also had something else in mind. He planned to build a mill to spin thread and weave cloth, a far more efficient arrangement than the "putting-out" system in which thread was distributed to weavers tending hand-powered looms at home. In 1813, Lowell and Boston merchant Patrick T. Jackson formed the Boston Manufacturing Company (BMC). The firm's capital was set at $100,000. To raise money, Lowell and Jackson asked ten other relatives and friends to invest. One of them was Appleton, who was reluctant at first to support such a speculative venture. "To see the experiment fairly tried," however, he agreed to purchase five shares at $1,000 each and to serve on the board of directors. The BMC purchased a mill site on the Charles River in Waltham, Massachusetts, and by 1814 Lowell's loom was ready for demonstration. "I well recollect the state of admiration and satisfaction with which we sat by the hour," Appleton later wrote, "watching the beautiful movement of this new and wonderful machine." The BMC's mill, the world's first vertically integrated* textile factory, was up and running by early 1815. Under the roof of the four-story, ninety-by-forty-foot building, cotton was cleaned, corded, spun into thread, and woven into cloth.

Meanwhile, the company's directors had devoted considerable thought to securing workers. A mere village in 1814, Waltham suffered from a lack of housing and a shortage of labor. Lowell and Appleton also realized that manufacturing itself posed a unique and potentially disastrous problem. Both men were concerned about manufacturing's possible effects on the character of workers. In that regard, neither Lowell nor Appleton had been reassured by Britain's textile mills. Appleton was especially appalled by the conditions in the textile center of Manchester, England, where a scarcity of labor had resulted in higher wages, which Appleton considered "a serious evil." Workers could get by on only four days' labor and spent the rest of their time "drinking & spending what they [had] earned." To Appleton, such behavior proved that workers were unwilling to improve themselves even "where they [had] the means."

Lowell and Appleton believed that employing farmers' daughters from the New England countryside would solve the labor shortage in Waltham and avoid these problems. Female workers would command much lower wages

---

Vertically integrated: A vertically integrated factory is one that performs all the steps needed to transform raw materials into finished products.

than their male counterparts, and as products of patriarchal households, they could be expected to respect male authority. In addition, they would never form a permanent laboring class because the young women would work in the mills for only a few years before marrying. Getting them to Waltham, however, required special measures. Early-nineteenth-century women were confined to domestic roles, and young single women did not generally leave home until marriage. To attract these workers to Waltham, the company had to build boarding houses and staff them with matrons to protect the girls' morals. Schools, churches, libraries, and a bank where workers could deposit their savings soon followed. Such company paternalism would reassure nervous parents about their daughters' safety outside the domestic sphere. At the same time, it would make it possible to have factories without debasing workers and disrupting the social order. [See Source 1.]

The BMC's success made such benevolence easier. By 1817, profits were high enough for the company to pay its first dividend of 17 percent, and for the next nine years, dividends averaged 18.75 percent. Appleton's share in 1817 alone totaled $5,540, at a time when many of his mill hands made less than a dollar a day. Such returns no doubt accounted for his flagging interest in imports and his growing role in the BMC's affairs, especially after Lowell's death in 1817. Increasingly, the company came to bear Appleton's imprint. A frequent witness to commercial bankruptcies, Appleton knew that inadequate funding often spelled doom for a business. As Waltham expanded to three mills by 1821, he insisted that the BMC not tie up all its capital in buildings and other fixed assets. As he had in his own firm, he also established careful accounting procedures. Appleton's trading ventures had led him into domestic markets far removed from New England. Thus he was perfectly suited to handle the sales of textiles, which had to be distributed over a broad market as well. The BMC's exclusive sales agent, Appleton's own firm garnered a 1 percent commission on the sale of goods. When sales ran into the millions of dollars, even such a low commission made for "a desirable and profitable business."

Soon an optimistic Appleton was ready to apply the Waltham method on a larger scale. With Patrick Jackson, he found a site on the Merrimack River where the waterpower could accommodate many more mills. In 1821, Jackson and Appleton created the Merrimack Manufacturing Company (MMC). They envisioned a town of fifty mills that would be laid out according to plans developed by Francis Cabot Lowell and named after him. The first mill opened in less than three years. To speed the construction of others, Appleton and his associates established a separate company to own Lowell's mill sites and to build canals, sell land, and lease waterpower to new firms. In this way, other wealthy Boston merchants who had not invested in the BMC or MMC could participate in Lowell's growth and help make sure that the mills were sufficiently capitalized. As a principal owner of the new firms, Appleton would naturally reap the benefits of that growth.

The soundness of this plan was soon apparent. Within another decade, the growing group of Boston Associates had $6 million invested in 19 mills operating 84,000 spindles and 3,000 looms. By 1833, Lowell's population topped

12,000, and 5,000 workers, called operatives, labored in the mills, including 3,000 women. Yet Lowell was more than a sound investment. It was also a showcase. Following Waltham's paternalistic model, Appleton and the other mill owners provided boarding houses and matrons for the female operatives. By 1833, Lowell claimed 10 churches, schools, a savings bank, a library, and a lyceum,* which offered lectures for 50 cents. It had also attracted numerous visitors who could not help comparing this industrial paradise to the dismal cities of Europe. Setting his eyes for the first time on Lowell's tree-lined streets, red-brick mills, trim dormitories, and "little wooden houses, painted white," one awestruck European visitor could hardly believe it was real. "It was new and fresh," he exclaimed, "like the setting at an opera."

More than the massive mills and tidy houses, however, it was Lowell's "acres of girlhood," as New England poet John Greenleaf Whittier put it, that attracted the notice of admiring observers. Especially impressive was Lowell's success in safeguarding the morals of its female operatives. Only three cases of illicit relations had occurred, one company director informed a visitor in 1834. In "all three cases," he quickly added, "the parties were married immediately." The mill girls seemed not only virtuous but also industrious and content. Thrifty depositors at the Lowell Savings Bank, they could return home after several years with enough money to marry. They were so different from European workers "clamoring for work, starving unless employed, and hence ready for a riot," another admirer noted. It was no accident that President Andrew Jackson was greeted by a procession of twenty-five hundred mill girls, each wearing a white muslin dress and carrying a parasol, when he visited in 1833. After filing past the president, the girls marched to their respective mills, where Jackson later observed them tending their machines. As Appleton and his associates realized, what "Old Hickory" called the "very pretty women" of Lowell had become its biggest selling point.

"Doomed to Eternal Slavery"

Four years after Andrew Jackson visited Lowell, a middle-aged woman from the village of Meredith Bridge (now Laconia), New Hampshire, arrived there. We do not know much about Sarah Bagley's youth, except that she was born in 1806, probably the third of five children, and was likely educated in common schools. Her father farmed in Candia and then Gilford, New Hampshire. At thirty-one, Sarah was older than most of the mill girls, whose ranks had swollen even since Jackson's visit. (About sixty-four hundred women, typically between seventeen and twenty-four years old, worked in Lowell by 1840.) Perhaps she was drawn by Lowell's glowing reputation, or maybe she had been recruited by an agent hired by one of the mills to scour the countryside for workers. Or perhaps she just needed the work.

By the 1830s, the region's farm families faced declining futures as the rich

---

Lyceum: A hall where public lectures or concerts are held; also, an organization that presents such activities.

farmland of the Old Northwest was put to the plow. In addition, farmers' daughters had previously spent much of their time assisting their mothers with spinning and weaving, but cheap cloth from Waltham, Lowell, and elsewhere now made their work unnecessary. For these or other reasons, the Bagleys' fortunes, like those of so many other rural New England families, seem to have been declining. Thus Sarah decided that it made sense to seek a job in the mills.

When Bagley arrived in Lowell in the fall of 1837, she went to work tending the power looms in the weaving room of a mill owned by the Hamilton Manufacturing Company, one of the new firms founded by Appleton. She found accommodations in a boarding house run by a widow. Board came to $1.25 a week, and like the fifty or so other women living there, she was expected to follow strict regulations set by Appleton. **[See Source 2.]** In the summer, she would be awakened by the bells at 4:30 A.M. and work until 7:00 P.M., with only a half-hour for meals. In the winter, the hours were shorter, but work was often performed by the light of whale-oil lamps. Only on Sundays and four annual holidays did the noisy mills fall silent.

Like other newcomers, Bagley earned about fifty cents a day, although by her second year, her wages had doubled. In 1840, she moved to the dressing room, which required intricate handwork to prepare the warps for weaving. The pay was lower, but the pace of work was slower. The slower pace may have appealed to Bagley, whose health had begun to deteriorate, possibly because of the poor ventilation in the mills. In the coming years, Bagley missed work for long periods of time, during which she returned to her family in New Hampshire. Already, though, she had achieved some financial success. On a trip home in 1840, she purchased a piece of property that became the family's residence. She put down $371 of the $1,071 purchase price, no doubt savings from her work in the mills. Although many observers believed that mill work provided female operatives with money only for wedding dresses and dowries, in Bagley's case it represented essential support for her family.

Still, to a remarkable degree, Bagley fit the image of the Lowell girls that Appleton and his associates wished to project. They pointed proudly to the $100,000 deposited by female operatives in the Lowell Savings Bank by the 1840s. In only a few years, Bagley had put her name on a deed, proving it was possible for thrifty, hard-working employees to accumulate property. They believed that Lowell morally uplifted its female workers by enforcing discipline and order and offering numerous opportunities for education and refinement. Like many other female operatives, Bagley eagerly pursued self-improvement on Sundays and at the end of the long workdays. In the evenings, she helped other boarders compose letters. She attended the lyceum, where the philosopher and poet Ralph Waldo Emerson, John Greenleaf Whittier, and other visiting luminaries delivered lectures. She was active in temperance work and joined one of Lowell's many "Improvement Circles," where operatives read and corrected their own literary compositions.

Bagley even saw her essays published in the *Lowell Offering*, a literary magazine founded in 1840 by a minister to give a voice to the women who toiled in the mills. Soon funded by the mill owners, the *Lowell Offering* further enhanced Lowell's image by demonstrating that factory workers could take up literary pursuits in their spare time. In fact, in "The Pleasures of Factory Life," Bagley offered an account of life as a female operative that Nathan Appleton himself would have endorsed. **[See Source 3.]** Yet Bagley's views were already changing. In 1840, she also wrote an article, rejected by the *Lowell Offering*, that referred to the mill owners as a "mushroom aristocracy." By then, she had been in the mills long enough for the novelty to have worn off and to see that Lowell itself was changing.

By the 1830s, expanding textile production had led to falling prices and lower dividends for a growing number of stockholders. The mill owners countered by lowering wages and lengthening the workday. In response to wage cuts in 1834, a fledgling Lowell Factory Girls Association led about eight hundred operatives in a walkout. Their protest lasted for only a few days, but two years later twice as many female workers took to the streets to protest an increase in their board. The mill owners fired the strike leaders and blacklisted them from other mills. Evicted from their boarding houses and without funds, the strikers straggled back into the mills as the Lowell Factory Girls Association collapsed. Hard times quickly put a damper on further mill girl militance. By the time Bagley arrived in Lowell, the Panic of 1837* had ushered in a severe depression that lasted through the early 1840s. With one-third of the nation's labor force out of work, operatives were less likely to voice their grievances. Not until the economy recovered fully in the mid-1840s did widespread labor unrest erupt once again at Lowell. When it did, Bagley was at its center.

In late 1844, Bagley and four other female operatives met in a dimly lit room after work to form the first trade union of industrial women in the United States. The Lowell Female Labor Reform Association (LFLRA) intended to fight for a ten-hour workday. At that time, mill girls worked on average seventy-five hours a week. Even British mill workers worked fewer hours. Lowell operatives also were required to tend three or four machines instead of one or two and, as time went on, twice as many spindles. As mechanics and laborers associations in the Northeast revived with the return of prosperity, Lowell's female operatives joined with them in demanding a ten-hour day. In 1843 and 1844, several thousand Lowell operatives had signed petitions calling on the state legislature to pass a ten-hour law. By early 1845, the LFLRA was busy collecting several thousand signatures on yet another petition. Signed first by Bagley, it declared, "We the undersigned peaceable, industrious and hard working men and women of Lowell, . . . [work] from 13 to 14 hours per day, confined to unhealthy apartments, exposed to the poisonous contagion of air."

A legislative committee met in early 1845 to investigate the complaint. It was headed by William Schouler, a representative from Lowell and a financial benefactor of the *Lowell Offering*. Bagley, one of the eight operatives invited to testify, told the legislators that her health had begun to fail, forcing her to return home for frequent rests. The short meal breaks and long days, she said, offered little time to cultivate the mind. When one committee member demanded that

---

Panic of 1837: A financial panic, caused by a contraction in bank lending and in the money supply, that led to a collapse of the national economy.

she provide evidence that "these girls want to improve their mental capacities," Bagley explained that after working all day, she instructed many of them "in simple branches of education." When the committee released its report several months later, it declared that the mills were "neat and clean" and the girls "healthy and robust." It recommended that the legislature take no action to limit the hours of labor. The report also distorted the operatives' testimony. It said, for instance, that Bagley "had kept school during the winter months, for four years and thought that this extra labor must have injured her health." Bagley was livid. "If they gave the operatives the same protection as they gave animals," she said, "our condition would be greatly improved."

Despite the legislature's inaction, the LFLRA's ranks and Bagley's stature in the labor movement continued to grow. Bagley and other LFLRA officers helped form the New England Workingmen's Association (NEWA), which united numerous local labor organizations and admitted male and female groups on an equal basis. When the NEWA met in Boston for its first convention, Bagley represented the LFLRA and addressed the delegates. "For the last half century, it has been deemed a violation of woman's sphere to appear before the public as a speaker," she said, "but when our rights are trampled upon what shall we do but appeal to the people?" Several months later, Bagley, now an NEWA vice president, addressed the members at a picnic in Woburn, Massachusetts, where some two thousand male and female workers gathered to celebrate the Fourth of July. According to one witness, when she spoke, the crowd was so quiet that you could hear the rustling of the leaves as she paused to catch her breath. The mill proprietors, she proclaimed, were trying to lengthen the hours of work, ending all hope that workers could improve their condition. They were, she went on, "doomed to eternal slavery." Bagley saved her harshest words for the *Lowell Offering*, charging that it was "controlled by the manufacturing interest to give a glow to their inhumanity."

Bagley's attacks had an impact. By the end of 1845, declining subscriptions forced the *Lowell Offering* to shut down. By then, Bagley had lent her support to a labor newspaper called the *Voice of Industry*, which the NEWA made its official organ. As president of the LFLRA, Bagley joined the *Voice*'s publishing committee and on occasion even served as its editor. She also contributed articles condemning the conditions in the mills. **[See Source 4.]** While LFLRA members recruited subscribers in the mills, the *Voice* publicized the activities of the association. By 1846, it had more than two thousand subscribers, and the LFLRA claimed six hundred members. Together, they used their influence to defeat William Schouler when he ran for reelection to the state legislature in 1846. Meanwhile, Bagley had not given up the fight for a ten-hour day. In 1846, the LFLRA presented the legislature with another petition, with Bagley's name heading up 4,500 signatures on a scroll 130 feet long. Ten thousand more signatures on petitions from other towns were not enough, however, to budge the legislature, which declared that a ten-hour law would only harm business and "deprive the citizen of his freedom of contract."

By that time, Bagley had quit the mills to open a dress shop and devote more time to the *Voice* and labor organizing. As female operatives elsewhere requested the LFLRA's assistance, Bagley took her campaign to other towns with mills owned by the Lowell corporations. She presided over a meeting at the

Manchester, New Hampshire, Town Hall that was attended by a thousand workers, most of them women. Within months, three hundred operatives had joined the Manchester branch of the FLRA, and soon branches also were established in Dover, Nashua, and other New Hampshire towns. As Bagley traveled throughout New England, she visited several prisons, ostensibly to report to the *Voice's* readers about prison reform. In one article, she noted that the inmates had a good library and "time to read" because they worked four hours less a day than workers in Lowell. In another article, she observed that a man incarcerated for forgery should have been more careful in his choice of crime. He could have robbed, she observed, without committing forgery. Then he could have "passed as an Appleton."

"High Priced, . . . Intelligent Labor"

The object of Bagley's attack was little concerned with the living and working conditions of his operatives in the 1840s. Long removed from active management of the mills, Nathan Appleton spent more time on family matters after the death of his first wife in 1833 and his remarriage six years later. Increasingly active in politics, he was elected repeatedly to the Massachusetts legislature and once to the U.S. House of Representatives. Meanwhile, his investments in banking, insurance, and railroads required more time, as did his numerous philanthropic endeavors. Appleton supported institutions such as the Massachusetts General Hospital, the Massachusetts Historical Society, the Boston Atheneum,* and the Boston Public Library. Committed to self-improvement, he also pursued various intellectual interests, traveled widely, and wrote on a variety of topics.

Thus Appleton only occasionally dropped by Lowell to show off the factories to a visiting dignitary or to dine with his partners at the Merrimack Hotel. And then he did not see a labor problem. The Boston Associates had erected Lowell with built-in safeguards to protect their operatives. Of course, workers had suffered wage cuts, especially in the difficult years following the Panic of 1837. Appleton himself had approved one such cut in 1840. Still, wages had risen 33 percent between 1842 and 1845 as the textile industry gradually recovered with the rest of the economy. If workers shared in the prosperity of the enterprise, then should they not also share in its losses? When sales and dividends fell, should wages not fall, too?

Guided by such assumptions, Appleton's companies threatened to fire workers who supported a ten-hour law. Such legislation would only bring harmful state interference in business enterprise and impede material progress. The protests of the LFLRA and other troublemakers, Appleton believed, were the result of incompetence or lack of ambition. Clinging to an ideology forged in the small shops and farmsteads of the eighteenth century, he saw no obstacles to the advancement of virtuous individuals. In America, he declared after visiting Britain's bleak industrial towns as a young man, even the "poorest [of] sons *knows* that by industry and economy he can acquire property & respectability."

Atheneum: A literary or scientific club named after the temple of Athena, where ancient Greek writers and scholars met.

Appleton never abandoned this faith in individual mobility. Much later in life, he recalled how he had arrived in Boston to start work at his brother's firm carrying his clothes with "a pocket-handkerchief in . . . hand." The point of his reminiscence was clear: Industrious boys from humble backgrounds could rise dramatically in life through hard work and perseverance.

In fact, only when it came to the federal tariff did Appleton see a need for state intervention to protect labor. As a merchant, he had opposed the tariff because it made imported items more expensive. Even after he invested in textiles, Appleton did not embrace protectionism.* He was "perfectly satisfied," he declared in 1827, that American textile manufacturers could compete with the British because female labor in American mills kept wages down. By 1830, however, when Appleton, a Whig, defeated a staunch free-trade Democrat for a seat in the House of Representatives, he was a vocal advocate of protection for American industry. (Massachusetts Whig Daniel Webster also became a defender of the tariff in the Senate after the Boston Associates gave him shares in the Merrimack Manufacturing Company and other financial assistance.) Even as the tariff became an explosive issue during the administration of Andrew Jackson, Appleton continued to denounce free trade. He supported the Tariff of 1832, which provoked opponents of the tax in South Carolina to nullify the law. When the standoff between Jackson and South Carolina, known as the nullification crisis, was over, Appleton railed against the Compromise Tariff of 1833, which lowered duties to appease the earlier tariff's opponents. In widely circulated articles, he defended protectionism in the name of higher wages, not higher profits. The choice, he argued, was between "high priced, well fed, intelligent labor" protected by tariffs and "cheap, starving" labor mercilessly exposed to free trade. Protectionism was the answer to attacks on the factory system by labor leaders such as Sarah Bagley. Unlike Europe, where an aristocracy exploited its workers, America honored labor and provided the opportunity for wage earners to become capitalists. By promoting higher wages, tariffs guaranteed ambitious individuals the opportunity to advance themselves. **[See Source 5.]**

Appleton trumpeted tariffs as a means of preserving upward mobility in the emerging factory system. Bagley, however, was far less certain how to respond to that system. In 1846, when one of the Lowell companies cut wages while requiring weavers to tend more looms, female operatives walked out. It was the only strike begun by members of the LFLRA, but the union was not responsible for it. In fact, the LFLRA declared itself opposed to "all hostile measures, strikes and turn-outs until all pacific measures prove abortive." Unlike modern unions, it was not able to negotiate wages and contracts and was thus more interested in petitions and conventions than in direct action. In fact, by 1847 the LFLRA was renamed the Female Labor Reform and Mutual Aid Society, reflecting its new goal of offering sick pay and other benefits to its members.

The turn away from militant action was hastened by the involvement of numerous social reformers in the labor movement. Bagley used the *Voice of Industry* and the LFLRA to promote a variety of reform causes. She frequently pro-

---

Protectionism: The policy of protecting American products by placing high tariffs on competing foreign imports; the opposite of a free-trade policy.

vided a forum for speakers such as abolitionist William Lloyd Garrison, journalist Horace Greeley, and transcendentalist* George Ripley. In time, causes such as abolition, land reform, and utopian socialism drew many operatives away from the labor movement. In 1846, Bagley became a vice president of the Lowell Union of Associationists, a group influenced by the utopian social theorist Charles Fourier, who proposed reorganizing society into communal living groups. Indeed, one of her last contributions to the *Voice of Industry* was a letter written as a delegate to the convention of the American Union of Associationists.

The Massachusetts legislature did not pass a ten-hour law until 1874. By that time, the LFLRA was long gone, as was the *Voice of Industry*. By the 1850s, most of the native-born mill girls had been replaced by Irish operatives, victims of English oppression and the Irish potato famine. In Lowell, they found a city of rundown tenements and little evidence of Appleton's paternalistic impulses. An abundance of cheap labor had made the Boston Associates' earlier efforts to attract and safeguard female workers unnecessary.

"For the Happiness of Our Country"

Late in life, Nathan Appleton hoped to be remembered for more than making a lot of money. He need not have worried. When he died in 1861, he was widely lauded for his benevolence. Practically forgotten was his role in the founding of Lowell. Sarah Bagley, however, was not remembered at all. After serving in Lowell as America's first female telegraph operator, she returned home in 1847 to care for her dying father. She quickly slipped into obscurity, and today even the date of her death remains a mystery.

Although their fates were different, Appleton and Bagley were more alike than either of them would have been willing to admit. Both came from rural New England stock and demonstrated a lifelong Yankee commitment to self-improvement. More important, both were transitional figures as a new industrial society emerged out of an older agrarian one. Neither of them, it seems, could quite come to terms with that new society.

As a businessman, Appleton epitomized the shift from an economy dominated by merchants to one ruled by industrialists. He also represented the transfer of control from owners to managers. Among the first industrialists to relinquish the responsibilities of factory management, Appleton eventually had no more to do with making cloth than J. P. Morgan* would have to do with managing blast furnaces. He also ushered in a factory system that closed off opportunity for most workers to become independent. In doing so, he helped make his own social philosophy obsolete. Appleton looked fondly to the past, but he pointed to a future in which those receiving the dividends were far removed from the means of production and few workers became "capitalists." He held up an ideal of individual mobility formed in a commercial economy in which

---

Transcendentalist: A member of a nineteenth-century literary and philosophical movement associated with Ralph Waldo Emerson, Margaret Fuller, and others.

J. P. Morgan: The New York financier who created the U.S. Steel Corporation in 1901. Morgan was the symbol of late-nineteenth-century finance capitalism, in which bankers seized control of companies from the industrialists who had founded and run them.

capital and labor were often indistinguishable. At the same time, he was unable to see the rise of a permanent factory labor force right before his eyes.

Bagley's career also pointed to things to come. Later in the nineteenth century, millions of workers would find strength in unions. By then, they confronted a fully developed industrial system dominated by powerful corporations that had long since shed any concern for the moral uplift of their workers. Yet Bagley, like Appleton, failed to grasp the factory's full impact on society. Also holding dear the ideal of individual advancement, she championed the ten-hour day and other reforms so that women could have more time for their own improvement. Bagley simply could not see that many workers faced the prospect of permanent factory work. Like Appleton, therefore, she was incapable of preventing Lowell from becoming the kind of English factory town that he had hoped, "for the happiness of our country," would never come to America.

PRIMARY SOURCES

Source 1:   Nathan Appleton, *"The Introduction of the Power Loom, and Origin of Lowell"* (1858)

In 1858, Nathan Appleton wrote a history of the power loom and the beginnings of textile manufacturing in Waltham and Lowell. What does Appleton reveal here about the motivation behind the Boston Associates' paternalistic approach to factory labor?

The introduction of the cotton manufacture in this country, on a large scale, was a new idea. What would be its effect on the character of our population was a matter of deep interest. The operatives in the manufacturing cities of Europe were notoriously of the lowest character for intelligence and morals. The question therefore arose, and was deeply considered, whether this degradation was the result of the peculiar occupation, or of other and distinct causes. We could not perceive why this peculiar description of labor should vary in its effects upon character from all other occupations.

There was little demand for female labor, as household manufacture was superseded by the improvements in machinery. Here was in New England a fund of labor, well educated and virtuous. It was not perceived how a profitable employment has any tendency to deteriorate the character. The most efficient guards were adopted in establishing boarding houses, at the cost of the Company, under the charge of respectable women, with every provision for religious worship. Under these circumstances, the daughters of respectable farmers were readily induced to come into these mills for a temporary period.

Source: Reprinted in Alfred D. Chandler, Jr. and Richard S. Tedlow, *The Coming of Managerial Capitalism: A Casebook on the History of American Economic Institutions* (Homewood, Ill.: Richard D. Irwin, 1985), pp. 160–161; originally from Nathan Appleton, "The Introduction of the Power Loom, and Origin of Lowell" (Lowell, Mass.: B. H. Penhallow, 1858).

The contrast in the character of our manufacturing population compared with that of Europe has been the admiration of the most intelligent strangers who have visited us. The effect has been to more than double the wages of that description of labor from what they were before the introduction of this manufacture. This had been, in some measure, counteracted for the last few years, by the free trade policy of the government; a policy which fully carried out, will reduce the value of labor with us, to an equality with that of Europe.

SOURCE 2: *Regulations of the Appleton Company* (1833)

The Appleton Company posted strict rules for its employees. What do these regulations reveal about life and work in the Lowell mills?

REGULATIONS

TO BE OBSERVED BY ALL PERSONS EMPLOYED IN THE FACTORIES OF THE

APPLETON COMPANY.

THE Overseers are to be punctually in their rooms at the starting of the mill, and not to be absent unnecessarily during working hours. They are to see that all those employed in their rooms are in their places in due season. They may grant leave of absence to those employed under them, when there are spare hands in the room to supply their places ; otherwise they are not to grant leave of absence, except in cases of absolute necessity.

ALL persons in the employ of the APPLETON COMPANY are required to observe the regulations of the overseer of the room where they are employed. They are not to be absent from their work, without his consent, except in case of sickness, and then they are to send him word of the cause of their absence.

THEY are to board in one of the boarding houses belonging to the Company, and conform to the regulations of the house where they board.

A regular attendance on public worship on the Sabbath is necessary for the preservation of good order. The Company will not employ any person who is habitually absent.

ALL persons entering into the employment of the Company are considered as engaging to work twelve months, and those who leave sooner will not receive a discharge unless they had sufficient experience when they commenced, to enable them to do full work.

ALL persons intending to leave the employment of the Company, are to give two weeks' notice of their intention to their overseer ; and their engagement with the Company is not considered as fulfilled, unless they comply with this regulation.

PAYMENTS will be made monthly, including board and wages, which will be made up to the last Saturday in every month, and paid in the course of the following week.

THESE regulations are considered part of the contract with all persons entering into the employment of the APPLETON COMPANY.

G. W. LYMAN, *Agent.*

Tompc & Press, Gorham-Street.

SOURCE: Reprinted in Benita Eisler, ed., *The Lowell Offering: Writings by New England Mill Women (1840–1845)* (New York: W. W. Norton & Company, 1998), p. 25; originally from Merrimack Valley Textile Museum, Lowell, Mass.

Source 3:   Sarah Bagley, *"The Pleasures of Factory Life"* (1840)

Sarah Bagley wrote several articles for the Lowell Offering. *In this article, what does she see as the "pleasures" of factory life? What does she reveal about her values?*

Pleasures, did you say? What! pleasures in *factory* life? From many scenes with which I have become acquainted, I should judge that the pleasures of factory life were like "Angels visits, few and far between"—said a lady whom fortune had placed above labor. [Indolence, or idleness, is not *above* labor, but *below* it.—Eds.] I could not endure such a constant clatter of machinery, that I could neither speak to be heard, nor think to be understood, even by myself. And then you have so little leisure—I could not bear such a life of fatigue. Call it by any other name rather than pleasure.

But stop, friend, we have some few things to offer here, and we are quite sure our views of the matter are just,—having been engaged as an operative the last four years. Pleasures there are, even in factory life; and we have many, known only to those of like employment. To be sure it is not so convenient to converse in the mills with those unaccustomed to them; yet we suffer no inconvenience among ourselves. But, aside from the talking, where can you find a more pleasant place for contemplation? There all the powers of the mind are made active by our animating exercise; and having but one kind of labor to perform, we need not give all our thoughts to that, but leave them measurably free for reflection on other matters.

The subjects for pleasurable contemplation, while attending to our work, are numerous and various. Many of them are immediately around us. For example: In the mill we see displays of the wonderful power of the mind. Who can closely examine all the movements of the complicated, curious machinery, and not be led to the reflection, that the mind is boundless, and is destined to rise higher and still higher; and that it can accomplish almost any thing on which it fixes its attention!

In the mills, we are not so far from God and nature, as many persons might suppose. We cultivate, and enjoy much pleasure in cultivating flowers and plants. A large and beautiful variety of plants is placed around the walls of the rooms, giving them more the appearance of a flower garden than a workshop. It is there we inhale the sweet perfume of the rose, the lily, and geranium; and, with them, send the sweet incense of sincere gratitude to the bountiful Giver of these rich blessings. And who can live with such a rich and pleasant source of instruction opened to him, and not be wiser and better, and consequently more happy.

Another great source of pleasure is, that by becoming operatives, we are often enabled to assist aged parents who have become too infirm to provide for themselves; or perhaps to educate some orphan brother or sister, and fit them for future usefulness. . . .

Source: Reprinted in Philip S. Foner, *The Factory Girls* (Urbana: University of Illinois Press, 1977), pp. 36–37; originally from the *Lowell Offering*, December 1840.

Let no one suppose that the "factory girls" are without guardian. We are placed in the care of overseers who feel under moral obligations to look after our interests; and, if we are sick, to acquaint themselves with our situation and wants; and, if need be, to remove us to the Hospital, where we are sure to have the best attendance, provided by the benevolence of our Agents and Superintendents.

In Lowell, we enjoy abundant means of information, especially in the way of public lectures. The time of lecturing is appointed to suit the convenience of the operatives; and sad indeed would be the picture of our Lyceums, Institutes, and scientific Lecture rooms, if all the operatives should absent themselves.

And last, though not least, is the pleasure of being associated with the institutions of religion, and thereby availing ourselves of the Library, Bible Class, Sabbath School, and all other means of religious instruction. Most of us, when at home, live in the country, and therefore cannot enjoy these privileges to the same extent; and many of us not at all. And surely we ought to regard these as sources of pleasure.

S.G.B.

SOURCE 4:   Sarah Bagley, *"Voluntary?"*   (1845)

In this essay from the Voice of Industry, *Sarah Bagley discusses the condition of Lowell's female operatives. How have her views changed since 1840 (see Source 3)?*

Whenever I raise the point that it is immoral to shut us up in a close room twelve hours a day in the most monotonous and tedious of employment, I am told that we have come to the mills voluntarily and we can leave when we will. Voluntary! Let us look a little at this remarkable form of human freedom. Do we from mere choice leave our fathers' dwellings, the firesides where all of our friends, where too our earliest and fondest recollections cluster, for the factory and the Corporations boarding house? By what charm do these great companies immure human creatures in the bloom of youth and first glow of life within their mills, away from their homes and kindred? A slave too goes voluntarily to his task, but his will is in some manner quickened by the whip of the overseer. The whip which brings us to Lowell is NECESSITY. We must have money; a father's debts are to be paid, an aged mother to be supported, a brother's ambition to be aided, and so the factories are supplied. Is this to act from free will? When a man is starving he is compelled to pay his neighbor, who happens to have bread, the most exorbitant price for it, and his neighbor may appease his conscience, if conscience he chance to have, by the reflection that it is altogether a voluntary bargain. Is any one such a fool as to suppose that out of six thousand factory girls of Lowell, sixty would be there if they could help it? Every body knows that it is necessity alone, in some form or other, that takes us to Lowell and keeps us there. Is this freedom? To my mind it is slavery quite as

SOURCE: Reprinted in Philip S. Foner, *The Factory Girls* (Urbana: University of Illinois Press, 1977), pp. 160–161; originally from *Voice of Industry*, September 18, 1845.

really as any in Turkey or Carolina. It matters little as to the fact of slavery, whether the slave be compelled to his task by the whip of the overseer or the wages of the Lowell Corporation. In either case it is not free will, leading the laborer to work, but an outward necessity that puts free will out of the question.

S.G.B.

SOURCE 5: Nathan Appleton, *"Labor, Its Relations, in Europe and the United States, Compared"* (1844)

In this defense of tariffs, Nathan Appleton discusses their impact on labor. What does he argue about the relationship between labor and capital? Is he consistent about the desirability of government interference in business enterprise?

The founders of the American colonies, brought with them, neither wealth nor titles of nobility. They had no accumulated stores of either wealth or honors, on which to subsist. Nature offered them this fertile domain, on the sole condition of appropriation by labor. Their earliest political institutions, establishing perfect equality, left no avenue open to wealth or power, but labor. Under these circumstances, it followed, of course, that active industry should be in the highest esteem. Industry was the only road to wealth, and wealth is power, in every part of the world. There are instances of fortunes accumulated in large masses, during the life of an individual, but, subject to our laws of equal distribution, they are sure to be absorbed or dissipated, in the course of one or two generations.

In this state of things, it is not surprising that the acquisition of property, by one's own labor and skill, should be held in equal, or even higher estimation, than the inheritance by the accident of birth. It is true, that the sons of the rich usually receive a better education than their fathers; and we award higher honors to the successful efforts of intellect, than to those of mere industry in the accumulation of wealth. Such an estimation, is, however, wholly founded on personal character.

Manual labor has a position with us, which it has never possessed in any period of the world.

Agricultural labor is, in a very great measure, performed by the owners of the soil and their sons. The universal diffusion of education, places our mechanics higher in the scale of intelligence, than the same class has ever stood in any country. They have the elements of character, which enable them to rise to any position in society.

The high reward of labor, in all its branches, is the great, the important distinction, which diffuses comfort, intelligence, self-respect, through the whole mass of the community, in a degree unknown in the previous history of civilization. . . .

With us, labor is, in fact, the great accumulator. It goes to work, without dif-

SOURCE: *Hunt's Merchants' Magazine and Commercial Review,* September 1844, pp. 217, 218–219, 220–222.

ficulty, on its own account. It is, therefore, perfectly clear, that that legislation which calls most labor into action, which gives it its fullest scope, is, with us, most productive of wealth. The doctrine of free trade, is founded upon the assumption, that labor is everywhere in excess, waiting to be employed by capital, in itself powerless, dependent, only asking to live. With us, labor assumes a higher tone—it treats with capital on equal terms—it shares in the profits, hand in hand with capital. The protective system rests as its basis, on the principle of an enlarged field for labor, resulting from that legislation which restricts or shuts out the competition of the cheaper and more degraded labor of Europe. The opposition comes from capital, which alleges that this system gives to labor too great an advantage, in the power of levying a contribution in the prices of the commodities consumed by capital. The answer is, that, with us, labor and capital are so mixed together, that, in the general prosperity resulting from an active, well-paid industry, capital is sure to get its share. All writers on political economy, recognise the high reward of labor as indicating the highest measure of general prosperity. It elevates the industrial classes in the scale of society, by giving them a power and a taste, in the enjoyments of civilized life, and in the cultivation of their minds. With us, it does more. In addition to all this, it enables them to lay by a surplus as capital.

QUESTIONS TO CONSIDER

1. One historian has argued that to portray Nathan Appleton "as a bloated capitalist grinding his heel into the necks of downtrodden workers would be the grossest caricature." Do you agree? How would you characterize him?

2. Sarah Bagley's activities as an antebellum labor leader have only recently begun to be fully appreciated, prompting one historian to predict that eventually she "will be seen as one of the true heroines of her time." Do you agree? Should she be studied for that reason or others?

3. How do you account for the transformation of Lowell from a "model" factory town to one that resembled those that Appleton had seen in Britain? In explaining this change, how important were the attitudes of mill owners like Appleton and labor reformers like Bagley, as opposed to other factors? Do you agree with the conclusion of this chapter's essay that neither Appleton nor Bagley was capable of preventing the transformation of Lowell? What would have made Lowell turn out differently in the end?

4. Given the increasing globalization of business and the controversy surrounding American trade with countries such as Mexico and Japan today, do you think Appleton was correct in arguing that a tariff on imported goods was the key to "high priced" and "intelligent" labor in the United States?

FOR FURTHER READING

Thomas Dublin, *Women at Work: The Transformation of Work and Community in Lowell, Massachusetts, 1826–1860* (New York: Columbia University Press, 1979), provides a thorough discussion of the lives and work of Lowell's female workers and how both changed.

Frances W. Gregory, *Nathan Appleton: Merchant and Entrepreneur, 1779–1861* (Charlottesville: University Press of Virginia, 1975), the only full-length biography of Appleton, focuses on his career as a merchant and manufacturer.

Hannah Josephson, *The Golden Threads: New England's Mill Girls and Magnates* (New York: Russell & Russell, 1967), offers a highly readable account of Appleton's life and the activities of Sarah Bagley and other female operatives in Lowell.

Bernice Selden, *The Mill Girls: Lucy Larcom, Harriet Hanson Robinson, Sarah Bagley* (New York: Atheneum, 1983), provides brief biographical sketches of three female operatives in Lowell.

CHAPTER
11

Manifest Destiny and Conquest:
Thomas Larkin and Juan Bautista Alvarado

Thomas Larkin

Juan Bautista Alvarado

It was a fine September evening in 1842 when Thomas Larkin stepped onto his veranda and watched the excited men rush in and out of his neighbor's house. The unusual activity across the street, Larkin knew, could affect him dramatically. Earlier that day, two American warships had sailed into Monterey Bay, and Larkin had escorted a landing party to see Juan Bautista Alvarado, the governor of Mexican California. As an American, Larkin had thought it unwise to enter the governor's residence with the military visitors. So he had walked back to his own house, where he kept a close eye on the comings and goings. He was desperate to know what was happening, though. As Monterey's leading merchant, Larkin was well aware of the growing American interest in California. He had heard the periodic talk of war between the United States and Mexico ever since Texas had won its independence from Mexico in 1836. In recent weeks, rumors had been rampant: British and French fleets had left South American ports for unknown destinations; Mexico and the United States were at war; Mexico was prepared to sell California to settle a debt with Britain. Such rumors had sent Commodore Thomas Jones racing to California. Now two of his ships were anchored in Monterey Bay, and one of his officers was inside the governor's house.

Finally, Larkin's curiosity got the best of him, and he walked across the dusty street to Alvarado's door. The governor greeted Larkin as cordially as ever. Born in Monterey, Juan Alvarado was a true Californio. In fact, his loyalty to California exceeded any feelings he had for Mexico. Far removed from Mexico City, Alvarado and many other Californios believed that they were not treated with the respect they deserved. Following the example of Texas, he had led a revolt against Mexico six years before and declared California an independent state. Although Alvarado's independence movement was short-lived, he stayed on as governor and developed a close business and personal relationship with Larkin. Now Larkin listened silently as an American naval officer demanded that Alvarado surrender California. Larkin noticed that Alvarado was agitated as he insisted that he had no authority to do so. His curiosity satisfied, Larkin walked back across the street to go to bed. Before he could retire, though, he was summoned aboard the American flagship. There, as he translated, the governor's representatives negotiated the surrender of California.

A few hours later, Larkin was summoned again—this time to Alvarado's house, where the governor was beside himself. "[N]one the better or clearer for wine or brandy," Larkin reported later, "he fairly raved." Alvarado wanted Larkin to obtain Commodore Jones's permission for the governor and his family to leave Monterey unmolested. The next morning, Larkin again boarded the American warship. No sooner had Jones denied Alvarado's request than American forces landed and occupied the town. They were not there long before the commodore realized that he had blundered. Convinced now that war had not been declared, the commodore promptly signed a new treaty that handed authority back to Alvarado.

The bizarre American takeover of California in September 1842, Larkin later said, "appeared at the time a dream." Yet it was Alvarado's worst nightmare. To him, it only confirmed the Americans' desire for his beloved California. In the end, Alvarado knew that Yankee greed was a far bigger threat to California than the disdain and neglect of Mexican authorities.

"Viva la Libertad!"

The Spaniards had been settled in Alta California* for forty years when Juan Bautista Alvarado was born in Monterey in 1809. California was then a remote province of New Spain, home to no more than 1,500 people of Spanish descent and perhaps 200,000 Indians. As elsewhere in the New World, priests and soldiers had spearheaded the Spanish occupation of California. Concerned about English and Russian encroachment on the Pacific coast, Spanish authorities had sent Franciscan* friar Junípero Serra and military leader Gaspar de Portolá on a colonizing expedition from Mexico in 1769. By the next summer, Serra and Portolá had established a mission and presidio (fort) on the broad Monterey Bay,

---

Alta California: Upper California, a province whose southern boundary was located near San Diego. It was settled about seventy-five years after Baja (Lower) California.

Franciscan: A member of the Catholic religious order founded by St. Francis of Assisi in the thirteenth century.

pushing the Spanish frontier four hundred miles to the north. Monterey was quickly designated the capital of Alta California, a vast area eventually dotted with a handful of presidios, pueblos (towns), and ranchos (ranches). Serra found Monterey's climate and magnificent surroundings to his liking and soon made it the headquarters for Spanish California's most powerful institution—the missions that would soon stretch from San Diego to San Francisco Bay. As Serra wrote to a friend after moving his Monterey mission five miles over the hills to Carmel, "I shall be content to live and die in this spot."

A half century later, Juan Alvarado also was drawn to Monterey's extraordinary natural features. Even as a boy, he loved to walk into the pine-covered hills overlooking the cluster of adobe dwellings that housed three hundred or so Montereños. On these walks, he was often joined by Pablo Vicente Solá, the last Spanish governor of California. Solá, a wealthy aristocrat, took an interest in the boy's education and often loaned him books. Even though Alvarado's father was only a sergeant in the army, his mother was a member of the powerful Vallejo family, and this was a society in which status was based on ancestry, not achievement. Thus, along with his uncle Mariano Vallejo and his cousin José Castro, Alvarado attended a special school that Solá established.

Although Franciscan friars and royal officials still reigned supreme in California, new ideas such as republicanism—the right of the people to rule themselves through their own representatives—had begun to penetrate the region. In fact, one year after Alvarado's birth, Mexico had rebelled against Spanish colonial rule. Eleven years later, in 1821, Mexico had won its independence. As a boy, Alvarado had witnessed the meeting of California's first provincial assembly. His own boyhood hero was the father of the new American republic, George Washington. With Vallejo and Castro, he had formed a secret group to study "radical" political ideas. Later, when Vallejo obtained several banned books from a passing ship, a priest demanded that the trio turn them over. When they refused, they were unofficially excommunicated from the church.

The youthful Alvarado may have harbored some dangerous ideas, but as an educated Montereño, he had opportunities unavailable to other Californios. He mixed freely with foreigners and learned some English. He also worked for an American named Nathan Spear, a Yankee merchant who had set up shop in Monterey in the early 1820s. Spear was one of a growing number of New England traders who moved to California, and Alvarado listened eagerly as the American shared his knowledge. Doors opened for Alvarado in the government as well. At eighteen, he was named secretary of the territorial legislature, where he served for six years, keeping a record of the proceedings and debates. Later, he was territorial treasurer, inspector at the customhouse, and a representative in the legislature. Finally, in 1836, he was named president of the legislature.

By then, Alvarado had had ample opportunity to see firsthand California's political instability. Occasionally, Mexico would send governors to the remote province, but most ruled for only a few years, and some for only a few weeks. Often they fell victim to Californios' resentment of Mexico City's interference. In 1836 alone, California had six governors. Two of them were supporters of the new centralist constitution of Mexico, which replaced the old federalist constitution in 1836. Most Californios knew little about Mexican politics and cared less, but they understood that centralism meant less autonomy for them.

Many Californios' resentment of outside political interference reflected their ambivalence toward Mexico itself. They had enough contact with foreigners to know about the country's backwardness. In addition, the authorities' periodic attempts to colonize California with *cholos* (scoundrels) from Mexican jails outraged Californians and made them even more determined to preserve their own identity. As a result, they no longer called themselves Españoles or Mexicanos, but Californios. Emboldened by the expulsion of two recent governors, many Californios believed that the time had come for them to choose their own governor.

Thus when Nicolás Gutiérrez was appointed governor in 1836 (for the second time in six months), Californios reacted with force. Their leader was the twenty-seven-year-old Alvarado, who had gained a following as an articulate opponent of centralization. Educated, magnetic, and well connected, he was a natural choice. With José Castro, Alvarado assembled a force of about a hundred men. He also sought the aid of a rough Tennessee trapper named Isaac Graham, who opposed Mexican rule in California and controlled a motley "army" of about fifty *cholos*, Indians, and American backwoodsmen. Apparently, Alvarado told Graham that he sought independence from Mexico and once it was won he would help repeal the law preventing foreigners from owning land. In truth, however, Alvarado and his supporters sought recognition of California as a state *within* Mexico. In any case, the rebels had little trouble deposing Gutiérrez. Marching on Monterey, they seized the presidio and fired one cannonball, which smashed into the roof of the governor's residence. Covered with dust and broken tiles, the terrified Gutiérrez stumbled out and surrendered immediately. "Everybody shouts *vivas*, for California is free," Alvarado wrote to Mariano Vallejo after the coup. Meanwhile, the territorial legislature named Alvarado governor and proclaimed California a "free and sovereign State" until the old federalist constitution was restored. Amid cries of *"Viva la Libertad!* (Long live Liberty!), Californios had halfheartedly declared their independence from Mexico.

Alvarado moved quickly to consolidate his political control. First he confronted the growing rivalry between northern and southern Californios. The southerners were angry that the capital was in Monterey rather than Los Angeles and suspicious that the northerners had relied on Yankees for assistance in overthrowing Gutiérrez. In 1838, determined to govern all of California, Alvarado marched toward Los Angeles with an army of about a hundred men and defeated a force of hostile southerners. When he received word that Mexico City had named him governor, he quickly swore allegiance to Mexico, and California resumed its territorial status. About the same time, he decided that it would be politically expedient to marry. Already the father of three children by mistresses in Monterey and Los Angeles, Alvarado married Martina Castro, whose prominent family traced its roots in California to 1776. He also gave generous grants of mission lands to his friends. Under Mexican law, the missions were to be secularized and their lands distributed to the Indians. In reality, however, few Indians received any land, and those who did quickly lost it. Alvarado also gave a large land grant on the Sacramento River to the Swiss immigrant John Sutter.* Although Alvarado claimed that he had not enriched himself, others were suspicious of his motives. As one California newspaper said in 1848, "The whole period of Alvarado administration was a perpetual struggle to maintain himself in office."

Generous land grants might have won the support of Californios, but they did little to counter the threat posed by the four hundred or so Americans who now lived in California. Like previous governors, Alvarado granted land to Yankees who became naturalized citizens. Many recent newcomers, however, were different from the New England merchants who had arrived earlier by sea. Rough frontiersmen, they had worked their way overland, following in the footsteps of the trapper Jedediah Smith, who had traveled to California 1826. More numerous every year, these "gringos" demonstrated no intention of becoming Mexican citizens. Like Isaac Graham, who wore buckskin and swilled brandy, they also showed little respect for authority and even less for Governor Alvarado.

By 1840, Alvarado was fed up with these unruly foreigners. When he heard that Graham was planning a revolt, he quickly rounded up the Tennessean and many of his friends and sent forty-six of them off to Mexico as prisoners. The next year, however, Graham and nineteen of his companions were back in Monterey. Alvarado was horrified, for he had expected never to see this unsavory character again. As Graham traipsed through town, Alvarado may have been tempted to feel animosity toward all Americans. And yet what about his friend Thomas Larkin? California was Larkin's adopted home. Surely, *he* respected Californios and their way of life.

"We Must Have It, Others Must Not"

Long after California fell to the invading Americans, Juan Alvarado concluded that they came from a nation whose "creed" was "time is money." For years before the American conquest, Thomas Larkin gave him no reason to think otherwise. Born in 1802 in Charlestown, Massachusetts, Larkin demonstrated an early interest in money. As a young man, he confessed that he would "stoop to any means & measures to gain it," a predilection he apparently gained from his stepfather. Larkin's father had died when Thomas was six; then his mother married an acquisitive banker named Amariah Childs. A clue to Childs's, and perhaps Larkin's, character is a letter Larkin received from a cousin years later. Childs, it read, "has no charity for those who owe him . . . & is as eager for money as he ever was." Larkin soon demonstrated a similar passion.

While still a teen, Larkin moved to Boston to take up book publishing. Quickly learning that printing books was "poor business" and selling them not much better, he decided to sail off with a friend in 1821 to seek his fortune. They chose Wilmington, North Carolina, as their destination. There Larkin found a job as a clerk and soon opened a small store. Three years later, he moved to Duplin

---

*John Sutter: The discovery of gold on his land in 1848 would spark the California gold rush.

County, North Carolina, where he opened another store and was appointed postmaster and magistrate. "If I attend to all," he observed, "I shall hardly ever be idle." By 1830, Larkin had achieved some success. In addition to his store, he owned a small plantation and six slaves. Yet the young New Englander was not satisfied in his new home. Southerners, he believed, were "a miserable, dis[si]pated lot." Nor was he content with his modest wealth. "Why . . . was I not born with a fortune[?]" he lamented. To gain one, he sold his store and invested in a sawmill, only to lose all his money. Larkin was shattered, saying, "My first prospects are blasted. . . . All I have accumulated has gone to the winds."

Frustrated in business, he had better luck with women. "[I] hear I am a Ladies man," he boasted about the same time. "[A] Lady told me . . . I could get any one." Yet if Larkin found romantic dalliances amusing, he also realized they were no substitute for money. "All love and no capital will never do for me," he said. A decade after arriving in the South, he wanted to return to Massachusetts and marry a rich cousin. When she expressed no interest, Larkin sought a post office appointment in Washington through another cousin. When that failed to materialize, he turned to his third and least desirable alternative. He would join a half brother, John Cooper, who lived in far-off Mexican California. A sea captain and trader, Cooper had settled in Monterey eight years earlier and now needed a clerk. Larkin knew little about California except that, as he confessed to Cooper, moving there would require him to "forget my Mother tongue" and live among "a people that I always d[e]spised and detested." Yet he also knew that Cooper had settled down, converted to Catholicism, and, like many early Yankee traders in California, married a local woman. But he had not married just anyone. His wife was the daughter of the wealthy Vallejo family. Larkin's imagination caught fire. If he went to Monterey, he observed, he would marry a local woman, provided she had "loot enough for me."

In September 1831, the twenty-nine-year-old Larkin sailed out of Boston on the *Newcastle* bound for Oahu and Monterey. Also on board was a young woman from Ipswich, Massachusetts. Rachel Hobson Holmes had married a sea captain only a short time before he left for Monterey. She sailed now to join him, but when the *Newcastle* arrived in Monterey the following April, Holmes discovered that her husband had just departed on a voyage to South America. By then, whatever relationship had developed between Holmes and Larkin on the long voyage from Massachusetts had been consummated. Several months later, she departed for Santa Barbara, where, in early 1833, she gave birth to a baby girl. After Holmes learned of her husband's death at sea, Larkin found himself under growing pressure to marry her. If he did, his dream of coming into wealth by taking the hand of a California woman would be shattered. Six months after the birth of their daughter, he relented, only to watch their baby die one month later.

Land and cattle would not be Larkin's through marriage, but Captain Holmes's estate of at least three thousand dollars was. It proved to be the stake on which Larkin would build his fortune. After a stint as Cooper's clerk, Larkin began trading for himself. His timing could not have been better. In the mid-1830s, the missions' vast lands and cattle herds were undergoing secularization. California's wealth was slipping from the hands of padres into those of rancheros. These men proved more adept than the mission fathers at producing cowhides, and they were far more anxious to secure the manufactured goods that Yankee traders supplied. By the late 1830s, California was experiencing an economic boom, as a growing shoe industry in Massachusetts fueled the demand for hides. Larkin was perfectly positioned to take advantage of the situation. From his store, he sold cloth, clothing, furniture, tools, china, sugar, and other goods brought by the "Boston ships" that regularly called on Monterey. Most of all, he sold liquor, much of which was consumed at a grog shop in his store. He commanded prices at least four times higher than those in Boston, and patrons mostly paid in "California bank notes": hides. Nor was the enterprising Yankee's business confined to his store. He quickly built a flour mill so he could also receive wheat for payment. Soon he added a bakery, and still later, he owned a blacksmith shop and a soap factory.

As his business grew, Larkin sometimes traveled to Mazatlán and Mexico City to purchase goods and regularly sold lumber and other items as far away as Los Angeles and Honolulu. He also became a frontier financier and by 1844 frequently served as a banker to the often cash-strapped California government. He even had a cousin in Boston begin to invest his surplus capital in stocks. The acquisitive Larkin watched his net worth soar from $2,650 in 1835 to more than $66,600 a decade later. It was never enough, though, for the man described by one contemporary as "active, nervous, quick moving, [and] busy." Larkin confessed, "As I am not up high enough, I keep moving, trying to get up."

There was more to Larkin's success than Yankee industry and a favorable location, however. As many business associates discovered, he also could drive a hard bargain. "[Y]ou have decidedly the most convenient memory for your own interest I have heard for some time," one associate told him. Another was more blunt, declaring that Larkin was "an infernal ass." Above all, Larkin thrived because he could adapt to Californio culture. Unlike his half brother and many other Yankee immigrants, Larkin did not marry a local woman or convert to Catholicism. Nor did he secure a land grant by becoming a Mexican citizen. Yet he also did not exhibit the deep prejudice that many of his countrymen brought to California. **[See Source 1.]** Despite his earlier expression of disdain for Mexicans, he later explained to his wife that he did not "look on [them] so ill as many foreigners do." Profiting handsomely in Monterey, in part from his association with Governor Alvarado and other officials, Larkin developed a tolerance born of necessity. "I am remarkably well situated with this Government and its people," he explained to a friend in 1842. "I never speak against their laws, modes or religion."

Larkin's ability to adjust to life in Mexican California was reflected in the home he built in Monterey. The Larkins would eventually have five surviving children and a number of Indian servants. To accommodate the growing family and business, Thomas and Rachel wanted to build a traditional New England Colonial house. The local building material, a mixture of straw and clay known as adobe, was unlikely to produce the desired effect. So Larkin improvised. On top of the adobe walls, he placed an American-style roof, which sloped in four directions rather than just two. Then he extended the roof with four-foot eaves to protect the adobe blocks from the winter rains. He added a veranda on two sides, then whitewashed the walls to give it the look of a traditional New England residence. Soon Juan Alvarado and other prominent Californios were building their houses in this so-called Monterey style. Melding New England and Hispanic architectural elements, Larkin's house symbolized the meeting of two distinct cultures on the California coast and was, appropriately, the scene of lavish entertainment of Californios and foreigners alike. It was "continually frequented by the most respectable citizens," observed Juan Alvarado, who was a frequent recipient of Larkin's hospitality and alcohol.

Larkin built with adobe and entertained as extravagantly as any California don. He even declared that he "wanted no more foreigners to come into the country" after Alvarado sent Isaac Graham packing. Yet he was still a Yankee. As time went on, he grumbled more about California's weak and unstable government than about the Tennessee trapper and his ilk. Americans and their property had to be protected, and he had little faith in the ability of the local authorities to do that. His confidence was further weakened when Alvarado's successor, Manuel Micheltorena, arrived from Mexico in 1842 with an army of three hundred *cholos*. When Alvarado and his old schoolmate José Castro led angry Californios in a revolt that overthrew Micheltorena, Larkin became even more critical of Mexico's administration of the province. Larkin had loaned Micheltorena a large sum of money. Now he was anxious to see California secured for the United States.

Larkin's hopes were shared by many other Americans by the 1840s. Since the 1830s, land fever had driven thousands of Americans into Texas and Oregon. By the early 1840s, westward migration had stoked a raging desire for national expansion. Many Americans believed that extending the nation to the Pacific Ocean represented nothing less than the fulfillment of its God-given destiny. The assumption that Americans had a divine duty to spread across the continent was neatly encapsulated in the term *manifest destiny*, coined by an eastern newspaperman in the 1840s. By then, of course, manifest destiny was already an old idea. It extended back to the seventeenth-century Puritans, who believed that God had set aside land for them to build their holy commonwealth. Now, however, it was reinforced by eighteenth-century assumptions about the superiority of republican political institutions and by virulent nineteenth-century racism. It also supported far more sweeping conclusions regarding the amount of land set aside for Americans' exclusive use. A boiling stew of political and racial assumptions, ethnocentrism, and land hunger, manifest destiny provided Americans with a powerful justification for getting the Indians, British, or Mexicans out of their way. As they looked longingly toward the Pacific, many Americans would apply it with equal force to the Californios. As one commentator wrote, the Spanish-speaking natives of California were "unfit to control the destinies of that beautiful country."

In the mid-1840s, expansion had become a burning political issue. In 1844, the expansionist-minded Democrat James K. Polk was elected president on a platform calling for America to take the Oregon Territory* and a now-independent

---

Oregon Territory: The area stretching from California to the Yukon, Oregon had been jointly occupied by Britain and the United States since 1818.

Texas. By that time, Larkin had been hard at work for years trying to fulfill manifest destiny in California. Already in 1840, he had headed a group in Monterey to lobby the United States to establish a consulate there. Three years later, he was appointed the first American consul to Mexican California. In his new post, Larkin took up his pen to inform American newspaper readers of the wonders of California. "Solomon in all his glory," he declared in the *New York Herald* in 1845, "was not more happy than a Californian." Alerting his eastern readers about British and French designs on the province, he left them a clear conclusion. "We must have it," he warned, "others must not." At the same time, he sent the American government a stream of reports on California's political and economic conditions that were also intended to stimulate interest in the Mexican province. **[See Source 2.]**

By 1845, Larkin's detailed reports from Monterey had caught the eye of President Polk, who also cast a covetous eye toward California. The new president quickly appointed Larkin a "Confidential Agent." He was instructed to gather intelligence, warn Californians of the danger of foreign intervention, and "arouse in their bosoms that love of liberty and independence so natural to the American Continent." Larkin's appointment letter arrived in Monterey in April 1846, carried by a marine officer posing as an associate of William Appleton & Company.* Not just a businessman but now a secret agent of America's destiny, Larkin received the letter with "unfeigned satisfaction." He quickly wrote back that Californios would be receptive to an American takeover. He told the American vice consul in San Francisco, "The pear is near ripe for falling."

If the attitudes of Larkin's old friend Alvarado were any indication, though, no fruit was going to fall without some shaking. Like many other Californios, Alvarado was tired of American meddling in the province and ready to take up arms to defend it. When John C. Frémont* entered California with a force of sixty men and a howitzer early in 1846, Alvarado was forced to do just that. Frémont's men were allegedly on a mapping expedition. When they began to build a fort northeast of Monterey, however, José Castro and Alvarado met them with an army of two hundred men. Although Frémont was forced to retreat to Oregon, he returned to northern California that summer. There he abetted an armed uprising of disgruntled Yankee settlers in Sonoma who hoisted the Bear Flag and proclaimed California an independent republic. By then, Alvarado was livid about the Yankees' obvious designs on California. "I think I shall be down in my grave without forgiving them for the insults which they gave to the flag and authorities of my country," he declared.

Before Alvarado could even attempt to crush this Bear Flag Revolt, he learned that the United States and Mexico were at war. In May 1846, the Polk administration had provoked a border dispute between the two countries over Texas, which had been annexed by the United States the previous year. Two

---

William Appleton & Company: One of four Boston firms that dominated the California cowhide trade before it collapsed in the late 1840s. It was owned by Nathan Appleton's cousin. (See Chapter 10.)

John C. Frémont: A soldier and explorer who traveled through the West and later turned to politics, running as the Republican Party's first presidential candidate in 1856.

months after the war began, Commodore John Sloat sailed into Monterey Bay and demanded that Mexican authorities turn over the province. The next day, Larkin sent Sloat's request for a meeting "for accomplishing the tranquility of the Country" to José Castro. At the same time, Larkin sent a letter to Alvarado expressing his hope for a peaceful American annexation of California. Such a move, he assured Alvarado, was in the Californios' best interests. Larkin's old friend did not see it that way. He replied by asking Larkin to consider what he would do in Alvarado's place "in circumstances like the present."

"Halcyon Days They Were"

During the brief skirmishes between American and Mexican forces in California, Larkin and Alvarado were both captured by the enemy. Retreating from the Monterey Bay area in the face of an overwhelming American force, Castro and Alvarado's army was pursued southward to Los Angeles, where it eventually dissolved. Fleeing back toward Monterey, Alvarado and a small contingent were captured by Frémont. Freed later with a pledge that he would cease resistance, Alvarado returned to Monterey, where he was greeted by a party hosted by Commodore Sloat's replacement, Commodore Robert Stockton. "[T]he Americans tried in this way to show me that they were not indifferent to my welfare," Alvarado concluded. Meanwhile, Larkin, traveling to San Francisco shortly after the war started, had been captured by Californios conducting guerrilla raids against Americans. Transported to Los Angeles, he was not released until early 1847, when American forces arrived in the area. As he was let go, one of his captors told him that he had been held because he was "the most active of enemies against Mexico."

By the time Larkin was set free, the American conquest of California was virtually complete. "I shall require days to be myself again," Larkin wrote the U.S. secretary of state shortly after his release. His belief that business would "increase astonishingly" after the American takeover no doubt sped his recovery. Already he had sold Frémont's force $3,600 in goods and would sell the U.S. Navy even more. Anticipating a rising demand for supplies, he invested all his capital in California-bound goods. Once again, he was perfectly positioned for profit. The discovery of gold in early 1848 sent thousands of fortune seekers streaming into California, providing Larkin with a host of new customers and, just as quickly, phenomenal returns. Convinced that a "Yankefied" California would bring untold economic benefits, Larkin saw a path to even greater wealth in real estate. Soon he began buying and selling lots in San Francisco, where prices rose from $600 to $10,000 or more in two years. "My head swirls with speculation," he declared. Looking farther afield, he purchased farms in Carmel, a huge rancho in Sonoma, and another along the Feather River north of Sacramento. Some properties Larkin bought from fellow Americans. Others, like the large tract near the mouth of the Sacramento River belonging to Mariano Vallejo, he gained due to the uncertainty many Californios now faced in an American California.

Altogether, Larkin and his children owned at one time or another about 250,000 acres. He was soon rich enough to return to the East and live in style. In 1849, he put his Monterey home on the market and the next year moved his family to New York City. They were greeted by old California friends who put on a California "Jubilee," the most "elegant, dignified affair that had ever been got up in New York," according to one newspaper. The Larkins lived in New York for only three years. Larkin's homesickness and growing conviction that California held more promise "under go ahead Yankees" drove them back.

Larkin built a mansion in San Francisco, began once again to buy and sell real estate, and became active in California railroad promotion. Even then, his success was not enough. He brooded that he was not really rich and lamented that he was no longer the mover and shaker he had been in the old days in Monterey. He began to miss what had been lost in Yankee California. He bemoaned the influx of Americans even as he grew rich off them. Pining for the old days, he declared to a friend, "Halcyon days they were. *We* shall not enjoy there [*sic*] like again." Larkin lived in California until his death, probably from typhoid fever, in 1858.

As for Larkin's old friend Juan Alvarado, the American conquest proved disastrous for him. At first the conquerors recognized Alvarado's importance in smoothing the transition to American control, offering to name him interim governor or secretary of state. Although Alvarado declined both posts, the new military government named him to the governor's legislative council along with Larkin and five other prominent Californians. The body never met, however, and it was soon clear that Californios were to have little influence in the new political order. For his part, Alvarado had already grown disillusioned with politics. The only honor he had ever received, he complained, was that his landlord addressed him as "Your Excellency, the Governor" when he came by to collect the rent. Only thirty-seven in 1846, Alvarado had seen his time pass. Paunchy from a fondness for alcohol, he settled down to live the quiet life of a ranchero.

Yet his struggle with the Americans was not over. No sooner had he returned home than Larkin was at his door, demanding that he sell his Mariposa rancho near Yosemite to settle his debts. Alvarado had acquired the huge tract at the end of his administration. Acting as an agent for Frémont, Larkin bought the property for three thousand dollars. After deducting his own commission, he passed the parcel to Frémont, who was delighted to learn a short time later of the discovery of gold there. The loss of the Mariposa rancho was only the beginning of Alvarado's woes. Over the next twenty years, he struggled with American squatters on what remained of his land. The problem arose from the Land Act of 1851, passed by Congress to settle the question of land ownership in California. Claims there frequently went back to Mexican government grants, but under the law, the burden of proving legal title fell to the claimant rather than the squatter. After two decades of legal battles, Alvarado managed to hold on to only a small portion of his land. He spent his last years on the rancho that his wife had inherited. Like Larkin, he also turned nostalgically to the past. His *Historia de California*, published in 1876, six years before his death, revealed Alvarado's ambivalence toward the idea of an American California. [**See Source 3.**]

Alvarado's fate mirrored that of most Californios. In 1848, the Treaty of Guadalupe Hidalgo ended the Mexican War and forced Mexico to cede to the United States land stretching from the Texas border to the Pacific. It also guaranteed that former Mexican citizens now under American rule "shall be maintained and protected in the free enjoyment of their liberty and property." That safeguard, however, flew in the face of Americans' land hunger and their assumptions about racial and cultural superiority. Manifest destiny had led the United States to conquer California and seize the northern half of Mexico in the first place. Its fulfillment did not bode well for Californios, who soon began to lose their land, influence, and position. Making matters worse, Anglos made no distinction between Californios of Spanish descent and the Mexicans of mixed Indian and Spanish blood who were targets of frequent violence and widespread discrimination. [See Source 4.]

In an effort to separate themselves from the despised Mexicans, Californios began to refer to themselves as "Spanish" and to the period before the conquest as "Spanish California," a term that evoked the romantic image of a lost paradise. In time, this semantic sleight of hand had the desired effect. Even as they continued to despise those of Mexican descent, nostalgic Anglo-Californians eventually embraced the Californios and the myth of Spanish California as a pastoral Eden. David Starr Jordan, president of Stanford University and a champion of Anglo-Saxon supremacy, demonstrated in 1893 how completely the conquerors had adopted this myth by the end of the nineteenth century. Jordan had named several streets on the Stanford campus after prominent Californios, including Juan Alvarado. Speaking about California's Hispanic heritage to a Monterey audience, he explained the allure of those names. "The 'color of romance' . . . ," he said, "hangs over everything Spanish."

PRIMARY SOURCES

SOURCE 1:   *Richard Henry Dana Assesses the Californios* (1840)

New Englander Richard Henry Dana sailed to California in the 1830s and later wrote about his journey in the classic Two Years Before the Mast, *one of the first books to introduce American readers to California. What does Dana reveal about Yankee prejudices toward Californio society?*

The Californians are an idle, thriftless people, and can make nothing for themselves. The country abounds in grapes, yet they buy bad wine made in Boston and brought round by us, at an immense price, and retail it among themselves at a real (12½ cents) by the small wineglass. Their hides, too, which they value at two dollars in money, they give for something which costs seventy-five cents in Boston—and buy shoes (as like as not made of their own hides, which have been carried twice round Cape Horn) at three and four dollars, and "chicken-

SOURCE: Reprinted in Richard Henry Dana, *Two Years Before the Mast* (Garden City, N.Y.: Doubleday & Company, 1944), pp. 75–76, 78, 81, 83.

skin" boots at fifteen dollars apiece. Things sell, on an average, at an advance of nearly 300 per cent upon the Boston prices. This is partly owing to the heavy duties which the government, in their wisdom—with the intent, no doubt, of keeping the silver in the country—has laid upon imports. These duties, and the enormous expenses of so long a voyage, keep all merchants but those of heavy capital from engaging in the trade. . . .

The fondness for dress among the women is excessive and is often the ruin of many of them. A present of a fine mantle, or of a necklace or pair of earrings, gains the favor of the greater part of them. Nothing is more common than to see a woman living in a house of only two rooms, and the ground for a floor, dressed in spangled satin shoes, silk gown, high comb, and gilt, if not gold, earrings and necklace. If their husbands do not dress them well enough, they will soon receive presents from others. They used to spend whole days on board our vessel examining the fine clothes and ornaments, and frequently made purchases at a rate which would have made a seamstress or waiting maid in Boston open her eyes. . . .

In Monterey there are a number of English and Americans . . . who have married Californians, become united to the Catholic Church, and acquired considerable property. Having more industry, frugality, and enterprise than the natives, they soon get nearly all the trade into their hands. They usually keep shops in which they retail the goods purchased in larger quantities from our vessels, and also send a good deal into the interior, taking hides in pay, which they again barter with our vessels. In every town on the coast there are foreigners engaged in this kind of trade, while I recollect but two shops kept by natives. The people are naturally suspicious of foreigners, and they would not be allowed to remain were it not that they become good Catholics and by marrying natives, and bringing up their children as Catholics and Spaniards, and not teaching them the English language, they quiet suspicion, and even become popular and leading men. . . .

Monterey is also a great place for cockfighting, gambling of all sorts, fandangos, and every kind of amusement and knavery. Trappers and hunters, who occasionally arrive here from over the Rocky Mountains with their valuable skins and furs, are often entertained with every sort of amusement and dissipation until they have wasted their time and their money, and go back stripped of everything.

Nothing but the character of the people prevents Monterey from becoming a great town. The soil is as rich as man could wish, climate as good as any in the world, water abundant, and situation extremely beautiful.

Source 2: *Thomas Larkin on the Situation in California*
(1845)

In this report, Larkin attempts to stimulate interest in California among Americans in the East. How does he justify an American takeover?

California July 1845

By almost evry newspaper from the united States and many from England we find extracts and surmises respectng the sale of this country. One month England is the purchaser the next month the U. States. In the meantime the prorgress of Califonia is onward, and would still be more so if Mexico would not send eviry few years a band of theivng soldiers and rapacous officers. . . .

There are many owners of large tracts of land in C. who hold them under the idea of the Country chang owners, havng no preset use for thm, as the Indians tame & wild steal several thousand head of Horses yearly from the Rancho. Most of these horses are stole for food. The Indins cut up the meat in strips and dry it in the sun. While this continue Grazng of Cattle can not be profitible conducted. There is no expectiation that this Govt. will find a prevntive—nothng but the fear of the Indian for the American Settlers will prevent it. They steal but a few horse from Foreigner as there is to much danger of bng followed. Mexico may fret and treatent as much as she pleases but all her Cal. Gov & Gen. give Cal land to all who apply for thm and from the nature of thigs will continue to do so. Foreignrs arring here expect to live & die in the Country, Mexican officers to remain 2 or 3 years & be shipt off by force unless they choose to marry a Native and becone a Californian, Body & Soul. This Ports in C. with the exceptin of Mazalan are the only Mexican Pacific Ports that are flourishng. All othrs are fallig & fallig fast. Here there is much advance in every thng and the Country present each year a bolder front to the world. It must change owners. Its of no use to Mexico. To hir its but a eye sore a shame and bone of Contentin. Here are are many fine Ports, the land produces wheat over 100 fold. Cotten & hemp will grow here and every kind of fruit there is in New Eng—granes in abundance of the furst qualuty. Wine of many kinds are made, yet there is no faciluty of makng. Much of it will pass for Port. The Bays are full of fish, the Woods of game. Bears, and Whales can be seen from one view. The latter are offen in the way of the Boats near the Beach. Finaly there is San Francisco with its rivers. This Bay will hold all the ship in the U. S. The entranc is verry narrow between two mountains easly defended and prehaps the most magnuficnt Harbour in the World and at present of as much use to the civi- lized world as if it did not exist. Some day or other this will belong to som Naval power. This every Native is prepared for. When Capt armstrng called on the Gov. (a Native) to give up the Contry in the name of Com Jons, Gen Mich & forces whre expected here in a month to take the Command. The Gov. said he preferd Com Jons should retain the Command in preferens to Gen M. Letters nor words can not express the advantag and importance of San F. to a Naval power.

Source: Reprinted in George P. Hammond, ed., *The Larkin Papers* (Berkeley: University of California Press, 1952), III, 292, 294.

SOURCE 3:   *Juan Bautista Alvarado on the Conquest of California*   (1876)

Thirty years after the start of the Mexican War, Alvarado offered his justification for many Californios' resistance to the invading Americans. On what grounds does he defend it? Do you think his circumstances after the Mexican War influenced his explanation?

Commodore Sloat . . . whenever he had occasion to speak in public always showed himself disposed to protect the rights of all the inhabitants of the country, irrespective of which language they spoke, the religion they professed or their place of birth. At the same time, however, that Commodore Sloat expressed his satisfaction with the behavior of the inhabitants of Monterey, he complained very bitterly of the political and judicial authorities who, instead of remaining steadfastly at their posts and trying to preserve order, had fled to the hills and were trying to gather men together to rescue the capital from the hands of the enemy. In regard to the conduct of the Monterey authorities, Commodore Sloat used to say,

> . . . I came with good intentions; I bring wealth and a brilliant future;
> and they do not appreciate those gifts. Truly, this procedure is more
> that of insane people than of persons in their right minds, because if
> they used common sense they would understand that I am too strong
> to allow myself to be forced to give up what I have acquired.

It may be that this reasoning was in accord with the way of thinking of a nation whose creed is summed up in the phrase "time is money," but we, who from youth up had been reared in the school of adversity, and who loved our country most dearly because we had only been able by dint of immense sacrifices to maintain it at the level of contemporary civilization, felt very differently from that which characterized the thoughts of the renowned Sloat. Even though we knew that nothing short of a Divine miracle would enable us to force the frigate *Savannah* and her consorts to abandon the port of Monterey, not even for this reason would we desist from making a supreme effort to show the world that although we had strong motives for complaint against Mexico, which had for so many years been the bane of our existence and had robbed us unmercifully, we, ever generous, were not willing to take advantage of an occasion when the Mexican Republic was engaged in a foreign war to settle our family differences; nor were my fellow citizens and I who had read the papers and knew the constitution of the United States, unaware that Alta California stood to gain a great deal by the change in flag, for it was well-known that the enterprising spirit of the North Americans . . . would know how to make their influence felt on California soil and make towns grow where there had been only rocks before. Although we knew all of the advantages which would accrue to us from the new alliance which Commodore Sloat was proposing, we preferred the life of privation, uncertainty and snares which we expected to continue

SOURCE: Juan Bautista Alvarado, *Historia de California* (1876), V, 219–222.

until the mother country had come out defeated or victorious in the unequal contest to which she had rashly provoked her powerful neighbor. Our resistance was not motivated by the hatred we had for the North Americans, or their government and institutions, but was dictated by a conscience which aspired to fulfilling as far as possible our duties as Mexican citizens.

SOURCE 4:   *Vigilante Justice in Los Angeles*   (1857)

This account of Anglo vigilante activity in Los Angeles in response to actions by a gang of thieves appeared in El Clamor Público, *a Spanish-language newspaper. What does it reveal about the status of Hispanics in American California?*

For three months a band of thieves has run about the streets and outlying areas of this city by night, abandoning themselves to all kinds of wickedness, including the most refined highway robbery. Various persons have complained to the authorities, but the authorities respond: "Do you have witnesses? Do you want to pay to have them arrested?" And the band continued robbing and killing with all security, by the light of day and in the middle of the city under the chin of the police officials who seem to view this as a comedy. This is not strange; [they say] "the Mexicans are killing each other." . . . Four or five Americans have established a Vigilante Committee, made a call to all the population for the public security, and named captains of a company to go in pursuit of the bandits. Here is where the drama begins with all its horrors, and wrapped in a mystery so strange that one is obliged to believe that the bandits were not the persecuted ones. In a few words, a company (all Americans), its captain Sanford, headed toward the Mission of San Gabriel. All the Mexican residents in that place were arrested and treated with unequalled brutality. Two of these unfortunates had been arrested at the entrance of the Mission. They had to submit to an interrogation of the most provocative sort. Intimidated by the threats, and impelled by the instinct of self preservation, they began to run, especially when they saw the captain draw his pistol. But, ay! at the first movement that they made, a general volley followed. One fell wounded from various shots. The other was able to reach a lake or marsh. He abandoned his horse and concealed himself in the rushes. Vain efforts. The American band arrived, set fire to the marsh, and very soon, among the general cries of gaiety, they discovered the head of the unfortunate above the flames. A second volley and all was done.—I deceive myself. It was not finished so quickly. The body, loaded over a horse, was transported to the Mission in the midst of cries and shouts of joy and gaiety. Here, overtaken by horror, thought stops because it is impossible to find expressions to describe the scene which took place and was related to me by many

SOURCE: Reprinted in David J. Weber, ed., *Foreigners in Their Native Land: Historical Roots of the Mexican Americans* (Albuquerque: University of New Mexico Press, 1973), pp. 175–176; originally from *El Clamor Público,* March 21, 1857.

witnesses worthy of trust. The body was thrown to the ground in the midst of the mob. One being, with a human face, stepped forward with a knife in his hand. . . . With one hand he took the head of the dead man by its long hair, separated it from the body, flung it a short distance and stuck his dagger in the heart of the cadaver. Afterward, returning to the head, he made it roll with his foot into the middle of his band and the rabble, amidst the cries and the hurrahs of the greater number. . . . Is it not horrible? But wait, we have not yet seen all. Another band arrived from another place with two Californios. They had been arrested as suspects, one of them going in search of some oxen, the other to his daily work. They were conducted into the middle of the mob. The cries of "To death! To death!" were heard from all sides. The cutter of heads entered his house, coming out with some ropes, and the two unfortunates were hanged— despite the protests of their countrymen and their families. Once hanged from the tree, the ropes broke and the hapless ones were finished being murdered by shots or knife thrusts. The cutter of heads was fatigued, or his knife did not now cut! Perhaps you will believe that this very cruel person was an Indian from the mountains, one of those barbarians who lives far from all civilization in the Sierra Nevada! Wrong. That barbarian, that mutilator of cadavers, is the Justice of the Peace of San Gabriel! . . . He is a citizen of the United States, an American of pure blood. . . .

Afterwards, two Mexicans were found hanging from a tree, and near there another with two bullets in the head.

On the road from Tejon another company had encountered two poor peddlers (always Mexicans) who were arrested and hanged as suspects.

QUESTIONS TO CONSIDER

1. "Lost causes," one historian has written, "have a way of illuminating winning ones." Juan Bautista Alvarado and the Californios lost control of California to Thomas Larkin and the Americans. What does their "lost cause" reveal about the Americans' winning one?

2. Alvarado's boyhood hero was George Washington. Why do you think Alvarado failed to become the George Washington of California? Did forces or circumstances beyond his control dictate his fate, or was it something about Alvarado himself that prevented him from being the father of a free California?

3. One study of Larkin concluded that he was "exuberantly American." Do you agree? What typically American traits did he possess?

4. Some historians have argued that the ethnically diverse American West was a fertile field for cultural fusion, while others have viewed it as a place of cultural conflict and conquest. What light do the lives of Larkin and Alvarado shed on this issue?

FOR FURTHER READING

Harlan Hague and David J. Langum, *Thomas O. Larkin: A Life of Patriotism and Profit in Old California* (Norman: University of Oklahoma Press, 1990), provides a thorough account of Larkin's rise in business and his role as an agent of the Americanization of California.

Robert Ryal Miller, *Juan Alvarado: Governor of California, 1836–1842* (Norman: University of Oklahoma Press, 1998), is the only full-length biography of Alvarado.

Douglas Monroy, *Thrown Among Strangers: The Making of Mexican Culture in Frontier California* (Berkeley: University of California Press, 1990), discusses the cultural conflict that resulted in the degradation of Indians and Hispanics in California.

Leonard Pitt, *The Decline of the Californios: A Social History of the Spanish-Speaking Californians, 1846–1890* (Berkeley: University of California Press, 1970), offers a thorough yet highly readable account of the Californios and their downfall in the nineteenth century.

David J. Weber, *The Mexican Frontier, 1821–1846: The American Southwest Under Mexico* (Albuquerque: University of New Mexico Press, 1982), examines Mexico's northern frontier and its relations with both the United States and Mexico.

CHAPTER
12

The South and the Slavery Debate:
Hinton Rowan Helper and George Fitzhugh

Hinton Rowan Helper

George Fitzhugh

As far as we know, Hinton Rowan Helper never set eyes on George Fitzhugh's house. If he had, all his worst fears for the South would have been confirmed. The Fitzhugh home was located in Port Royal, Caroline County, Virginia. By the 1850s, it had seen better days. As one neighbor put it, the place was a "rickety old mansion" located on the worst end of a "once noble estate." In fact, the house had actually belonged to Fitzhugh's wife, and he had moved there only after their marriage. Fitzhugh fell in love with his new home and spent most of his time there with his large family, but he was little concerned about keeping it up. More than anything, he wished to spend time in his library. Amid the piles of books and papers, he worked tirelessly to promote the very foundation of the South's economy and the heart of its society: slavery.

A prolific author, Fitzhugh believed that slavery was a positive good. It was good for the master, the slave, and the nonslaveholding white person. It was the basis for an orderly, paternalistic society that honored traditional values and took care of the weak. Northern capitalist society, with its factories and free labor, was a disorderly, individualistic, competitive jungle in which the strong devoured the weak. Free laborers, left to fend for themselves or die, were the true "slaves" in American society. In fact, Fitzhugh suggested, slavery's superiority as a social system was so obvious that many white people ought to be enslaved as well. Other writers made arguments in defense of the "peculiar institution" in the years before the Civil War. None, however, did so as boldly as Fitzhugh.

Hinton Rowan Helper was also a son of the South. The North Carolina native had seen firsthand the effects of slavery on the region. It had dragged the South down, he concluded, economically, socially, and culturally. The very sight of Fitzhugh's broken-down mansion might have offered him proof of that. Helper would not have wasted too many tears on Fitzhugh, though. And he would have shed none at all for Fitzhugh's few slaves. As a nonslaveholder, Helper was little concerned about slavery's impact on the master class or its black bondsmen. He feared instead its effects on the South's yeomen farmers. He was convinced that slavery had mired ordinary whites in poverty and backwardness. Worse, it had closed off their opportunities for advancement. Just as Fitzhugh eagerly took up the pen to defend slavery, Helper assailed it. On the eve of the Civil War, Helper launched a printed attack on slavery that caught the attention of North and South alike. Others had blasted slavery before, but never quite like this. In the words of Helper's publisher, his assault came as a "heavy artillery of statistics" and "rolling volley and dashing charges of argument and rhetoric." And just as Fitzhugh's defense of slave labor did not go unnoticed in the North, Helper's fusillade provoked a violent reaction in the South. Like the North and South, Fitzhugh and Helper were joined in a bitter war of words. In the late 1850s, those words helped nudge the two sections closer to real war.

"The Freest People in the World"

George Fitzhugh was a child of Virginia. Unfortunately, by the time Fitzhugh was born in Prince William County in 1806, the state's best years were behind it. Generations of tobacco cultivation had taken a toll on the Old Dominion's soil by the beginning of the nineteenth century. Nowhere was that more evident than in Prince William County, located between the Potomac and Rappahannock Rivers. In 1800, nearly seven thousand whites lived in the county, along with about fifty-four hundred slaves. Twenty years later, the white population had declined by more than two thousand and the slave population by more than one thousand. The Fitzhughs were among those who left.

When George was six, his father purchased a plantation in Alexandria near the banks of the Potomac. The move did little to revive the family's fortunes. George's father, a small planter and physician, fell victim to worn-out soil, debt, and mismanagement. Given the family's difficult financial circumstances, George's opportunity for formal education was limited to a few years at a neighborhood school. Most of what he learned came from reading. "We are no regular built scholar," he confessed later. "We have . . . picked up our information by the wayside."

George Fitzhugh went on to read law under a local attorney and practice before the bar. With little appetite for the law or legal routine, however, he proved to be a mediocre lawyer. Fitzhugh's rural practice brought him little income, and the problem of making a living became a matter of great urgency. That problem was compounded in 1829 when his father died and the Fitzhugh family lost its estate. Quickly, however, things took a turn for the better. The same year, Fitzhugh married and took control of his wife's inheritance, a small plantation not far from Port Royal on the Rappahannock River. He continued to practice law, but he never prospered. He disliked many of his clients and often tried criminal cases rather than more lucrative civil suits because criminal defendants talked less. Listening too much to clients, he declared, "would make a man idiotic."

As it happened, Port Royal had also been the home of John Taylor of Caroline, a leading defender of slavery and spokesman for the rejuvenation of the soil as the key to the South's prosperity. (See Chapter 6.) Taylor had died just five years before Fitzhugh moved to Port Royal. Taylor's writings had failed to revive the area's tobacco economy, and the town's battered wharf stood as a silent reminder of a once thriving tobacco trade. As a defender of slavery and the South's plantation economy, however, his influence was still widely felt. Taylor's books graced the shelves of Fitzhugh's library, and their impact would be clearly evident in his own work. Fitzhugh was impressed by Taylor's agrarian philosophy, which held up agriculture as the "natural interest" of society. He was equally impressed with Taylor's faded Port Royal and in time came to associate it with the finest aspects of a slaveholding society. Here, he boasted, murder, ignorance, starvation, and unemployment were nonexistent. Instead, the village's four hundred to five hundred residents—about half black and half white—enjoyed peace, order, and plenty. "Come and see Port Royal . . . ," he rhapsodized, "when the crops are growing, the flowers blooming, the birds singing, and the placid lakelike river just rippling into smiles."

Like many southerners by the 1840s, Fitzhugh was increasingly troubled by the growing attacks of abolitionists. He was intimately familiar with their arguments because he read them all, from William Lloyd Garrison's (see Chapter 8) to Fanny Wright's (see Chapter 9). "We have whole files of infidel and abolition papers," he declared. "[They] are our daily companions." He also had developed close friendships with such defenders of slavery as George Frederick Holmes, a professor of history and literature at the University of Virginia, and James D. B. DeBow, the well-known publisher of *DeBow's Review* and a leading voice for southern rights. He had read with intense interest the works of the Scottish philosopher and historian Thomas Carlyle, a critic of abolitionists and life in Britain's emerging industrial society. Modern society, Carlyle charged, tore the very fabric of the community by turning labor into a commodity to be let go when it was no longer needed. The Scot struck an obvious chord in Fitzhugh. As he encountered Carlyle's idealized vision of premodern society, Port Royal no doubt came easily to mind.

By the late 1840s, Fitzhugh was ready to defend slavery publicly. At the end of the Mexican War, slavery had emerged once again as an explosive political issue dividing the North and South. Before the guns fell silent in 1848, northerners and southerners had already divided over slavery's extension into any territory taken from Mexico. Fitzhugh realized that the South was involved in a war for Americans' hearts and minds. And as a propagandist, he knew that he could not be completely honest. "I assure you Sir," he confessed to George Frederick Holmes, "I see great evils in slavery, but in a controversial work I ought not to admit them." Instead, Fitzhugh went on the offensive. Beginning with two pamphlets published in the early 1850s, he advanced themes he would develop in his later work. "Liberty and equality," he declared in *Slavery Justified* (1850), were failed concepts. Because "half of mankind are but grown-up children," liberty "is as fatal to them as it would be to children." Slaves needed the protection of the plantation, for the slave "is never without the master to maintain him." The wage-labor system devoured the weak and created social chaos. The South, by contrast, had "no mobs, no trades unions, no strikes for higher wages, no armed resistance to the law, but little jealousy of the rich by the poor. We have but few in our jails, and fewer in our poor houses." **[See Source 1.]** If Fitzhugh believed that many whites were better off under slavery, he had no doubts about blacks. In "What Shall Be Done with the Free Negroes?" (1851), he declared that the wretched condition of the thousands of free blacks in both the North and South proved that liberty was a failed experiment. Slavery, he concluded, was "the only condition" for which blacks were suited.

With these pamphlets, Fitzhugh announced himself not just as another voice in the growing proslavery chorus but as one of the country's most radical philosophers. In fact, his thought represented a clear departure from any previous defense of slavery. Men such as John Taylor of Caroline and fellow Virginian Edmund Ruffin defended slavery in terms of "natural rights" theory. The philosophical underpinnings of this theory sprang from the Enlightenment thought of the seventeenth and eighteenth centuries. Enlightenment theorists assumed that an orderly universe was governed by certain "natural laws" and that individuals possessed "natural rights." In the seventeenth century, English political philosopher John Locke had identified the most important of these rights as "life, liberty, and property." In the next century, of course, Thomas Jefferson proclaimed that citizens were equal in their possession of such natural rights. Both Locke and Jefferson further believed that citizens and their government had entered into a contract: governments were charged with protecting natural rights and the people retained the right to replace governments when they did not. Given these assumptions, slavery's earlier defenders saw themselves as heirs of John Locke. In their view, broad ownership of property was essential because it provided citizens with economic and thus political independence. By securing this independence for planters, slavery helped protect the liberty of free citizens against the encroachment of government power. Slavery thus represented the best defense of "natural rights."

Fitzhugh would have none of this. In his first book, *Sociology for the South, or the Failure of Free Society* (1854), he offered a radical alternative to the American belief that "all men" were created equal—even if they *were* white. Here he rejected outright a defense of slavery based on natural rights theory. And he spurned the idea that government's duty was to protect liberty, especially the rights associated with the ownership of private property. Humanity, Fitzhugh insisted, was part of an organic—or interconnected and mutually dependent—universe created by God. Society, too, was organically connected. Each part depended on every other part. He argued that individualism, equality, and liberty threatened this organic society. Especially dangerous was the individual's unrestrained liberty to acquire property in a capitalist economic system. Left unchecked, this principle would lead to the collapse of the natural order

that God had designed. Capitalism as practiced in the northern states unleashed selfishness and allowed the rich to exploit the poor.

Fitzhugh also rejected the ideas of the eighteenth-century Scottish econo-
mist Adam Smith. According to Smith, the public good was achieved when individuals pursued their own self-interest. Thus he called for the government to
curtail its regulation of the economy and allow the profit motive and the laws of
supply and demand to work. The result, Fitzhugh countered, was human misery and social chaos. Instead, the best alternative was a society based on slavery
and inequality. In Fitzhugh's paternalistic society, the aristocrats had the power
and the right to rule and protect society. The majority of the population needed
the protection offered by these masters because inequality, not equality, was the
natural state of humankind. It was self-evident that men were not born equal.
Rather, he declared, "it would be far nearer the truth to say, 'that some were
born with saddles on their backs, and others booted and spurred to ride
them,'—and the riding does them good."

Three years later, Fitzhugh extended his argument in what would be his
best-known attack on equality, natural rights, and liberty. In *Cannibals All! or
Slaves Without Masters* (1857), he challenged Americans' faith in progress, their
assumptions about the goodness of human nature, and their belief in individualism. In short, to defend race-based slavery, he turned their intellectual world
upside down. Northern material "progress" was actually a descent into social
chaos. What northerners thought was slavery was actually freedom. Their freedom was nothing more than slavery. And what they thought was good was actually evil. All "good and respectable people," he declared, "are 'Cannibals
all.'" They do nothing but live off others' labor. By contrast, the "low, bad, and
disreputable people" were forced to labor for themselves and support others
besides. Thus free labor was more profitable than slavery, because masters took
care of their slaves, while capitalist employers exploited their workers. The capitalist was "a slave owner—a master, without the obligations of a master,"
Fitzhugh wrote. "They who work for you, who create your income, are slaves,
without the rights of slaves. Slaves without a master!" The slaves of the South,
however, "are the happiest, and, in some sense, the freest people in the world."
[See Source 2.]

"Sunk . . . in Galling Poverty and Ignorance"

On one point Hinton Rowan Helper would not disagree with George Fitzhugh:
Blacks were inferior to whites. In all other ways, though, the two men's views—
and visions for American society—could not have been more different. Fitzhugh
and Helper stand as reminders that white southerners were not united on the
question of slavery. They also remind us that there was more than one South before the Civil War.

Helper was not just a son of North Carolina but a son of *western* North Carolina. Born in 1829 in Rowan (now Davie) County, he was the child of a small
farmer who owned about two hundred acres along the Yadkin River. The area
may have influenced Helper's views about slavery in two ways. First, the Yadkin Valley was a land of nonslaveholding yeomen farmers. Remote from the

area of large plantations farther east, the county boasted more than fourteen thousand residents in 1860, but among them were only three dozen or so planters with twenty or more slaves. Second, it was an area settled by many German pioneers. In fact, Hinton's father, Jacob Helfer (as the family name was originally spelled), had emigrated from Germany in the middle of the previous century. Although Helper later claimed that his father owned several slaves, Germans in North Carolina and elsewhere in the South demonstrated a marked preference for free labor. Practicing the sort of self-sufficiency and diversified agriculture they had often known in the old country, many German settlers had little inclination to embrace slavery.

Whatever views regarding slavery Helper imbibed in the Yadkin Valley, he was introduced at an early age to the hard life of a yeoman farmer. When he was only nine months old, his father died. Hinton, the fifth son and seventh child, grew up in poverty. As a boy, he spent plenty of time walking behind a plow. He also attended a local school and passed the time on winter nights by reading. It was his escape, he later said, from "those loathsome dungeons of illiteracy in which it has been the constant policy of the oligarchy to keep the masses." After graduation, he was apprenticed as a clerk to a nearby storekeeper. After stealing three hundred dollars from his employer, which he later claimed to have repaid, he headed to New York City, hoping to make his fortune. Unable to find a good job there, Helper soon came down with "goldfever" and traveled to California. After two and a half years in the goldfields, success still eluded him. By 1854, he was back in North Carolina.

Frustrated in his two attempts to advance himself, Helper decided to capitalize on his horrible experience in California by writing a book revealing the state as a moral cesspool. In *The Land of Gold*, published in 1855, Helper laid out "the truth" about California: "its rottenness and its corruption, its squalor and its misery, its crime and its shame, its gold and its dross." California's most appalling feature, however, was its racial diversity, and Helper spared no nonwhite group from savage criticism. Blacks and Mexicans lived in "filth and degradation," Indians were "filthy and abominable," and the Chinese "semi-barbarians." California's ethnic and racial "ingredients," he concluded, "cannot be compounded into a harmonious, perfect, and complete whole." **[See Source 3.]**

Like George Fitzhugh's early writings, Helper's demonstrated themes that would dominate his later, more famous works. Thus *The Land of Gold* revealed the basis for Helper's later assault on slavery. California's racial and ethnic diversity, he concluded, was holding back the state's development. Here Helper had an explanation for his own failure to succeed in the goldfields: the presence of a motley population of "inferior" races. In a few years, Helper would turn his intense racism—and the same conclusions about social advancement—on slavery.

He knew, of course, that the debate over slavery was heating up. In 1854, the year he returned to North Carolina, Fitzhugh published his *Sociology for the South*. More important, Congress passed the Kansas-Nebraska Act, overturning the prohibition on slavery north of 36° 30' north latitude established by the Missouri Compromise. By opening up the possibility that most of the Louisiana Purchase could become slave territory if the settlers there allowed it, the act inflamed many white northerners. They viewed the Kansas-Nebraska Act as proof that slaveholders were conspiring to take over the government and spread slavery everywhere. These fears in turn fueled the growth of the new Republican Party, which called for a halt to slavery's westward expansion. Helper realized that many northerners, fearful about the prospect of competition with slave labor in the West, were ready to hear what slavery had done to the *white* man. Two years before, Harriet Beecher Stowe had published her antislavery novel *Uncle Tom's Cabin*. Stowe's work made blacks the central characters and focused on slavery's inhumanity. Helper dismissed such abolitionist propaganda as sentimental. It might be appropriate for women, he thought, but not for men. "[I]t is all well enough for women to give the fictions of slavery," he declared. "[M]en should give the facts." What the antislavery cause needed was a factual study of slavery, based on a statistical comparison with the free labor system of the North.

Published in 1857, *The Impending Crisis of the South* was just such a study. Rather than show "friendliness or sympathy for the blacks," Helper's book concentrated on slavery's impact on whites. His main arguments rested on the supposition that the North and South had been roughly equal in economic and cultural terms at the time of the signing of the U.S. Constitution in 1787. Since then, however, the North had dramatically increased its power and was now dominant. He rolled out the numbers in relation to population, agriculture, manufactures, the value of real estate, and literacy. The South, he concluded, had grown dependent on the North in nearly every way. Northern factories produced the goods made from southern resources and sold to southern consumers. The North dominated domestic and foreign trade. It produced most of the country's art, literature, and culture. It invented new technologies and new systems of production. The South offered little or nothing in return. Southerners did not write books, nor did they read them. They did not build factories, nor did they care to. Instead, they depended on the North to provide the necessities, as well as the luxuries, of life. Why was this so? Helper's answer was clear: Slavery had "impeded the progress and prosperity of the South" and had "sunk a large majority of our people in galling poverty and ignorance." **[See Source 4.]**

As abolitionist propaganda, *The Impending Crisis* was not totally honest. In demonstrating slavery's impoverishment of the white nonslaveholding class, Helper presented only those facts that suited his arguments. For instance, he did not consider the vast differences in climate, culture, proximity to transportation, and other aspects that might be responsible for the economic imbalance. He compared North Carolina to Massachusetts, and Pennsylvania to South Carolina, but he ignored the West, which had attracted thousands of people in great migrations out of the eastern states. This especially hurt the South in his comparative analysis. Although areas of eastern migration, such as the Midwest, were prosperous, they still lagged behind New England and the Mid-Atlantic States. By contrast, the most prosperous area of the South was the Deep South, stretching from western Georgia to eastern Texas. There slavery and cotton were thriving, and the population was growing. Only in the eastern slave states had competition and soil exhaustion brought population decline and economic malaise.

Helper's argument was not exactly original. In fact, many northern observers had made much the same point about the South's economic, social, and cultural backwardness. **[See Source 5.]** In addition, he ignored the moral issue of slavery. To this "side of the question," he wrote, "Northern writers have already done full and timely justice." In fact, Helper was totally unmoved by any "humanitarian" considerations regarding slavery. Rather, he was steeped in the new "scientific" racism of the mid-nineteenth century, which declared blacks a separate and inferior species. Following the Swiss-born Harvard natural scientist Louis Agassiz, writers in the American School of Ethnology argued that blacks were not descended from Adam and Eve, but instead were the product of a separate creation. Helper embraced this theory and thus declared in *The Impending Crisis* that he did not believe in the "unity of the races." Unlike many southern writers, however, he did not use this conclusion to justify slavery. Instead, he agreed with many other ethnographers that various climatic regions determined the appropriate habitations for the different "types of mankind." Thus the temperate climate of the United States created an inappropriate home for blacks. Those of African descent belonged in the tropics. In *The Impending Crisis,* he wrote, "It is too cold for negroes [in the United States], and we long to see the day arrive when the latter shall have entirely receded from their uncongenial homes in America."

Although Helper believed that blacks were "an undesirable population," he downplayed the question of race in *The Impending Crisis.* Instead, he focused almost exclusively on slavery's ill effects. As he was directing his argument to northern whites, perhaps he thought it wise to submerge his own racial views. If so, he seriously misjudged his audience. Racism, a fear of slavery, and hopes for economic advancement were as intimately in many northerners' minds as they were in Helper's. That was especially true by 1857, when the Supreme Court declared in the Dred Scott decision* that Congress could not pass a law barring slavery from the territories. The court's ruling further aroused the fears of northern whites about competing with slave labor. At the same time, Helper gave them a powerful demonstration of slavery's impact on free labor. By pushing race into the background, *The Impending Crisis* confirmed northerners' worst fears about slavery and their own economic opportunity without forcing them to confront their racism.

"Purposely Kept . . . in Ignorance"

Published amid the growing controversy over the extension of slavery into the territories, Fitzhugh's and Helper's books only heightened the tensions between North and South in the late 1850s. They fed common misunderstandings and raised fears on both sides, thus increasing the resistance to compromise.

The proslavery views of Fitzhugh enjoyed widespread acclaim in the South. Reviewers praised *Sociology for the South* for its "bold assertion of uni-

---

Dred Scott decision: The Supreme Court ruling based on the case of a slave named Dred Scott, who argued that living for four years in free territory made him free. The Court denied this and went on to rule that the Missouri Compromise of 1820 was unconstitutional because Congress had no power to bar slavery from federal territories.

versal principles" and its "profound views on the comparison of slavery with what is miscalled 'free society.'" Southern editors and readers likewise praised *Cannibals All!* and adopted its arguments and rhetoric as their own. Northern reviewers denounced Fitzhugh's books in the strongest terms. New York newspaper editor and abolitionist Horace Greeley wrote that Fitzhugh was an example of the barren wasteland of southern literature. Abolitionist William Lloyd Garrison called *Sociology for the South* "a shallow, impudent, and thoroughly satanic work." Indeed, in the minds of many northerners, Fitzhugh became the symbol of proslavery thought, especially after he traveled north to debate leading abolitionists. By the late 1850s, many northerners viewed him as representative of all southerners. His ideas, they incorrectly believed, were typical southern ideas. In 1860, abolitionist senator Charles Sumner used Fitzhugh's work as his main target in a speech titled "The Barbarism of Slavery." Abraham Lincoln read *Sociology for the South* and used Fitzhugh's statements as proof of southern extremism. He also borrowed ideas from Fitzhugh, such as in his famous "House divided" speech. It was the Virginian's rhetorical assertion, after all, that "domestic slavery and (attempted) universal liberty cannot long coexist in the Great Republic of Christendom."

Helper's book, meanwhile, raised friends and foes in exactly opposite quarters. Nonslaveholders—about three-quarters of the white South—were often illiterate and thus never heard his argument at all. The slaveholding class, however, found his arguments troubling. It did not help that Helper had drawn his statistics from the Census of 1850. Ironically, that census had been compiled under the direction of James D. B. DeBow, the well-known newspaper editor who was an ardent defender of slavery and a close friend of George Fitzhugh. Outraged Southerners often denounced Helper as a renegade scoundrel and a traitor. One North Carolina newspaper even urged the author of *The Impending Crisis* to throw himself into the arms of the famous black abolitionist Frederick Douglass and "mix with that dark, infidel, and traitorous crew upon whose purses all your highest hopes now depend." The accusation that Helper was in favor of interracial relations—sexual or otherwise—was nonsense, of course. Yet it demonstrates how he had touched a sensitive nerve in the white South. Helper may have exaggerated the case, but few southerners could deny that they were "compelled to go to the North for almost every article of utility and adornment, from matches, shoepegs, and paintings up to cotton-mills, steamships and statuary."

Even worse, Helper had called for "an exterminating war" against slavery. Nonslaveholders, he suggested, should join together and rise up again slaveholders. They "have hoodwinked you, trifled with you, and used you," he declared. "They have purposely kept you in ignorance, and have, by moulding your passions and prejudices to suit themselves, induced you to act in direct opposition to your dearest rights and interests." Helper's plan for abolishing slavery called for banning slaveholders from politics. The actual abolition of slavery would be accomplished through legislation making slaveholding a crime and by taxes on slaveholders who did not immediately comply. The money raised by these taxes would be used to colonize the emancipated slaves in Africa or Central and South America. To bring this about, Helper called for nonslaveholding southerners to change their political allegiance. They had supported the proslavery Democratic Party for far too long. The time had come to join the new Republican Party and vote for its presidential candidate in 1860. The Republicans, he believed, would keep slavery out of the territories and open the door for abolition.

Helper's prescription confirmed slaveholders' fears about the rising Republican menace in the North. If Republicans triumphed at the polls, they believed, slavery was doomed. Northerners liked Helper's work as much as they hated Fitzhugh's. William Lloyd Garrison praised his arguments, claiming that they were irrefutable. Horace Greeley printed an eight-page review of the book in his *New York Tribune* and called it one of the most remarkable antislavery works ever written. *The Impending Crisis* sold more than 13,000 copies in its first year. It received even greater exposure when the Republican Party distributed more than 140,000 copies of the book in the 1860 campaign.

The impact of Helper's publication on Abraham Lincoln's election in 1860 is impossible to determine. But as a result of the election, the southern slaveholding states seceded from the Union, thus triggering the Civil War. During the war, most of Helper's yeomen farmers fought for the Confederacy, motivated no doubt in part by the same racial fears that possessed Helper. Slavery, after all, was more than a labor system. It was also a powerful way to control blacks and assert white superiority. At the same time, however, large pockets of the South remained loyal to the Union. Populated mostly by nonslaveholding whites, these areas demonstrated that many southern whites did not see the slaveholders' interests as their own.

The Civil War, of course, would destroy Fitzhugh's allegedly paternalistic slave system. Yet after the war, he had little difficulty finding friends, even among northern Republicans. Fitzhugh privately lamented postwar Republican policies in the South. At the same time, he became a judge in the Freedmen's Bureau, the federal agency set up by Republicans to aid former slaves in their transition from slavery to freedom. Here he was able to act on his paternalistic views by assisting helpless blacks who could not fend for themselves. Before he died in 1881, Fitzhugh even grew fond of the industrial capitalism he had so vehemently attacked. Monopolistic capitalism, he came to believe, was a social system that reflected the natural inequality of humankind.

Helper also found a position with the triumphant Republicans. They had not forgotten the political value of *The Impending Crisis,* and in 1861 Lincoln rewarded him with an appointment as consul to Argentina. There, despite his virulent anti-Catholicism and racism, he married a local woman. When he resigned in 1866, his accounts were short by six thousand dollars, although the Republicans further rewarded him by ignoring the missing funds. Still convinced that the United States was a white man's country, Helper would go on to publish a trilogy of books designed to "write the negro out of America" and "out of existence." Completed in 1871, they established Helper as one of the era's most fanatical white supremacists. Meanwhile, as before the Civil War, his schemes to get rich never quite paid off. Abandoned by his wife and suffering from depression and loneliness, Helper was filled with despair over his failed business ventures. Unable to cope with his own crisis, he committed suicide in 1909.

In the postwar years, the abiding racism of Fitzhugh and Helper was shared by most Americans. At the same time, however, postwar society would not live up to the hopes of either man. Americans rejected Fitzhugh's views about individualism, competition, liberty, and equality. Although Helper's vision seemed fulfilled with the election of Republicans in the postwar South, Republican rule would not last beyond the 1870s. Moreover, Helper never saw the removal from the United States of the "undesirable" black population. In the end, both men's dreams regarding slavery and society were shattered.

PRIMARY SOURCES

SOURCE 1: George Fitzhugh, *Slavery Justified* (1850)

In Slavery Justified, *George Fitzhugh compares northern and southern society. Why does he believe that life in the South is better?*

The bestowing upon men equality of rights, is but giving license to the strong to oppress the weak. It begets the grossest inequalities of condition. Menials and day laborers are and must be as numerous as in a land of slavery. And these menials and laborers are only taken care of while young, strong and healthy. If the laborer gets sick, his wages cease just as his demands are greatest. If two of the poor get married, who being young and healthy, are getting good wages, in a few years they may have four children. Their wants have increased, but the mother has enough to do to nurse the four children, and the wages of the husband must support six. There is no equality, except in theory, in such society, and there is no liberty. The men of property, those who own lands and money, are masters of the poor; masters, with none of the feelings, interests or sympathies of masters; they employ them when they please, and for what they please, and may leave them to die in the highway, for it is the only home to which the poor in free countries are entitled. . . .

There is no rivalry, no competition to get employment among slaves, as among free laborers. Nor is there a war between master and slave. The master's interest prevents his reducing the slave's allowance or wages in infancy or sickness, for he might lose the slave by so doing. His feeling for his slave never permits him to stint him in old age. The slaves are all well fed, well clad, have plenty of fuel, and are happy. They have no dread of the future—no fear of want. A state of dependence is the only condition in which reciprocal affection can exist among human beings—the only situation in which the war of competition ceases, and peace, amity and good will arise. A state of independence always begets more or less of jealous rivalry and hostility. A man loves his children because they are weak, helpless and dependent. He loves his wife for similar reasons. When his children grow up and assert their independence, he

SOURCE: Reprinted in Eric McKitrick, ed., *Slavery Defended: The Views of the Old South* (Englewood Cliffs, N.J.: Prentice-Hall, 1963), pp. 38–39, 45, 47–48; originally from George Fitzhugh, *Slavery Justified, by a Southerner* (Fredericksburg, Va.: Recorder Printing Office, 1850); later included in *Sociology for the South, or the Failure of Free Society* (Richmond, Va.: A. Morris, 1854).

is apt to transfer his affection to his grandchildren. He ceases to love his wife when she becomes masculine or rebellious; but slaves are always dependent, never the rivals of their master. Hence, though men are often found at variance with wife or children, we never saw one who did not like his slaves, and rarely a slave who was not devoted to his master. . . .

At the slaveholding South all is peace, quiet, plenty and contentment. We have no mobs, no trades unions, no strikes for higher wages, no armed resistance to the law, but little jealousy of the rich by the poor. We have but few in our jails, and fewer in our poor houses. We produce enough of the comforts and necessaries of life for a population three or four times as numerous as ours. We are wholly exempt from the torrent of pauperism, crime, agrarianism, and infidelity which Europe is pouring from her jails and alms houses on the already crowded North. Population increases slowly, wealth rapidly. . . . Wealth is more equally distributed than at the North, where a few millionaires own most of the property of the country. (These millionaires are men of cold hearts and weak minds; they know how to make money, but not how to use it, either for the benefit of themselves or of others.) High intellectual and moral attainments, refinement of head and heart, give standing to a man in the South, however poor he may be. Money is, with few exceptions, the only thing that ennobles at the North. We have poor among us, but none who are over-worked and under-fed. We do not crowd cities because lands are abundant and their owners kind, merciful and hospitable. The poor are as hospitable as the rich, the negro as the white man. Nobody dreams of turning a friend, a relative, or a stranger from his door. The very negro who deems it no crime to steal, would scorn to sell his hospitality. We have no loafers, because the poor relative or friend who borrows our horse, or spends a week under our roof, is a welcome guest. The loose economy, the wasteful mode of living at the South, is a blessing when rightly considered; it keeps want, scarcity and famine at a distance, because it leaves room for retrenchment. The nice, accurate economy of France, England and New England, keeps society always on the verge of famine, because it leaves no room to retrench, that is to live on a part only of what they now consume. Our society exhibits no appearance of precocity, no symptoms of decay. A long course of continuing improvement is in prospect before us, with no limits which human foresight can descry. Actual liberty and equality with our white population has been approached much nearer than in the free States. Few of our whites ever work as day laborers, none as cooks, scullions,* ostlers,* body servants, or in other menial capacities. One free citizen does not lord it over another; hence that feeling of independence and equality that distinguishes us; hence that pride of character, that self-respect, that gives us ascendancy when we come in contact with Northerners. It is a distinction to be a Southerner, as it was once to be a Roman citizen.

Scullions: A household servant of the lowest rank.

Ostlers: People who take care of horses.

Source 2:   George Fitzhugh, *Cannibals All!*   (1857)

George Fitzhugh defends slavery in these passages from Cannibals All! *On what grounds does he do so?*

The respectable way of living is to make other people work for you, and to pay them nothing for so doing—and to have no concern about them after their work is done. Hence, white slave-holding is much more respectable than negro slavery—for the master works nearly as hard for the negro as he for the master. But you, my virtuous, respectable reader, exact three thousand dollars per annum from white labor (for your income is the product of white labor) and make not one cent of return in any form. You retain your capital, and never labor, and yet live in luxury on the labor of others. Capital commands labor, as the master does the slave. Neither pays for labor; but the master permits the slave to retain a larger allowance from the proceeds of his own labor, and hence "free labor is cheaper than slave labor." You, with the command over labor which your capital gives you, are a slave owner—a master, without the obligations of a master. They who work for you, who create your income, are slaves, without the rights of slaves. Slaves without a master! Whilst you were engaged in amassing your capital, in seeking to become independent, you were in the White Slave Trade. To become independent is to be able to make other people support you, without being obliged to labor for *them*. Now, what man in society is not seeking to attain this situation? He who attains it is a slave owner, in the worst sense. He who is in pursuit of it is engaged in the slave trade. You, reader, belong to the one or other class. The men without property, in free society, are theoretically in a worse condition than slaves. Practically, their condition corresponds with this theory, as history and statistics everywhere demonstrate. The capitalists, in free society, live in ten times the luxury and show that Southern masters do, because the slaves to capital work harder and cost less than negro slaves.

    The negro slaves of the South are the happiest, and, in some sense, the freest people in the world. The children and the aged and infirm work not at all, and yet have all the comforts and necessaries of life provided for them. They enjoy liberty, because they are oppressed neither by care nor labor. The women do little hard work, and are protected from the despotism of their husbands by their masters. The negro men and stout boys work, on the average, in good weather, not more than nine hours a day. The balance of their time is spent in perfect abandon. Besides, they have their Sabbaths and holidays. White men, with so much of license and liberty, would die of ennui; but negroes luxuriate in corporeal and mental repose. With their faces upturned to the sun, they can sleep at any hour; and quiet sleep is the greatest of human enjoyments. "Blessed be the man who invented sleep." 'Tis happiness in itself—and results from contentment with the present, and confident assurance of the future. We do not know

Source: George Fitzhugh, *Cannibals All! or Slaves Without Masters* (1857; reprint, Cambridge: Harvard University Press, 1960), pp. 17–19, 243–244.

whether free laborers ever sleep. They are fools to do so; for, whilst they sleep, the wily and watchful capitalist is devising means to ensnare and exploitate them. The free laborer must work or starve. He is more of a slave than the negro, because he works longer and harder for less allowance than the slave, and has no holiday, because the cares of life with him begin when its labors end. He has no liberty, and not a single right. . . .

We do not agree with the authors of the Declaration of Independence, that governments "derive their just powers from the consent of the governed." The women, the children, the negroes, and but few of the non-property holders were consulted, or consented to the Revolution, or the governments that ensued from its success. As to these, the new governments were self-elected despotisms, and the governing class self-elected despots. Those governments originated in force, and have been continued by force. All governments must originate in force, and be continued by force. The very term, government, implies that it is carried on against the consent of the governed. Fathers do not derive their authority, as heads of families, from the consent of wife and children, nor do they govern their families by their consent. They never take the vote of the family as to the labors to be performed, the moneys to be expended, or as to anything else. Masters dare not take the vote of slaves as to their government. If they did, constant holiday, dissipation, and extravagance would be the result. . . . Not even in the most democratic countries are soldiers governed by their consent, nor is their vote taken on the eve of battle. They have some how lost (or never had) the "inalienable rights of life, liberty, and the pursuit of happiness," and, whether Americans or Russians, are forced into battle without and often against their consent. . . . The governments of Europe could not exist a week without the positive force of standing armies.

They are all governments of force, not of consent. Even in our North, the women, children, and free negroes, constitute four-fifths of the population; and they are all governed without their consent. But they mean to correct this gross and glaring iniquity at the North. They hold that all men, women, and negroes, and smart children are equals, and entitled to equal rights. The widows and free negroes begin to vote in some of those States, and they will have to let all colors and sexes and ages vote soon, or give up the glorious principles of human equality and universal emancipation.

The experiment which they will make, we fear, is absurd in theory, and the symptoms of approaching anarchy . . . among them leave no doubt that its practical operation will be no better than its theory.

SOURCE 3: *Hinton Rowan Helper on Chinese Immigrants* (1855)

In this excerpt from The Land of Gold, *Hinton Rowan Helper discusses Chinese immigrants in California. Why does he object to them? What do his fears about the Chinese have to do with his concerns for whites?*

The national habits and traits of Chinese character, to which they cling with uncompromising tenacity in this country, are strikingly distinct from those of all other nations. There is a marked identity about their features, person, manners and costume, so unmistakable that it betrays their nationality in a moment. Particular fashions and modes of dress give them no concern whatever. All their garments look as if they were made after the same pattern out of the same material and from the same piece of cloth. In short, one Chinaman looks almost exactly like another, but very unlike any body else. . . .

The Chinese are more objectionable than other foreigners because they refuse to have dealing or intercourse with us. Consequently there is no chance of making any thing of them either in the way of trade or labor. They are ready to take all they can get from us but are not willing to give any thing in return. They did not aid in the acquisition or settlement of California and they do not intend to make it their future home. They will not become permanent citizens nor identify their lives and interests with the country. They neither build nor buy, nor invest capital in any way that conduces to the advantage of any one but themselves. They have thousands of good-for-nothing gewgaws and worthless articles of *virtu** for sale, and our people are foolish enough to buy them.

Though they hold themselves aloof from us, contemn and disdain us, they have guaranteed to them the same privileges that we enjoy and are allowed to exhaust the mines that should be reserved for us and our posterity—that is if they are worth reserving at all. Their places could and should be filled with worthier immigrants—Europeans who would take the oath of allegiance to the country, work both for themselves and for the commonwealth, fraternize with us, and finally, become a part of us. . . .

However, they have neither the strength of body nor the power of mind to cope with us in the common affairs of life and our people will not always treat them with undue complaisance. They must work for themselves, or we will make them work for us. No inferior race of men can exist in these United States without becoming subordinate to the will of the Anglo-Americans. It was so with the negroes and the Indians and it will be so with the Chinese in California.

SOURCE: Reprinted in Lucius Beebe and Charles M. Clegg, eds., *Dreadful California* (Indianapolis: Bobbs-Merrill, 1948), pp. 70, 74–75, 77; originally from Hinton Helper, *The Land of Gold* (Baltimore: H. Taylor, 1855).

**Virtu:* Curios or antiques.

SOURCE 4:   Hinton Rowan Helper, *The Impending Crisis of the South*   (1857)

In this passage, Hinton Rowan Helper discusses the South's dependence on the North. How does he explain southern backwardness? Do you think this argument would have been effective at the time? Why?

The North is the Mecca of our merchants, and to it they must and do make two pilgrimages per annum—one in the spring and one in the fall. All our commercial, mechanical, manufactural, and literary supplies come from there. We want Bibles, brooms, buckets and books, and we go to the North; we want pens, ink, paper, wafers and envelopes, and we go to the North; we want shoes, hats, handkerchiefs, umbrellas and pocket knives, and we go to the North; we want furniture, crockery, glassware and pianos, and we go to the North; we want toys, primers, school books, fashionable apparel, machinery, medicines, tombstones, and a thousand other things, and we go to the North for them all. Instead of keeping our money in circulation at home, by patronizing our own mechanics, manufacturers, and laborers, we send it all away to the North, and there it remains; it never falls into our hands again.

In one way or another we are more or less subservient to the North every day of our lives. In infancy we are swaddled in Northern muslin; in childhood we are humored with Northern gewgaws; in youth we are instructed out of Northern books; at the age of maturity we sow our "wild oats" on Northern soil; in middle-life we exhaust our wealth, energies and talents in the dishonorable vocation of entailing our dependence on our children and on our children's children, and, to the neglect of our own interests and the interests of those around us, in giving aid and succor to every department of Northern power; in the decline of life we remedy our eye-sight with Northern spectacles, and support our infirmities with Northern canes; in old age we are drugged with Northern physic; and, finally, when we die, our inanimate bodies, shrouded in Northern cambric, are stretched upon the bier, borne to the grave in a Northern carriage, entombed with a Northern spade, and memorized with a Northern slab!

But it can hardly be necessary to say more in illustration of this unmanly and unnational dependence, which is so glaring that it cannot fail to be apparent to even the most careless and superficial observer. All the world sees, or ought to see, that in a commercial, mechanical, manufactural, financial, and literary point of view, we are as helpless as babes; that, in comparison with the Free States, our agricultural resources have been greatly exaggerated, misunderstood and mismanaged; and that, instead of cultivating among ourselves a wise policy of mutual assistance and co-operation with respect to individuals, and of self-reliance with respect to the South at large, instead of giving countenance and encouragement to the industrial enterprises projected in our midst, and instead of building up, aggrandizing and beautifying our own States, cities

SOURCE: Hinton Rowan Helper, *The Impending Crisis of the South* (1857; reprint, Cambridge: Harvard University Press, 1968), pp. 22–24, 25, 33–35.

and towns, we have been spending our substance at the North, and are daily augmenting and strengthening the very power which now has us so completely under its thumb. . . .

And now to the point. In our opinion, an opinion which has been formed from data obtained by assiduous researches, and comparisons, from laborious investigation, logical reasoning, and earnest reflection, the causes which have impeded the progress and prosperity of the South, which have dwindled our commerce, and other similar pursuits, into the most contemptible insignificance; sunk a large majority of our people in galling poverty and ignorance, rendered a small minority conceited and tyrannical, and driven the rest away from their homes; entailed upon us a humiliating dependence on the Free States; disgraced us in the recesses of our own souls, and brought us under reproach in the eyes of all civilized and enlightened nations—may all be traced to one common source, and there find solution in the most hateful and horrible word, that was ever incorporated into the vocabulary of human economy—*Slavery!* . . .

By taking a sort of inventory of the agricultural products of the free and slave States in 1850, we now propose to correct a most extraordinary and mischievous error into which the people of the South have unconsciously fallen. Agriculture, it is well known, is the sole boast of the South; and, strange to say, many pro-slavery Southerners, who, in our latitude, pass for intelligent men, are so puffed up with the idea of our importance in this respect, that they speak of the North as a sterile region, unfit for cultivation, and quite dependent on the South for the necessaries of life! Such rampant ignorance ought to be knocked in the head! We can prove that the North produces greater quantities of breadstuffs than the South! Figures shall show the facts. Properly, the South has nothing left to boast of; the North has surpassed her in everything, and is going farther and farther ahead of her every day. We ask the reader's careful attention to the following tables, which we have prepared at no little cost of time and trouble, and which, when duly considered in connection with the foregoing and subsequent portions of our work, will, we believe, carry conviction to the mind that the downward tendency of the South can be arrested only by the abolition of slavery.

TABLE NO. I.

Agricultural Products of the Free States—1850.

States.	Wheat, bushels.	Oats, bushels.	Indian Corn, bushels.
California	17,228		12,236
Connecticut	41,762	1,258,738	1,935,043
Illinois	9,414,575	10,087,241	57,646,984
Indiana	6,214,458	5,655,014	52,964,363
Iowa	1,530,581	1,524,345	8,656,799
Maine	296,259	2,181,037	1,750,056
Massachusetts	31,211	1,165,146	2,345,490
Michigan	4,925,889	2,866,056	5,641,420
New Hampshire	185,658	973,381	1,573,670
New Jersey	1,601,190	3,378,063	8,759,704
New York	13,121,498	26,552,814	17,858,400
Ohio	14,487,351	13,472,742	59,078,695
Pennsylvania	15,367,691	21,538,156	19,835,214
Rhode Island	49	215,232	539,201
Vermont	535,955	2,307,734	2,032,396
Wisconsin	4,286,131	3,414,672	1,988,979
	72,157,486	96,590,371	242,618,650

TABLE NO. II.

Agricultural Products of the Slave States—1850.

States.	Wheat, bushels.	Oats, bushels.	Indian Corn, bushels.
Alabama	294,044	2,965,696	28,754,048
Arkansas	199,639	656,183	8,893,939
Delaware	482,511	604,518	3,145,542
Florida	1,027	66,586	1,996,809
Georgia	1,088,534	3,820,044	30,080,099
Kentucky	2,142,822	8,201,311	58,672,591
Louisiana	417	89,637	10,266,373
Maryland	4,494,680	2,242,151	10,749,858
Mississippi	137,990	1,503,288	22,446,552
Missouri	2,981,652	5,278,079	36,214,537
North Carolina	2,130,102	4,052,078	27,941,051
South Carolina	1,066,277	2,322,155	16,271,454
Tennessee	1,619,386	7,703,086	52,276,223
Texas	41,729	199,017	6,028,876
Virginia	11,212,616	10,179,144	35,254,319
	27,904,476	49,882,979	348,992,282

Source 5:   Emily Burke, *Reminiscences of Georgia*   (1850)

New Englander Emily Burke taught for eight years in Savannah, Georgia, in the 1840s. After returning to the North, she joined a growing list of northerners who published accounts of their experiences in the South—and who often found southerners deficient in numerous ways. What is Burke's view of the white people of northern Georgia? How does she explain their character?

There are but a few water-mills in the south part of Georgia, owing to a want of falls; but in the upper part of the State it is owing to a want of enterprise in the people. The northern part of Georgia, I have been told, very much resembles New Hampshire, being hilly and rocky. Those who have traveled much in that section of country, say that when compared with New England its inhabitants are all of one hundred years behind the times in education, and in all kinds of improvements. In building their houses, they change little, if any more, from one generation to another, than the robins do, who build their nests now just as the first robin did that gathered her sticks and moss, and hatched her innocent brood in the garden of Eden. As it respects conveniences for cooking, they have none. Ovens built of brick are seldom seen; when they are used, they are built out of doors, separated from any building. Iron kettles with covers, sometimes called Dutch ovens, are used when any thing of the kind is needed. Most of the bread is baked before the fire on a piece of wood or earthenware. Cellars, which we consider so indispensable, are never dug, to my knowledge. I never saw one either in the city or country; consequently, we never see good butter there in the warm season; its fluid state always required a deep dish when it came upon the table. Meat is not salted and barreled as here, but smoked and dried, and generally tainted during the process. I never saw any meat preserved in this way that I could eat; and it was more than I wished to do, to sit at the table where it was. I was once passing a corn-house on a plantation with a servant woman, where I observed the smell of putrid flesh; and on making inquiry what it was, the woman informed me that it was beef drying upon the top of the house; for they dry all their meat in the summer, when they can have the benefit of a good hot July or August sun. To those educated in New England, the ignorance that is seen in many portions of the northern part of Georgia is truly astonishing; many cannot read a word, or write their own names. I have heard merchants say, that in transacting business with many men of great wealth, they have found them obliged to use a mark for their signature. This deplorable state of ignorance is owing to the circumstance, that the government has made no provision for common schools, and no children can be educated, unless they are sent from home; and board and tuition in the Southern cities are so expensive, that it requires a large fortune to educate a child; consequently but a few are educated. . . .

This part of the population of Georgia and some of the contiguous States . . . have no ambition to do any thing more than just what is necessary to procure

Source: Reprinted in Alan Gallay, ed., *Voices of the Old South: Eyewitness Accounts, 1528–1861* (Athens: University of Georgia Press, 1994), pp. 277–278; originally from Emily P. Burke, *Reminiscences of Georgia* (Oberlin, Ohio: J. M. Fitch, 1850).

food enough of the coarsest kind to supply the wants of the appetite, and a scanty wardrobe of a fabric they manufacture themselves. If they should ever cherish a desire for any other life than such as the brutes might lead, it would be all in vain, for the present institutions and state of society at the South are calculated to paralyze every energy of both body and mind. They are not treated with half the respect by the rich people that the slaves are, and even the slaves themselves look upon them as their inferiors. I have seen the servants when one of these poor women came into a planter's house, dressed in her homespun frock, bonnet and shawl, collect together in an adjoining room or on the piazza and indulge in a fit of laughter and ridicule about her "cracker gown and bonnet," as they would call them.

Slavery renders labor so disreputable, and wages of slave labor so low, that if places could be found where they might hire out to service, there would be but little inducement to do so.

Questions to Consider

1. How would you compare George Fitzhugh's and Hinton Rowan Helper's analyses of slavery? Both men assumed that blacks were inferior to whites, but they came to very different conclusions about slavery. How do you account for that?

2. What were the most important influences or factors in the lives or backgrounds of Fitzhugh and Helper in shaping their views about slavery? In what ways were they representative voices in the slavery debate before the Civil War? In what ways were their arguments unique?

3. Fitzhugh defended slavery by pointing to the worst features of northern society, while Helper attacked slavery by pointing to the worst features of southern society. How would you compare the men's treatments of life in the North and South? From your understanding of American society in the mid-nineteenth century, whose views do you think are more accurate?

4. Do you think Fitzhugh's or Helper's argument about slavery is more effective? How would you assess the influence of these two propagandists?

5. Helper argued for the abolition of slavery on different grounds than many other abolitionists. How would you compare his arguments to those of Benjamin Lundy and David Walker (see Chapter 8)?

For Further Reading

Hugh C. Bailey, *Hinton Rowan Helper: Abolitionist-Racist* (Tuskaloosa: University of Alabama Press, 1965), is the standard biography of Helper.

David F. Ericson, *The Debate over Slavery: Antislavery and Proslavery Liberalism in Antebellum America* (New York: New York University Press, 2000), studies the impact of antislavery and proslavery rhetoric on the sectional crisis.

Eugene D. Genovese, *The World the Slaveholders Made: Two Essays in Interpretation* (Hanover, N.H.: Wesleyan University Press, 1969), offers an important interpretation of Fitzhugh's anticapitalist views.

Larry E. Tise, *Proslavery: A History of the Defense of Slavery in America, 1701–1840* (Athens: University of Georgia Press, 1987), explores the development of proslavery thought.

Harvey Wish, ed., *Ante-Bellum Writings of George Fitzhugh and Hinton Rowan Helper on Slavery* (New York: Capricorn Books, 1960), provides a concise selection of the two men's writings, with a valuable introduction by the editor.

CHAPTER
13

Free Blacks and the Struggle for Equality:
Mary Ann Shadd and Henry Bibb

Mary Ann Shadd   *Henry Bibb*

Henry Bibb and Mary Ann Shadd had made their decisions. Like other im-migrants, they were determined to pull up stakes and leave the country of their birth for a new life in another land. Like those who went before them, they sought economic opportunity and escape from oppression. And like so many others, they were encouraged by glowing reports about their new home. It of-fered everything their own country did not: freedom, equality before the law, and a chance to improve their lot in life. To get to this promised land, they merely had to leave the United States. For Bibb, Shadd, and thousands of other African Americans, their Canaan was right across the border in Canada.

From 1850 to 1860, between 15,000 and 20,000 African Americans fled to Canada. For them, the decision to emigrate made perfect sense. In 1850, Con-gress passed a fugitive slave law, one of a series of acts designed to resolve a sec-tional crisis sparked by California's proposed admission to the Union as a free state. As a concession to the slave states, Congress approved a law that made it possible for alleged runaways to be taken into the South merely on the sworn statement of a white claimant. Now virtually all of the roughly 200,000 free blacks in northern states could be accused of being runaways. Unable to defend themselves in court, they were, as the African-American historian W. E. B. Du

Bois put it, "hunted blacks." Like Bibb and Shadd, most of the blacks who moved to Canada in the 1850s settled in the southwestern part of what is now the province of Ontario. Some, like Bibb, were runaways from slavery. Others, like Shadd, had been born free. Yet it made no difference now how far one was removed from slavery. Bibb and Shadd were equal in the eyes of the fugitive slave law.

Once in Canada, though, African Americans did not necessarily agree on the best way to achieve equality. Few disagreed more vehemently than Bibb and Shadd. Bibb believed that blacks had to withdraw from white society and build their own separate institutions to achieve true equality. Such thinking appalled Shadd. Convinced that segregation only reinforced white misperceptions of black inferiority, she maintained that integration was the only way for blacks to realize the full promise of life in their new home. The fight between these two refugees attracts attention today because it was so acrimonious. Yet their story also merits our interest because it reveals so much about the challenges facing free blacks and the conflicts that still divide African Americans.

"The Slimy Reptile"

As a free man, Henry Bibb had no interest in running away from slave catchers. Educated "in the school of adversity, whips[,] and chains," he had already run away numerous times as a slave. In fact, his narrative told a harrowing tale of repeated escape and capture. Born in Kentucky in 1815, the son of a white father and a slave mother, Bibb was by his own account a "wretched slave." Continually insubordinate, he claimed that he was not brought up but rather "flogged up." As a boy, he was frequently hired out to others and "compelled to work under the lash without wages." He attempted his first escape at the age of twenty while working for another family. "They would abuse me for going off," he declared, "but it did no good." Sometime later, Bibb heard about Canada, "a land of liberty, somewhere in the North."

For the next seven years, Bibb's life was marked by an unrelenting effort to break "the bands of slavery" and get to Canada, where he believed that he would be "regarded as a man, and not as a thing." His intense desire for freedom did not prevent him from marrying another slave, named Malinda. "I suffered myself," he admitted, "to be turned aside by the fascinating charms of a female." The willful Bibb changed hands several times and was eventually purchased by William Gatewood, Malinda's master and the owner of a nearby plantation. Gatewood proved to be particularly cruel, and Bibb, now the father of a daughter, was determined to escape slavery for good. Walking the short distance to the Ohio River on Christmas Day, 1837, allegedly to work in a slaughterhouse, he escaped to Indiana. There, with a complexion "near the color of a slaveholder," he was not detected as he boarded a Cincinnati-bound steamboat.

Bibb spent the winter in Ohio, planning to rescue his wife and daughter the following spring. Before he could execute his plan, however, he was apprehended by slave catchers hired by Gatewood. Brought back to Kentucky, where Gatewood intended to sell him, Bibb escaped again but was captured when he returned for his wife and child the next summer. Sold by Gatewood and sent down the Mississippi, Bibb and his family were purchased in Vicksburg by a planter named Francis Whitfield for $2,200. By Bibb's account, the Whitfield plantation, fifty miles up the Red River in Louisiana, was a hellhole of rattlesnakes, alligators, and flogging. After more attempts to escape, Bibb was sold again, this time separated for good from Malinda and his daughter. He was taken into Indian Territory, west of the Mississippi River, where he finally passed into the hands of a Cherokee. When the Indian died, Bibb fled again, this time with some of his late master's money. By 1842, Bibb had made it back across Missouri, up the Ohio River to Cincinnati, and all the way to Detroit. Just across the Detroit River from Canada, the Michigan town would be his home for the next eight years.

In Detroit, Bibb joined a black community numbering several hundred. Most of its residents had originally come from Virginia, where harsh enforcement of slave codes* sent free blacks fleeing northward in search of a haven. As elsewhere in the North, they found that while whites enjoyed the increasing democratization of American society in the 1830s, conditions for African Americans had only worsened. Most northern states denied blacks the vote, and many prohibited them from testifying in court against whites. Until 1860, blacks could serve on juries only in Massachusetts. Often states also barred African Americans from certain occupations, prohibited them from buying or selling alcoholic beverages, and even prevented them from moving freely from one county to another. Such discrimination reflected a rising fear of blacks among whites in the North. This growing Negrophobia in the late 1830s and early 1840s led to at least six race riots, the burning of black homes and churches, and frequent beatings of African Americans.

Bibb found racial animosity and second-class citizenship for blacks in Detroit as well. Few longtime residents had forgotten an incident nine years earlier when slave hunters from Kentucky had arrived in search of two fugitives. Blacks had responded by threatening to burn down the town. After a club-wielding mob beat the sheriff, grabbed one of the fugitives, and spirited him off to Canada, racial hatred only deepened. A committee appointed to investigate the incident summed up the feelings of most white residents when it concluded that "neither [blacks'] habits, nor their morals, with a few exceptions make them a safe or desirable addition to our population." As Detroit's black population grew in the 1840s, more white residents came to share that view. In 1850, one White Detroiter described blacks as "dark bipeds—a species not equal to ourselves."

Such attitudes underlay the segregation and discrimination that Bibb and other blacks faced in Detroit. Because voting in Michigan was limited to white males, he was barred from the ballot box. When the Michigan Constitutional Convention submitted the question of black suffrage to the electorate in 1850, Detroit's residents voted it down by a wide margin. Blacks would not be enfranchised in Michigan until the ratification of the Fifteenth Amendment in 1870. African Americans also were not welcome in Detroit's all-white schools. When the self-taught Bibb sought to further his education, he had to attend a black school run by the Reverend William Monroe. Barred from tax-supported white schools, blacks raised money for Monroe's school while also paying the

---

Slave codes: Laws that defined slaves as property and denied them basic rights.

tax for the white ones. When the state created segregated public schools for blacks in 1842, Detroit's board of education quickly assumed control of Monroe's school and replaced him with a white teacher. Praising Monroe for guiding their children's "morals and intellect" and declaring the "utmost confidence in his ability and integrity," black parents started another school. Meanwhile, similar segregation prevailed in Detroit's churches. The town's first black church was founded in 1837 (with William Monroe as its pastor) when black worshipers at the First Baptist Church were relegated to the gallery during services.

This segregation and discrimination sped the formation of numerous black organizations: a library and reading room, a debating club, a temperance society, and a young men's society. It also led to a growing commitment in the black community to fight slavery and second-class citizenship. In 1837, abolitionists founded the Detroit Anti-Slavery Society. A few years later, blacks held a mass meeting to protest their disfranchisement, proclaiming "no taxation without representation." Declaring that "the long lost rights of our people in this community, or any other, could only be gained by our own exertion," black community leaders also organized the Colored Vigilant Committee. Similar to vigilance committees in other northern communities, the group provided assistance to fugitives and campaigned for black suffrage and an end to slavery.

As such committees indicated, Bibb's arrival in Detroit coincided with a growing abolitionist movement throughout the North. For blacks, organized abolitionism had begun in response to the formation of the American Colonization Society, founded in 1817 by northern white abolitionists and southern politicians to colonize blacks outside the United States. (See Chapter 8.) Northern free blacks quickly organized to protest these efforts to send them into exile. Their work, which soon gave rise to scores of black abolitionist societies, was reinforced in the early 1830s by the emergence of more militant white abolitionists, epitomized by the fiery William Lloyd Garrison. The founder of the antislavery newspaper the *Liberator* in 1831 and one of the organizers of the American Anti-Slavery Society two years later, Garrison denounced colonization and the gradual emancipation favored by earlier abolitionists. To Garrison and many other militant abolitionists, slavery was a moral question. Southern slaveholders needed to be convinced through moral persuasion to end this sinful institution. Although few southerners converted to abolitionism, perhaps several hundred thousand whites and blacks joined the crusade against slavery by the 1850s.

Supporting himself with jobs that "varied according to circumstances," Bibb put his considerable talents to work in this growing fight against slavery and inequality. He joined the Colored Vigilant Committee. In 1843, he attended a state convention of "colored citizens" in Detroit that called for the immediate abolition of slavery and demanded "equal rights and political privileges," including the right to vote. He was involved in a secret organization known as the Order of the Men of Oppression or the Order of Emancipation. Although its activities remain a mystery, it was probably part of the Underground Railroad,* aiding

---

Underground Railroad: A secret network of several thousand people who helped slaves escape to free states and to Canada.

fugitive slaves who made their way to Detroit. Concerned about the economic lot of free blacks, Bibb also became an agent for a manual-labor school for blacks.

It was as an antislavery speaker, however, that Bibb made his biggest mark. By 1844, he was spending much of his time outside Detroit speaking for candidates of the antislavery Liberty Party.* With Frederick Douglass and other black abolitionist leaders, he attended the first meeting of the Free-Soil Party* in 1848. When a convention of blacks met in 1850, it chose Bibb to send to the Michigan Constitutional Convention to speak for equality and enfranchisement. Although his formal education had been limited to a two-week stint at William Monroe's school, the former slave was an effective speaker. Once, standing before a crowd of a thousand people, he saw "many of them shedding tears while I related the sad story of my wrongs."

Such activities sometimes provoked angry crowds and drew the ire of the *Detroit Free Press,* which called him a "rascal" who was "unworthy of belief." Nevertheless, Bibb was undeterred and even delivered his antislavery message to southerners. He was convinced that the Christian Gospel was opposed to slavery, and he backed the American Missionary Association's* efforts to distribute Bibles to slaves. Traveling in southern Ohio, he frequently spoke to Virginians who crossed the Ohio River to attend his lectures. He also spoke to whites in his native Kentucky. After the 1843 convention, Bibb sent copies of the proceedings to several Kentucky slaveholders, including William Gatewood. His old master responded with a letter informing him that his "mother is still here and she is well." After consulting antislavery friends, Bibb wrote back, clearly conveying his attitudes toward Gatewood and slavery itself. **[See Source 1.]**

In 1849, Bibb published *Narrative of the Life and Adventures of Henry Bibb, an American Slave,* a powerful indictment of the "peculiar institution." In the antislavery cause, he found not only his life's work but a partner for life. While at an antislavery meeting in New York City in 1847, he met Mary Miles, a Rhode Island native and only child of Quaker parents. Mary had graduated from the normal school in Albany, New York, and had taught school in Massachusetts, Pennsylvania, and Ohio. Bibb found that their principles "were nearly one and the same," and the next year they were married.

One principle that Henry and Mary soon agreed on was the need for blacks to leave the United States. Years earlier, Bibb had introduced a resolution at a black convention declaring that delegates would "never consent to emigrate or be colonized from this, our native soil, while there exists one drop of African blood in bondage." By 1850, however, the Bibbs were ready to do just that. Like the estimated three thousand African Americans who fled to Canada in the first three months after the passage of the Fugitive Slave Act, they were concerned about their safety. Yet their desire to emigrate reflected not just fear of capture but also a loss of faith in the United States. Bibb was annoyed at the racism he

Liberty Party: The first antislavery political party, formed in 1840.

Free Soil Party: A political party founded in the 1848 to oppose the extension of slavery in territory taken by the United States in the Mexican War.

American Missionary Association: An organization run by white, antislavery Protestants to assist fugitive slaves.

perceived among white abolitionists, disillusioned with William Lloyd Garrison's policy of ending slavery through moral persuasion, and increasingly gloomy about the prospects for free blacks.

Settling in Sandwich, outside Windsor, in what would become Ontario, the Bibbs quickly became leaders in the black community, now swelling with refugees from the United States. They helped found antislavery, temperance, and educational societies and became active in the Methodist Church. Mary started a day school in her home for the children of fugitive slaves, as well as a Sunday school. Meanwhile, Henry began publication of the *Voice of the Fugitive,* the first black newspaper in Canada, which he intended to be "a mouthpiece" for the black refugees. In its pages, he advocated immigration to Canada, where blacks faced no discriminatory legislation and were entitled to citizenship and voting rights. "[U]nder this government . . . ," he declared, "we participate in all the rights and privileges which other men enjoy."

The Bibbs and other refugees quickly learned, however, that attitudes and conditions in Canada were in many ways little different from those in the northern United States. Blacks were discriminated against socially and economically. They were barred from many jobs and excluded from white churches. Because Canadian law left the decision to segregate schools up to the local districts, they also were excluded from white schools. As more refugees moved into western Ontario, racism among whites increased, an attitude both reflected in and fanned by the Canadian press. "Already, we have a far greater number of negroes in the province than the good of the country requires," a Toronto newspaper observed. Conceding nothing to his American counterparts when it came to racist attacks, one editor declared that when he was referring to whites, he was "speaking now of human beings, the link between the celestial and terrestrial [*sic*] and not of negroes who connected the orangoutang [*sic*] with the monkey." Bibb used his newspaper to respond to this growing Negrophobia. Comparing Canadian prejudice to a snake, he declared that it was "biting and poisoning every one that [it] can without being seen." The *Voice of the Fugitive,* he added, "shall endeavor to keep [its] eye upon the slimy reptile."

Canadian racism helped convince Bibb that leaving the United States was only the first step toward freedom. He now believed that to achieve "independence and self-respect," blacks had to create a separate black community as free as possible from interaction with the larger society. It was not a new idea. Ever since David Walker had published his *Appeal to the Coloured Citizens of the World* in 1829 (see Chapter 8), many blacks had struggled with the question of black separatism. Although Walker condemned racial oppression, he refused to endorse separatism. Many of his followers, however, called for the formation of independent and self-sufficient black communities. For example, in the 1830s, former slave Lewis Woodson, a Pittsburgh minister and teacher, proposed that blacks separate from white society. Sometimes called the father of black nationalism, Woodson argued that integration would never work and blacks should form their own communities. By the 1840s, Woodson's message had inspired the formation of several black communities in the United States and Canada. After the passage of the Fugitive Slave Act in 1850, many more blacks had turned with new interest to Woodson's concept of separate black agricultural communities.

Bibb was one of them. After settling in Canada, he became a leader and promoter of the Refugee Home Society (RHS), a Detroit-based organization founded in 1851 to help fugitive slaves become farmers. The RHS proposed to settle black refugee families on twenty-five-acre plots, which it would sell for $1.50 an acre. Two-thirds of the revenue from these sales would be reinvested, creating a perpetual revolving fund for the purchase of additional land from the government. Soon the organization had purchased two thousand acres near Windsor, reselling half of the land to 150 blacks who had already moved there. The RHS had other ambitious plans. It intended not only to purchase fifty thousand more acres for resale but also to transform fugitives by instilling within them the virtues of self-reliance and industry. By promoting temperance, education, and religion, Bibb predicted, the RHS would bring about nothing less than the elevation of the fugitives and ultimately their acceptance in society. **[See Source 2.]** Little did he know that a black woman and fellow refugee would be this bold scheme's biggest foe.

"Dead and in Hell"

Henry Bibb and Mary Ann Shadd traveled very different paths to Canada. While Bibb entered the world a slave, Shadd was born in 1823 into a small, slave-state, black elite. Her father, Abraham, was a Wilmington, Delaware, shoemaker who had followed his own father's occupation and inherited part of his thirteen-hundred-dollar estate. As a skilled craftsman, Abraham acquired even more property. By 1830, he was a vocal abolitionist, and later became a member of the American Anti-Slavery Society. An opponent of the American Colonization Society's program of black emigration from the United States to Africa, Abraham was convinced that African Americans would achieve equality only through education, hard work, thrift, and integration. A believer in mutual aid as well as self-help, he sheltered fugitive slaves fleeing to the North on the Underground Railroad. Perhaps for the same reason, he moved his family in 1833 to Pennsylvania, where Mary Ann, the oldest child, would have the opportunity for an education denied her in Delaware.

Mary Ann's career reflected her father's views. Like Abraham, she was convinced that literacy was the first step toward independence. After attending a Quaker school for six years, she returned to Wilmington to start a school for blacks. Later, at schools in New York and Pennsylvania, she continued to stress the need for hard work, thrift, and education. In 1849, she published a pamphlet that revealed her emphasis on self-help and, perhaps, her exposure to the Quakers' focus on simple living and commitment to moral activism. In *Hints to the Colored People of the North*, she analyzed how blacks were kept down in northern society, counseled them to shun the showy display and materialism of whites, and advised them not to wait for whites to take up the antislavery cause.

Shadd taught for twelve years, until the passage of the Fugitive Slave Act changed her views about the desirability of emigration. In 1851, she traveled to Toronto to attend the North American Convention of Colored People, organized by Bibb to promote emigration from the United States to Canada. Impressed by the condition of blacks in Canada, Shadd quickly decided to leave the United States. In Canada, she wrote her brother, she did not "feel prejudice."

Encouraged by Bibb to seek out a new home in Sandwich, the twenty-eight-year-old Shadd soon found herself headed west across Lake Erie on a steamboat. Arriving in Sandwich later that fall, she immediately moved a few miles north to Windsor, where she found a poverty-stricken black community. Local residents had invited her to establish a school, which she soon opened in a former military barracks. Just as quickly, she would learn that she and other black refugees in Canada were bitterly divided over the best way for them to survive in their new home. Bibb, Lewis Woodson's student Martin Delany, and other black leaders called for self-segregation based on a common black culture and experience. Shadd vehemently opposed it. She may have come to accept emigration, but the woman who quit the African Methodist Episcopal Church "because of its distinctive [segregated] character" was not ready to give up her belief in integration as the only hope for black equality.

These conflicting views put Shadd in a nasty and protracted struggle with the very man who had invited her to come west. The initial problem was Shadd's school, which reflected her integrationist views by accepting both blacks and whites. At first Bibb seemed pleased with Shadd and her work, calling her a "lady of high literary attainments." Shortly after her school opened, however, it came under Mary Bibb's attack. Mary had already established a nearby school for blacks, and now she was arguing that blacks should demand a separate public school. When the government finally created a black school in 1853, Mary took it over. Denouncing the "pretended sympathizers in this vicinity," Shadd publicly accused Henry Bibb of undermining her school, which struggled for several years before finally being forced to close for lack of funds. Even then, Shadd refused to yield. "I stand alone," she declared, "in opposition to caste schools."

The struggle over segregated schools was just the beginning of the two refugees' battle. Although Shadd shared Henry Bibb's desire for black self-sufficiency, she was adamantly opposed to separation of the races in any form. In her mind, black schools and churches were bad, and separate communities were even worse. That view, of course, put her at odds with Bibb and his Refugee Home Society. Already by 1852, the RHS had settled 150 blacks on the land it had purchased near Windsor. Such separate black communities, Bibb argued, were necessary because black refugees in Canada were "strangers in a foreign land" and would "experience a greater degree of happiness" living together. Shadd was convinced that blacks need to function outside of insulated communities. Besides, if such experiments failed, that would only reinforce white perceptions that blacks were incapable of supporting themselves as free people.

For the same reason, Shadd blasted the RHS's practice of fundraising. Labeled a "begging system" by opponents, it involved the soliciting of clothing, supplies, and funds among whites, who were urged to help impoverished refugees. Shadd was appalled by such appeals, which she said made former slaves seem helpless and thus reinforced a degrading perception of blacks. The begging of RHS agents in white homes, churches, and antislavery gatherings, she noted, made blacks "objects of charity" and transformed them into "improvident, thriftless and imbecile paupers." Rather than make black refugees the recipients of welfare, she proposed, assistance should work to help them develop skills so they could support themselves. After only nine months in Canada, Shadd launched a frontal assault on Bibb. In a pamphlet titled *A Plea for Emigration, or Notes of Canada West, in its Moral, Social and Political Aspect,* she attacked separatism in general and the RHS in particular. Black communities, she argued, would arouse white Canadian prejudice by making black Canadians look like the "degraded men of like color in the United States." In addition, she thought that Bibb and other separatists exaggerated the extent of Canadian Negrophobia to scare fugitives into insulating themselves from society. By distorting and misconstruing whites' remarks, they merely increased blacks' prejudice against whites and made it more difficult for blacks to assimilate into Canadian society.

A Plea for Emigration further heightened the animosity between Shadd and Bibb, which had become personal as well as philosophical. Given Bibb's own history, it was easy for him to conclude that a freeborn, elite black woman like Shadd had little understanding of the needs of refugee slaves. Given the widespread assumptions about the need for women to defer to male authority, it also was easy to conclude that Shadd had overstepped her bounds. The *Voice of the Fugitive* regularly published what one historian called "Victorian homilies" designed to reinforce conventional assumptions about women's domestic role. As the battle between Shadd and Bibb continued, it did not take Bibb's newspaper long to observe that Shadd did not conform to them. "Miss Shadd has said and written many things," it noted in 1852, "which we think will add nothing to her credit as a lady." Like many white abolitionist women in the United States, Shadd discovered that her work on behalf of blacks brought her face-to-face with another kind of prejudice.

As the dispute between Shadd and Bibb escalated, it descended into petty insults and name-calling. The *Voice of the Fugitive* called Shadd "an insignificant scribbler in this village" who "merits the contempt" of the commuity. Shadd and her supporters, it went on, were "vile creatures." After Shadd published *A Plea for Emigration,* Bibb attacked her for having it printed by a white publisher in Detroit and pointed to its numerous printing errors. Later, he disclosed Shadd's acceptance of American Missionary Association funds for her school, undercutting her attacks on the RHS's reliance on white philanthropy. Such attacks only sharpened Shadd's pen. Mary Bibb, she charged, was "a *profane* swearer and drug taking woman," while Henry Bibb "says he could see me dead and in Hell." RHS agents, she said, took a large share of the money they raised through their abject begging among whites. Worse, the RHS often sold its land parcels to refugees at a higher cost than the government did for comparable land. Henry Bibb, she concluded, was "a dishonest man, and as such must be known to the world." **[See Source 3.]** Bibb countered these charges by accusing Shadd and her supporters of betraying their race. Those who accepted "the deluded sister'[s]" beliefs, he declared, were "vile traitors who give 'aid and comfort' to the enemies who attack us."

Shadd became increasingly frustrated by her inability to respond publicly to Bibb's attacks. In 1853, she started her own newspaper, the *Provincial Freeman,* which she moved to Toronto the next year. In its pages, she continued to preach her integrationist message and attack separatism. Only by becoming independent and productive members within society would refugees prove "the fitness of slaves for freedom" and the ability of blacks to live "upon terms of political and social equality with the anglo-saxon race." As the first black female newspaper editor in North America, Shadd realized that she had broken "the Editorial ice" and urged other black women to "go to editing." Yet she also realized that she had once again overstepped her bounds as a woman. While remaining firmly in control of the paper, she appointed a male editor to pacify critics who, like Bibb, were often quick to complain that she was entirely too outspoken for a "lady."

Unfortunately for Bibb, mismanagement of the RHS provided Shadd's paper with ample fodder. The RHS, for instance, sold land to poor fugitives and then brought suit against them when they were unable to make payments. At the same time, the fugitives saw little evidence of the RHS's ambitious programs for education and moral uplift. Gradually, Shadd's assault turned public opinion against Bibb and the RHS. One Canadian antislavery organization, for instance, denounced what it called "the general begging schemes in the name of the Colored people of this country." Bibb's cause received another setback when a fire destroyed the office of the *Voice of the Fugitive* in 1853. Convinced that the blaze was the result of arson, he promised readers that the paper was not dead. For a time, he published a one-page *Voice*, but the paper never recovered from the fire.

The cause of black Canadian separatism received an even bigger blow the following year. On August 1, 1854, Bibb died at the age of thirty-nine. The date was an important one to Canadian blacks, for it marked the end of slavery in the British West Indies. On Emancipation Day, they reveled in parades, speeches, and picnics reminiscent of the slaveholders' celebration of the Fourth of July. Several years later, Mary Bibb married Isaac Cary, a fellow refugee. Cary, an agent for the *Provincial Freeman*, was Shadd's brother-in-law. Perhaps Bibb found significance in her marriage to Cary, a Shadd associate and in-law. If nothing else, it reflected the black refugee community's isolation from the rest of Canadian society. It was that very isolation that had made the accusations and recriminations between Shadd and Henry Bibb so destructive. As in other communities in similar circumstances—confronted with prejudice and yet dependent on the larger society—it was only too easy for members to take their frustrations out on one another.

"Ignorance, Conceit and Ambition"

After the main target of Mary Ann Shadd's wrath died, her paper continued to attack black separatism and the RHS. Its new leader in Canada was a white man named Charles Foote. Shadd found Foote's begging for funds and patronizing attitude toward blacks reprehensible. In fact, anything that she considered an obstacle to the full assimilation of blacks into Canadian life drew her scorn. The paper repeatedly attacked the racism of white Canadians, publicizing examples of discrimination and prejudice in scathing terms. Shadd singled out one town as a "contemptible . . . little place in the bush" and advised blacks to steer clear of it if they wished to avoid "lessons in colorphobia." Even Canadian abolitionists, whom she accused of a "despotic, dictatorial, snobbish air of superiority" over blacks, did not escape her wrath. At the same time, Shadd never argued that whites alone were responsible for blacks' woeful position in Canadian society. Rather she continued to preach that refugees had to take it upon themselves to improve their lot and ignore the "pretended" leaders who were nothing more than "men of great ignorance, conceit and ambition." **[See Source 4.]**

Such outspokenness no doubt contributed to the demise of the RHS, which was never able to fulfill Henry Bibb's dream of a separate, thriving black community. By 1860, only sixty black families lived on land purchased from the RHS. By the next year, the society began to liquidate its assets and soon joined a growing list of failed black separatist communities. At the same time, Shadd's acerbic style did little to aid the *Provincial Freeman*'s shaky finances. By 1856, it had ceased regular publication. To make ends meet, Shadd's new husband, a Toronto barber and fellow refugee named Thomas Cary (the brother of Mary Bibb's new husband), was forced to sell lamps and lamp oil. Meanwhile, Shadd went on an antislavery lecture tour to sign up subscribers and found it necessary—just as Henry Bibb had earlier—to issue a public plea for funds. "Any *Donations* in funds sent by friends to our address," it read, "will be duly and gratefully acknowledged." Such appeals did little good. The paper was published only intermittently until 1860, when it ceased publication for good.

Shadd returned to teaching, establishing a school with her sister-in-law in Chatham. Like her earlier school in Windsor, the new school would make "no complexional differences," but it quickly ran into financial difficulties. Many of the parents were unable to pay, and Shadd was forced to accept funds from the American Missionary Association. Such support must have been especially galling for Shadd, who believed that the association had withdrawn support from her Windsor school six years earlier because she had dared to criticize the RHS. Worse, she again found herself involved in the very "begging" that she had condemned. In accepting funds from the American Missionary Association and others, Shadd demonstrated that she, like Bibb, had to sacrifice principle for self-interest.

When the Civil War began in 1861, Shadd found her principles put to the test again. She had invested much in the dream of establishing an integrated community north of the border. In 1863, though, she eagerly accepted an offer from Martin Delany to become a recruiter for the Union army. By the end of the war, thousands of black refugees in Canada had returned to the United States. Believing that the cause of racial equality held greater promise in her native land, Shadd decided to join them. After teaching for several years in Detroit, she moved to Washington, D.C., which she called "the Mecca of the colored pilgrim." By the time she died in 1893, she had served as the principal of a black grammar school, earned a law degree from Howard University, lectured frequently on the need for black self-help and the dangers of white benevolence, and become an active supporter of women's rights. Shadd also lived long enough to see that her optimism about race relations after the Civil War had been misplaced. By the end of the nineteenth century, virtually all of the political gains freedmen won during Reconstruction, including the right to vote, had been lost, and blacks remained second-class citizens.

Although Shadd's and Bibb's dreams of equality were unrealized, their struggles were important nonetheless. The very issues that they fought over—integration, black nationalism, and self-help—would confront African Americans throughout the next century, dividing such leaders as W. E. B. Du Bois and Booker T. Washington, Martin Luther King Jr. and Malcolm X, and Jesse Jackson and Louis Farrakhan. In addition, the struggles that Shadd and Bibb faced illustrate the kinds of obstacles those fighting for full racial equality would continue to confront. Battling the seemingly intractable problems of white racism and black poverty, Bibb and Shadd made compromises that violated their principles. Bibb championed black separatism but relied on a white-controlled organization and accepted white charity to achieve it. Shadd preached self-help but also was reduced to "begging" for funds. Bibb saw himself as a fugitive but stayed in Canada until it became his final resting place. Shadd believed that refugees needed to think of Canada as their permanent home but returned to the land she had fled. In the end, both refugees' fates demonstrated that America's racial problems could not be solved by fleeing from them.

PRIMARY SOURCES

SOURCE 1:   Henry Bibb, *Letter to His Former Master*   (1844)

William Gatewood wrote a letter to Henry Bibb after Bibb sent his former master a pamphlet containing the proceedings of a black state convention in Detroit. What does the tone of Bibb's reply suggest about his attitudes toward slavery?

Dear Sir:—I am happy to inform you that you are not mistaken in the man whom you sold as property, and received pay for as such. But I thank God that I am not property now, but am regarded as a man like yourself, and although I live far north, I am enjoying a comfortable living by my own industry. If you should ever chance to be traveling this way, and will call on me, I will use you better than you did me while you held me as a slave. Think not that I have any malice against you, for the cruel treatment which you inflicted on me while I was in your power. As it was the custom of your country, to treat your fellow men as you did me and my little family, I can freely forgive you.

I wish to be remembered in love to my aged mother, and friends; please tell her that if we should never meet again in this life, my prayer shall be to God that we may meet in Heaven, where parting shall be no more.

You wish to be remembered to King and Jack. I am pleased, sir, to inform you that they are both here, well, and doing well. They are both living in

SOURCE: Reprinted in Gilbert Osofsky, ed., *Puttin' On Ole Massa: The Slave Narratives of Henry Bibb, William Wells Brown, and Solomon Northup* (New York: Harper & Row, 1969), pp. 155–156; originally from Henry Bibb, *Narrative of the Life and Adventures of Henry Bibb, an American Slave* (New York, 1850).

Canada West.* They are now the owners of better farms than the men are who once owned them.

You may perhaps think hard of us for running away from slavery, but as to myself, I have but one apology to make for it, which is this: I have only to regret that I did not start at an earlier period. I might have been free long before I was. But you had it in your power to have kept me there much longer than you did. I think it is very probable that I should have been a toiling slave on your plantation to-day, if you had treated me differently.

To be compelled to stand by and see you whip and slash my wife without mercy, when I could afford her no protection, not even by offering myself to suffer the lash in her place, was more than I felt it to be the duty of a slave husband to endure, while the way was open to Canada. My infant child was also frequently flogged by Mrs. Gatewood, for crying, until its skin was bruised literally purple. This kind of treatment was what drove me from home and family, to seek a better home for them. But I am willing to forget the past. I should be pleased to hear from you again, on the reception of this, and should also be very happy to correspond with you often, if it should be agreeable to yourself. I subscribe myself a friend to the oppressed, and Liberty forever.

Henry Bibb.

WILLIAM GATEWOOD.
Detroit, March 23d, 1844.

SOURCE 2:   *Henry Bibb on the Refugee Home Society*   (1851)

In this editorial from the Voice of the Fugitive, *Henry Bibb discusses the Refugee Home Society's plans for the settlement of black fugitives on the land. Why does Bibb think such a settlement scheme is necessary? What does this source reveal about Bibb's hopes for the society?*

It was generally supposed before the passage of the fugitive slave law that there were from 25 to 35 thousand who had taken refuge here, and since that enactment the number has greatly augmented[1]—from the fact that it is now well understood that there is no protection to the liberty of a refugee slave in America, until the Canadian line is drawn between him and his pursuer. . . .

The condition of this people in Canada, as a general thing, is that they are here in a strange land from necessity, uneducated, poverty stricken, without homes or any permanent means of self support; however willing they may be to work they have no means to work with or land to work upon. The natural in-

---

SOURCE: Reprinted in C. Peter Ripley, ed., *The Black Abolitionist Papers* (Chapel Hill: University of North Carolina Press, 1986), II, 143–145; originally from *Voice of the Fugitive*, June 18, 1851.

*Canada West: Now the province of Ontario.

---

1. Bibb no doubt exaggerated the number of refugees in Canada.

ference is that they must either beg, starve or steal. To prevent this much has been sent to Canada during the last 7 months by the friends of humanity, in the way of food and clothing for the fugitives. But such help is only temporary and must be repeated again and again, while it is degrading to some extent to all who are recipients thereof—for no people can be respected who live beneath the dignity of manhood. Ignorance, dissipation and pauperism are the landmarks of slavery, and the great aim and object, therefore, should be to enable this people to arise above it by their own industry. The remedy for the physical wants of this people, those especially specified, lies slumbering in the virgin soil of C[anada] W[est]. To improve the moral, mental and political condition of a poverty stricken and degraded people, they must become owners and tillers of the soil—and PRODUCE WHAT THEY CONSUME.

It is no exaggeration for us to say that more than two-thirds of the refugees in Canada understand agricultural labor and would follow it for a livelihood, had they land or the means to purchase it. They would also gladly open schools for their children that they might be educated for usefulness in life, had they the means with which to do it.

Without homes or employment they are poorly qualified to produce the necessaries of life, to educate the youth or extend the hospitable hand to the gradual emigration of other fugitives who are constantly arriving here, who go up and down these shores hunting shelter and employment but finding none. In order that there may be a permanent asylum to conduct such persons to on the Queen's soil, where the cause of education, industry and morality may be promoted, the friends of humanity in Michigan have organized a state society for the purpose of making an "effort at home and abroad" to purchase 50,000 acres of Canada land for this object, and they propose to deed to the family of every actual settler 5 acres of said land and to leave adjoining it 20 acres which may be purchased by said settler at cost and that one-third of all money paid in for said land by settlers should be appropriated for the support of schools for their children, and that the balance should be kept at interest in the bank for the purchase of more land for the same object from time to time while slavery exists in the United States . . . .

H. BIBB

SOURCE 3:   *Mary Ann Shadd on the Refugee Home Society* (1852)

The American Missionary Association provided funds for Mary Ann Shadd's school while also supporting the Refugee Home Society. Shadd wrote this letter to the association's secretary in response to Henry Bibb's charges against her. What are her main complaints about the RHS? Does this source suggest that the dispute between Bibb and Shadd was mostly personal or philosophical?

Windsor, C[anada] W[est]
Dec[ember] 28, [18]52

Professor G. Whipple
Dear Sir—

Yours of the 15th has been received for which and the enclosed draft you will please accept my thanks.

I am not at all surprised that your attention should be called to my case, indeed the many assertions made by Mr. and Mrs. Bibb, publicly and privately, of my being "nearly down [now]" with the certainty of a still more dishonorable position, and over all, the confident way in which they expressed themselves, made their dishonorable actions both in supplying Rev. C. C. Foote* with falsehoods concern[ing m]e, and in endeavoring to make my residence here an impossibility too apparent. I am surprised though that the Rev. C. C. Foote should accuse me of "outrageous slanders." . . .

In "affirming that the ~~fugitises~~ fugitives do <u>not</u> need help" there is no slander, but a fact known to every one who knows much about them, and continually insisted upon by fugitives themselves. I will here call your attention to a large meeting held, in this place, by fugitives on this very subject: it was one of a number of the same kind held in different parts of the province. "That they get but little of what is raised" is no slander, but is strictly true, whether it refers to begging for old and new clothes, money &c., or for the <u>Refugees</u> [sic] <u>Home Society</u>. Agents of the clothes and money, in most cases give out very little to destitute fugitives, and fugitives in this district, never <u>heard</u> of money being given to them—some have had it taken <u>away</u>. . . .

I deny ever having said or written that the Society was "got up" for the benefit of the agents. . . . I do not know that it was <u>gotten up</u> only for the benefit of the agents and officers, but I believ[e] it is for their benifit now only; I <u>know</u> that if the agents have not been benefitted, the black people have <u>not</u>. . . .

The prominent objections to the Society are: It is not needed <u>at all</u> as Government offers land <u>cheaper</u> and on better conditions: many families of fugitives own farms near the Refugees Home, and not one of whom gave as much per acre as the Society charges. . . .

SOURCE: C. Peter Ripley, ed., *The Black Abolitionist Papers* (Chapel Hill: University of North Carolina Press, 1986), II, 245, 247–249, 250, 251; originally from American Missionary Association Archives, Amistad Research Centers, New Orleans.

Charles C. Foote: A Presbyterian minister and an associate of Henry Bibb's in the Refugee Home Society. After Bibb died, he became the leader of the society.

It keeps active the begging system, and thus diverts the gifts of benevolent persons from their proper course. By claiming to be a "<u>Missionary Society</u>," funds are diverted from efficient missionary organizations. It fosters exclusive institutions; making a line between black men even. Though one half is said to be applied to educational and religious purposes, fugitives only may be so benefitted, if it can be called a benefit in such a case. . . . Instead of the settlers being men of "good character," . . . the testimony of respectable fugitives is that they come to [word crossed out] town whenever they can get a few shillings, spend them in the liquor stores for whiskey, and depend upon borrowing a little meal etc., from their neighbors. The Home is looked upon as a lounging place for worthless thriftless men, and is calle[d] "Bibbs plantation," "Nigger quarter" and other names indicative of their hatred of oppression. . . .

It is no slander to say that Henry Bibb has hundreds of dollars belonging to fugitives—probably thousands would be nearer the truth. Henry Bibb is a dishonest man, and as such must be known to the world. To expose him is a duty which though painful . . . must nevertheless be performed . . .

Within the present year, and during the time he has been asking for "donations" etc. to help him out of difficulty, he has built a house, bought a vessel, bought a house and lots leased on which he lives, leased another, and Mrs. Bibb has purchased a farm, and there are other business operations I can mention, besides the paper and being in receipt of several hundreds per annum for buildings and lots in Detroit. This is the man who is "making sacrifices" for the fugitives. The man who travels West with toes and elbows out, to create sympathy—who has a smile a prayer or billingsgate* ready on the instant, and who at home, wraps up in purple and fine linen by warm fires, and sends from his door naked fugitives, on the plea that "abolitionists have left it discretionary with him to give or not." Fugitives have come to me to inquire what steps must be taken to secure money given to them by friends in his house and withheld by him, on the pretence that <u>they would not know</u> how to expend it. . . .

In conclusion I can only say I have endeavored to do my duty here as your teacher, and have studiously sought to so act as not to bring contempt upon our Lord's cause. I have spoken out what I and others know of the Refugees' Home Society, and of Henry Bibb, but not until silence was no longer safe nor right. . . . In doing what I have done I repeat no one has been slandered; facts and statements made by persons of veracity have been given; and I trust the cause of truth has been subserved and the interests of fugitives promoted measurably.

May God and not man decide for you in this matter, that exact justice may be given to all parties. Yours very respectfully,

Mary A. Shadd

Billingsgate: Foul, abusive language.

Source 4:   Mary Ann Shadd, *"Obstacles to the Progress of Colored Canadians"* (1857)

In this editorial from the Provincial Freeman, *Mary Ann Shadd discusses why black Canadians have made so little progress in their new home. What does she see as the primary obstacles facing the black community?*

The colored people of these Provinces live in a land of equal laws—equal rights, and yet, no people that we know of are given to complaint more than they. In certain localities, parties can be found, who, taking advantage of the prevalent ignorance among the colored population, administer the law in a way clearly prejudicial to the interests of the latter; but, how far the former are censurable under the circumstances is with us a question, when viewed in the light of an ordinary transaction for the exact extent of the censure to be attached to the colored people themselves is not quite clear, we are convinced however, that the fault is not all on one side, but that to them belongs a fair share of blame. We make these remarks with no intention to shield white men from merited blame at all; but that the colored people may not take to themselves complete exemption from rebuke for their great indifference to their interests.

Courts of justice, corrupt judges nor any other grievance of which we may complain can injure them a tithe in comparison, with the treachery, want of confidence and down right wickedness one towards the other. . . .

Try any community—our own, to begin with, and seek out if you can among its teeming hundreds, twenty men who see eye to eye upon the subject of their interests! They cannot be found! While upon one question some may unite, there will be the most rancorous and bitter division, upon others equally clear and conclusive; and rather than yield an opinion for the general good; their entire interests may go by the poor. . . .

Take a retrospect of the colored people of Canada for the last thirty years. Their institutions—their divisions—the knots and "squads"—their white and colored beggars—begging in public for lands, clothes, schools, churches—the quarrels of these beggars, white and colored—the contentions about their lands— among their churches—the *immorality* among missionaries white and colored, teachers and preachers, male and female—the caucuses, conventions, resolutions, and after all, the return of the pretended leaders of the people, "Like the dog to his vomit, or the sow to her wallowing in the mire," and that too, after years or weeks or months of sin, and after having before "God and the sun" foresworn for the twentieth time such vile deeds.

And now good reader, and friend to your race, look at the *condition* of the same churches, schools, institutions. Calculate if you can, the vast sums drawn from the benevolent of England and America, enough to have installed an empire; then, too, turn to the "mussy fussy" creatures who have been at this work—this business of degrading an entire people, back almost to their [first]

Source: Reprinted in C. Peter Ripley, ed., *The Black Abolitionist Papers* (Chapel Hill: University of North Carolina Press, 1986), II, 360, 361–362; originally from the *Provincial Freeman*, January 31, 1857.

estate, as fast as British law could make men of them, and what do we see? Who are these Atlases upon whose powerful shoulders rests this *colored* world? Men generally among the whites, who could not be made available for any good work at home—men of fallen fortunes or of no fortunes, who have chosen this field to replenish empty purses, or to fill purses always empty; and among black men, knavish tools of these first named, or men of great ignorance, conceit and ambition, whose highest recommendation, whose certificate of reputation, is their ability to instal beggars and begging, and to squander the same. Think of it! The destiny of thousands of people to be confided to such keeping. Think of a people who when on the other side, was said by one of the greatest philanthropists of the county to be a "nation of servants," and when under British rule aspire to be a nation of beggars. . . . Instead of treachery, ignorance[,] servility, we want to see confidence, intelligence, independence and instead of a host of cold refugees formerly bond and free, aiming . . . to curse their people, with a proslavery—yankee training. We shall aim to persuade these "suffering" people, to cease hankering after the "flesh pots of Egypt," and as they have come under British rule from necessity, to become British at heart in reality.

M.A.S.C.

Questions to Consider

1. How would you compare the approaches of Henry Bibb and Mary Ann Shadd to dealing with the plight of African Americans? For all of their differences, did they seek the same thing and share the same values? What factors may have helped to influence their thinking about the best way to achieve racial equality? Do you think Shadd would have thought differently about this problem if she had been a slave?

2. One study has argued that abolitionists had "a noble dream and no practical program" for achieving racial equality. Do Bibb and Shadd contradict or reinforce that generalization?

3. Like other antebellum black-separatist groups, the Refugee Home Society failed to establish a permanent, successful community on the land. How do you explain its failure? Was Shadd correct in her analysis of its problems, or were other factors more important in determining its fate?

4. The authors of one study of Shadd said that they wrote it "in the hope that the best ideas of the 19th century will be realized in the 20th." Do you think that Bibb or Shadd had better ideas for addressing the situation confronting African Americans in the mid-nineteenth century? To what extent have those ideas been realized in our own time?

For Further Reading

Jim Bearden and Linda Jean Butler, *Shadd: The Life and Times of Mary Shadd Cary* (Toronto: NC Press, 1977), presents the story of Shadd largely through her own words.

Henry Bibb, *Narrative of the Life and Adventures of Henry Bibb, an American Slave*, in Gilbert Osofsky, ed., *Puttin' On Ole Massa: The Slave Narratives of Henry Bibb, William Wells Brown, and Solomon Northup* (New York: Harper & Row, 1969), is a gripping account of Bibb's slave experience and his eventual escape.

James Oliver Horton, *Free People of Color: Inside the African American Community* (Washington, D.C.: Smithsonian Institution Press, 1993), provides an overview of the lives of free blacks in the nineteenth-century North.

William H. Pease and Jane H. Pease, *Black Utopia: Negro Communal Experiments in America* (Madison: State Historical Society of Wisconsin, 1963), discusses nineteenth-century black-separatist communities in the United States and Canada, including the Refugee Home Society.

Benjamin Quarles, *Black Abolitionists* (New York: Oxford University Press, 1968), examines the unique position of black abolitionists, including Henry Bibb and Mary Ann Shadd.

Jane Rhodes, *Mary Ann Shadd Cary: The Black Press in the Nineteenth Century* (Bloomington: Indiana University Press, 1998), offers a comprehensive biography of Shadd, focusing on her pioneering role as a black female journalist.

Jason H. Silverman, *Unwelcome Guests: Canada West's Response to American Fugitive Slaves, 1800–1865* (Milwood, N.Y.: Associated Faculty Press, 1985), discusses the impact of racism on black refugees in what is now the province of Ontario and the refugees' responses to it.

14

Mr. Lincoln's War:
Clement Vallandigham and Benjamin Wade

Clement Vallandigham

Benjamin Wade

Clement L. Vallandigham knew that Abraham Lincoln was a tyrant. In the name of fighting a war to save the Union, Lincoln had violated the very principles that formed the basis of that Union. Since taking office in 1861, he had broken the laws of the land and ridden roughshod over the U.S. Constitution. Those who dared to oppose him were smeared with derogatory labels, attacked as sympathizers with the rebellion, and even jailed or exiled. Indeed, Vallandigham had experienced firsthand Lincoln's oppressive power. The Ohio congressman believed that he had no choice but to stand up to Lincoln's villainy.

Benjamin F. Wade disagreed. Lincoln was no tyrant, but he was an incompetent fool. Lincoln refused to seize the opportunity for social, economic, and political reform presented by the Civil War. The United States could be made to live up to its professed principles of liberty and equality for all, if Lincoln would adopt Wade's agenda. But Lincoln would not cooperate. He could not see the possibilities open to him and his party. Instead of vigorously pushing the Ohio senator's program forward, Lincoln was an obstacle to it.

Like the nation itself, the North was divided during the Civil War. Few people better illustrate that division than Vallandigham and Wade. Unlike most northern Democrats, who supported the Union's war efforts, Vallandigham opposed the war entirely. The congressman was the leader of the antiwar Democrats, or Copperheads, as the Republicans called them. Some Copperheads wanted to end the war and let the South have its independence. Vallandigham wanted peace and reconciliation—a return to prewar conditions. He wanted the Republic reunited, even if it meant that slavery would be preserved. Most of all, he wanted the Constitution upheld. Wade believed that Lincoln had not exercised enough power during the Civil War. Like many other Republicans, he wanted to punish the South, free the slaves, and transform southern society. Together, Vallandigham and Wade had Lincoln in a bind. While he led the fight to defeat the Confederacy, the president also had to secure enough unity on the home front to see the Union through to victory. To do that, he had to keep these two men at bay. Only then would the North have a chance to defeat the South.

"Valiant Val"

Clement Vallandigham was proud to call himself a Jacksonian Democrat. Like Jacksonians earlier in the nineteenth century, he was a representative of the "common man" fighting the forces of "special privilege" and the encroachments of federal power. Thus he criticized banks, which he believed operated with government support to enrich the few at the expense of the many. He also opposed the nation's budding industrial interests, which demanded favors from government such as high tariffs. Taxes on imports, Vallandigham believed, only made manufactured products more expensive for the people. Like most good Democrats in the early nineteenth century, he was a staunch defender of limited government and states' rights. Following Thomas Jefferson, the Democrats believed that the states were sovereign. The federal government, therefore, had no business interfering with slavery. Because slavery was sanctioned by the Constitution, Vallandigham argued, it was a matter for the states to decide.

At first glance, this son of an Ohio Presbyterian minister was an unlikely Jacksonian. Born in 1820, Vallandigham was only a boy when Andrew Jackson was elected president in 1828. He was far too young for "Old Hickory's" presidency to have an impact on him. More important, Presbyterian ministers' sons did not generally flock to Jackson's Democratic Party. Instead, they favored the Whigs, who believed that government had a positive role to play in promoting the moral welfare of the nation. Worried about the moral degeneration of society, New England Protestants such as Lyman Beecher were naturally drawn to the Whigs. (See Chapter 9.) Interested in reforming the character and behavior of Americans, the Whigs were especially interested in temperance—the restriction or outright elimination of alcohol consumption. The Democrats, by contrast, believed that religion and politics should be separate.

Perhaps Vallandigham's family background determined his fierce partisan loyalties. His father's family traced its roots back to Jefferson's Virginia. Among their ancestors, the Vallandighams counted Indian fighters, Revolutionary War officers, and participants in the Whiskey Rebellion of 1794 (see Chapter 6). A revolt against a Federalist tax on whiskey, this rebellion was centered in western Pennsylvania among small farmers who distrusted the central government. Like many other "common people," the Vallandighams had moved west with the advancing frontier, from Virginia to Pennsylvania to New Lisbon, Ohio. Here were people who understood Jackson's message that government's role was a negative one: to remove obstacles from the path of the common people. They certainly had no use for the Whig conception of government.

Ethnic ties also may have shaped Vallandigham's views. Whereas the Whig Party's moral appeal attracted primarily Protestants of English descent, the Vallandighams were of Dutch extraction. (A colonial ancestor had changed the name from Van Landegham.) Like many other non-English ethnic groups, Dutch immigrants as far back as the eighteenth century had resented the dominance of English Americans in their colonies or states. In the early nineteenth century, the Democratic Party had attracted many of these non-English groups who felt alienated from an Anglo-Saxon establishment. For similar reasons, Vallandigham's Scots-Irish mother also may have played a role in shaping his political outlook. Immigrants to the colonies in the eighteenth century, the Scots-Irish were Protestants from Scotland who had moved to Ireland in the seventeenth century. Although the Vallandighams were devout Presbyterians, many Scots-Irish were hard-drinking, hard-fighting, and fiercely independent people who opposed government regulation of morals. Like Jackson, also of Scots-Irish descent, Vallandigham saw a powerful central government not as a benevolent force for reform, but as a dangerous enemy of personal freedom.

Whatever political impact Vallandigham's parents had on him, they most certainly instilled in him a love of learning. His mother read to him at an early age, and his father operated a school in the family's home. When the eloquent and self-confident Vallandigham entered Pennsylvania's Jefferson College, it was as a member of the junior class. He dropped out after a year to teach school in Maryland, only to return and drop out again. Yet books would be his lifelong companions. Back in New Lisbon, he began to study law. After passing the bar in 1842, he joined his brother's legal practice. Personable and analytical, Vallandigham would use his impressive legal talents to great advantage.

His talents also suited him perfectly for politics. In 1840, he campaigned for the Democratic Party. The following year, he served as a delegate to a county Democratic Party convention. This early entrance into politics whetted his appetite for more, and his legal career helped him get it. As an ambitious lawyer, he frequently defended people against merchants, land speculators, and bankers. Many of his clients were poor Irish Americans and German Americans, who invariably voted Democratic. In 1844, he campaigned for the Democratic presidential candidate, James K. Polk. The following year, he won election to the Ohio assembly. As a Jacksonian watchdog, he attacked bankers and manufacturers. When Polk and the Democrats in Congress took the country to war against Mexico in 1846, he attacked Whig legislators who opposed what they derisively called "Mr. Polk's War." Pouncing on Whig opponents of the war, he declared that "by the blood of its slain ye shall have no part in its glories."

Over the next several years, Vallandigham turned from politics to personal affairs. Married in 1846, he moved to Dayton the next year. He devoted himself to his legal practice, his new wife and child, and the many books he purchased for his library. He was inevitably drawn back to politics, though. Within a couple of years, the controversy surrounding the Compromise of 1850* ignited concern among many northerners about slavery. Vallandigham vocally supported the compromise on behalf of Democrats. Back in the political arena, he ran for office over the next several years but without success. He lost a bid for lieutenant governor in 1851 and two congressional elections in 1852 and 1854. He ran for Congress again in 1856, this time with a different outcome.

By the mid-1850s, the Whig Party was falling victim to the growing sectional conflict over slavery. The passage of the Kansas-Nebraska Act in 1854 had heightened northerners' fears about the spread of slavery. The measure, introduced in Congress by Democrat Stephen A. Douglas, overturned the Missouri Compromise's prohibition on slavery in most of the Louisiana Purchase by allowing voters in the area to decide the issue under the principle of popular sovereignty. After the passage of the Kansas-Nebraska Act, northern antislavery Whigs no longer trusted their southern colleagues and vice versa. As the Whig Party disintegrated, the opponents of the Kansas-Nebraska Act met in 1854 to found the Republican Party, which attracted both abolitionists and those who sought to exclude slavery from the western territories. Unlike the Whigs, this exclusively northern party was open to the potent Democratic charge that it was friendly to blacks.

In 1856, Vallandigham's opponent for Congress was a member of the new Republican Party. Vallandigham lost the election by nineteen votes, but he challenged the results, claiming that the Republican had won because of invalid ballots cast by African Americans. In Ohio, as in many other northern states, blacks were free but did not have the right to vote. When a congressional investigation supported by southern Democrats overturned the election, Vallandigham had his victory. He would be reelected twice more, in 1858 and 1860.

From his seat in Congress, Vallandigham watched in despair the growing sectional crisis between the North and South. For the sake of preserving the Union, he took a moderate position. Although he saw slavery as morally wrong, he believed that the federal government had no right to move against it in the states because it was sanctioned by the Constitution. In this regard, Vallandigham agreed with the Republican Party's rising star, Abraham Lincoln. He disagreed with Lincoln and the Republicans, however, on the issue of the expansion of slavery into the western territories. Lincoln and most Republicans called for the containment of slavery in the states where it already existed. Vallandigham placed his faith in popular sovereignty, the solution championed by Stephen Douglas. Embodied in the Kansas-Nebraska Act, popular sovereignty called for voters in the territories to decide the issue of slavery themselves. Like most other Democrats, Vallandigham believed that if the Republicans won the

Compromise of 1850: A congressional deal forged by Whig Henry Clay and Democrat Stephen A. Douglas to resolve sectional conflict between the North and South over the issue of the expansion of slavery into the territories taken in the Mexican War. Its provisions included the admission of California as a free state, the end of the slave trade in the District of Columbia, and a stronger Fugitive Slave Act.

presidential election in 1860, frightened southerners would secede from the Union. While running for reelection in 1860, he launched an all-out assault on the Republicans by playing on his constituents' racial fears. If the Republicans won, he declared, "stinking niggers" would sit next to them in jury boxes and at workbenches, and their daughters would marry "black boys" and have "black babies."

Such tactics worked for Vallandigham but failed to carry the day for Douglas. Shortly after Douglas lost the presidential election to Lincoln, the southern states began to secede. The Republicans were determined to use force to preserve the Union. Vallandigham decried the breakup of the Union but also opposed war as a means for preserving it. He believed that peace could be achieved and the Union restored through compromise and negotiation. Armed coercion, he declared, would be "destructive of republican liberty." Clinging to the doctrine of state sovereignty, Vallandigham reflected the view of many northern Democrats, especially the poorer ones of the lower Midwest, an area originally settled by southerners. They wanted the Union preserved as much as they disliked blacks and feared abolition. When the war started in 1861, many of them turned to "Valiant Val" to express their fears.

"Bluff Ben"

Politically, Benjamin Franklin Wade also was a product of his early environment. Born in 1800 in western Massachusetts to old Yankee stock, he was a descendant of the New England Puritan tradition. Although the Wades were poor farmers, their Protestant faith instilled in them the value of education. Thus Benjamin was taught to read the Bible by his mother, the daughter of a Congregational minister. As a young man, he rejected his parents' emphasis on formal religion, but he could not escape the effects of his Puritan upbringing. He approached life as a struggle between right and wrong and believed that compromising on fundamentals was tantamount to sin. Those who disagreed about such matters were not merely misguided but evil. Society, moreover, was capable of moral improvement. Thus Wade was as committed to the righteous exercise of government power as Vallandigham was opposed to it. That attitude dovetailed perfectly with the economic changes he noticed while growing up. As cotton mills and other businesses sprang up in New England after the War of 1812, the entire area seemed to benefit from more jobs and greater commerce. When he later backed government support for industry, he did not forget the favorable impact these enterprises had had on his boyhood environment.

Wade's Puritan background influenced him in other ways, too. Industriousness, he believed, was a virtue and idleness a sin. To earn his keep, the ambitious young Wade hired himself out to other farm families. Later, he worked as a laborer on the construction of the Erie Canal in upstate New York. And when his family moved to northeastern Ohio in 1821, he worked as a farmer and drover and even taught school for a while. Driven to succeed, he set his sights on becoming a lawyer, so he began studying law under a local attorney. In 1828, he was admitted to the bar.

Wade was a natural Whig, as were many of the other settlers in northeastern

Ohio. With their backing, in 1837 Wade won election to the state senate in a landslide. The young legislator sometimes broke with his party on policies such as subsidies for corporations that he believed favored business interests too much. Otherwise, he was a staunch Whig. He favored tariffs for industry and shared many Whigs' views about slavery. To Wade, slavery was not just an economic issue but a moral wrong.

By the early 1840s, Wade was married with two children. Meanwhile, he continued to serve in the state legislature and developed a lucrative law practice. In 1847, he was elected to a judgeship. Three years later, when Congress passed the Fugitive Slave Act, he was catapulted onto the national stage. Passed as part of the Compromise of 1850, the act compelled northerners to assist southern slave catchers. Alleged runaways could now be taken into slavery solely on the sworn statement of a slave owner. Accused blacks had no right to testify for themselves in court. Wade declared that as a district judge, he would refuse to uphold the law. That position had a lot to do with his election by the state legislature to the U.S. Senate in 1851.

When Wade arrived in the Senate, he joined a small group of antislavery senators in attacking the Fugitive Slave Act. His firm antislavery views quickly established his reputation as a fearless radical. His debates with southerners were often characterized by blunt talk and taunts of his slaveholding colleagues. **[See Source 1.]** His outspoken manner soon earned him the nickname "Bluff Ben." Although he also earned the respect of his southern opponents, he fought them on slavery at every turn. Thus, when the Kansas-Nebraska Act opened to the door to the westward expansion of slavery, Wade and his fellow antislavery Whigs joined the new Republican Party. By this time, he had adopted most of the Whig economic program as his own, including protective tariffs and federal funding for internal improvements such as roads and canals. As a Republican, he continued to promote these policies. At the same time, he continued to oppose policies that favored a particular industry or put business above all other interests. Most of all, he fought against the "sin" of slavery and the northerners and southerners in Congress who supported it.

Easily winning reelection in 1857, Wade soon established himself as a rising star in the new Republican Party. By 1860, he was a prominent member of the Senate and a Republican presidential candidate. Although he lost the nomination to Lincoln, when Lincoln won the election, Wade would have his day. Serving on the Senate committee that tried to head off secession, he opposed any compromise with the South. In late 1860, for instance, Senator John Crittenden of Kentucky proposed that 36°30' north latitude, established as the boundary between slave and free territory in the Louisiana Purchase, be extended to the Pacific. Wade urged Lincoln to reject the so-called Crittenden Compromise. The Republicans, he believed, had been fairly elected on a platform to exclude slavery from the territories. They could not now ignore the majority will. Lincoln agreed, and the last hope for compromise between the North and South was gone.

Once the Civil War began, however, Wade was not pleased with his president. The moderate Lincoln was more concerned with repairing the Union than ending slavery. As the political leader of the Union, Lincoln knew that there was a wide range of opinions on slavery in the North, from those of radical abolitionists to those of slaveholders in the loyal slave states. He knew, too, that many Democrats sympathized with their southern brethren and feared the prospect of competing with black labor. Moving quickly to satisfy Wade and his supporters would only alienate northern Democrats such as Clement Vallandigham and their backers. And if most northerners did not stay committed to the fight for the Union, the North's tremendous advantages in resources and manpower would not matter. **[See Source 2.]**

Wade and other Radical Republicans, however, had high expectations. Mostly abolitionists, they wanted immediate emancipation of slaves and punishment for southern secessionists. They envisioned a complete social restructuring of the South after it was defeated. They believed that the government should redistribute plantation owners' land to former slaves, strip all Confederates of political rights, destroy the economic basis of the southern planter aristocracy, and replace that aristocracy with a more democratic and egalitarian social order. Serving as chairman of the Joint Committee on the Conduct of the War, Wade quickly emerged as a leader of the Radical Republicans. The Union war effort in 1861 had proved disastrous, and the Radicals used this oversight committee to challenge Lincoln's conduct of the war. Indeed, it would be their main weapon in the battle to shape the Union's wartime policies. For Wade and other leaders of the faction, including Thaddeus Stevens, Wendell Phillips, and Charles Sumner, Lincoln was being too cautious. When he delayed emancipation and supported Democratic generals, they were outraged.

Lincoln's support for General George McClellan was especially outrageous to Wade. A longtime Democrat, the general had taken command of the Army of the Potomac following the disastrous Union defeat at Bull Run in July 1861. Wade had joined the many Washington residents who had gone to the battlefield to watch what they had assumed would be the only battle of the war. In the midst of the ensuing rout, the enraged senator had used his carriage to block the road back to the capital and threatened the retreating Union soldiers with his rifle. Now, as McClellan's overly cautious nature made him reluctant to fight, Wade stepped up the pressure on Lincoln. He even worked with Ambrose Burnside and other officers under McClellan to gather ammunition against the general. In return for the information, Wade would ignore charges that Burnside had moved too slowly at the Battle of Antietam in 1862.

Wade's attacks on McClellan reflected the Ohio senator's views about the proper way to conduct the war in general. He constantly badgered Lincoln to move faster, carry the fight to the South, and crush the rebellion quickly. At one point, he said that the president was not smart enough to lead the nation during the crisis and cynically noted, "I do not wonder that people desert to [Confederate president] Jeff Davis as he has brains; I may desert myself." When the Lincolns hosted a ball at the White House, Wade refused to attend and released to the press his brutal reply to the Lincolns' invitation: "Are the President and Mrs. Lincoln aware that there is a civil war? If they are not, Mr. and Mrs. Wade are, and for that reason decline to participate in feasting and dancing." Every action Lincoln took exposed him to Wade's withering scrutiny. Lacking military or administrative experience, the senator did not realize that the armies often could not have moved faster even if their leaders had ordered them to.

More than Lincoln's conservative conduct of the war, Wade and other

Radicals were concerned with the administration's foot-dragging on slavery. The Radicals urged Lincoln to abolish slavery as the first step toward the dramatic reform of American society. They called for full and immediate emancipation, land redistribution, and political rights for freedmen. As Union armies won victories and occupied portions of the South, Lincoln carried out a much more moderate plan. First, Union generals administered no clear policy of abolition. Some commanders, such as John C. Frémont, pursued their own policies for emancipation by freeing the slaves in occupied territories. The Radicals applauded such efforts and were dismayed when Lincoln overturned military emancipation. Only a person who came from "poor white trash," Wade sneered, would reverse emancipation. Soon rumors of the president's negotiations with southern Unionists in the conquered territories of Louisiana and Arkansas flew about the capital. One claimed that Lincoln had struck a bargain that would bring those states back into the Union and preserve slavery. Wade fully believed such rumors. Lincoln's next annual message to Congress, he declared, would include a recommendation "to give each rebel who shall serve during the war a hundred and sixty acres of land." Beneath the sneers and sarcasm, Wade and his allies worried that Lincoln had sold them out.

In fact, the president was walking a political tightrope. He had to try to keep the slaveholding border states—Missouri, Kentucky, Maryland, and Delaware—in the Union. The loss of these strategically placed states would be a major blow to the North's war effort. Lincoln himself acknowledged the strategic importance of these states when he declared that he would *like* to have God on his side, but he *must* have Kentucky. Any bold approach toward emancipation might well force it and the other border states right out of the Union. Furthermore, white racism made emancipation very unpopular in the North. Many northern workers did not like slavery because they agreed with Hinton Rowan Helper and other antislavery agitators that it degraded free labor. (See Chapter 12.) At the same time, they did not want to compete with free blacks for jobs and land. Lincoln also had an eye on the complicated constitutional and legal questions surrounding emancipation. Could the government abolish slavery legally? If so, which branch of the national government had the power to do so? If the state governments had sovereignty over the matter, how could the Republicans convince state leaders to carry out emancipation? Would slave owners have to be compensated financially for the freedom of their workers? If so, where would the money come from?

Whatever Wade and the Radical Republicans thought about the matter, Lincoln knew that emancipation was a complex and dangerous issue. Thus, when he finally did move against slavery, it was in a hedged and halfhearted way. Lincoln's Emancipation Proclamation, which went into effect in 1863, pertained only to slavery in rebellious territory. In other words, it excluded the loyal slave states and those areas in Confederate states already under the control of Union forces. It freed only those slaves behind enemy lines, where the Confederates were not about to carry out Lincoln's order.

Wade and his fellow Radicals saw the Emancipation Proclamation as more evidence of Lincoln's conservatism. They were not any happier with his proposed plan for Reconstruction of the defeated Confederate states. Lincoln called for each state to create a new government after only a small fraction of its male citizens swore allegiance to the United States. Fearful that Democrats would gain control of the reconstructed states under the president's plan, Wade offered an alternative. With congressman Henry Davis of Maryland, he introduced legislation requiring a majority of citizens in former Confederate states to take such an oath. Although the Wade-Davis bill passed in Congress, Lincoln vetoed it. The bill's authors promptly issued the Wade-Davis Manifesto, a heated denunciation of Lincoln's policies. [See Source 3.]

The manifesto was one of the Ohio senator's greatest political blunders. The majority of northerners agreed with Lincoln that the Civil War was above all a crusade to preserve the Union. They approved his moderate course on slavery and his plans to bring the rebellious states back into the Union as quickly as possible. Thus many of them reacted with disgust to the manifesto. Moderate Republicans began to suspect that the Radicals wished to divide the party. If a Democrat were elected in 1864, they reasoned, the Radicals could rid themselves of the South once and for all. The Democrats looked as if they were heading for a victory in the fall elections, and if they carried the day, there might be a negotiated peace with the South after all.

"Exact and Equal Justice"

Moderate Republican fears about a negotiated peace backed by the Radicals did not seem far-fetched in 1864. By then, war weariness across the North created a groundswell of Democratic support. The leaders of the Democratic resurgence were Vallandigham and his fellow Peace Democrats. These Copperheads were convinced that Lincoln's war policies were destroying American liberty. Lincoln had extended federal power at the expense of the states and individual citizens. Early in the war, he had acted without congressional approval, unilaterally mobilizing the country for war. They believed that he had inappropriately moved at the federal level against slavery. And, they charged, he had assumed dictatorial powers. In 1861, he had suspended the writ of habeas corpus,* taking away the constitutional right of citizens to a speedy trial. Although the Constitution allowed the writ to be suspended during times of rebellion or invasion, congressional leaders argued that only the legislative branch had the authority to do so. Thus Lincoln was extending his executive powers beyond constitutional bounds. In fact, when the chief justice of the Supreme Court had ruled that Lincoln's suspension of habeas corpus was unconstitutional, Lincoln had simply ignored the ruling.

The president also had declared martial law and subjected "disloyal" persons to imprisonment. As a result, perhaps as many as thirteen thousand people were detained, many of them for long periods. They were never brought to trial, and the government never presented evidence against them. Many of them were guilty of demonstrating Confederate sympathies or opposing administration policies. At one point, Union forces even arrested thirty-one Maryland state legislators to prevent them from voting for the state to secede. Meanwhile, the administration's draft policy forced citizens to serve in the army. It also allowed

---

Habeas corpus: The legal right of jailed persons to be brought before a court to determine whether they should be charged with a crime or released.

those who could afford to do so to buy their way out of service or hire another man to take their place for three hundred dollars. The rich were exempt from military duty, while the poor had to fight.

In Vallandigham's view, the administration's financial policies took tyranny even further. Lincoln raised taxes to pay for the war. He even instituted an income tax that was later found to be unconstitutional. He reorganized the currency system through the establishment of a national bank and the introduction of paper money not backed by gold. A national bank and paper money had long been supported by the old Whig Party, to which Lincoln had belonged. They also were part of the Republican Party platform. Now the president argued that such measures were necessary to conduct the war. To Lincoln, crushing dissent, drafting poor men to fight the war, raising taxes, and creating an economic climate favorable to business were all part of his plans to win the war. To Vallandigham and many other Democrats, it seemed that he was using the conflict as a way to enact policies favorable to business interests. They argued that these moves only proved that Lincoln was power hungry and oppressive.

Already by 1862, Vallandigham's fiery oratory and relentless criticism of Lincoln had made him the most prominent Peace Democrat. His slogan, "The Constitution as it is, the Union as it was," became the rallying cry for antiwar protesters across the country. As the war continued and the casualties mounted, Vallandigham found a receptive audience. He roused his supporters with slashing attacks on Lincoln's suspension of civil liberties and his tax policies. With the Union war effort bogged down by late 1862, Vallandigham's oratory grew more heated. Appealing to the racist sentiments of northerners, the Copperhead leader declared that Lincoln's policies would bring a flood of blacks to the North. The South, he asserted, could not be conquered. The only trophies of war that the North had to show for its efforts were "defeat, debt, taxation, sepulchers . . . the suspension of *habeas corpus,* the violation . . . of freedom of the press and of speech." Lincoln and his cronies had "made this country one of the worst despotisms on earth." The Republicans had made the war for Union a war for abolition, he cried, and what had it accomplished? "Let the dead at Fredericksburg and Vicksburg answer," he declared. [**See Source 4.**]

With the cry "Rich man's war, poor man's fight," Vallandigham also attacked the draft with great effect. Quick to sense the unfairness of Lincoln's policy, many workers and farmers responded favorably to Vallandigham's slogan. Republicans, in turn, were quick to blame Vallandigham for helping to stir up draft resistance. Some even blamed him for the New York draft riot in 1863. Sparked by the Lincoln administration's draft, the riot left 120 people dead and resulted in millions of dollars' worth of property damage. It also exposed the racial and ethnic tensions in northern society. Much of the rioters' violence, like "Valiant Val's" rhetoric, was directed against blacks. And most of the rioters were workers and immigrants—people generally receptive to his message. The charge that Vallandigham had incited this violence, however, was far-fetched.

Yet even for Benjamin Wade and other Radical Republicans, Vallandigham's rhetoric and actions proved too much. To counter the Peace Democrats' growing support, Wade publicly declared Vallandigham a traitor. The Ohio Democrat's "every breath," he argued, was devoted to the destruction of the republic.

Vallandigham, Wade charged on the Senate floor, was a member of the Knights of the Golden Circle, a secret prosouthern organization dedicated to helping the Confederacy via sabotage. A number of knights had been arrested for treasonous activities, and Vallandigham could not afford to let Wade's charges go unanswered. On the floor of the House of Representatives, he responded. Vallandigham opened his speech by reading Wade's slanderous charges and then shouted out at the top of his lungs, "Now, sir, here in my place in the House, and as a Representative, I denounce—and I speak it advisedly—the author of that speech as a liar, a scoundrel, and a coward. His name is BENJAMIN F. WADE!" **[See Source 5.]**

Republican attempts to discredit Vallandigham continued, but Wade's charges of treason would not stick. In fact, Vallandigham's popularity grew as Union armies suffered more setbacks on the battlefield. In 1863, he delivered a series of antiwar, antiadministration, anti-Lincoln speeches that enraged the Republicans. Already Wade's old friend Ambrose Burnside, now serving as military governor of Ohio, had issued various orders to clamp down on Copperhead activity. In May 1863, he ordered Vallandigham's arrest. The Ohio representative was charged with "publicly expressing . . . his sympathies for those in arms against the Government of the United States, declaring disloyal sentiments and opinions, with the object and purpose of weakening the power of the Government in its efforts to suppress an unlawful rebellion."

Vallandigham was tried by court-martial, convicted, and sentenced to a term in a military prison "during the continuance of the war." While cries of outrage swept the Democratic areas of the North, Vallandigham's attorneys appealed his case. The federal courts refused to overturn the decision because the judges could not decide whether the government had been justified in its action against him. Later, the Supreme Court decided in Ex parte *Vallandigham* in 1864 that it could not hear the case because it had no jurisdiction to hear appeals from a military commission. His legal options were exhausted, but not his political chances. From behind bars, Vallandigham managed to rally his supporters to continue their efforts. In fact, his arrest only validated Vallandigham's arguments that the Lincoln administration was indeed tyrannical. Imprisoned, he was now a martyr and a symbol of the injustices of "Mr. Lincoln's War."

To head off the political damage already suffered in the Vallandigham case, Lincoln and his cabinet decided to exile him to the South. Released from prison shortly after his arrest, he was carried to Confederate lines in Tennessee. Although southerners received him warmly, they did not want him to stay. They realized that he had more value as a Copperhead than as a Confederate. After a month in the South, he made his way to Canada, where he continued to lead the Peace Democrats from exile. Then he secretly returned to Ohio in defiance of federal authority. While he campaigned publicly for George McClellan, the Democratic nominee for president in 1864, the Republicans conveniently ignored his presence. Vallandigham's actions were in vain, however, for the election was ultimately decided on the battlefield. When General William T. Sherman captured Atlanta in September, flagging Union spirits were revived and Democratic hopes for electoral victory shattered. Lincoln and the Republicans won reelection that fall, and Union armies won the war the following spring.

In the end, Vallandigham and the Copperheads lost. Their hopes for a Union restored on prewar terms were dashed. After the war, Vallandigham attempted unsuccessfully to rejuvenate his political career. Returning to his law practice, he again proved his superb legal abilities. His fiery oratory continued to mesmerize juries. His courtroom dramatics, however, finally killed him. In 1871, while defending a man accused of murder, Vallandigham argued that the victim had actually shot himself by accident. The famous attorney planned to make his case by dramatically reenacting the scene. While demonstrating for his colleagues what he intended to do in the courtroom, he shot himself fatally with a pistol he mistakenly thought was unloaded.

For a time, it seemed that Wade and the Radicals had won. During the presidency of Lincoln's successor, Andrew Johnson, they seized control of Reconstruction. Wade hoped that Congress would now help ensure blacks' economic security and political equality. The Confederates would finally be punished. During congressional Reconstruction, many former Confederates did lose their political rights, and freedmen won the right to vote. Wade's dream of a radical restructuring of southern society, however, was never fulfilled. Most blacks were left impoverished and never got the chance to purchase their own land. Left in dire economic circumstances, they were politically vulnerable. In time, resurgent southern Democrats would find it easy to strip them of their voting rights and impose a rigid racial caste system on them.

Long before then, Wade experienced his own defeat. He knew that voting rights for blacks were unpopular in Ohio even after the Civil War, but he would not waver from his belief in "exact and equal justice for all men without reference to color, condition, or race." Instead, he enthusiastically "waved the bloody shirt" of the Civil War by reminding voters about pro-Confederate Democrats like "the bold, convicted traitor" Clement Vallandigham. By 1867, however, Wade found that such tactics would not work. Ohio voters elected a Democratic legislature that year. When the legislature in turn elected a Democratic senator, Wade's political career was over. After leaving the Senate in 1869, he returned to his law practice and became involved in railroad building. He lived until 1878, long enough to see Reconstruction overturned and his hopes for "exact and equal justice" for blacks dashed. In the end, Wade had to wonder whether he or Vallandigham had actually accomplished more as a result of "Mr. Lincoln's War."

PRIMARY SOURCES

SOURCE 1: *Benjamin Wade Assaults a Southern Colleague (1854)*

In 1854, the Kansas-Nebraska Act proposed to resolve the issue of slavery in Kansas and Nebraska by letting the settlers there decide whether or not to allow slavery. In debates in the Senate, Benjamin Wade blasted the bill and colleagues who supported it. What does this attack on a senator from North Carolina reveal about Wade's approach to politics?

There was one argument made by the Senator from North Carolina, which struck me as exceedingly singular. He has set forth all the beauties of the patriarchal institution, as he calls it, to show the affectionate relation existing between him and his slaves, with whom he grew up from boyhood, with whom he was intimate and familiar, and whom he pronounced the best friends he had upon earth. He said, "Do you want to make us hard-hearted? Now sir," said he, "[i]f I can better my condition and the condition of my slaves by going into Nebraska, where the soil is better, and where we will have a better supply of all things, in the name of God, do you want to stand forth and prevent me?" Did anyone notice the force with which he urged that appeal? So wedded was he to the idea that he could not exist anywhere without his old friends, as he called them, and yet he could not take his old "mammy," as he called her, who nursed him and brought him up to manhood, into that Territory. Why? Notwithstanding these intimate relations, he could not take her there, because he could not have the right to sell her when he got there. There could not be any other reasons for it; for, most assuredly, if he wanted to take his affectionate old mammy there and give her her freedom, there would be nothing in the way, either in a slave law or anything else.

SOURCE: Reprinted in Hans Louis Trefousse, *Benjamin Franklin Wade: Radical Republican from Ohio* (New York: Twayne Publishers, 1963), pp. 88–89; originally from *Congressional Globe*, 33d Cong., 1st sess., 1854, appendix, 313.

Source 2:   Abraham Lincoln, *Letter to Horace Greeley* (1862)

In this letter to Republican newspaper editor Horace Greeley, Lincoln explains his view of the Civil War. What does Lincoln identify as the paramount issue of the war?

Executive Mansion
August 22, 1862
Hon. Horace Greeley.
DEAR SIR

I have just read yours of the 19th addressed to myself through the New-York Tribune. If there be in it any statements, or assumptions of fact which I may know to be erroneous, I do not, now and here, controvert them. If there be in it any inferences which I may believe to be falsely drawn, I do not now and here, argue against them. If there be perceptable [*sic*] in it an impatient and dictatorial tone I waive it in deference to an old friend whose heart I have always supposed to be right.

As to the policy I "seem to be pursuing" as you say, I have not meant to leave any one in doubt.

I would save the Union. I would save it the shortest way under the Constitution. The sooner the national authority can be restored, the nearer the Union will be "the Union as it was." If there be those who would not save the Union unless they could at the same time *save* slavery, I do not agree with them. If there be those who would not save the Union unless they could at the same time *destroy* slavery, I do not agree with them. My paramount object in this struggle *is* to save the Union, and is *not* either to save or to destroy slavery. If I could save the Union without freeing *any* slave I would do it, and if I could save it by freeing *all* the slaves I would do it and if I could save it by freeing some and leaving others alone I would also do that. What I do about slavery and the colored race, I do because I believe it helps to save the Union; and what I forbear, I forbear because I do *not* believe it would help to save the Union. I shall do *less* whenever I shall believe what I am doing hurts the cause and I shall do *more* whenever I shall believe doing more will help the cause. I shall try to correct errors when shown to be errors, and I shall adopt new views so fast as they shall appear to be true views.

I have here stated my purpose according to my view of *official* duty; and I intend no modification of my oft-expressed *personal* wish that all men every where could be free. Yours,

A. Lincoln

Source: Reprinted in Richard N. Current, ed., *The Political Thought of Abraham Lincoln* (Indianapolis: Bobbs-Merrill, 1967), pp. 214–215; originally from *New York Tribune*, August 25, 1862.

SOURCE 3: Benjamin Wade and Henry Davis, *The Wade-Davis Manifesto* (1864)

In the following excerpt from the Wade-Davis Manifesto of August 5, 1864, Senator Benjamin Wade and Congressman Henry Davis attack President Lincoln's veto of the Wade-Davis bill. What arguments do they use against Lincoln?

We have read without surprise, but not without indignation, the Proclamation of the President of the 8th of July. . . .

The President, by preventing this bill from becoming a law, holds the electoral votes of the rebel States at the dictation of his personal ambition.

If those votes turn the balance in his favor, is it to be supposed that his competitor, defeated by such means, will acquiesce?

If the rebel majority assert their supremacy in those States, and send votes which elect an enemy of the Government, will we not repel his claims?

And is not that civil war for the Presidency inaugurated by the votes of rebel States?

Seriously impressed with these dangers, Congress, *"the proper constituted authority,"* formally declared that there are no State governments in the rebel States, and provided for their erection at a proper time, and both the Senate and the House of Representatives rejected the Senators and Representatives chosen under the authority of what the President calls the free constitution and government of Arkansas.

The President's proclamation *"holds for naught"* this judgment, and discards the authority of the Supreme Court, and strides headlong toward the anarchy his proclamation of the 8th of December inaugurated.

If electors for President be allowed to be chosen in either of those States, a sinister light will be cast on the motives which induced the President to "hold for naught" the will of Congress rather than his government in Louisiana and Arkansas.

That judgment of Congress which the President defies was the exercise of an authority exclusively vested in Congress by the Constitution to determine what is the established government in a State, and in its own nature and by the highest judicial authority binding on all other departments of the Government. . . .

A more studied outrage on the legislative authority of the people has never been perpetrated.

Congress passed a bill, the President refused to approve it, and then by proclamation puts as much of it in force as he sees fit, and proposes to execute those parts by officers unknown to the laws of the United States and not subject to the confirmation of the Senate!

The bill directed the appointment of Provisional Governors by and with the advice and consent of the Senate.

The President, after defeating the law, proposes to appoint without law,

SOURCE: Reprinted in Melvin I. Urofsky, *Documents of American Constitutional and Legal History* (Philadelphia: Temple University Press, 1989), I, 481–482.

and without the advice and consent of the Senate, *Military* Governors for the rebel States!

He has already exercised this dictatorial usurpation in Louisiana, and he defeated the bill to prevent its limitation. . . . The President has greatly presumed on the forbearance which the supporters of his Administration have so long practiced, in view of the arduous conflict in which we are engaged, and the reckless ferocity of our political opponents.

But he must understand that our support is of a cause and not of a man, that the authority of Congress is paramount and must be respected, that the whole body of the Union men of Congress will not submit to be impeached by him of rash and unconstitutional legislation, and if he wishes our support, he must confine himself to his executive duties—to obey and execute, not make the laws—to suppress by arms armed rebellion, and leave political reorganization to Congress.

If the supporters of the Government fail to insist on this, they become responsible for the usurpations which they fail to rebuke, and are justly liable to the indignation of the people whose rights and security, committed to their keeping, they sacrifice.

Let them consider the remedy for these usurpations, and, having found it, fearlessly execute it.

SOURCE 4:   Clement Vallandigham, *"The Great Civil War in America"*   (1863)

In this excerpt from his speech before the House of Representatives on January 14, 1863, Clement Vallandigham condemns the war effort. What arguments does he use to attack the war? How do his attacks on Lincoln's war policies compare to Benjamin Wade and Henry Davis's arguments in the previous source?

Money and credit, then, you have had in prodigal profusion. And were men wanted? More than a million rushed to arms! Seventy-five thousand first, (and the country stood aghast at the multitude,) then eighty-three thousand more were demanded, and three hundred and ten thousand responded to the call. The President next asked for four hundred thousand, and Congress, in their generous confidence, gave him five hundred thousand, and, not to be outdone, he took six hundred and thirty-seven thousand. Half of these melted away in their first campaign, and the President demanded three hundred thousand more for the war, and then drafted yet another three hundred thousand for nine months. . . . And yet victory strangely follows the standard of the foe. From Great Bethel to Vicksburg, the battle has not been to the strong. Yet every disaster, except the last, has been followed by a call for more troops, and every time, so far, they have been promptly furnished. From the beginning the war has been

SOURCE: *Congressional Globe*, 37th Cong., 2d sess., 1863, appendix, 54–55.

conducted like a political campaign, and it has been the folly of the party in power that they have assumed, that numbers alone would win the field in a contest not with ballots but with musket and sword. But numbers, you have had almost without number—the largest, best appointed, best armed, fed and clad host of brave men, well organized and well disciplined, ever marshaled. A Navy, too, not the most formidable perhaps, but the most numerous and gallant, and the costliest in the world, and against a foe, almost without a navy at all. Thus, with twenty millions of people, and every element of strength and force at command—power, patronage, influence, unanimity, enthusiasm, confidence, credit, money, men, an Army and a Navy the largest and the noblest ever set in the field, or afloat upon the sea; with the support, almost servile, of every State, county, and municipality in the North and West, with a Congress swift to do the bidding of the Executive, without opposition anywhere at home, and with an arbitrary power which neither the Czar of Russia, nor the Emperor of Austria dare exercise, yet after nearly two years of more vigorous prosecution of war than ever recorded in history, after more skirmishes, combats and battles than Alexander, Caesar, or the first Napoleon ever fought in any five years of their military career, you have utterly, signally, disastrously—I will not say ignominiously—failed to subdue ten millions of "rebels," whom you had taught the people of the North and West not only to hate, but to despise. Rebels, did I say? Yes, your fathers were rebels or your grandfathers. He, who now before me on canvas looks down so sadly upon us, the false, degenerate, and imbecile guardians of the great Republic which he founded, was a rebel. And yet we, cradled ourselves in rebellion, and who have fostered and fraternized with every insurrection in the nineteenth century everywhere throughout the globe, would now forsooth, make the word "rebel" a reproach. Rebels certainly they are; but all the persistent and stupendous efforts of the most gigantic warfare of modern times have through your incompetency and folly availed nothing to crush them out, cut off though they have been, by our blockade, from all the world, and dependent only upon their own courage and resources. And yet, they were to be utterly conquered and subdued in six weeks, or three months! Sir, my judgment was made up, and expressed from the first I learned it from [William Pitt the Elder, Earl of] Chatham, "My lords, you can not conquer America." And you have not conquered the South. You never will. It is not in the nature of things possible, much less under your auspices. But money you have expended without limit, and blood poured out like water. Defeat, debt, taxation, sepulchers, these are your trophies. In vain, the people gave you treasure, and the soldier yielded up his life. "Fight, tax, emancipate, let these," said the gentleman from Maine, [Mr. Pike,] at the last session, "be the trinity of our salvation." Sir, they have become the trinity of your deep damnation. The war for the Union is, in your hands, a most bloody and costly failure. The President confessed it on the 22d of September [with the promulgation of the Preliminary Emancipation Proclamation] solemnly, officially, and under the broad seal of the United States. And he has now repeated the confession. The priests and rabbis of abolition taught him that God would not prosper such a cause. War for the Union was abandoned, war for the negro openly begun, and with stronger battalions than before. With what success? Let the dead at Fredericksburg and Vicksburg answer.

Source 5:   *Clement Vallandigham Attacks Benjamin Wade* (1862)

In response to an attack by Benjamin Wade, Clement Vallandigham denounced Wade on the floor of the House of Representatives. As a result, a Wade ally introduced an unsuccessful resolution of censure against Vallandigham. What do Vallandigham's remarks reveal about his situation as a dissenter during the Civil War? What do they reveal about Vallandigham himself?

Mr. Chairman, I have waited patiently for three days for this the earliest occasion presented for a personal explanation.

In a speech delivered in this city the other day—not in this House—certainly not in the Senate—no such speech could have been tolerated in an American Senate—I find the following:

"I accuse them [the Democratic Party] of a deliberate purpose to assail, through the judicial tribunals and through the Senate and the House of Representatives of the United States, and everywhere else, and to overawe, intimidate, and trample under foot, if they can, the men who boldly stand forth in defense of their country, now imperiled by this gigantic rebellion. I have watched it long. I have seen it in secret. I have seen its movements ever since that party got together, with a colleague of mine in the other House as chairman of the committee on resolutions—*a man who never had any sympathy with this Republic, but whose every breath is devoted to its destruction, just as far as his heart dare permit him to go.*"

Now, sir, here in my place in the House, and as a Representative, I denounce—and I speak it advisedly—the author of that speech as a liar, a scoundrel, and a coward. His name is BENJAMIN F. WADE. . . .

A convention was held in Dayton, where I reside, by the party to which my colleague now belongs, a combination or fusion of Republicans and other elements of a mixed character, opposed now to the Democratic party. This regularly-called city convention, in nominating its candidates, adopted a platform containing but a single point. It was extraordinary, sir, indeed, that such a platform should have been made, forgetting the high purposes of an election, and containing but a single issue, and that merely personal to a fellow-citizen, appealing to the people of that city to vote for candidates solely upon that personal issue. But the platform was in these words:

"*Resolved*, That we will take the occasion of our ensuing city election to make it known to all men that the city of Dayton REPUDIATES CLEMENT L. VALLANDIGHAM and his organ, the Dayton Empire, and REBUKES them for their refusal to support the Government in its death struggle with treason; and to the end that this rebuke may be made the more emphatic, we call upon all loyal men, without respect to party, to vote for the Union, ANTI-VALLANDIGHAM, anti-Empire ticket this day nominated."

Sir, that direct issue thus proffered was openly, flatly, and boldly accepted

SOURCE: *Congressional Globe*, 37th Cong., 2d sess., 1862, 1828–29, 1830.

by my friends, and after a violent contest of three weeks, the election resulted in the success of the entire Democratic ticket, from mayor down, upon that sole question, by an average majority of some two hundred, against four hundred and ninety-two fusion majority at the State election that fall. . . .

Now, in the first place, I deny that I have violated any rule. I took a paper, and read from a printed speech that which related to me personally, and which contained a foul and infamous libel which the utterer knew, at the time, to be false and slanderous. He, the member from Ohio, talk now, indeed! of the opprobrium of the epithets, "liar," "scoundrel," and "coward"! Does he not know that the word "traitor" enters here now covered ten times over with the leprosy of reproach; and am I to sit in this Hall unmoved while that epithet is insinuated against me, in all its taint and foulness, by a member of the Senate, it may be, where I have no chance to meet and hurl it back on the spot as it deserves? Am I to bear it calmly any longer, uttered by any responsible person? I tell you, nay. And when I choose to meet and brand it as a man and as a gentleman should meet and brand it, am I to be called in question here and the first offender go acquit? Sir, I referred to the man, not to the Senator. My manner of allusion was in accordance with ancient parliamentary usage; and if the member from Ohio had known anything about parliamentary usage, he would have known that, following the practice of the Irish and the British Parliaments, I said nothing for which I could properly be called to order in debate. I put a supposititious case, and no man can, under parliamentary precedent, object to it. That, sir, is my first answer.

But I scorn to stand upon that point alone. If what I said has been out of order, let the member from Ohio go to the Senate first and there vindicate the violated obligations of parliamentary decorum. Is it disorderly for a member of this House to refer to a member of the Senate, and yet exactly in order for a Senator to denounce a member of this House, who sits here not by your consent—although you have the right to expel him, two thirds concurring, if he has been guilty of a sufficiently grave offense—but under the same Constitution and laws, and by the equal, nay, better title of the will of the people—to denounce him as "a man who never had any sympathy with this Republic, and whose every breath is devoted to its destruction, just as far as his heart dare permit him to go?" And has the member from Ohio no holy indignation against a Senator who has thus wantonly, and in violation of all parliamentary law, slandered a Representative in this House? Sir, let him go to the Senate, where those false words were uttered, if they were uttered in the Senate, and let him see to it that that body shall first vindicate its obligations to the members of this House, before he dares to call me to a reckoning for words spoken in retort here. How does he know that the words spoken by me had reference to a Senator? But no; suppose they had, what of it? Was not the retaliation just what he deserved? Could anything less have expiated the offense? Sir, I spoke of him as BENJAMIN F. WADE, an individual, a citizen of my own State, and made no allusion to him as a Senator. . . .

I have not finished the sentence. Whenever BENJAMIN F. WADE shall take back the false and slanderous accusation which he has made against me, I will take back the language I have applied to him; but not before.

Questions to Consider

1. How would you compare Clement Vallandigham's and Benjamin Wade's political views? How do you account for the differences? What were the most important influences shaping each man's outlook?

2. Some historians have argued that Vallandigham was a traitor to the Union cause, while others view him as a loyal and legitimate political opponent. Which view do you think is correct? Why?

3. Wade was one of the most radical politicians of his time. What was so radical about his views? What threat did they pose to Abraham Lincoln during the Civil War?

4. Wars often result in the narrowing of civil liberties. The Civil War was no exception. Do you think Lincoln was justified in dealing with Vallandigham as he did? What do the careers of Vallandigham and Wade reveal about the political pressures confronting Lincoln during the war?

For Further Reading

Frank L. Klement, *The Limits of Dissent: Clement L. Vallandigham and the Civil War* (New York: Fordham University Press, 1998), provides a balanced study of Vallandigham's role in the war.

Mark E. Neely Jr., *The Fate of Liberty: Abraham Lincoln and Civil Liberties* (New York: Oxford University Press, 1991), is a Pulitzer Prize–winning study of Lincoln's constitutional policies that offers a sympathetic view of his actions.

Phillip S. Paludan, *The Presidency of Abraham Lincoln* (Lawrence: University Press of Kansas, 1994), provides a balanced interpretation of the constitutional issues confronting Lincoln.

Hans Louis Trefousse, *Benjamin Franklin Wade: Radical Republican from Ohio* (New York: Twayne Publishers, 1963), remains the classic biography of Wade.

15

Race and Redemption in the Reconstructed South:
Robert Smalls and Carl Schurz

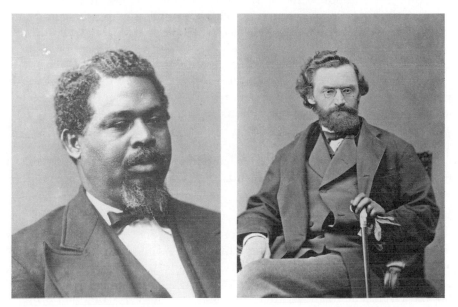

Robert Smalls   Carl Schurz

In the predawn hours of May 13, 1862, the small Confederate ship *Planter* made its way out of Charleston Harbor. As it steamed toward the ships blockading the South Carolina port, Union lookouts strained their eyes, then prepared to sound the alarm to open fire on the small vessel. Suddenly, one lookout spotted a white flag flying on the boat, and the Union ships held their fire. As the *Planter* came alongside, Union naval officers were shocked. No whites were on board. Instead, they saw only black men, women, and children, who were dancing, singing, and shouting for joy. When a Union officer boarded, a well-dressed black man stepped forward to address him. "Good morning, sir! I've brought you some of the old United States guns, sir!" Indeed he had. An armed Confederate vessel, the *Planter* contained a cargo of unmounted cannon and sixteen slaves who had captured the boat and escaped to freedom. The man who had organized the capture was the ship's pilot, a twenty-three-year-old slave named Robert Smalls.

About three months later in Virginia, a thirty-three-year-old German immigrant named Carl Schurz met Confederate forces at the Second Battle of Bull Run. In the First Battle of Bull Run a year earlier, Union forces had been routed.

The second battle ended the same way. Brigadier General Schurz, however, performed with distinction. After the battle, he was promoted to major general and given command of a division composed mostly of German Americans. The next year, Schurz and his troops made a gallant stand on Cemetery Ridge at the Battle of Gettysburg. Still later, he saw action against Confederate forces in Tennessee.

By the time the Civil War was over, Robert Smalls and Carl Schurz had served the Union well. That was not all they had in common, though. Both men were committed Republicans. Both would go into politics after the war and serve in Congress—Smalls as a representative from South Carolina and Schurz as a senator from Missouri. Both men also would support their party's efforts to reconstruct the South and guarantee political equality to the freedmen. But before the period known as Reconstruction was over, they had split over what to do with the South and the freedmen. One would hold fast to his hopes for the former slaves; the other would retreat from his commitment to them. Smalls and Schurz were only two of the millions of Americans who contributed in one way or another to the Union victory in the Civil War. Like so many of their countrymen, they did not necessarily agree about the meaning of that victory. For that reason, the stories of these two Union veterans may help us understand why Reconstruction turned out as it did.

"The Smartest *Cullud* Man"

Robert Smalls had something in common with Carl Schurz and with the leader of his own Republican Party, Abraham Lincoln. Like Lincoln, Smalls had arisen from utter obscurity. He was born in 1839 in Beaufort, South Carolina, to a slave woman who worked as a domestic servant. His father was an unknown white man, although many believed that he was John McKee, his mother's master. John McKee died when Robert was six, and his son Henry sent Smalls to live with relatives in Charleston when was twelve. He lived in the home of his master's sister-in-law, working as a waiter, a lamplighter, and a stevedore. Smalls was "hired out," meaning that he worked for wages. He kept some of his pay for himself and sent the rest to his master. This situation gave the young slave relative autonomy. He may even have had enough freedom to pursue an education during his years in the city. Smalls apparently taught himself to read and possibly attended for a few months a school run by one of Charleston's many black societies. Formed in violation of the South Carolina law that prohibited more than four slaves from assembling at one time, such societies often provided education and other services to the African-American community.

In 1858, Smalls married Hannah Jones, a hotel maid who was also a slave. He was nineteen; she was thirty-one. Smalls said he married Hannah because he wanted "to have a wife to prevent me from running around—to have somebody to do for me and to keep me." Slaves, of course, were not allowed to marry legally, but Smalls made a deal with his master. He would pay McKee fifteen dollars a month so that he could marry Hannah. Smalls made a similar deal with Hannah's master, paying him five dollars a month. This allowed the two slaves to keep enough money to support themselves and even have children. Smalls later agreed to purchase his wife and daughter for eight hundred dollars. When he fled the city in 1862, he had seven hundred dollars, having never paid any of the agreed-upon amount to his wife's owner. How he accumulated this sum and managed to keep his household running is difficult to imagine. His own wages as a deck hand in 1861 amounted to only sixteen dollars a month, and Hannah probably made no more than ten dollars a month as a maid, assuming that she continued to work after their marriage.

Somehow the little family managed to make it, probably due to Smalls's abilities as a trader. His position as a deck hand on the *Planter* allowed him even greater autonomy than his job on the docks. Traveling on the river and coastal steamer, Smalls was able to make regular visits to friends and associates in a wider area. He traded goods within the slave community and probably with whites as well. As a sailor, Smalls acquired valuable skills. He learned to handle the ship and eventually became a wheelman. (Actually, he was a pilot, a title white southerners refused to give blacks.) When the Civil War offered him the opportunity to escape bondage, his skills, education, and position served him well. Smalls carefully planned the escape of his family and friends. One night when the ship's three white officers were on shore, he pulled off his plan in dramatic fashion.

The theft of the *Planter* brought not only freedom but also an economic windfall. The northern press jumped on the story of Smalls's heroic action. *Harper's Weekly,* for instance, ran a picture of Smalls and an article on the "plucky Africans." One New York newspaper commented that few events during the Civil War "produced a heartier chuckle of satisfaction" than the theft of the *Planter.* The "fellow" behind the feat, it observed, "is no Small man." Given such favorable reaction, Smalls and his fellow hijackers were awarded a bounty by Congress for liberating the *Planter.* As leader of the party, Smalls got the largest share, fifteen hundred dollars. He continued to work as a pilot on the *Planter,* which was now operating as a troop transport for the Union. The ship shuttled men and supplies between the Sea Islands* off South Carolina and mainland areas occupied by Union forces. In addition, he piloted other ships, including some engaged in unsuccessful attacks on Charleston.

At the same time, Smalls worked to improve the condition of fellow blacks. In Union-occupied Beaufort, he engaged in fundraising to assist freedmen with education and employment. He also traveled to New York during the war to raise awareness of the condition of the growing ranks of free blacks in the South. He had been sent north by freedmen in Beaufort County who were eager to help themselves rather than wait for charity or government assistance. Such efforts were widespread throughout the postwar South, but African Americans in Beaufort County became organized—and politicized—several years before those in most other areas. A highly concentrated black population, early occupation by Union forces, and a large number of black soldiers and white teachers and missionaries contributed to their efforts. Already in 1864, blacks in the area

Sea Islands: Low-lying islands off the coast of South Carolina and Georgia. Occupied early in the war by Union forces, the islands were home to a large number of blacks who worked on the rice plantations there.

had expressed their political preferences by organizing a delegation to the Republican convention in Baltimore. Although the delegates could not secure official representation at the convention, they made it clear that they were ready to "fight for the Union [and] die for it" and that they also wanted the right to "vote for it."

Unfortunately, that right was not immediately forthcoming, even when the Civil War ended. When Andrew Johnson became president after Lincoln's assassination in April 1865, he promoted a Reconstruction plan that excluded blacks from politics. Committed to white rule in the South, Johnson wanted a policy that would bring the rebellious states back into the Union without a fundamental restructuring of southern society. Under his Reconstruction plan, white Southerners—often former Confederates—quickly reorganized state governments. By early 1866, southern state legislatures elected under the president's plan had passed Black Codes. These laws severely limited the rights of African Americans to own property, assemble, move about freely, and vote. Often they prevented interracial marriage and upheld labor contracts that favored white landowners. The Black Codes in South Carolina legalized harsh labor practices regarding blacks and placed severe restrictions on freedmen. At a convention in late 1865, South Carolina blacks protested the new laws. In an address to the state's whites, the convention demanded that blacks "be governed by the same laws that control other men." **[See Source 1.]**

For several years after the war, Smalls was more concerned with improving his own position than with getting involved in politics. Even before the war ended, he returned to Beaufort and opened a store. He did well enough to purchase his former master's house by paying the back taxes on it. In 1867, he purchased an eight-room building at a government tax sale and deeded it "to the Colored children" of Beaufort as a school. These actions are a measure of his status in the community. One observer, capturing the dialect of Sea Island blacks, noted that Smalls was "regarded by all the other negroes as immensely rich, and decidedly 'the smartest *cullud* man in Souf Car'lina.'" Widely known, well-off, obviously intelligent, and self-possessed, Smalls was a natural leader in his community. His emergence as a prominent black politician during Reconstruction was almost inevitable.

"Their Minds Were Fully Made Up"

When Carl Schurz was born in Prussia (now Germany) in 1829, few would have predicted that he would have an impact on a former slave like Robert Smalls. Certainly, his early circumstances were far removed from Smalls's oppressive world. Schurz's father was a teacher and businessman with minor connections to the local nobility. Carl was educated at schools in the nearby city of Cologne, then went on to the University of Bonn. He entered the university in the fall of 1847, just in time to become embroiled in the Revolutions of 1848, uprisings against the monarchies and oppressive regimes that controlled much of Europe. Some of the rebels hoped to create nations based on republican principles and free-market economies; others advocated socialism. Along with other revolutionaries, Schurz wrote articles, organized workers, and made rousing speeches in support of revolution. After a failed attempt to capture an arsenal, he barely escaped arrest. Forced to hide in attics and crawl through sewers, he fled to France. Later, he returned to Germany, bribed a prison guard, and assisted one of his jailed professors in a dramatic escape. By the time he made his way to England, he was a famous man. For the next few years, he made his living as a journalist and teacher in England and France. In 1852, he married the daughter of a wealthy Hamburg cane merchant and moved to the United States, where he hoped to write a history of his adopted country that would appeal to both Americans and Europeans.

Schurz and his wife settled in Philadelphia, where he wrote and lectured. His wife's inheritance also gave him the freedom to travel. As he journeyed across the northern United States, he had an opportunity to learn about his new country. He also found a more suitable home in the upper Midwest, where many other Germans had migrated in the early nineteenth century. In 1856, Schurz and a growing family moved to Watertown, Wisconsin, where he went into real estate, dabbled in other businesses, bought a farm, and continued to write. His real calling, however, was politics. Before long, he joined the Republican Party, largely because of his opposition to the expansion of slavery. As a young revolutionary fighting European despotism, Schurz was a fervent opponent of an institution that violated the principles of political equality. Although many Republicans were staunchly anti-immigrant, Schurz believed that the new party offered possibilities for the German immigrant community to gain political power. Energetic, charismatic, famous, and bilingual, Schurz was the perfect leader to build Republican strength in an important ethnic community. He could use his background to counter the appeal the Democrats had for many German Americans and then forge them into a powerful Republican bloc.

In the following years, Schurz worked tirelessly for the Republican Party. He attempted unsuccessfully to become Wisconsin's lieutenant governor and even its governor. In 1860, he led the Wisconsin delegation at the Republican National Convention and quickly threw his support to Abraham Lincoln. After Lincoln won the Republican nomination, the party elected Schurz to the Republican National Committee in hopes that he would be able to secure the German-American vote. Schurz helped deliver enough German-American votes to be awarded a post as minister to Spain in 1861. Watching the war from Europe, he decided that emancipating the slaves might be the only way to keep the European powers out of the war. Thus he lent his voice to the cause of the Radical Republicans,* who urged Lincoln to free the slaves and transform the conflict from a war for the Union into one for freedom.

It was a natural position for Schurz. As a revolutionary, he had fought tyranny and oppression in Europe. He had joined the Republican Party because of the Democrats' support of slavery. Now his belief in liberty and equality

---

Radical Republicans: Those Republicans who wanted the abolition of slavery, an extension of citizenship to former slaves, and punishment of Confederate leaders. After the war, the Radicals believed that Reconstruction could not be achieved without a restructuring of southern society.

led him to give up his diplomatic post and return to the United States to fight. He was commissioned as a brigadier general just in time to see action at the Second Battle of Bull Run in August 1862. Rewarded for his performance with a command over a largely German-American division, Schurz saw action in many major campaigns, including Chancellorsville, Gettysburg, and Chattanooga. He frequently squabbled with his commanders, though, and was later removed from action at the front. In fact, Schurz was constantly politicking. In the fall of 1864, he campaigned for Lincoln's reelection, and at the end of the war, he looked forward to helping Lincoln carry out his Reconstruction policy. After Lincoln's assassination, Schurz hoped for a close relationship with Andrew Johnson. When the new president's Reconstruction plan resulted in new southern state governments committed to white supremacy, Schurz joined with other Republicans intent on bringing about radical changes in southern society and politics. Led by politicians such as Benjamin Wade of Ohio (see Chapter 14) and Thaddeus Stevens of Pennsylvania, the Radical Republicans called for legislation that would enfranchise the freedmen, distribute to them land confiscated from former Confederates, and establish legal and social equality for blacks.

Schurz played a critical role in helping the Radicals seize control of Reconstruction policy. As white southerners began to organize new governments by the summer of 1865, Schurz took an inspection tour of the South. He reported that Johnson's policies allowed former Confederates to keep their hold on power and that the new governments were passing Black Codes severely limiting the freedom of blacks. Although the Thirteenth Amendment had abolished slavery in 1865, a new labor system had arisen that made African Americans slaves in all but name. Moreover, white supremacists were using violence to keep down those who opposed the new governments. Schurz's report presented ample evidence of the attitudes of many white southerners toward blacks. The slightest resistance on the part of freedmen to white control was merely proof in whites' minds that blacks were unfit for freedom. One Georgia planter came to that conclusion because "one of his negroes had . . . impudently refused to submit to a whipping." Schurz came away from his contact with white southerners convinced that in most cases "their minds were fully made up" about the failure of the South's new free labor system. [See Source 2.]

"This . . . Untutored Multitude"

Published later in 1865, Schurz's report fed the growing alarm of many northerners about the new southern state governments. It also helped rally the Radical Republicans to action. In 1866, the Fourteenth Amendment was passed in Congress and submitted to the states for ratification. The amendment extended citizenship to African Americans, barred former Confederates from holding office, and penalized states that did not allow blacks to vote by reducing their representation in Congress. All but one of the former Confederate states rejected the amendment (although it was ratified in 1868). The governor of South Carolina expressed the sentiment of many southern whites when he declared that blacks were "steeped in ignorance, crime, and vice" and should not be allowed to vote. This resistance to the wishes of Congress further angered many northerners, who now believed that Johnson and the southern politicians were overturning the Union's victory in the war. In late 1866, therefore, Republicans made big gains in the congressional elections, and the Radicals in Congress seized the initiative. Early the next year, they passed the first of the Reconstruction Acts,* which overturned the governments established under Johnson's plan and imposed military rule on most of the former Confederate states. Under the watchful eye of the military, the freedmen would be registered to vote, new state constitutions drafted, and new elections held. Across the South, Republicans were swept into power.

In South Carolina, the overturning of the Johnson government finally gave the freedmen a chance to exercise the citizenship rights they had long desired. After helping to form the Beaufort Republican Club, Robert Smalls received its nomination as a delegate to the state's constitutional convention. Meeting early in 1868, the convention brought together 124 delegates, 78 of whom were black. Although one South Carolina newspaper charged that the black delegates were "misguided as to their true welfare," South Carolina's new constitution was revolutionary for the South and reflected the concerns of the state's black majority. It called, for instance, for state assistance to help people in "their homeless and landless condition." It declared that "no person shall be deprived of the right of suffrage for non-payment of the poll tax."* It abolished segregation. The delegates also recognized that the maintenance of a government "faithful to the interests and liberties of the people" depended "in great measure on the intelligence of the people themselves." Thus, following a resolution offered by Smalls, the constitution provided for free elementary schooling for all children.

Submitted to South Carolina's now largely black electorate, the new constitution was overwhelmingly approved. Shortly after that, new elections brought Republicans to power. Smalls won a seat in the lower house of the legislature—the only one in the reconstructed South made up of a majority of black legislators. In fact, the majority of the state's legislators were ex-slaves. Smalls and the other freedmen often deferred to whites and the better-educated freeborn blacks, but Smalls continued to fight for issues that affected his black constituents. He served on a commission "to establish and maintain a system of free common schools" and sponsored a bill to enforce the Civil Rights Act of 1866, which granted the same civil rights to all persons born in the United States. He also served on a panel that investigated the intimidation, even murder, of Republican voters in the state during the 1868 election.

Smalls devoted much of his energy in the legislature to mundane issues that benefited his constituents in Beaufort County. He championed the construction of roads, railroads, government buildings, and docks in his district.

Reconstruction Acts: Passed in 1867 and 1868, the Reconstruction Acts divided the former Confederate states into five military districts, subjected them to martial law, and gave military commanders the power to register voters and oversee elections.

Poll tax: A tax established in many southern states as a requirement for voting in order to discourage blacks from casting ballots.

He mobilized voters with brass bands and torchlight parades, and he knew how to arouse them with passionate rhetoric. He called on black voters to "bury the democratic party so deep that there will not be seen even a bubble coming from the spot where the burial took place," and he vowed to "pour hot shot into the ranks of traitors." At the same time, his financial support of the widow and family of his former master built up the goodwill of many whites in the county. All these efforts paid off, as Smalls built a political machine* based largely on the loyalty of his constituents. As one observer put it, "The men, women and children seem to regard him with a feeling akin to worship." Although Smalls was not highly educated, another noted, he was "a thoroughly representative man among the people" and had "their unlimited confidence." That confidence was evident in 1870, when he handily won election to the upper house of the state legislature. Smalls sat in the state senate for four years and then in 1874 won election to the U.S. House of Representatives. Mobilizing his Beaufort County machine, he swamped his opponent by a margin of more than four to one.

Taking his seat in Congress in 1875, Smalls continued to mind the needs of his South Carolina constituents—white and black. In 1876, for example, Smalls fought a minor battle over federal control of the Citadel, the military school in Charleston that had been seized by the national government during the war. The takeover of the school had upset many white South Carolinians, and Smalls demanded that the secretary of war at least pay rent to the city of Charleston for use of the grounds. As in the state legislature, however, much of his energy was devoted to the passage of bills concerning such mundane matters as appropriating funds for the maintenance of harbors. Although such work was not glamorous, Smalls recognized its importance for his district's well-being. At the same time, he had not lost his commitment to Reconstruction. In 1876, he fought against a bill calling for the reduction of the army in South Carolina. Such a move, he knew, would make it easier for white vigilante groups to terrorize black voters in an effort to overthrow Republican control of the state. In one particularly gruesome incident that summer in Hamburg (now North Augusta), South Carolina, a mob of about a thousand armed whites surrounded a black militia unit and murdered a number of the militiamen after they surrendered. As one newspaper put it, they "were shot down like rabbits." Shortly after, Smalls unsuccessfully attempted to amend the force-reduction bill, arguing that no military forces should be withdrawn from South Carolina "so long as the militia of that State . . . are assaulted, disarmed, and taken prisoners, and then massacred in cold blood by lawless bands of men." [See Source 3.]

Eight years after formally entering politics, Smalls was at the height of his power. Yet the Hamburg incident and others like it did not bode well for Smalls or Reconstruction. The bastion of anti-Reconstruction whites, the Democratic Party, had made a remarkable comeback by 1876. In fact, when Smalls first took his seat in Congress that year, the Democrats had a majority in the House of Representatives for the first time in eighteen years. About two-thirds of the

---

*Political machine: A type of political organization that often dominated city and state politics in the late nineteenth century. The bosses who ran these machines often built up support by dispensing favors to constituents.

Democrats in the House were southerners, and eighty of them were veterans of the Confederate military. Calling themselves Redeemers,* these southern Democrats launched a violent assault against Republican rule. As white terrorist organizations such as the Ku Klux Klan and the Red Shirts used violence and even murder to intimidate Republican voters, the Democrats began to regain political control in one state after another.

South Carolina was a particularly fertile field for the growth of vigilante groups. By 1876, whites in South Carolina had organized about three hundred rifle clubs, with twenty-four in mostly black Beaufort County alone. Often organized by former Confederate officers, these clubs were nothing more than armed bands of nightriders. At the same time, South Carolina Democrats launched a vocal propaganda campaign against the alleged corruption and mismanagement of the Republican-controlled state government. As with the Reconstruction governments in other states, South Carolina's legislature had made large expenditures to help rebuild the war-torn South. Increased spending on a shrunken, war-ravaged tax base made these Republican regimes inviting targets. So did the presence in them of northerners, who were derisively called carpetbaggers.* The Redeemers railed against the wasteful excesses of "carpetbag" governments that had spent once responsible states to the brink of bankruptcy. Most of all, though, the Redeemers played on the deeply held racism of the white southerners. "Ignorant" blacks, they charged, had been taken advantage of by grasping "Yankees," and the result was a disgraceful riot of incompetence and theft. With its black-majority legislature, South Carolina was especially vulnerable to this charge. *New York Tribune* reporter James Pike wrote an influential book titled *The Prostrate State: South Carolina Under Negro Government*, in which he referred to the actions of the legislature as a "shocking burlesque upon legislative proceedings" and to the black legislators themselves as an "uncouth and untutored multitude." **[See Source 4.]**

The next year, the Democrats were victorious in the three southern states not already "redeemed," including South Carolina. The deadlocked presidential election in late 1876 gave the Redeemers their opening. The Democratic candidate, Samuel J. Tilden, won the popular vote, but twenty electoral votes in the Deep South were in dispute. When a special commission appointed by Congress met to resolve the issue, it awarded all twenty electoral votes—and the presidency—to the Republican candidate, Rutherford B. Hayes. The Democrats lost the presidency by one electoral vote, but they had gained something, too. Although the Republicans retained control of the presidency, the Democrats got federal troops withdrawn from the remaining Republican states in the South. Without the protection provided by these forces, the Republican governments

---

Redeemers: Conservative white Democrats who vowed to save, or redeem, the South from Republican rule.

Carpetbaggers: The label applied by white southerners to northerners in the South during Reconstruction. The term was used to suggest that these "Yankees" carried their worldly goods in their carpetbags (suitcases) and therefore had no roots in the community. Because some of the northerners were involved in Reconstruction politics, the label also implied that they were corrupt—that is, out to enrich themselves at the public's expense.

were doomed. With the so-called Compromise of 1877,* conservative Democratic rule was restored across the South. Reconstruction was over.

Smalls was one of the Redeemers' victims. After the Democrats won control of the South Carolina government in 1877, they set out to prove the corruption of the prior Republican regimes. In his second term in Congress, Smalls was a prime target of their investigations. While serving in the state senate, he had chaired the Printing Committee, which oversaw the government's printing contracts. Now the Democrats accused him of accepting a bribe in connection with those contracts. Smalls said that he was innocent, but he was convicted by a jury and sentenced to three years in prison "with hard labor." He appealed the verdict before the state supreme court and lost, but the Democratic governor pardoned him when the Republicans promised to drop their investigation into Democratic election fraud. In reality, Smalls probably had overstepped the bounds of legality, but the evidence was scanty, others also were involved, and his crime paled in comparison to those committed by other politicians of the day. It was obvious that Smalls had been a political target and that the Democrats wanted control of his congressional district.

The Democrats had not seen the last of Smalls, however. In 1878, he ran for reelection to Congress. As they had done throughout the South, the Democrats influenced the election by frightening voters away from the polls. Smalls lost, but he was undeterred. Two years later, he ran for Congress again. Despite all their advantages, the Democrats realized that it would be a close race. To counter Smalls's popularity among black voters, the Democrats stuffed the ballot boxes. The fraud was so obvious that Smalls was awarded the victory when he challenged the results. By the time he took his seat, however, his term was almost over. To ensure their victory when Smalls ran again in 1882, the Democrats in control of the state legislature redrew the boundaries of his congressional district so that he was unable even to win the Republican primary. Denied the nomination, he would regain his seat in 1884 when the Republican winner died in office and a party convention selected him to finish out the term. Later that year, he was reelected. The Democrats were still determined to have his seat, however, and in 1886 they once again resorted to violence, tossing out Republican ballots and forcing black voters away from the polls to defeat Smalls for good.

"Ignorance and Inexperience"

In the 1870s, Carl Schurz was far removed from the maneuvering in South Carolina that ultimately cost Smalls his office. In a way, though, Schurz also had something to do with Smalls's demise. After all, the fate of the Reconstruction governments was not determined solely by events in the South. The shifting attitudes of many prominent northern Republicans also played a big part, and few of them underwent a more dramatic change of heart regarding Reconstruction than the former German revolutionary.

In 1869, Schurz had ridden the Radical Republican cause right to the U.S.

Compromise of 1877: The political deal struck between Republicans and Democrats to break the deadlocked presidential election of 1876. It allowed federal troops to be removed from the South in exchange for the election of the Republican presidential candidate.

Senate. After the war, he had moved to St. Louis and helped rally the city's large German-American community for the Republicans in the 1868 presidential election. The next year, he was rewarded by the Missouri legislature with election to the Senate. With the election of Ulysses S. Grant as president in 1868, the Republicans now controlled the presidency, the Congress, and the reconstructed states of the South. From his new position, Schurz fully intended to support stern measures for former Confederates, as well as the Republican governments already established under congressional Reconstruction. Political practices in his own party began to disturb him, though. Schurz was disgusted by the use of patronage—the dispensing of government jobs as political rewards. The Civil War had greatly expanded the federal bureaucracy, and as it continued to grow after the war, both Republicans and Democrats used the spoils of office to their advantage. One of the powers of a political machine, such as the one Robert Smalls had built in South Carolina, was to give government jobs to supporters. A Republican machine in Missouri had secured Schurz's own election to the Senate. Increasingly, though, he was appalled by corruption in the Grant administration, and by the early 1870s he was leading the calls for civil service reform.*

Schurz's concerns about honesty in government made him especially vulnerable to the Redeemers' arguments about the Republican regimes in the South. In truth, these governments were no more corrupt than those that had preceded them or those that followed. Nonetheless, Schurz and many other northerners swallowed the argument that ignorant blacks in league with wily carpetbaggers were responsible for shocking corruption. His first public disagreements with the Radical Republicans arose over the readmission of Georgia to the Union in 1870. After the state was readmitted, Democrats in Georgia passed laws excluding blacks from the government. Republicans in Congress responded by insisting that Georgia ratify the Fifteenth Amendment,* which guaranteed freedmen the right to vote. Convinced that the South had been punished long enough, Schurz warned against continued federal interference in the states. Soon Schurz opposed every Radical bill, even the Ku Klux Klan Acts,* which were designed to curb the power of that terrorist, antiblack organization.

Schurz's new stance shocked many of his Republican friends: The Radical was now on the side of the Redeemers! Yet Schurz's shift was not as dramatic as it seemed. His radicalism was rooted in the idea of the political equality of free citizens. When placed against Old World monarchies and aristocracies, that belief seemed revolutionary indeed. Yet in the post–Civil War period, the empha-

---

Civil service reform: Changes that would result in the awarding of government jobs on the basis of merit rather than as political rewards, as under the so-called spoils system.

Fifteenth Amendment: Ratified in 1870, this constitutional amendment prohibited states from denying the right to vote on the basis of "race, color, or previous condition of servitude." Thus, unlike the Fourteenth Amendment, it did not give states the option of denying voting rights to blacks.

Ku Klux Klan Acts: Passed in Congress in 1870 and 1871, these acts resulted from overwhelming evidence of widespread white terrorism against blacks. They gave the president new powers to put down such violence, including the detention of whites.

sis on political equality also could lead to support for Reconstruction policies that stopped well short of a revolution in southern society. In fact, like most Republicans, Schurz believed that securing political equality for freedmen was the central goal of Reconstruction. Like most Americans, however, he associated political freedom with free enterprise and the protection of private property. Thus sweeping government action such as property redistribution to address the dire economic condition of the freedmen violated the economic rights of free citizens. With emancipation and ratification of the Fourteenth Amendment, blacks now stood with whites as free citizens. Just like whites, they were able to advance themselves in a free-market economy as far as their talents and abilities would take them. Unfortunately, it would not take much evidence to convince many northern whites that the condition of blacks reflected their abilities. And, in their minds, those alleged abilities seemed to justify the Redeemers' position. Thus it was relatively easy for Schurz to come to the conclusion that Republican Reconstruction had allowed "ignorance and inexperience" to have too much influence on "public affairs." **[See Source 5.]**

Schurz would pay a price for his pro-Redeemer views. In fact, his support of the restoration of former Confederates' voting rights helped Democrats regain control of Missouri's legislature, which then denied him reelection to the Senate in 1875. Yet he would not be denied political office. The next year, Schurz rallied the German-American vote for the Republican presidential candidate, Rutherford B. Hayes. Ironically, the proponent of civil service reform would enjoy the spoils of victory when Hayes appointed him secretary of the interior. By then, of course, Reconstruction was over, and Schurz, like other Americans, turned his attention to other matters. One of them was the "Indian problem" in the American West. Schurz's view of Native Americans was similar to his view of freedmen. Like many other white Americans, he saw them as another "ignorant and inexperienced" people. That widespread view was reflected in a federal policy that forced Indians onto reservations in the late nineteenth century—a policy that Schurz helped enforce.

At the same time, the Democratic Redeemers began to strip the freedmen of their political rights and erect a rigid system of legal racial segregation. Left impoverished, most African Americans were tied to small plots of land belonging to others. By the end of the nineteenth century, their dire circumstances once again caught the attention of Schurz, who had become close friends with Booker T. Washington, the foremost black leader at the turn of the century. Washington had helped found the Tuskegee Institute in Alabama, a vocational school for blacks. Throughout his career, Washington preached a self-help gospel that naturally appealed to Schurz. Blacks, Schurz continued to believe until his death in 1906, simply had to pull themselves up by their bootstraps to achieve equality. Perhaps Robert Smalls could have convinced Schurz otherwise. Appointed a collector of customs for the port of Beaufort when the Republicans won the presidency in 1888, he served in that position on and off until 1913, one of the few black officeholders in the South. Until the day he died in 1915, however, he was convinced that Reconstruction had been a failure.

PRIMARY SOURCES

SOURCE 1:   Zion Presbyterian Church, *"Memorial to the Senate and House of Representatives"* (1865)

The freed people of the South were at the heart of Reconstruction. In this document, African Americans from Zion Presbyterian Church in Charleston, South Carolina, present a list of demands to the U.S. Congress. What do these demands reveal about the people's desires?

Gentlemen:

We, the colored people of the State of South Carolina, in Convention assembled, respectfully present for your attention some prominent facts in relation to our present condition, and make a modest yet earnest appeal to your considerate judgment.

We, your memorialists, with profound gratitude to almighty God, recognize the great boon of freedom conferred upon us by the instrumentality of our late President, Abraham Lincoln, and the armies of the United States.

"The Fixed decree, which not all Heaven can move,
  Thou, Fate, fulfill it; and, ye Powers, approve."

We also recognize with liveliest gratitude the vast services of the Freedmen's Bureau together with the efforts of the good and wise throughout the land to raise up an oppressed and deeply injured people in the scale of civilized being, during the throbbings of a mighty revolution which must affect the future destiny of the world.

Conscious of the difficulties that surround our position, we would ask for no rights or privileges but such as rest upon the strong basis of justice and expediency, in view of the best interests of our entire country.

We ask first, that the strong arm of law and order be placed alike over the entire people of this State; that life and property be secured, and the laborer free to sell his labor as the merchant his goods.

We ask that a fair and impartial instruction be given to the pledges of the government to us concerning the land question.

We ask that the three great agents of civilized society—the school, the pulpit, the press—be as secure in South Carolina as in Massachusetts or Vermont.

We ask that equal suffrage be conferred upon us, in common with the white men of this State.

This we ask, because "all free governments derive their just powers from the consent of the governed"; and we are largely in the majority in this State,

SOURCE: Reprinted in James S. Allen, *Reconstruction: The Battle for Democracy, 1865–1876* (New York: International Publishers, 1937), appendix, 228–229; originally from South Carolina African Americans' Petition, November 24, 1865.

bearing for a long period the burden of onerous taxation, without a just representation. We ask for equal suffrage as a protection for the hostility evoked by our known faithfulness to our country and flag under all circumstances.

We ask that colored men shall not in every instance be tried by white men; and that neither by custom nor enactment shall we be excluded from the jury box.

We ask that, inasmuch as the Constitution of the United States explicitly declares that the right to keep and bear arms shall not be infringed and the Constitution is the Supreme law of the land—that the late efforts of the Legislature of this State to pass an act to deprive us of arms be forbidden, as a plain violation of the Constitution, and unjust to many of us in the highest degree, who have been soldiers, and purchased our muskets from the United States Government when mustered out of service.

We protest against any code of black laws the Legislature of this State may enact, and pray to be governed by the same laws that control other men. The right to assemble in peaceful convention, to discuss the political questions of the day; the right to enter upon all the avenues of agriculture, commerce, trade; to amass wealth by thrift and industry; the right to develop our whole being by all the appliances that belong to civilized society, cannot be questioned by any class of intelligent legislators.

We solemnly affirm and desire to live orderly and peacefully with all the people of this State; and commending this memorial to your considerate judgment.

Thus we ever pray.

Charleston, S.C. November 24, 1865
Zion Presbyterian Church.

SOURCE 2:   Carl Schurz, *Report on the Condition of the South*   (1865)

In 1865, Carl Schurz toured the South to investigate the conditions there. His report to Congress was published and became a powerful tool for the Radical Republicans. In this excerpt, Schurz describes the opinions of whites in the South regarding African Americans. What does this report reveal about the attitudes of conquered white southerners?

That the result of the free labor experiment made under circumstances so extremely unfavorable should at once be a perfect success, no reasonable person would expect. Nevertheless, a large majority of the southern men with whom I came into contact announced their opinions with so positive an assurance as to produce the impression that their minds were fully made up. In at least nineteen cases of twenty the reply I received to my inquiry about their views on the

SOURCE: Carl Schurz, *Report on the Condition of the South* (1865; reprint, New York: Arno Press, 1969), pp. 16–17.

new system was uniformly this: "You cannot make the negro work without physical compulsion." I heard this hundreds of times, heard it wherever I went, heard it in nearly the same words from so many different persons, that at last I came to the conclusion that this is the prevailing sentiment among the southern people. There are exceptions to this rule, but, as far as my information extends, far from enough to affect the rule. In the accompanying documents you will find an abundance of proof in support of this statement. There is hardly a paper relative to the negro question annexed to this report which does not, in some direct or indirect way, corroborate it. Unfortunately the disorders necessarily growing out of the transition state continually furnished food for argument. I found but few people who were willing to make due allowance for the adverse influence of exceptional circumstances. By a large majority of those I came in contact with, and they mostly belonged, to the more intelligent class, every irregularity that occurred was directly charged against the system of free labor. If negroes walked away from the plantations, it was conclusive proof of the incorrigible instability of the negro, and the impracticability of free negro labor. If some individual negroes violated the terms of their contract, it proved unanswerably that no negro had, or ever would have, a just conception of the binding force of a contract, and that this system of free negro labor was bound to be a failure. If some negroes shirked, or did not perform their task with sufficient alacrity, it was produced as irrefutable evidence to show that physical compulsion was actually indispensable to make the negro work. If negroes, idlers or refugees crawling about the towns, applied to the authorities for subsistence, it was quoted as incontestably establishing the point that the negro was too improvident to take care of himself, and must necessarily be consigned to the care of a master. I heard a Georgia planter argue most seriously that one of his negroes had shown himself certainly unfit for freedom because he impudently refused to submit to a whipping. I frequently went into an argument with those putting forth such general assertions, quoting instances in which negro laborers were working faithfully, and to the entire satisfaction of their employers, as the employers themselves had informed me. In a majority of cases the reply was that we northern people did not understand the negro, but that they (the southerners) did; that as to the particular instances I quoted I was probably mistaken; that I had not closely investigated the cases, or had been deceived by my informants; that they *knew* the negro would not work without compulsion, and that nobody could make them believe he would. Arguments like these naturally finished such discussions. It frequently struck me that persons who conversed about every other subject calmly and sensibly would lose their temper as soon as the negro question was touched.

SOURCE 3:   *Representative Robert Smalls Protests the Withdrawal of Federal Troops*   (1876)

In the face of rising vigilante action against blacks in South Carolina, Robert Smalls introduced an amendment to a bill in Congress that would have reduced federal military forces in the state. What does Smalls's testimony reveal about the threat to Republican rule in the state?

I offer the amendment which I send to the desk. The clerk read as follows:

Add to the first section the following:

Provided, That no troops for the purposes named in this section shall be drawn from the State of South Carolina so long as the militia of that State peaceably assembled are assaulted, disarmed, and taken prisoners, and then massacred in cold blood by lawless bands of men invading that State from the State of Georgia.

I hope the House will adopt that proviso as an amendment to the bill. As I have only five minutes I send to the desk a letter published in one of the newspapers here from an eye-witness of the massacre at Hamburgh [*sic*], and I ask the Clerk to read it.

The Clerk read as follows:

The origin of the difficulty, as I learn from the best and most reliable authority, is as follows: On the Fourth of July the colored people of the town were engaged in celebrating the day, and part of the celebration consisted in the parade of the colored militia company. After marching through the principal streets of the town, the company came to a halt across one of the roads leading out of the town. While resting there two white men drove up in a buggy, and with curses ordered the company to break ranks and let them pass through. The captain of the company replied that there was plenty of room on either side of the company, and they could pass that way. The white men continued cursing and refused to turn out. So the captain of the militia, to avoid difficulty, ordered his men to break ranks and permit the buggy to pass through. . . .

Late in the afternoon General M. C. Butler, one of the most malignant of the unreconstructed rebels, rode into the town, accompanied by a score of well-armed white men, and stated to the leading colored men that he came for the purpose of prosecuting the case on the part of the two white men, and he demanded that the militia company should give up their arms and also surrender their officers. This demand the militia was ready to comply with for the purpose of avoiding a difficulty if General Butler would guarantee them entire safety from molestation by the crowd of white desperadoes. This Butler refused to do, and persisted in his demand for the surrender of the guns and officers, and threatened that if the surrender was not immediately made he would take the guns and officers by force of arms. This threat aroused the militia company to a realizing sense of their impending danger, and they at once repaired to a large

SOURCE: *Congressional Record,* 44th Cong., 1st sess., 1876, 5, pt. 5: 4641–42.

brick building, some two hundred yards from the river, used by them as an armory, and there took refuge. They numbered in all about forty men and had a very small quantity of ammunition. During this time, while the militia were taking refuge in their armory the white desperadoes were coming into the town in large numbers, not only from the adjacent county of Edgefield, but also from the city of Augusta, Georgia, until they numbered over fifteen hundred well-armed and ruffianly men, who were under the immediate command and direction of the ex-rebel chief, M. C. Butler. After the entire force had arrived, the building where the militia had taken refuge was entirely surrounded and a brisk fire opened upon it. This fire was kept up for some two hours, when, finding that the militia could not be dislodged by small arms, a messenger was sent to Augusta for artillery. During all this time not a shot had been fired by the militiamen. The artillery arrived and was posted on the bank of the river and opened fire on the building with grape and canister.

[An attempt to interrupt reading fails.]

The militia now realized that it was necessary to evacuate the armory at once. They proceeded to do so, getting out of a back window into a cornfield. They were soon discovered by the ruffians, and a rush was made for them. Fortunately, by hiding and hard fighting, a portion of the command escaped, but twenty-one were captured by the bushwhackers and taken immediately to a place near the railroad station.

Here a quasi-drumhead court-martial* was organized by the blood-hunters, and the last scene of the horrible drama began. It must now be remembered that not one of the twenty-one colored men had a pistol or gun about them. The moment they were captured their arms were taken from them, and they were absolutely defenseless. The orderly sergeant of the militia company was ordered to call the roll, and the first name called out to be shot in cold blood was Allan T. Attaway, the first lieutenant of the company, and holding the position of county commissioner of Aiken County, in which county Hamburgh is situated. He pleaded for his life, as only one in his position could plead, but his pleading were met with curses and blows, and he was taken from the sight of his comrades and a file of twelve men fired upon him. He was penetrated by four balls, one entering his brain, and the other three the lower portion of his body. He was instantly killed and after he was dead the brutes in human shape struck him over the head with their guns and stabbed him in the face with their bayonets. Three other men were treated in the same brutal manner. The fifth man when taken out made a dash for his life, and luckily escaped with only a slight wound in his leg.

In another portion of the town the chief of police, a colored man named James Cook, was taken from his house and while begging for his life brutally murdered. Not satisfied with this, the inhuman fiends beat him over the head with their muskets and cut out his tongue.

Another colored man, one of the marshals of the town, surrendered and was immediately shot through the body and mortally wounded. He has since

---

Drumhead court-martial: A court-martial held in the field for the purpose of trying offenses during military operations.

died. So far as I[1] have been able to learn only one white man was killed. It will thus be seen that six colored men were brutally murdered and one wounded, while on the side of the whites only one white man was killed. After this holocaust of blood was over the desperadoes in large bodies entered the houses of most of the prominent colored men of the town and completely gutted them. They stole all they possibly could, and what they could not steal they destroyed. Furniture was smashed, books torn to pieces, pictures cut from their frames, and every-thing that could be destroyed was given up to the demon of destruction. . . .

Are the southern colored citizens to be protected or are they to be left at the mercy of such ruffians as massacred the poor men of Hamburgh? Murdered At-taway was a man of considerable prominence in the republican party of the county. He was a law-abiding citizen, held a responsible office, and was well thought of by very many people. The other murdered men were good citizens and have never been known to infringe the law. The whole affair was a well and secretly planned scheme to destroy all the leading republicans of the county of Aiken living in Hamburgh. M. C. Butler, who lost a leg while fighting in the ranks of the rebels, and who is to-day the bitterest of Ku-Klux democrats, was the instigator of the whole affair and the blood-thirsty leader of the massacre. He boasted in Hamburgh during the fight that that was only the beginning; that the end should not be until after the elections in November. Such a man should be dealt with without pity or without hesitation. The United States Government is not powerless, and surely she will not be silent in an emergency like this, the parallel of which pen cannot describe. In this centennial year will she stand idly by and see her soil stained with the blood of defenseless citizens, and witness the bitter tears of women and children falling upon the murdered bodies of their loved ones? God forbid that such an attitude will be assumed toward the colored people of the South by the "best Government the world ever saw." Something must be done, and that quickly, or South Carolina will shed tears of blood and her limbs be shackled by democratic chains.

What I have written in this letter are facts which I vouch for entirely, and are not distorted in any degree. It's a "plain, unvarnished" narration of painful and horrible truths.

---

1. When a Democrat, Mr. Cochrane of Pennsylvania, demanded that Smalls name the correspon-dent, he replied: "I will say to the gentleman that if he is desirous that the name shall be given in order to have another Negro killed, he will not get it from me."

SOURCE 4:   James Pike, *The Prostrate State*   (1874)

In 1873, New York Tribune *correspondent James Pike traveled to South Carolina to report on conditions under the state's Republican government. Many whites in the North seized on his articles and book,* The Prostrate State: South Carolina Under Negro Government, *as evidence that Reconstruction was a failure. What is Pike's view of the South Carolina legislature in this excerpt from* The Prostrate State? *Why do you think many white northerners were so ready to accept it?*

We will enter the House of Representatives. Here sit one hundred and twenty-four members. Of these, twenty-three are white men, representing the remains of the old civilization. These are good-looking, substantial citizens. They are men of weight and standing in the communities they represent. They are all from the hill country. The frosts of sixty and seventy winters whiten the heads of some among them. There they sit, grim and silent. They feel themselves to be but loose stones, thrown in to partially obstruct a current they are powerless to resist. They say little and do little as the days go by. They simply watch the rising tide, and mark the progressive steps of the inundation. . . .

This dense negro crowd they confront do the debating, the squabbling, the law-making, and create all the clamor and disorder of the body. These twenty-three white men are but the observers, the enforced auditors of the dull and clumsy imitation of a deliberative body, whose appearance in their present capacity is at once a wonder and a shame to modern civilization. . . .

Their struggles to get the floor, their bellowings and physical contortions, baffle description. The Speaker's hammer plays a perpetual tattoo all to no purpose. The talking and the interruptions from all quarters go on with the utmost license. Every one esteems himself as good as his neighbor, and puts in his oar, apparently as often for love of riot and confusion as for any thing else. It is easy to imagine what are his ideas of propriety and dignity among a crowd of his own color, and these are illustrated without reserve. The Speaker orders a member whom he has discovered to be particularly unruly to take his seat. The member obeys, and with the same motion that he sits down, throws his feet on to his desk, hiding himself from the Speaker by the soles of his boots. In an instant he appears again on the floor. After a few experiences of this sort, the Speaker threatens, in a laugh, to call "the gemman" to order. This is considered a capital joke, and a guffaw follows. The laugh goes round, and then the peanuts are cracked and munched faster than ever; one hand being employed in fortifying the inner man with this nutriment of universal use, while the other enforces the views of the orator. This laughing propensity of the sable crowd is a great cause of disorder. They laugh as hens cackle—one begins and all follow.

But underneath all this shocking burlesque upon legislative proceedings, we must not forget that there is something very real to this uncouth and untutored multitude. It is not all sham, nor all burlesque. They have a genuine interest and a genuine earnestness in the business of the assembly which we are

SOURCE: James S. Pike, *The Prostrate State: South Carolina Under Negro Government* (New York: D. Appleton and Company, 1874), pp. 10–15, 19–21.

bound to recognize and respect, unless we would be accounted shallow critics. They have an earnest purpose, born of a conviction that their position and condition are not fully assured, which lends a sort of dignity to their proceedings. The barbarous, animated jargon in which they so often indulge is on occasion seen to be so transparently sincere and weighty in their own minds that sympathy supplants disgust. The whole thing is a wonderful novelty to them as well as to observers.

SOURCE 5:   Carl Schurz, *Speech in the Senate*   (1872)

By the early 1870s, Carl Schurz had reversed his stand on Reconstruction. In this excerpt from a speech in the U.S. Senate on January 30, 1872, how does Schurz attack the Republican governments in the South?

But the stubborn fact remains that they [Southern black voters and officeholders] were ignorant and inexperienced; that the public business was an unknown world to them, and that in spite of the best intentions they were easily misled, not infrequently by the most reckless rascality which had found a way to their confidence. Thus their political rights and privileges were undoubtedly well calculated, and even necessary, to protect their rights as free laborers and citizens; but they were not well calculated to secure a successful administration of other public interests.

I do not blame the colored people for it; still less do I say that for this reason their political rights and privileges should have been denied them. Nay, sir, I deemed it necessary then, and I now reaffirm that opinion, that they should possess those rights and privileges for the permanent establishment of the logical and legitimate results of the war and the protection of their new position in society. But, while never losing sight of this necessity, I do say that the inevitable consequence of the admission of so large an uneducated and inexperienced class to political power, as to the probable mismanagement of the material interests of the social body, should at least have been mitigated by a counterbalancing policy. When ignorance and inexperience were admitted to so large an influence upon public affairs, intelligence ought no longer to so large an extent have been excluded. In other words, when universal suffrage was granted to secure the equal rights of all, universal amnesty ought to have been granted to make all the resources of political intelligence and experience available for the promotion of the welfare of all.

But what did we do? To the uneducated and inexperienced classes—uneducated and inexperienced, I repeat, entirely without their fault—we opened the road to power; and, at the same time, we condemned a large proportion of the intelligence of those States, of the property-holding, the industrial, the profes-

SOURCE: Reprinted in Frederic Bancroft, ed., *Speeches, Correspondence and Political Papers of Carl Schurz* (New York: G. P. Putnam's & Co., 1913), pp. 326–327; originally from Carl Schurz speech in Senate, January 30, 1872.

sional, the tax-paying interest, to a worse than passive attitude. We made it, as it were, easy for rascals who had gone South in quest of profitable adventure to gain the control of masses so easily misled, by permitting them to appear as the exponents and representatives of the National power and of our policy; and at the same time we branded a large number of men of intelligence, and many of them of personal integrity, whose material interests were so largely involved in honest government, and many of whom would have cooperated in managing the public business with care and foresight—we branded them, I say, as outcasts, telling them that they ought not to be suffered to exercise any influence upon the management of the public business, and that it would be unwarrantable presumption in them to attempt it.

I ask you, sir, could such things fail to contribute to the results we read today in the political corruption and demoralization, and in the financial ruin of some of the Southern States? These results are now before us. The mistaken policy may have been pardonable when these consequences were still a matter of conjecture and speculation; but what excuse have we now for continuing it when those results are clear before our eyes, beyond the reach of contradiction?

QUESTIONS TO CONSIDER

1. What does the career of Robert Smalls reveal about the goals of blacks at the end of the Civil War? What role did Carl Schurz play in the achievement of those goals during Reconstruction? What role did he play in undermining them?

2. What do the essay and sources in this chapter reveal about some of the factors influencing the outcome of Reconstruction? What would have been required to change the outcome?

3. Some historians argue that the Reconstruction governments in the South were overturned because the Republicans paid too much attention to securing political rights for the freedmen and not enough attention to their economic security. On the basis of the material in this chapter, do you agree with that assessment?

4. If Smalls and Schurz had met at the end of the nineteenth century, what do you think each would have said to the other? Do you think each would have blamed the other for the way Reconstruction turned out? If so, on what grounds?

FOR FURTHER READING

Eric Foner, *Reconstruction: America's Unfinished Revolution, 1863–1877* (New York: Harper & Row, 1988), offers a recent synthesis of the Reconstruction era. Foner argues that Reconstruction provided opportunities for reform that were not taken and correctly places African Americans at the center of the story.

Edward A. Miller Jr., *Gullah Statesman: Robert Smalls from Slavery to Congress, 1839–1915* (Columbia: University of South Carolina Press, 1995), is a useful biography of the African-American leader.

Kenneth M. Stampp, *The Era of Reconstruction, 1865–1877* (New York: Random House, 1965), views Reconstruction as a positive and successful policy.

Hans L. Trefousse, *Carl Schurz: A Biography* (New York: Fordham University Press, 1998), emphasizes the importance of ethnic politics in Schurz's political career.